PENGUIN BOOKS

MUTINY

John Prebble was born in Middlesex in 1915, but spent his boyhood in Saskatchewan, Canada. He entered journalism in 1934 and is now a novelist, a film-writer (*Zulu* amongst others), and the author of highly praised plays and dramatized documentaries for television, including contributions to *Henry VIII* and *Elizabeth R.*

During the war he served for six years in the ranks with the Royal Artillery, from which experience he wrote his successful war novel *The Edge of Darkness* (1948). His other novels include *Where the Sea Breaks* (1944) and *The Buffalo Soldiers* (1959), which won an award in the United States for the best historical novel of the American West.

He has also written several books on the history of Scotland. These include *Culloden* (1961), a subject in which he became interested when he was a boy in a predominantly Scottish township in Canada. *Culloden* was subsequently made into a successful television film. This was followed by its natural successors, *The Highland Clearances* (1963), *Glencoe* (1966), *The Darien Disaster* (1968) and *The Lion in the North* (1971). (All these books have been published in Penguins.) John Prebble is a Fellow of the Royal Society of Literature. He is married, with two sons and a daughter.

JOHN PREBBLE

MUTINY

HIGHLAND REGIMENTS
IN REVOLT
1743–1804

*"If I were as I used to be,
amongst the hills,
I would not mount guard
as long as I lived,
nor would I stand on parade
nor for the rest of my life
would I ever put on a red coat."*

PENGUIN BOOKS

Penguin Books Ltd, Harmondsworth, Middlesex, England
Penguin Books, 625 Madison Avenue, New York, New York 10022, U.S.A.
Penguin Books Australia Ltd, Ringwood, Victoria, Australia
Penguin Books Canada Ltd, 2801 John Street, Markham, Ontario, Canada L3R 1B4
Penguin Books (N.Z.) Ltd, 182–190 Wairau Road, Auckland 10, New Zealand

—

First published by Martin Secker & Warburg 1975
Published in Penguin Books 1977
Reprinted 1978, 1980

—

—

Made and printed in Great Britain by
by Richard Clay (The Chaucer Press) Ltd,
Bungay, Suffolk
Set in Monotype Bembo

To
the Private Soldiers of the 15th Scottish
Division – Highland, Lowland, and English
Northwest Europe 1944–1945

Contents

List of Plates

1

MEN BRED IN THE ROUGH BOUNDS

43rd Highland Regiment (Black Watch)
Ladywood, May 1743

"They think themselves in southern air accurs'd . . ."

BEFORE DAWN ON Whitsunday Major John Creed rode again to Ladywood, this time with a clerk, with ink, paper and quills. It was his second visit and there had been no opportunity for sleep since his first on Saturday night. He was not a young man, he was nearing the end of his scriptural span and the physical strain of the past hours must have been great, but he rode again to the wood because of a promise he had given the mutineers and because he hoped to persuade them to surrender before there was "a good deal of blood shedding".

He told the Lords Regent this, in a letter written by candlelight before mounting his horse, and with a touch of pride when he said that whereas the Army had so far failed to find the Highlanders he knew where they were. The little vainglory was justified. Nineteen troops of dragoons were dispersed across the countryside between London and Northampton, four of them riding hard for the Forest of Rockingham where Brigadier-general Blakeney believed the scoundrel Scots would hide if they could, yet it was an aging Justice of the Peace, a half-pay officer long past campaigning, who was able to tell the Regents that the mutineers were in fact standing to arms among the bright spring leaves of Ladywood, four miles from Oundle. They had themselves made their presence known. A startled countryman, walking along the skirt of the wood on Saturday, was stopped by strange men in scarlet and tartan who politely asked him to inform a Justice of the Peace that they were willing to discuss the terms of their surrender.

This message was carried to Oundle and to John Creed in the

rich comfort of Cobthorne House above the river. The Major was a worthy man, said a contemporary encomium, "whose love of liberty, whose loyalty to the present royal family, and whose affection for the true interest of his country are as well known as his courage, prudence, and beneficence". Like much praise of this headstone nature the words obscured more than they revealed. His youth had been selfish and spendthrift, his middle age a long and embittered wait for his inheritance. The military glory he had once sought in Flanders and Spain had gone to his elder brother, whose heroic corpse he had carried from the battlefield of Blenheim. His parents' disapproval of his wasted life had endured beyond their deathbeds. His father's will deplored his profligacy, and a quarter of a century later his mother certainly declared him the heir to much of her wealth and lands but in the same testament accused him of stealing from her while she lived. John Creed senior probably thought that his own life should have been a model to a wayward son. A Parliamentarian turned Royalist at the Restoration, a retainer of the Montagu family, he had secured Government office by their preferment and had prospered further by marrying their distant kinswoman. Samuel Pepys, with whom he drank and ogled play-actresses, despised his low-born cunning and marvelled that a fellow who could drink so much would once have hanged himself rather than touch a cup of Lambeth ale. The Major's mother, who was a cousin of Pepys and John Dryden as well as the niece of the Earl of Sandwich, seemed to survive in order to spite her son, devoting her widowhood to philanthropy and the painting of altar-pieces and dying when he was beyond the pleasures his inheritance could once have brought him.

Such a disappointed man might have had little sympathy and a high contempt for the mutineers he met in Ladywood, but he treated them with respect and won their trust, and his concern for them may have been sincere for all his determination to secure the whole credit for their surrender. When he went to the wood in the dark of Saturday he did not know what he might find. Reports from London that week had spoken of fifty, two hundred, even a thousand armed men marching northward, outlandishly dressed and speaking no English. At that first meeting Creed saw and learnt little. Shadowy figures spoke to him in gentle English, offering to submit upon their own terms and asking him to write to London for their pardon. He promised to return as soon as he could with a scrivener, and he went back to Oundle where he awoke his clerk and ordered the Town Constable to ride at once to the nearest officer of dragoons with the news that Major John Creed had found the Highlanders.

It was past four o'clock and the air full of birdsong when he returned to the wood on Sunday morning. He was allowed to speak freely with any of the Highlanders who understood English and he was impressed by their boldness and courage. The trees hid the main body of the mutineers, the shine of broadsword and musket-barrel behind the pale green leaf, but he saw that they were well-placed beyond a ditch and if they were set upon resistance it would indeed be bloody. Although he did not know it, they had beer, bacon and bread for a week, and each man with ammunition had fourteen rounds of ball cartridge in his pouch. The two mutineers whom others appeared to accept as their leaders were both corporals, young men in bonnet, scarlet and plaid, and they spoke to Creed as his equals. He accepted the presumption without protest, calling them "gentlemen High- landers" in his dispatch, and although this was dictated in their hearing the context does not suggest that the words were used to flatter their vanity and thereby obtain their submission. He advised them to depend unconditionally upon the Crown's clemency, and when they refused he ordered his clerk to write to the Duke of Montagu, one of the King's Regents and the largest landowner in the county.

I did assure them that your Grace would stand their friend as much as possible. They acknowledged that they had forfeited their lives according to the laws of the land and therefore were not willing to lay down their arms without being assured of a pardon; and in that case they would be willing to return to

their Regiment again and promise fidelity for the future; and
in this case they desire that one of their officers may be sent
down with a route for them to march by, otherwise they
cannot be provided for upon the road.

He asked Montagu to reply by the first post, for the matter
was urgent and the Highlanders would be satisfied with nothing
less than a pardon signed by the Regents and the Secretary at
War. He ended by asking the Duke to excuse him for not writing
the letter himself because – and this with old memories stirring
and as if he were campaigning again – "it is in the field, in the
presence of the Highlanders".

Then, to his certain chagrin, he discovered that he was in danger
of losing that coveted distinction of bringing the mutineers back
to a proper sense of their duty. They told him that an hour or so
before his arrival they had been visited by a man called Stanley
whom Creed knew to be the steward of the Duke of Montagu's
estate at Boughton. Stanley had been gathering casual intelligence
of the Highlanders' movements since they entered the county on
Thursday morning, sending it to the nearest officer of dragoons.
When he heard that they were in Ladywood, perhaps from the
same man who took the news to Creed, he boldly rode there at
once with a demand for their surrender written by Major Charles
Otway of Montagu's Carabineers. Creed's clerk, who must have
hoped that this potentially dangerous business was over, was now
ordered to take up his pen again and he crouched at the Major's
feet to write a peremptory note to Otway in which the dragoon
was asked to commit "no act of hostility" until Creed received a
reply from the Duke. He was also warned that the mutineers
were resolved not to submit until their pardon came, and so that
he might understand what next was expected of him he was told
that Creed would be glad to see him at Oundle.

If Otway received this letter at his quarters in Kettering he did
not acknowledge it in his reports. Britain had been at peace when
he became a cornet of Horse and since he had seen little excitement
in nearly thirty years of service he was probably unwilling to be

robbed of it now by a civil officer. He commanded the four troops of dragoons who had ridden seventy-four miles in two and a half days to cut the roads to the Forest of Rockingham, and although men and mounts had suffered less than he expected they were in no condition to undertake another forced march. He was prepared to wait until he heard from Blakeney, whom he understood to be at Stamford thirty miles to the north-east, but when the indefatigable Mr. Stanley came to him at breakfast he immediately ordered Captain Renkine's troop to mount and ride. They were to make no hostile contact with the mutineers, they were to surround and scout Ladywood at a discreet distance, but Renkine should treat with the Highlanders if this were possible.

John Creed had returned to Oundle by the time Renkine's horsemen rode into Sudborough and deployed on the fields to the west and north of the timbered high ground. They took up their positions by twos, well-spaced and with carbines unslung, their red coats and dock-tailed chestnut horses clearly visible, and when this was done Anthony Renkine rode alone up the gentle slope and into the wood. He had been in the Army longer than Otway, with less advancement, but he seems to have had no bitterness and genuinely wished to save the Highlanders from a bloody encounter with his regiment. He had followed them closely northwards from Barnet and was impressed by the fact that not once had he heard of any violence committed by them. He was welcomed courteously when he dismounted in the wood, and he later reported that the Highlanders told him "several things they accounted unjust and ill usage which provoked them to this madness, as that many of them being as well born as some of their officers, were never listed by them, nor received any pay, but were desired to come up only and be reviewed by the King and then return to Scotland, whereas they were informed they were to be sold for slaves".

One of the corporals, who said his name was Macpherson, gave Renkine a letter for Otway, a reply to the demand brought earlier by Stanley, and although its wording indicated that he had written it he said that it should be regarded as the unanimous resolution of all in the wood. It regretted that they had put His Majesty's troops to such trouble and they could now see the folly of what they had done, but they would submit on no other conditions than those they had given John Creed.

We are all of us fully determined never to surrender otherwise then upon this terms while we live, tho' our chance is but small: seeing we must suffer for our disobedience by returning captives we chuse loose our lives in making our way if our pardon will not be granted. I expect your Honour will see this reasonable and will be assisting in procuring the same. You'l be pleas'd let us hear your opinion in the mater. This is by the general consent of the whole party.

Renkine took the appeal to Otway before noon, and the Major wrote at once to Montagu and the Secretary at War, sending the letters by express in the saddle holster of one of his lieutenants. He said that the "poor wretches" in the wood had promised not to move until they knew the mercy of the Lords Regent and he would not molest them until he had further orders, but should they attempt to leave then his scouts would follow. Upon his instructions, Renkine had assured them of the Duke's "great compassion for unfortunate tho' infatuated people" and he believed this had induced them to submit.

A third officer was that morning eager to be the man who brought the mutineers to submission, and he more harsh in the resolve than either Otway or Creed. Captain John Ball commanded a squadron of Wade's Dragoons and had marched them at a sweating pace to reach Uppingham by Saturday, knowing that country about and believing that the Highlanders would pass through Rutland on their way north. He was an old, sour-tempered cavalryman who had secured his cornet's commission in the year of Malplaquet, who remembered the rebellion of the clans in 1715 and 1719, and who had no patience with mutineers whatever their peculiar grievances or fanciful notions about their gentility. His contempt for the Highlanders was shared by many Englishmen to whom a Scot was a creature of fun and a Highland

Regiment more curious than a raree-show. A rhymester in the *London Magazine* that week said that the mutineers were like the leprous tribes of Israel who had rejected the quails and manna sent by God in favour of chains and garlic. England was well rid of such ingrates who could not have been trusted to defend the land of good roast beef and pudding, and it was not surprising that men unused to sunshine, fed on nothing but cold oatmeal and animal's blood, should run away when confronted by the blessings of a superior civilisation.

> Away false northern kern, well you deserve
> The greatest punishment – at home to starve.
> Midst barren rocks and dreary mountains nurs'd
> They think themselves in southern air accurs'd.
> Surely the land where milk and honey flowed,
> On thankless Israelites was ill bestowed.

John Ball might have been less pleased with himself had he known that when his tired riders passed through the village of Brigstock in the early light of Saturday morning those Israelites were watching him from the western edge of Ladywood. At Uppingham he sent a keeper from the Earl of Gainsborough's estate into the timbered hills and at noon on Sunday this man, with the travel-worn Town Constable of Oundle, brought him news that the mutineers were ten miles behind him. Without waiting for his pickets to answer his recall he put the remainder of his three troops on the road to the south-east. At Brigstock he divided the squadron, sending half to the east of the wood and leading the rest across the open fields below the trees in the west. He ignored Renkine's listless scouts who had been in the saddle and in the heat for four hours now, and he deployed his troopers in line, the officers reining back to dress with the front rank. He then rode up to the silent wood with his Quartermaster, determined to browbeat the Highlanders into surrender or to drive them from the trees with the sabre.

"Men of élan and mettle, with blue blade in pommel"

HIGHLAND SOLDIERS WERE the first of Britain's colonial levies, called to arms to police their own hills and then to fight in the Crown's imperial wars. Until they were disciplined and regimented like any English battalion of the line, until their peculiar identity had become a harmless military caricature, they were treated with suspicion and distrust. During the reign of William and Mary, growing old at his garrison in Lochaber, Colonel John Hill had bitterly resented the sullen men of Clan Grant who were drafted into his regiment. They were brutish, he thought, quarrelsome and intractable, inclined to desert upon some fancied injury to their pride, and so attached to their own customs of warfare that they would never be able to stand and give fire in the reliable manner of English Foot. The wasteful slaughter of breeched Highlanders at the battle of Steinkirk, and in the hot July assault on the redoubts of Dottignies, did not change John Hill's opinion nor that of many of his countrymen. Scotland had been England's bloody enemy for centuries, and even when the union of parliaments made it a despised political partner its mountain people were plainly determined upon further banditry, murder, and rebellion.

The Parliament of Great Britain, which sometimes behaved as if it were still the defunct legislature of England, was slow to realise that the Union of 1707 had brought the Crown an astonishing and seemingly inexhaustible source of manpower for its wars, but once this was recognised – largely as a result of earnest representations from Highland chiefs and Lowland lairds – an artery was opened and the heart of the land was bled dry. In the begin-

ning the Highlanders were regarded as a constant threat to the
security of the nation, an opinion their behaviour frequently
justified, and it was believed that if their troublesome savagery
could not be eliminated it was best retained in their mountains
where they would cut no throats but their own. As early as 1690,
however, the first Earl of Breadalbane, a slippery and intriguing
Campbell, submitted to William III his *Proposals Concerning the
Highlanders*, a summary of the strength of the principal clans
("four thousand good and effective men") and some cynical
advice on the use to which it could be put: "To take up arms for
your majesty in case of any insurrection at home, or invasion
from abroad, or that your majesty think fit to use some of them
in foreign parts. . . . Your majesty has these forces without any
charge, except for a few officers." It was too early for the Crown
to adopt such a scheme, or for the Highlanders to accept it, but
William did raise four line regiments from the clans he could
trust and used one in an attempt to exterminate the MacDonalds
of Glencoe before he committed all to the slaughterhouse of
Flanders.

The tribal structure of the Highland people made them
peculiarly fitted to Breadalbane's proposals, and to similar
schemes devised by other men later. The word *clann* means
children, and the chief of the clan was the father of the family,
loved and feared, benevolent at best and exercising his terrible
power of pit and gallows at the worst. In a mystical sense the
clansmen thought of the land as theirs, personifying its rocks and
waters, but they were their father's tenants-at-will, paying him
rent in kind or by service in the clan regiment, fighting his
battles, sharing his grief and joy, obeying those of his kinsmen to
whom he gave tacks, leasehold upon the land and thereby
superiority over them. Their obsessive pride came from a belief
in a common ancestry and an exclusive identity that placed them
above other races outside the *Gaidhealtachd*, and as the influence
of those races began to erode the fabric of their society that pride
became fiercest in their attachment to their language and dress
and to the solacing companionship of their fellows. In his proposals

Breadalbane advised William to leave them these things should
he make them his soldiers, and the advice was rejected then as it
would be tragically ignored later.

For most Highlanders existence was bleak and hard, alternating
between famine and gluttony. The land held by the smaller clans
was a thin skin of soil on a skeleton of mountainous rock, and
since their herds of shaggy black cattle were always inadequate
to sustain life they filled their larders by raids upon their neighbours' glens or by a swirling descent on the Lowlands. Need
made robbery a necessity, skill at arms an instrument of that
need, and warfare the ultimate in masculine achievement. The
more robust of Gaelic verse throbs with the love of weaponry,
blue-bladed swords like lightning flames, three-grooved swords
in well-sinewed hands, bright-sparking pistols and dark brown
muskets, silver-studded shields and the crescent sweep of axes.
The bards who used such imagery were often warriors themselves
and had seen what their weapons could do to unresisting flesh,
but their enthusiasm was spurred rather than curbed by experience. Poets who sang of the musk-like fragrance of their beloved's
breath, the swansdown of her breasts, were also passionately
delighted by the thought of necks cut like thistle-stems, arms
hewn from white bodies and skulls cleft to the back-bone marrow.
Their clean-limbed young men are ever dauntless and gay,
stepping lightly upon the heather with plaids belted, bonnets
cocked and eyes bright. Even where it is stylistic and repetitious
the verse is always vibrant, pulsing with admiration, and its
strange alchemy worked upon the bewildered Highlandmen long
after grape-shot had proved more deadly than the lightning-
flame, and the purse of the *ceann-cinnidh* more persuasive than his
ancient obligations as the father of the family.

Killing and death in Gaelic verse are always heroic and grief
is a shining laurel for the slain. Between the vision and the reality
there was of course an obscene truth, but it would not be seen
by the Highlanders until they were betrayed into the Government's red coat and the valour that had been an essential part of
their now decaying society became a commodity to be bought

and sold by the English-speakers. Lagging behind the Lowlands and lightly affected by the social, political and economic changes of the seventeenth and early eighteenth centuries the Highland people still fed upon the fat of their past, unaware of or unwilling to acknowledge the beginning of that decay. There were as yet no highways in their hills, no large towns, no formal education of an influential kind, nothing that would bring those changes without pain, but their chiefs had already taken a pace into the future and away from their children at a time when they were perhaps most needed.

Until the last of them left the Palace of Holyroodhouse for the softer comforts of Whitehall successive kings of Scotland had failed to do more than contain the lawlessness of the clans, and James VI had perpetuated the evil he hoped to eliminate by granting writs of Fire and Sword to ennobled chiefs, the Draconian power to destroy those whom the King's Council considered pestilential and irredeemable. Understandably this power was frequently used to strengthen the holder's own position, private quarrels were given legal sanction and the aggressive nature of the people was maintained. Although the Highlander's apparently mindless attachment to robbery and bloodshed was deplored in stable times, it was eagerly called upon when it could be put to bloodier work in the name of the Crown, Parliament or Kirk. The Gaels themselves, paying their rents by service in arms, were rarely motivated by the political or religious cause to which their chiefs had summoned them, innocently seeing it as an opportunity to demonstrate and preserve their own way of life, believing this even when they died in the ditches outside Worcester or were cut down by English dragoons in the streets of Preston.

The example of the writs of Fire and Sword, the practice of using Highlander against Highlander, was a precedent for subtler measures taken in the eighteenth century. Britain's small standing army, superb in the performance of clockwork movements on a Flanders battlefield, was ill-trained and unequipped to police the mountains. The battalions sent to the garrisons at Fort William,

Bernera or Ruthven were often prisoners in their bleak stone barracks, awed by the great amphitheatre of hills and unable to check the reiving and the levying of black mail* by which the hungrier clans supported themselves. It was evident that the deer-footed men of Rannoch and Lochaber could not be effectually restrained by pipe-clayed foot-soldiers from Lothian or Lincolnshire, nor was it ever thought that these alone should be used. In 1667, when the standing army was as yet no more than the decorative troops of the Royal Household, Charles II had issued a commission to the second Earl of Atholl, authorising him to raise independent companies of clansmen to keep "watch upon the braes" along the scythe-blade of the Highland Line from the Moray Firth to Dunbartonshire. By definition this was containment rather than control, a protection for the Lowlands but with no real influence to the north-west of the Great Glen.

By the end of the century there were many such companies, captained by the gentry of Clan Campbell, Murray and Grant, Menzies, Fraser and Munro, and composed of "Highlanders cloathed in their ancient, proper, Caledonian Dress and armed all with Broad Swords, Targets, Guns, Side-pistols and Durks, alias Daggers". They were known as The Watch, from that felicitous phrase in Atholl's commission, but whom they watched, how they watched, and why they watched was not always within the spirit of the Crown's interest alone. The first military action to which they were committed in strength was a campaign led by the Campbell Earl of Argyll against his family's hereditary enemies the Macleans, the success of which happily extended his power over the mainland of Morvern and the isles of Mull, Coll and Tiree. On a less ambitious level, but giving the same personal satisfaction no doubt, a little laird who led a foray on the summer shielings of Strathearn might that autumn be serving in the Watch and harrying those who had foolishly taken reprisals against his glen. The power to exercise the King's writ by force of arms also offered novel opportunities to the Highlander's old

* An old tribute exacted by Highland and Border freebooters, payment in coin or kind in return for immunity.

taste for blackmail and extortion, disgusting Major-general George Wade whose road-making would soon be a far more effective method of pacification than the independent companies.

> For want of being put under proper regulations, corruptions were introduced, and some who commanded them instead of bringing criminals to justice (as I am informed) often compounded for the theft, and for a sum of money set them at liberty. They are said also to have defrauded the government by keeping not half their numbers in constant pay.

This was written to George I after the Watch had been disbanded in 1717, and it contains the first indication of what would later be the obstinate and axiomatic opinion of the War Office – that if Highlanders were taken into the King's service they should be subject to and given no preferential exemption from the conditions governing other battalions of the line. Their race, their language and dress, their belief that they should soldier with men from their own district and that promises made to them upon enlistment were honourably binding upon all who commanded them later, none of this should exclude them from the changing decisions of empirical government. Not until the Highlands had ceased to be a prodigal source of manpower, and perhaps not even then, did authority realise that but for these cherished things it would not have been able to raise so remarkable a force of men.

The existence of the Watch had failed to prevent the rebellion of the Jacobite clans in 1715. Indeed some of the men of the companies took part in it, there being no breach of honour in this since their only loyalty was to their *ceann-cinnidh* who had exercised his right to make them soldiers of the Watch and who now used it again to call them out in support of a Stuart restoration. By 1717 the companies had exhausted the fragile faith of the Crown, and once disbanded they were replaced by four garrisons of Lowland or English Foot, each with thirty Highlanders who were to be no more than guides. This measure was miserably ineffective. An attempt to strip the hillmen of their

arms was successful only among those who had been loyal to
the Government, and the wildness of outlawed or landless men
increased. In 1724, when an Act was passed to regulate the
disarming of the clans, the King ordered George Wade to examine
and report upon the state of the Highlands which that resolute
old campaigner did with thoroughness and candour. Of more
than twenty thousand fighting-men in the mountains, he said,
half were perhaps in sympathy with the Stuart cause. The garrison
forts were incapable of imposing the rule of law, and only one
murderer had been executed at Inverness in four years. The
worst depredations were committed by the MacGregors, by the
Camerons, Mackenzies, Keppoch MacDonells and Breadalbane
men, and the Camerons had sworn a holy oath on their dirks
not to accept the money which the Government was offering to
informers. They emphasised the solemnity of their word by
hanging one suspected traitor before his own door.

Forgetting the disapproval of an earlier paragraph, or hoping
that proper regulations might now be followed, Wade advised
the King to re-establish the Watch. He said that it should be
"employed in disarming the Highlanders, preventing depredations, bringing criminals to justice, and hinder rebels and attainted
persons from inhabiting that part of the kingdom". It should also
be composed of well-affected men, subject to martial law and
placed under the orders of the Commander-in-Chief in North
Britain, a post to which he was shortly and justly appointed. The
proposal received the King's authority in April 1725, and so that
the nation's book-keeping might not be over-burdened by the
extra expense of 550 private soldiers the strength of every troop
of Horse and every company of Foot was reduced by one or two
men. Determined that the men of the new Watch should at least
bear some resemblance to a uniformed battalion of the line, and
thereby be better soldiers, Wade ordered "the plaid of each
Company to be as near as they can of the same Sort and Colour".
The choice of sett was perhaps fortuitous, there is no contemporary evidence to support those who later believed the nine-
teenth-century myth of clan tartans and who claimed that the

Watch adopted a Campbell, a Grant, or a Munro pattern. The cloth most commonly worn was green and blue, from the natural dyes of heather and blaeberry, the colours merging into darkness at a few paces. Because of this, it was said, and with contempt or admiration according to their sympathies, the Highland people called its wearers *Am Freiceadan Dubh*, the Black Watch.*

In the second decade of the next century, remembering the tales of old men in his childhood, General David Stewart of Garth wrote with affection for those first six companies of the Black Watch. Although his *Sketches* are still rich in knowledge and anecdote, they have the sweet smell of the romantic anaesthesia that softened any guilty pain his class may have felt at the manner in which an old way of life had passed. Between him and those first men of the Watch was a black gulf across which the Gaelic people had been brutally dragged. Between his colourful pen and the past was the spine-breaking blow of Culloden, the despoiling of the glens, the bloody sewer of the French wars, the coming of the great Cheviot sheep and the beginning of eviction and dispersal. In his study at Garth House, wearing Highland dress and peering myopically through the small lenses of his spectacles, Stewart wrote as if he could feel the chill egalitarianism of the Industrial Age coming with the wind from Loch Tay.

> Many of the men who composed these companies were of a higher station in society than that from which soldiers in general are raised; cadets of gentlemen's families, sons of gentlemen farmers, and tacksmen, either immediately or distantly descended from gentlemen's families – men who felt themselves responsible for their conduct to high-minded and honourable families, as well as to a country for which they cherished a devoted affection. In addition to the advantages derived from their superior rank in life, they possessed, in an eminent degree, that of a commanding external deportment.

* A claim that the adjective originally referred to the companies' principal duty, to keep watch upon *black*mailers, is equally persuasive. Both explanations may be believed without conflict.

Gentlemen many of them were by their own accounting, although there was almost a millenium between the *duine-uasal* of a clan and the English squirearchy of Garth's description. But he was not conscious of any absurdity in his words, any more than he was aware of farce when arranging the Highland dress worn by George IV in Edinburgh, carefully placing the fall of kilt and plaid about the pink tights the fat king was wearing. The "higher station" of these men was more accurately described by a Highland minister called Campbell, who nobly served the mutineers in the Tower, but even so he used the language of emergent snobbery. "The officers took special care that none should be enlisted but the sons of the wealthiest and most reputable farmers in the country; and the second and younger sons of some of the lesser vassals were not ashamed to enlist." Edward Burt, an Englishman who worked with Wade's road-making gangs, said that the clansmen had such a conceit of themselves that almost all were genealogists, and he was amused by the soldiers of the Watch who "have Gillys, or Servants to attend them in Quarters, and upon a March to carry their Provisions and Fire-locks". By definition, however, a clan depended upon the strict observance of its family structure, the rights and duties of all, and at no time was its tribal character more clearly seen than when it gathered for war. The blood-proud men of the companies would have been insulted by any suggestion that an English foot-soldier was their equal, or that military rank should bar them from the privileges of birth. Duncan Ban Macintyre, the Glen Etive forester and bard who served with an independent company, did not speak of gentility when he composed his song in honour of the Watch. That all were superior men was implicit, "men bred in the Rough Bounds,* the host that is trustworthy . . . men of élan and mettle with blue blade in pommel. . . ."

* The wild and mountainous district of Knoydart northwest of Fort William. Few if any men were recruited there for the Black Watch at this time, but the impression the words give of a proud and independent body of men is exact and fitting.

Descendants of noble clans,
begotten of north men,
'twas their instinct in action
to advance at each step:
every foot was the swiftest,
every hand was the hardest,
and their pride was rampant
as they struck mighty blows;
for their foes it was usual
to lie still on the field,
while the part that escaped them
had pursuit on their trail.

Few of the young men thought of themselves as soldiers. "In the discipline to which they were at first subjected," wrote Garth, "there was much affinity with their ancient usages, so that their services seemed merely that of a clan, sanctioned by legal authority." It mattered little why they had been called upon, only that they had, and at a time when the glories of the past were apparently passing into the darkness of old men's dreams. While the Disarming Act forced another man to hide his sword in his roof-sod or a peat-bog, a member of the Watch could walk abroad as his ancestors had done, with a basket-hilt on his hip, a targe on his shoulder, and a long musket in his hand. Carrying the arms their fathers had used in the November charge at Sheriffmuir, the braeside descent of Killiecrankie, the young men were above and apart from the red soldiers, and the inspiring roll of English drums meant little to a race whose pipers cried to God for three hands, one for the claymore and two for the pipes. The southern world, three weeks away by foot-post, could as well have been separated by three centuries, and they did not think that they could or should be sent from the Highlands. Nor did their captains encourage them to believe it would ever happen. The author of an anonymous pamphlet, published in 1743 when the mutineers were awaiting death, said that they thought their only purpose had been to keep the peace in the mountains.

It is most certain that they always looked upon themselves from the time they were first raised as a corps destined to service in Scotland, or rather in the Highlands, and no where else. . . . They laid great stress upon their habit; to what purpose, said they, are we cloathed like Highlanders if we are not constantly to be employed in the Highlands; here indeed the dress is equally fit and commodious; it has a martial air, and it enables us to do our duty better; but all these reasons will cease elsewhere.

For fifteen years the men of the Black Watch helped to keep the peace in the Highlands, more successfully than their predecessors and better than General Wade may have hoped. Burt thought they grew soft from good pay and dry lodgings, losing the natural hardiness and agility of their kind. They were indulged by their officers, and he despised a captain who "is said to strip his other Tenants of their best Plaids wherewith to clothe his Soldiers against a Review", but he agreed they were useful in imposing the Disarming Act and in preventing the theft of cattle. The comparative calm of these years was due less to the efforts of the Watch, perhaps, than to the omnipresence of Wade's marching-regiments. The Jacobite chiefs accepted a harsh truth, that without military help from abroad there might never be another rising, and it may be that some of them were grateful for this. Their attachment to the Stuarts became a matter of melodramatic intrigue conducted by correspondence. They drank emotional toasts, sent their younger sons to serve in French regiments, gave promises of help if the Pretender came again and offered a prayer or two for God's charity in keeping him where he was for the time being. They surrendered some weapons when the regulars or the Watch came to their glens, and most of them put a snaffle on the eagerness of their young men. As if they felt the earth moving with change and feared to lose their balance, they accepted pardons from the Government and thereby retained their ancient powers. The fingers of the future were grasping at their mountains, Wade's inexorable roads, and the genial old man himself could sometimes be seen as he rode by on inspection, stopping his great coach to dine with his workmen where they roasted oxen whole in the red sandstone dust of his civilising highways.

Only the MacGregors and the outlawed men of Lochaber, Rannoch and Breadalbane remained intractable, and these the companies pursued as if they were wolves, exacting joyous payment for old grievances between their clans as much as serving the King's peace. In their own behaviour the men of the Watch were sometimes as bloody as the thieves they were supposed to control, molesting the innocent as well as the guilty, and on the Duke of Atholl's ground particularly they were hated and resented. "The country complains," reported the Duke's secretary, "that the soldiers of the Independent Companies are allowed to straggle through the country in arms, doing no good, whatever mischief." The officers supported their men, bound by clan obligations which came before any other. When two soldiers called Grant were accused of bayoneting a harmless fellow in a field near Dalnacardoch their captain, George Grant of Culbin, arrogantly defied the custom of the law and insisted that a lieutenant and a sergeant be present when evidence was taken from them, in the hope perhaps that the interrogator would be too frightened to proceed further. Between the companies there was often hostility based upon past enmities, and an ensign of the Grants who attempted to stop a tavern-house brawl among the Frasers was pistolled through the mouth and through the eye. Had the members of the court-martial not feared further violence as a result, they might have sentenced the murderer to hang instead of transportation.

The abuses which Wade had deplored in the earlier Watch probably continued, though less among the officers than before, and in one case at least the offence was more endearing, if the *Memoirs* of Sergeant Donald MacLeod are to be believed. He was the younger son of the tacksman of Ulinish on Skye and a descendant of chiefs. He was serving in the Royal Scots when he heard a woman hawking news of the formation of the Watch and he took his discharge, walking from Newcastle to Inverness to offer his services to Simon Fraser of Lovat. He enjoyed life in the companies, teaching the use of the broadsword at which he was most proficient, particularly against anyone called Maclean, "hunting after incorrigible robbers, shooting, hawking, fishing, drinking, dancing, and toying with the young women". Dalliance was more pleasurable than the pursuit of incorrigible robbers. In the high glens of Atholl one day his party surprised James Robertson, a notorious horse-stealer, but MacLeod's duty was deflected by his admiration for one of the outlaw's four handsome daughters.

> "Jamie," said he to her father, "I believe I must have one of your daughters to-night." "Yes, my dear," said James, "you are welcome to make yourself agreeable to any of my girls that you chuse. Make up matters between yourselves, and your courting shall not be disturbed by Jamie Robertson."

The heather-bed consummation of this sudden passion was indeed agreeable until it was violently disturbed by three of Robertson's companions with rusty swords, but these the Sergeant quickly dispersed, and further showed his magnanimity by allowing Robertson to escape, keeping only the daughter and the stolen horses. He married the girl, was as faithful to her as he could be while she lived, and remembered the incident with relish in his one hundred and third year. Lest his readers think he had less regard for his duty than his pleasures, he explained that "as British laws, made since the Union, had not yet free course in the Highlands, and depended for the execution on military aid, a great discretionary power, in cases of this kind, was assumed and exercised by military officers of all ranks".

The men of the Watch may have believed that they would never serve beyond the Highlands but greater men were beginning to see that there was a wider use for the aggressive spirit of the clans. In 1738, when it was apparent that Captain Robert Jenkins' aural loss could be revenged if not restored by war with Spain, Britain once again faced the usual problem of raising battalions to fight its campaigns. One of those who suggested an answer was the newly appointed Lord President of the Court of Session, Duncan Forbes of Culloden. He was an elegant and handsome jurist, an erudite man who was said to have read the Scriptures eight times in Hebrew alone, a merry man who was good company over a book or a bottle, and although he was compassionate by nature he would still be enough a creature of his age to recommend the inhuman transportation of Jacobite prisoners after the rebellion of 1745. From his fine house on the Moray Firth he could look north and west to that mountain mass so widely sown with dragon's teeth, and by marriage and friendship he had strong links with the loyal and the dissident clans. An old-fashioned Whig by conviction, dedicated to the maintenance of the Great Revolution, he was determined that the Stuarts should never again find support in the Highlands. In the year of Jenkins' Ear, perhaps without knowing that they were not original, he repeated the proposals made by Breadalbane half a century before. He sent the scheme to the Lord Justice Clerk, who sent it to the Lord Privy Seal of Scotland from whom it went in natural progression to the King's first minister, Sir Robert Walpole.

Forbes said that the Government should raise four or five regiments of the line from the clans, and although he thought that their colonels should be Englishmen, or at least Scots of proven loyalty to the Crown, the lieutenant-colonels, majors, captains and subalterns could be drawn from

> . . . the chiefs and chieftains of the disaffected clans, who are the very persons whom France and Spain will call upon in case of war to take up arms for the Pretender. If Government pre-engage the Highlanders in the manner I propose, they will not only serve well against the enemy abroad, but will be hostages for the good behaviour of their relatives at home, and I am persuaded it will be absolutely impossible to raise a rebellion in the Highlands.

Although Walpole approved of the scheme he opposed the war with Spain, and was at this moment fighting for his political life against both friends and enemies in the Commons. Forbes' proposals were undoubtedly a casualty of this struggle, rejected by other ministers who may also have thought that, hostages or not, the Jacobite chiefs were the last men to whom arms should be given. For years, however, general officers had either admired the Watch or been irritated by its lack of proper discipline, and some of them were anxious to bring it within the framework of the regular army. Its special qualities, the high standard of fitness which its captains maintained as a complement to their own competitive dignity, made it far superior to an English battalion recruited by the press or from the scourings of county gaols. A soldier bred in the traditions of warfare, albeit seditious and troublesome, might more easily be committed to battle than one who had taken the red coat as an alternative to the transports or the gallows. Persuaded by such arguments, and by the seemingly good sense of the Lord President's proposals, the King decided to translate the Watch into a regiment of the line. A Royal Warrant to that effect was signed in November 1739, raising the strength of the companies from six to ten, and a Letter of Service as Colonel was granted to the Earl of Crawford. This young man, a Lowlander but Highland-bred by the Duke of Argyll, was at that moment in the service of the Empress of Russia and seems to have regarded his colonelcy as a bank draft, shortly to be cashed for the purchase of a commission in the more congenial company of the Life Guards.

The officers of the Watch were no doubt pleased to become equal in rank with line officers as well as their natural superiors by race and birth, but no serious attempt was made to inform the men of the very great difference between their previous duties and those now expected of them. Until this time they had lived at home, gathering only for musters or when called out "in pursuit of robbers or disturbers of the peace", taking their eight-pence a day while under arms and despising the garrison redcoats with whom they were temporarily lodged. Like Malcolm Macpherson some may have sensed the coming change, and have had no taste for it. He was the son of the little leaseholder of

Driminard in Strathspey and had joined Simon Fraser's company two years before. He now asked for his discharge which Lovat either failed to obtain or forgot, with disastrous results for Macpherson. Most of the men accepted the new order as another rightful claim upon them as a clan levy, or welcomed the excitement of regular service in their mountains, but none of them can have fully understood the meaning of the King's Warrant which changed them overnight from Independent Companies of the Watch to the 43rd Highland Regiment.*

Crawford's enlistment orders authorised him to raise his four extra companies by beat of drum or otherwise "in any County or Part of Our Kingdom of Great Britain", an early indication of the fact that the Crown, while eager to employ Highland soldiers, would never stand in the way of colonels who found it easier or necessary to complete their numbers in the streets of Glasgow, Newcastle or Dublin. The phrase would appear in all Letters of Service for Highland regiments. Stewart of Garth evidently thought it humiliating. He ignored the beating order for the 43rd in his *Sketches*, and when he reprinted the Warrant he honoured his loyalty to his mountain land by inserting the words "the men to be natives of that country and none other to be taken". In the beginning the men of the 43rd were indeed all Highlanders, their officers predominantly those who had served with the companies and all sympathetic to the Government. The equivocating chief of Clan Fraser had been relieved of his command, it being suspected that he was loyal to no man's cause but his own. He was compelled to surrender his company to his brother-in-law Major Grant of Culbin, and was incensed when Grant rejected some of the men as "bairdless lads" and physically

---

* Better understood, perhaps, as the 43rd (Highland) Regiment. The number indicated a regiment's precedence among others of the line. It could change when senior regiments were disbanded and younger formations were given the honour of a lower number. Thus, ten years later, the 43rd became the 42nd, by which it is more commonly remembered. The old custom of calling regiments by their colonels' names was slowly being replaced by reference to their numbers.

unfit. Lovat was asked for replacements, and was unwilling or unable to find them from his own people. Like a shopkeeper anxious to replenish his shelves, and demonstrating what would soon be the common view of the chiefs – that clansmen were marketable cattle – he wrote appealing to his friends and kinsmen, to Cameron of Lochiel, MacDonell of Glengarry and Macpherson of Cluny. "I earnestly intreat you as you have any regard for my honour and interest you may send me, as soon as possible, two or three men at 5 ft 7 inches or above, and I will give you my word of honour that when you desire to get them back that I will send them to you if I should be obliged to pay ten guineas for each of their discharges."

In May 1740 the ten companies were mustered on a riverside field by Aberfeldy, where Wade's masons worked on the fine bridge William Adam had designed, and after a formal inspection the eight hundred and fifty officers and men were embodied into a regiment. Five of the private soldiers had spent the night as guests of Stewart's grandfather at Garth House four miles away. "The following morning they rode off in their usual dress, a tartan jacket and truis, ornamented with gold lace embroidery, or twisted gold cords, as was the fashion of the time, while their servants carried their military clothing and arms." That military clothing was the first modification of what would in time become a mockery of Highland dress, blue bonnets with a diced border of red, white and green, diced hose of red and white, short scarlet coats faced with buff, dark plaids hanging from the shoulder and black-belted about the waist to form the kilt, sporrans of deerskin or calfskin, and cartridge-boxes stamped with the Royal cipher. The arms they carried were largely their own property, and would still be so three years later. From their belts hung claw-butted pistols richly engraved, dirks with handles made from heather-root or bog-oak and intricately carved in Celtic patterns. Sheathed on a crossbelt was a basket-hilted broadsword a yard or more in length, grooved and double-edged, and although many of the muskets were regular issue from the Minories in London others were of Spanish origin, long in the barrel and graceful in design. Some men still had the round hide shields they had carried in the Watch, but a War Office order would soon abolish that military anachronism.

The companies stood on the green grass with an easy grace. Stalwart warriors, sang Duncan Ban Macintyre, youthful and gay, of good repute and so vigorous and comely, hunters of deer, proud in self-esteem. These characteristics, individual rather than military, were also contrary to regulations, and sergeants from other regiments were sent to teach the Highlanders the mysteries of drill, the complicated movements that created a machine of death. For fifteen months they remained on the banks of the Tay and the Lyon, tirelessly exercised by their lieutenant-colonel Sir Robert Munro of Foulis. They learnt to march by files, by platoons, by companies and in battalion order. They mastered the three motions for resting their firelocks, four for grounding, twenty-one for priming and loading, and nineteen for firing. They were taught to march upon the centre or wheel to the right and left about, to learn each ruffle of a grenadier drum and to obey its tapping permutations without hesitation. All this and more to replace the half-naked storm-charge that had been the only military tactic of their ancestors.

It may have seemed to some of them that their life had changed, if anything, for the better. They were still in their mountains and embodied "to take care of the country against thieving". They were paid for each day of the week instead of for musters and gatherings only, and they strutted like peacocks before the young women of Strathtay. It cannot be known how much they understood of the terms of their enlistment. Most of them spoke no English, and although the Articles of War should have been read to them regularly, translated into Gaelic, it is clear from evidence at the court-martial later that few captains bothered with this tedious duty. In addition to a natural impatience with military trivia, common enough at the time, the officers may also have been unwilling to risk their standing in the regiment and in their clans by allowing the men to realise that they had been deceived. Francis Grose knew some of these captains as a youth, and in his *Military Antiquities* he accused their superiors of dishonesty.

> Some of the chiefs in raising these companies had given them promises they were not authorised by government to make; among other inducements to enlist, thus improperly held forth, it is said, the men were assured they should not go out of their own country; under the faith of this promise many reputable farmer's and yeomen's sons entered themselves as privates in the corps who would not otherwise have thought of enlisting.

The results of this deception were yet to come, but within two years of their embodiment the men complained of a breach of faith and of promises made, of a cynical exploitation to which English foot-soldiers were long accustomed and which they accepted with spitting contempt. When Crawford went to the Life Guards the colonelcy of the 43rd was given to Hugh Sempill, twelfth lord of the name, a veteran of Marlborough's wars and later a brigadier-general. He was a man of courage and manners but he had no more attachment to the regiment than was usual for men of his rank, nor did that rank require him to concern himself with the affairs of the battalion in detail, this being the duty and responsibility of its lieutenant-colonel. It was customary, however, for general officers to make what money they could when supplying and clothing the regiments given them, indeed such appointments and the varying degrees of profit to be had were regarded as rewards. Crawford had promised the Highlanders that they would receive two shirts and two pairs of hose every year, Sempill gave them one of each. He reduced their brogue-money from a shilling to tenpence and stopped their pay to make up the past excess. The black plaids he supplied were of miserable quality, too narrow and an ell shorter than the twelve required by custom, ease and comfort. Highland soldiers throughout the 18th century would frequently complain of the inadequacy of their plaids, and it may be that their short kilts – which English and French cartoonists found so scatalogically amusing – were the result of such penny-profiting by their colonels and contractors. More than four hundred men of the 43rd carried their own broadswords and wished to send these treasured family weapons home, but they were never issued with the replacements promised. Sempill later produced papers to prove that the complaints were unjustified, and the War Office said that such assurances about shirts and hose and shoes exceeded the normal regulations for foot regiments, but no one in Whitehall realised that the issue was not the articles alone but that the promises which had accompanied them were regarded as inviolable by the Highlanders.

These grievances were for the moment endured and would not find angry voice until a greater injury was felt. At the beginning of winter in 1741, their training over, the companies were dispersed among the garrisons of the Great Glen. As they marched on the frost-white stones of Wade's roads, over Corrieyairack and the Devil's Staircase, there was no reason for them to believe that they would ever be called upon to serve beyond their mountains.

"To send for them to show their bare backsides in England"

A RUMOUR THAT the 43rd Regiment was to march into England, and to leave from the Thames for Flanders, was first heard in Edinburgh seven months before the companies were brought down from the hills. When a gentleman of Clan Grant sent that news to the north Sempill's senior officers had known for three weeks that it was true, or at least that they were to take their Highlanders across the Border. On July 29, 1742, Sir William Yonge the Secretary at War wrote to Major-general Jasper Clayton who had succeeded Wade in Scotland, "I am commanded by His Majesty to acquaint you that it is his intentions that the Highland Regiment should march into South Britain, and you will very soon receive orders accordingly". The ultimate destination of the battalion was probably made known privately to its colonel and lieutenant-colonel, for within a few days Munro's son told a kinsman that "Lord Sempill's Regiment goes for Flanders, and in a very short time we shall have a proclamation of war between us and France". The desultory brawl over Captain Jenkins' ear was about to be followed by a more spectacular dispute over Maria Theresa's right to the Austrian succession.

It is impossible to believe that the men of the regiment did not soon discover that they were to be sent to England. Before the end of the year newspapers in London and Edinburgh announced that the Highlanders were to be reviewed by the King on Hounslow Heath, and there were enough private soldiers of birth and education to have read this or heard of it from their families. But it would seem that they preferred not to believe the tattle of the journals, trusting their captains who informed them

40

of their marching orders before spring melted the snows on Dalnaspidal and Corrieyairack. The Reverend Mr. Campbell pursued this matter diligently with the mutineers in the Tower and he concluded that they had been decoyed to London, that they were first told that they would march to the links at Musselburgh, four miles from Edinburgh, where they would be reviewed by General Clayton. Once there they learnt that the General now wished to inspect them at Berwick-upon-Tweed, and only in the Border town and upon English ground were they told that "His Majesty designed to review them in person in London, and that then they would all return to their families." Whether they heard of the Royal review in the Highlands or when they stood above the Tweed, the progression of the deception practised upon them was cynical and deliberate, a breach of trust, and it culminated in the greatest lie that they would come back to their glens. Their captains may have rightly feared the consequences if the truth had been too early known, that the men would not have left the Highlands had they been told that they were to go to London, but not even the most junior ensign could claim that he did not know what was intended. When the companies were at Musselburgh Lieutenant Lewis Grant wrote happily to a cousin in Strathspey

> The Regiment is come this length on their march to London where we are to be reviewed by the King, and when that is over it's generally believed we shall return to the Highlands, tho' I must own I have no notion of our going back if any regiment goes abroad – which we have no reason to question as some has got their marching orders as well as our Regiment.

As early as the autumn of 1742 Duncan Forbes of Culloden also knew that the Government had decided to send the 43rd to Flanders, and despite his previous proposals he was alarmed that this should happen when the risk of another Jacobite rising, provoked and aided by the French, would be greatest. The Highland Regiment, he thought, was the one force which might prevent rebellion, not so much because of its strength but from the psychological effect its presence would have on other clansmen, and he wrote a troubled letter to Clayton. "Wou'd the Pretender's emissaries, or the Highlanders who might favour them, be in any apprehension from the regular troops?" This was not, perhaps, a tactful and persuasive argument to address to a general officer and an Englishman, but he persisted. "If France shou'd stumble upon such a design as I have been supposing, remove but that regiment and there is nothing to hinder the Agents of that Crown to have their full swing, and to tamper with the poor unthinking people of the Highlands." He said that he had at first been not unduly disturbed, believing that the men would return after they had been reviewed by the King, "but as I have been lately assured that they are destined for foreign service I cannot dissemble my uneasiness at a resolution that may, in my apprehension, be attended with very bad consequences."

The appeal was ignored, and the Government may well have thought that if there were to be a rebellion it would be foolish to make the Pretender a present of an armed and disciplined battalion. Horace Walpole said that when Robert Munro was ordered to march his men from Scotland he asked what would happen if the Jacobites were then to rise. "Why," he was told, "there will be eight hundred fewer rebels there." That rising did come two years later and the 43rd was recalled from Flanders, but it was not put into the field against the clans. Although it had suffered bloodily before the redoubts at Fontenoy, replacement companies had been raised in the Highlands. Since five officers and more men of these companies took their pride, loyalty and arms into the Jacobite service it would appear that for once the Government had more good sense than the Lord President.

The Black Watch came down from the north before March was out in 1743, from Inverness, Fort Augustus and Fort William, over the snow-deep passes beyond Blair and Rannoch. The five companies that marched from Inverness were uneasy and sullen, and although there is no substantiation for a curious report in the London *Daily Post* – that some of them mutinied and killed two of their officers – it does indicate that there was perhaps a violent manifestation of their resentment and suspicion. Their ill-humour increased as they came through Atholl. Their officers belonged to the Whig clans of Munro, Grant and Campbell, but many of the men were Macphersons, MacGregors, Camerons and Mac-Donalds, levies whom their chiefs had raised in the market manner of Lovat, and they had little affection for the Murray gentry and tenants of Strathtay. The Duchess of Atholl was unimpressed by their appearance and manner. She was a resolute old woman with a sharp tongue and a quick temper, living apart from her impoverished husband who was no doubt grateful for this respite, their emotional and intellectual contact having become no more subtle than the leg of mutton she once hurled at him. She wrote derisively of the Highlanders' straggling passage through Dunkeld on March 25, "stealing without sound of drum and pipe, but it seems their musick had retired on the way, and miserable and tattered fellows they were, for it's said they have sold all the clever fellows and filled up the companies with scrubs."

Not only had some of their pipers deserted, twenty more men of this division had slipped away since it left Inverness, either from a simple desire to stay in the Highlands or because they had heard and believed the stories that they were to be sent to Flanders. Those who remained expended some of their anger on the people of Atholl as they passed, shouting from the ranks that they would have their revenge upon the Duke whom they accused of selling them to the English. "One of our carts on Saturday sennight," said the Duchess, "meeting a parcel of them at the muir town, they asked the carter who he belonged to, which he telling, they fired to fright the horses twice, which had such effect that horses, man, and cart had like to have been destroyed." The principal leaders of such defiance, the "scrubs" she despised, were undoubtedly MacGregors, members of a proscribed and landless clan, victims of the rising power of the Murrays and Campbells whose miserable sub-tenants they now were, and by whom they had been drafted into the Watch and used against their own people.

When the ten companies assembled on the links of Musselburgh at the beginning of April the Edinburgh *Evening Courant*
thought they were "the best-looked Foot Regiment in the
service, being generally tall, well-bodied and stout". If the
information given to Mr. Campbell was correct – that they
were now told Clayton would review them at Berwick – the lie
was impudently bold, for he was long gone to take up a command
in Flanders. The defence of Scotland was in the trembling hands
of Lieutenant-general Joshua Guest, a rheumy-eyed dotard well
into his ninth decade who would later distinguish himself by
cannonading the city of Edinburgh from the walls of the castle,
in the apparent belief that whoever suffered as a result some of
the Young Pretender's clansmen were sure to be among the dead.
He came by coach to see the regiment at Musselburgh and gave
Sir Robert Munro the orders he had himself received four weeks
before. Since His Majesty had thought fit to send the 43rd on
foreign service it was to leave now for Berwick and the south.

A great crowd came from the city to watch as the Highlanders
marched away in the April sunshine. Far enough from their
mountains, among strangers in breeches, awed by the wide firth
and white-sailed ships, stone-black villages and dyked fields, few
of the soldiers knew the difference between Musselburgh and
Berwick, except that the southern sun was in their eyes as they
marched. Across the Border there was truth at last, or part of it.
At a chill morning parade, when the companies assembled before
the cottages in which they had been quartered for the night, the
captains walked along the ranks, talking familiarly to the men in
Gaelic and telling them that they were to go to London where
the King himself would review his brave lads.

It was well known that George II had more than the usual
royal interest in soldiers and soldiering, although he would be
the last monarch allowed to risk defeat as well as his own death
by leading an army in battle. Like most of his subjects he had
never seen a Highland warrior, and he and they had the same
proprietorial and paternal curiosity that Victorians would later
feel about a Rajput or a Pathan. The men of the 43rd, victims of

their own consuming self-esteem, were perhaps flattered by the honour and were not aware – as any English foot soldier could have told them, and some Lowland Scots shortly did – that it was customary for the King to review a battalion before it was embarked. One explanation for their willingness to march into England, apart from an assurance that they would return after the review, may be found in a story told by Garth. In response to an earlier wish to see a Highlander in arms, two private soldiers had been selected and sent to the King in London. Both were Breadalbane men of birth, John Campbell whose family held Duneaves, and a handsome MacGregor known as Gregor the Beautiful. They were presented to George II at St. James's Palace, before a scarlet-coated, gold-laced and white-cuffed audience that included the Duke of Cumberland, His Majesty's jolly son, and old George Wade who was now a field-marshal. Campbell and MacGregor gave a fierce display of exercises with the broadsword, and the delighted monarch presented each with a guinea. They silently forgave him the ignorant insult and handed the coins to a porter as they left. If the King did indeed see this small demonstration of their exceptional qualities, the rest of the regiment would have thought it ignoble to deny him the pleasure of beholding them all.

They left Berwick in three divisions, a day's march apart, resting on Sundays or upon every fourth day if their commander thought this necessary. Their route through dust or mud was by Alnwick, Newcastle and Richmond, Doncaster, Newark and Royston. They were nightly quartered on uneasy cottagers who were surprised to discover that these savages stood bonnet in hand for grace before they supped, and they marched at dawn when a grenadier drummer beat the General. There were more desertions, ten before the advance party of a sergeant's guard entered York, and more to make the total sixty before the unbelievable sight of London from Highgate Hill. The losses were not greatly regretted, except that "they carried off their clothes and a few their arms". Major Grant's orders instructed him to gather those deserters from other regiments whom he found in town gaols and to convey them to London. Any man of the 43rd who was still of a mind to be away home could learn a lesson from these sullen, manacled wretches who marched with the third division and who talked at night of the lash, the transports, and the killing fevers of the Savoy Prison above the Thames.

For the first few days the spirits of the Highlanders were high, and they strutted before the crowds who came to hear the barbaric music of their pipes, to see the billowing swing of their plaids. At Newcastle fifteen hundred mounted gentlemen of the county cantered up and down the columns, loudly expressing their admiration. Highlanders had not been seen this far south since the Jacobites surrendered in Lancashire nearly thirty years before, and further south they had not been seen for a century, when they had come to die on an autumn day for an unwanted King. The civil reception became less admiring and respectful. The contemporary author of *A Short History of the Highland Regiment* said that as they marched on and "met with the compliments of our true bred English clowns they grew more gloomy" and apparently reacted violently. He did not blame them for this, since men enlisted to avenge their country's wrongs abroad could not be expected to endure the grossest affronts at home, but he would not believe that they were stupid enough to think they were only coming south to be reviewed by the King.

> I say this on a supposition that their officers knew it to be an error, which is carrying the thing as far as can be, since in all human probability the officers thought in this respect like the private men, and never dream'd that such a whim could come into any body's head as to send for them to show their bare backsides in England.

Far more serious in effect than the jeering contempt of English villagers was a meeting with a party of the Royal Scots returning home to recruit. These sixty hollow-cheeked, yellow-faced men were all that was left of a battalion that had been sent to the West Indies, the rest being dead in the fever-graves of the islands. They were members of the first regiment of Foot in the British Army, proud to be known as Pontius Pilate's Bodyguard, and they were also Lowlanders whose contempt for the clans must have been salted by envy as they sat in the tavern smoke and looked at these young, vigorous, healthful Highlanders. Finally they were Old Soldiers whose custom and privilege it was to deflate the conceit of men who had yet to see a comrade beheaded by roundshot or choke to death on his own black vomit. They said that it was well known that when the 43rd reached London it would be sent to the Caribbean, all but the officers who would return to Scotland to recruit another regiment.

They spoke of death as a familiar, of rotting bodies in the West Indian sun, of men rising cheerfully at morning call and stepping into sudden eternity with one pace, of burials too numerous to remember, and graves lost in a week beneath jungle growth. The Highlanders knew more about the West Indies, perhaps, than they knew of London. The Caribbean was the nightmare of their recent history, a place of damned souls to which some of their ancestors, defeated in one rebellion or another, had been transported and lost. Within the lifetime of many of them an Act of Parliament had declared that such punishment upon Highland rebels should come second only to death. Service in the West Indies was also the omnipresent fear of the serving soldier, and for him a punishment too, awarded by courts-martial and so dreaded that many condemned men accepted a thousand or two thousand lashes as an alternative, believing their chances of survival under this murderous experience were greater than they could hope from the fever swamps of Jamaica. Nor could they be sure that, once embarked, they would reach the islands alive. Crammed aboard the transports, lying on deck-boards that stank of the diseased men the ships had recently brought home, existing in daily corruption and filth which frequent drenchings with vinegar and salt water could not remove, the soldiers died by tens, twenties and hundreds before the first green landfall of the Caribbean isles.

The losses suffered by the Royals were not exceptional. In the campaign they had been sent to fight more men had died from disease than from Spanish gunshot and bayonet, ten thousand in the ranks and nearly three hundred officers, including their general. In less than five weeks one regiment had four colonels, three lieutenant-colonels and three majors, each following his predecessor into a hill-top grave and forgotten with the echoes of a valedictory fusillade. Wolfe's battalion of Marines had been reduced to ninety-six men, and Blakeney's to eight. Death in battle would have been a charity, but there was little combat to bring this merciful release and to be wounded only was a greater terror. Aboard a hospital ship off Cartagena, Tobias Smollett heard men call upon death to deliver them from the filth in which they wallowed, from the maggots that hatched in their putrefying flesh. The survivors of a few wasteful engagements were used as labourers, building roads and entrenchments that were soon washed away by storms, succumbing more easily to fever as their spirits were weakened by exhaustion and despair. In the forgivable ignorance of the time regimental surgeons could do little, dying themselves as they wrote for more powdered Peruvian bark, more rhubarb, more vinegar. The horror grew worse throughout the century. Of a hundred thousand casualties suffered by the British Army in the last decade, two-thirds were dead men or broken men as a result of West Indian service, the equivalent of sixty battalions of Foot.

After that meeting with the Royals on the Great North Road the Highlanders no longer trusted their officers, and they now knew that the review by the King was not a special honour but proof that they were to be sent out of the country. They marched on in bitterness, conscious of a breach of faith, of dishonest assurances given by men of their own race. The discovery of those lies made it easy to believe a greater untruth, that they were to be abandoned by their officers and sold as slaves to the Indies. They saw their past and their future clearly. "It naturally came into their heads," said the *Short History*, "that they had been first used as rods to scourge their own countrymen, and after having sufficiently tamed them were now to be thrown into the fire."

"That they should not go out of their own country"

THE KING WAS gone to Flanders before the first division of the Highlanders marched down the Roman road into Hertfordshire. The only members of the regiment he might have seen were the distant figures of a baggage party standing on the deck of a ship that passed his yacht in the Thames estuary, a vessel from Inverness tacking upstream to St. Katharine's dock with the battalion's heavier equipment. He had not forgotten the 43rd however, or at least not before delegating the review to another. It was rumoured that this was to be his first son Frederick, a poor ill-tempered fellow with staring blue eyes, but the duty had been given to George Wade who had already reviewed the companies more times than he or they could recall. There were, of course, other matters upon the King's conscience and attention. The war was somewhat late in starting, due to the old man's uncertainty as to which candidate for the Austrian succession might best serve the interests of the Electorate of Hanover. To the relief of his Government he had at last decided to oppose the French, whose choice he had earlier supported, and had now left to join his soldiers in the field with more enthusiasm than his general officers felt appropriate to his age and experience. The public had been bewildered by the procrastination, and a hack poet expressed a popular ridicule.

> The Lord knows how our army'll fare,
> We're governed by the Lord knows who.
> Our King is gone the Lord knows where,
> And the Lord knows what we'll do.

49

They were in fact to be governed by a regency council of nineteen Lords Justices, headed by the Archbishop of Canterbury and including seven dukes and six earls. It did not feel obliged to meet until the King had been gone for more than a week, and one of the first entries in its minute-book for that day was a marching order to Lord Sempill, instructing him to quarter his men in the villages of Highgate, Hampstead, Finchley and Barnet. London society was delighted by this news, for the journals had previously said that the regiment would embark from Colchester, distressing many excited ladies who were eager to see these bare-shanked Apollos.

Six companies were quartered about Barnet and Highgate by May 6, and four in other villages. They attended their morning and evening parades dutifully enough, but sullenly, and they gathered in secretive groups before and after. Whatever was being planned among them, Patrick MacGregor of Sir Robert Munro's company could not wait. He exchanged his plaid and jacket for the small-clothes of a villager and set out for home one night, but he got no further than Royston where his awkwardness and lack of English caused him to be taken up and lodged in Cambridge Gaol. The Highlanders were objects of fashionable curiosity, not only to the respectable gentlefolk who had country residences on Church Row or Pond Square but also to others who took advantage of the gentle spring evenings to drive up from the city by Tottenham Court or Lamb's Conduit Fields. The wells at Highgate and Hampstead were diverting resorts, an escape from the sulphurous air of the city, and there were coffee-houses and dancing-rooms to compensate those visitors who were disappointed by the reserve or hostility of the soldiers. A correspondent of the *Gentleman's Magazine* did speak to some of the Highlanders, on matters of importance rather than the barbaric peculiarities of their dress, and he wrote later that they had intended to petition the King at the review, alleging that

> . . . they were retrenched of their pay; that they had not been regularly enlisted, and had been told that they should not go

out of their own country, and were only coming to England
to be reviewed; and that they were terrified for fear of going
to Jamaica, as some had told them, rather than which they
chose immediate death.

If the officers were aware of a growing discontent they did
nothing. The regiment would be in the field within a fortnight
and marching against the enemy, until then a gentleman could
enjoy the unfamiliar pleasures of the gaming-rooms at Belsize, the
houses of "dissipation and amusement" at Hampstead. Innocence
is an irresistible victim to the malicious, the fears of another a joke
to the unthreatened, and a linen-draper from Ludgate Hill took
as much delight as a potboy from Aldersgate in telling the Highlanders that they were indeed to be sent to the West Indies. As a
result of this ill-informed gossip, said Mr. Campbell, the soldiers
felt "a very great animosity against their officers whom they
groundlessly blamed for not informing them truly where they
were to go before they carried them from their own country, and
not allowing them time to settle their concerns".

A crowd of forty thousand came to see the review on Saturday,
May 14, gathering about the open ground of Finchley Common.
Two troops of Montagu's Dragoons and a company of the Third
Guards formed the perimeter of an open square, holding back the
press of riders, carriages and hackney-coaches, citizens on foot
with their families, ballad-singers and fiddlers, fire-eaters and
sword-swallowers, pie-sellers, fruit-vendors and milkmaids, pick-
pockets, thief-takers and professional duellists looking for a
quarrel. Those who could not see the square created their own
amusements by goading drunkards into bare-knuckle fights or
whores into screaming abuse, and those whose rank entitled
them to a privileged view ordered their sweating coachmen to
whip back the unprivileged who threatened to obscure it.

Their tapping drums scarcely heard above the noise, the
Highlanders marched on to the Common at seven o'clock, by
companies and each followed by a shouting tail of mocking
children. They formed in battalion line, three ranks of scarlet and

green, the Lieutenant-colonel's company on the left and the Major's, Colonel's and Grenadier's on the right, with the other six spaced between in order of seniority. The captains stood before their commands, flanked by their lieutenants and ensigns, and twelve paces to their front the drummers beat the Troop until the whole regiment was in line and properly dressed. And then a silent wait, each man with his musket at rest and one knee bent, enduring the ribald shouting of the mob. Between nine and ten, after breakfast in town, George Wade arrived with a party of gentlemen, including the Duke of Montagu who was there as a representative of the Lords Regent and thus all that the Highlanders could hope to see of the King's Majesty.

Wade ignored the indecent fairground behaviour of the crowd, and he carried out the review with conscientious diligence. This was a battalion made ready for war, for the business of killing, and it was his duty to see that it was well-equipped and fit for such serious employment. As he walked toward each company with Sempill its drummer beat a complimentary ruffle and its captain removed his bonnet with an elegant sweep of his arm. Wade carefully inspected every rank, remembering what contented or displeased him before returning to the reviewing post to watch the battalion at exercise. The complicated movements of drill and firing were greeted by the crowd with applause, laughter or mock alarm according to their humour, and when the bloodless simulation of battle was over Major George Grant advanced to the front and called "To the right, close your files by companies. . . .!" He waited until the officers, sergeants and drummers had taken their posts and then cried "*March!*", upon which the files closed upon their right-hand markers. This done, the companies were wheeled to the right, moving like the opening feathers of a fan and changing from a battalion in line to column of companies in line, the swinging green plaids softening the stiffness of the ranks. With drums beating, and field officers marching at the head of their own commands, the regiment finally moved past Wade in the Grand March of Review.

That afternoon Wade dictated his report to the Secretary at

War. The Highlanders were good-sized men and had marched and fired extremely well. He thought their uniforms were old and much worn, but he had been assured by Sempill that new clothing was coming from Scotland. Four hundred and more broadswords were still wanting to replace those owned by the men, but again Sempill had promised that these would come as soon as the contractor completed the order. Without comment, Wade noted that among the absent officers was the adjutant, John Lindsay, "said to be a minor of about 10 years of age". Lieutenant Lindsay, who had been commissioned three years before, was no doubt still at his lessons, but happy to have secured the earliest possible seniority in the Army List.

Before the companies were dismissed to their quarters they were given the orders that had come that afternoon from the Secretary at War. On the following Thursday they would march to the Isle of Dogs from which they would cross the river to Greenwich, be quartered there for the night and then proceed to other North Kent towns where they would await embarkation on transports already anchored in the Thames. The orders said nothing of their destination once at sea. Some of the Highlanders were informed by their officers that they were going to Flanders, but as they later told Campbell they knew this to be "only a blind to get them on board, in order to ship them really for the West Indies".

Angered by so many betrayals of trust, their pride injured by the King's failure to review them, and believing that they were thereby released from any obligation to soldier a day more, many of them were now determined to go home. How this decision was reached, by what communication between the dispersed companies, will never be known, but that there was an intelligent if naïve leadership cannot be doubted. No body of men could have acted as the mutineers behaved without such guidance. More than this, they were Highlanders and the family structure of the clan had bred in them the expectation of authority as much as obedience to it, so long as it kept faith with them. Without it they were lost. However, with one exception the hundred and

seven mutineers later brought to trial steadfastly and in almost
the same words declared that "they would not admit of any chief
or commander among them". The one man who did make such
an admission was a MacGregor, held in the Savoy Prison and thus
isolated from his companions in the Tower. He denied it the next
day, but that moment of lonely weakness was enough to take
the life of Corporal Samuel Macpherson.

Macpherson was born thirty years before in the parish of
Laggan, where the Spey comes down the western shoulder of
the grey Monadhliath and turns north-eastward into a widening
valley. His family was Jacobite if a choice of kings had to be made
in battle, and his uncle held the lands of Breakachie. His father
was descended from the ninth chief of the Macphersons and his
mother was probably a sister of the present holder of the title,
which gave him the right to claim a direct line through twenty-
one generations to the medieval parson who had given his people
their name. He was a quiet and undemonstrative man who had
obeyed his father and studied law in Edinburgh until he could no
longer endure such inaction, joining the Watch and earning
promotion in the company commanded by Grant of Culbin. His
cousin Malcolm Macpherson, whom the Army would rightly or
wrongly consider a ringleader also, was the son of the laird of
Driminard in Laggan, and he became a corporal in Simon Fraser's
company, serving without complaint until the embodiment of
the 43rd made him uneasy. He would never have faced the
killing muskets of the Scots Guards had Lovat honoured a promise
and secured his discharge. Both men were family-proud and clan-
proud, and it was they who told Renkine in Ladywood that they
were "as well-born as some of their officers". By Saturday afternoon, when they returned to their quarters from Finchley
Common, they had stomached enough injury from their equals.

The answer to the Highlanders' discontent was simple. A
contract of trust had been broken and they would soldier no
more. How they should return to their mountains was also easily
decided, they would march as they had come, defending themselves if necessary but molesting no one who let them pass, and

making payment for all they took. This peaceable intention, which they resolutely kept, would be regarded later as an example of the inherently superior qualities of the Highlander, it being the fancy of Victorian romantics to credit their favoured savages with the virtues of a drawing-room civilisation. What makes the mutineers' behaviour admirable, however, is that it was a contradiction of their natures and their history. Their fathers and grandfathers had lived on the land through which they forayed, and some of the soldiers – the MacGregors and the Breadalbane men particularly – had recently been raiders themselves. They had no love for southern peoples, and to take what they wanted from barn and byre would have seemed good sense as well as the pattern of an old way of life. An intelligent leadership, and an acceptance of discipline imposed by three years of regimental training, persuaded them to act otherwise. The Macpherson cousins knew that if they travelled with speed and cunning they might outwit the troops sent to restrain them, but if they provoked the hostility and resistance of countryfolk with whom they had no dispute they could not hope to pass through the southern shires of England.

When they should go was the most important decision, and three days passed before it was forced upon them. On Tuesday they were told that the first division would now march for Greenwich the following morning. The word passed quickly among the companies. They should gather on Finchley Common at midnight, with their arms and any ammunition they had in their pouches, and they should go home together to their mountains. Such a call, carried by word of mouth from village to village, could not be kept secret. At six o'clock an unhappy soldier of the grenadiers went to the sign of The Horns at Highgate where he found his sergeant, Alexander MacBean. He said that many of his comrades intended to desert that night. MacBean did not believe it, but he crossed the street to another inn and told Lieutenant John Menzies of Comrie who did not believe it either, or at least did nothing. His duty done, MacBean returned to The Horns and his ale.

The gathering began before midnight. Men came in small groups through the darkness, muskets and bayonets slanting against a dim glow from the whale-oil lamps outside the houses on the edge of the Common. One party attempted to bring the battalion colour with them but an ensign, in whose charge it was, stripped it from the staff before they got into his quarters, giving it to a woman who was providentially keeping him company. Midnight passed without the march beginning. The delay was due to some cheerful small-talk and debate, but also to Samuel Macpherson's reluctance to leave until he was sure that most if not all of the companies were present. Malcolm Macpherson told Campbell that he had not made up his mind when he came to the gathering "and then his reflection was so short that he scarce knew what he did", but he was forgetting what he wished to forget, and the statement does not explain why he went to the Common at all, or that he too believed the march should not begin until most of the battalion was willing to go. Lewis Mac-Farlane, a man of sublime equanimity, was bored by the waiting and went to sleep, awakening only when the others had gone. He then hurried after them, although the locomotive verb he used at his trial was "strolled". That he slept at all is astonishing, for there was a great noise of voices, the clattering of arms, and some of the men fired their muskets in the air. This was a *feu de joie* perhaps, or an impatient summons to the laggards. Two miles away, MacBean took it to be such an alarm and he belted on his plaid and went into the street. There he found Menzies, also aroused and no doubt regretting his earlier indifference. Together they ran toward the firing.

In Barnet to the north, Captain John Munro of Newmore heard the shots and at the same time was told that some of his company had left their quarters. He set out at once with a sergeant for Finchley and skirting the Common. A third officer was also alarmed. Between eleven and twelve a grenadier called Panton, who may have been the same man who reported to MacBean, went to The Bell at Highgate and told Lieutenant Malcolm Fraser that his brother was gone with other grenadiers to a meeting on the Common. Fraser called up two sergeants and on their way to the gathering they met Peter Farquharson, going home with his firelock on his shoulder and his sword at his side. They took him prisoner and held him until he was snatched from them. Fraser could see little in the moving darkness of the mob, but when he did recognise a face or a voice he appealed to the man to return to duty. One was willing to submit, but three others drew their broadswords and threatened to kill him if he took a step away from his comrades. At this Fraser pushed angrily into the crowd, but was held by bayonets charged at his chest and voices warning him to go no further at the risk of his life.

Elsewhere in the black confusion Menzies and MacBean were now calling upon the men to disperse. The presence of officers and sergeants changed the mood of the deserters. They became angry, anxious to be gone. They told Menzies to stand away, but he contemptuously seized one of their muskets and threw it behind him. MacBean grasped a shadow, believing that if he marched one man away the others would be ashamed of their behaviour. The shadow was Farquhar Shaw of the Colonel's company, son of a sub-tenant in Rothiemurchus, and he may have wondered later at the chance that made him MacBean's tragic choice and not another. As he tried to free his arm the Sergeant tightened the grasp, they grappled and fell. They struggled for a moment and then Shaw broke free, rising and losing himself among the other deserters.

By the time Munro of Newmore came to the Common with Sergeant Donald Grant the deserters were moving quickly northward on the Barnet road. He heard their hurrying shouts, the rattle of their weapons, and he ran after them, shouting for them to stop. Sixteen men did turn about, but with bayonets charged and crying "Stand off!" He ignored the weapons and walked forward, demanding a way through, but they said "it was not proper to suffer him to come amongst them, for that he would certainly delude some to desert from them". At this paradoxical use of the word he stepped forward impatiently, and half a dozen bayonets touched his body. A moment of silence and then the muskets were brought to the recover. Darkness moved across the dimly seen faces and the Highlanders were gone, running softly after their fellows. Newmore and Grant followed for three miles, into Barnet where other men of the companies were standing sullenly in the street. To keep them from deserting too, Munro broke off the pursuit.

It was long past dawn when the mutineers halted in the market street of St. Albans. They had marched ten miles, mostly in the dark and in a little over four hours, but this would be the slowest pace of their retreat. They had also kept to the road. Henceforward, travelling by night once they were far enough from London, they would take the cover of woods and parklands. They may have originally intended to return to Scotland by the route they had come, but either from intelligent design or from the angry haste in which they had finally left Finchley Common they were twenty miles to the west of that southward march, and in country none of them could have known. There was nobody abroad in St. Albans, although a window or two opened in astonishment and then closed quickly in alarm. Lodged in the town, some of them in the Fleur-de-lys and other inns off Market Place, were the two troops of Montagu's Dragoons commanded by Anthony Renkine. The Highlanders did not know this, and in the minutes before reveille the cavalry sentinels had gone to wash and rouse, unaware that the mutineers were standing on the cobbles a few yards from their quarters. The Macpherson cousins, who had begun to count heads at first light, could now see how few men had come from the Common, little more than a hundred of the whole battalion. Malcolm was gloomy and said they would all be wise to return and trust the mercy of their colonel. Samuel was of the same mind, but when the rest declared that they would march on or die with swords in their hands where they stood, both men agreed to go forward, although always, they said later, counselling their companions against further retreat. At the toll-gate outside the town they civilly asked its keeper to direct them toward Northampton and marched away up the Roman road to Bedfordshire.

An hour and a half later the toll-gate keeper decided that this strange incident was important enough to report to the captain of dragoons. Surprised at his breakfast Renkine knew nothing of the mutiny, but it was not difficult for him to guess what had happened. He sent a troop quartermaster in pursuit of the Highlanders, to talk to them if possible and to watch their route. Another rider was sent to the commander of any soldiers at Northampton, and a third to Barnet. Without orders he could do no more.

Lord Sempill had been awoken at four o'clock in his London chambers, by a manservant who told him that two of his company officers had come with dreadful news. Dressing as quickly as he could while the captains reported, Sempill then took a chair to Wade's house. Reacting like a machine in contrast to his visitor's growing panic, the old soldier told Sempill to get to Hampstead as quickly as he could, to draw out his regiment on the Heath, to list the absent men and to keep the rest under arms and firm discipline. That sharply said, and having urged Sempill on his way, Wade wrote a report to the Earl of Harrington, president of the regency council. The Earl responded with equal alacrity and called an immediate meeting of the council, to be held at his house "that no alarm might be given".

For all this haste, Sempill did not come before his assembled regiment until well past noon on Wednesday. The soldiers had been standing on the Heath for some hours in response to the order he had sent, and the temperature of their feelings was apparent as soon as he rode before them. Uncontrolled by officers or sergeants they waved their muskets and swords in the air, shouting that they had been cheated of their pay and clothing, that they had been sold to the Indies. Miserably hurt, Sempill dismounted and walked closer to them, asking for their trust, but they told him to stand off or he would be shot. Some men began to prime and load and others, already prepared, brought their muskets to the present, finger on the trigger and head inclined to the stock in the deadly affection of the aim. Sempill was shaken but he stood his ground, his voice unheard as he cautioned them against their folly, promising that all just grievances would be redressed. "Be dutiful," he cried, "be dutiful!" But it was the sweating exertion of his officers rather than this melancholy appeal that persuaded his own company and Major Grant's to recover their arms and march to quarters. The other companies broke ranks and would not leave the Heath.

Sempill turned away to his horse and rode hard to Sir William Yonge in Whitehall, stiffly informing the Secretary at War that he feared more mutiny and desertion. He then returned to his chambers and retired to bed, keeping to its solacing security for the rest of the week. He was much vexed, it was said, that Society should blame him and not his men for what they had done.

Yonge had been writing orders since the early morning. Once the Regents had interrogated Wade and Sir Robert Munro at Harrington House they began to issue instructions for the arrest of the deserters and the suppression of further mutiny. Six hundred men of the Third Foot Guards, with fifty riders from the Horse Grenadiers, were ordered to Barnet. Nineteen troops of dragoons, quartered at Loughborough, Leicester, Huntingdon, Northampton and other towns between London and York, were instructed to march upon the deserters wherever they might be found, "to surround and take them all or any part of them prisoners, and to bring them prisoners to the Tower of London". Brigadier-general William Blakeney was given command of this boot-and-saddle campaign, with orders to repel force by force. He was a rough, scarred Irishman well past seventy, and had been enjoying life in the capital since his return from the West Indies, but before nightfall he was riding north in joyous anger.

Upon the Regents' instructions Yonge also wrote to the senile commander in North Britain, telling him that a hundred men "in their Highland regimental habits" were disobediently returning to their own country, and he was to apprehend them should they reach it. Similar letters were sent to the commanders at Carlisle, Newcastle and Berwick. The Secretary then composed an *Advertisement as to the Mutiny and Desertion* for publication in the journals and display in public places, offering forty shillings above the usual reward to anyone bold enough to secure a deserter and bring him before a Justice of the Peace. Finally, at the end of this wrist-aching day, Yonge dispatched the Regents' command "that the whole Highland Regiment do march to Gravesend and embark there for Flanders as soon as possible".

The further desertions Sempill had feared, and did still fear as he lay in his unhappy bed, took place at twelve that night. Between sixty and seventy men gathered as before on Finchley Common and marched away in good order with all their weapons. At one o'clock they entered Barnet where they were halted by Captain Dugal Campbell of Craignish, Munro of Newmore, a lieutenant and an ensign. "I did all in my power to stop them," Campbell told Yonge, "but they, in an insolent manner, bade me stand off or they would shoot me and the officers with me, and thrust their bayonets at me." While he argued with them bravely, some of them beat on doors in the street, calling upon the men of his company and Newmore's to join them. At last he stepped aside, and the mutineers marched on. Still angered by his failure to stop the first desertion on Tuesday night, Newmore followed with the junior officers. Two hours later the Horse Grenadiers rode into Barnet, black horses, big men in poppy-red coats and mitre caps. Their captain was eager to put them to a fast trot in pursuit, but Campbell urged them to stay. In abject shame, he feared that if his Highlanders thought their companions were to be attacked they might leave their quarters and fall upon the troopers from the rear.

This night Munro of Newmore was successful. He and his two officers came up with the deserters eight miles beyond Barnet, and by appeal and threat, the promise of his intercession, he persuaded fifty-three of them to return with him. Twelve refused, of whom eight lost heart at dawn and turned back to surrender. The remaining four were stouter in resolve. They went on, and by a miracle of chance or skill they found the first party.

From his bed at eight o'clock on Wednesday night, and before he turned his face to the wall, Sempill had sent Yonge a numerical

return of the deserters – two corporals, one piper, one hundred
and nine private men. They had gone from all the companies, as
few as two from the Lieutenant-colonel's and as many as twenty-
one from that commanded by James Colquhoun of Luss. Sempill
had lost fourteen from his company. He did not give the names
of the missing men, and might not have thought them significant.
Not more than a dozen had the same surname or patronymic as
their officers, but sixty-five came from clans with a history of
Jacobite sympathies, of raiding or resistance to southern authority.
There were thirteen MacGregors from Breadalbane or Bal-
quhidder, thirteen from Clan Cameron, ten MacDonalds, eight
Frasers, and some Stewarts, Macleans and Macintyres. There
were men from the little clans of Atholl and twenty-six from the
great confederation of Clan Chattan of whom seventeen were
Macphersons. Although all the men of the battalion were
mutinous or resentful, these were understandably the most
obdurate in their decision to soldier no more. They had been
raised by their chiefs or feudal lords and sent to the Watch in
marketable parcels, and unlike the Grants, Munros and Campbells
they had no representative of their *ceann-cinnidh* among the
officers to demand ultimate obedience in his name.

Such niceties were of no consequence to the Regents, who
were English with two exceptions. It was more than enough that
a hundred men, skilled in arms and desperate in humour, were
marching northward and that five hundred others might follow
at any moment. The Lieutenant-colonel of the Third Guards at
Barnet, William Douglas, reported that the remaining men were
"extremely mortified with the madness and folly of their countrymen", but the Regents were not comforted. Douglas was told to
send one of his officers with the 43rd when it marched to the Isle
of Dogs, and at the first report of disorder to fall upon the Highlanders with his Lowland Scots. On Thursday Major George
Grant marched five companies of the first division from Highgate,
through excited crowds in Hornsey, Hackney and Bow, and an
hour later Douglas led his black-capped and white-gaitered
guardsmen on a parallel route through Islington to the Tower.

At half-past six that evening, when the barges brought the last of the men across to Greenwich, Grant sent Yonge the news that all the companies had behaved very civilly. However, an hour since Sergeant MacBean had brought him "a message in the name of the whole men that they would not march to-morrow morning without which they had one shirt more and sixteen pence yearly for shoes". It was late at night, Yonge had been at his desk since early morning and his response was testy and bureaucratic. He sent Grant a printed copy of the rules governing shoes and clothing, with instructions to arrest any man who disputed them. He also wrote a hurried letter to Colonel Edward Wolfe, ordering him to take command of all regiments of Marines in Kent and to march them immediately to Greenwich, there to quell any mutiny or disturbance.

On Friday, Munro of Foulis brought the second division over the Thames, and his friendly assurances or the arrival of so many battalions of Marines persuaded the Highlanders to parade on Blackheath the next day. As the companies stood at ease, their captains went among them making notes of their complaints, of plaids very poor and narrow, of shirts lacking and shoe money unpaid, of missing buckles and frayed sword-belts. Munro knew that their real discontent came from that fear of being sent to the Indies, and he was anxious to get them aboard before their smouldering unease burnt into new anger. To his relief they marched obediently to Dartford and Gravesend, and before noon on the following Tuesday they were all aboard the transports.

They had believed his promise that they would be relieved of all their just grievances and they did not know what he had written to Sempill, that he "took in writing the demands they made that the world might see how unreasonable they were".

"You see now what situation you are in . . ."

WILLIAM BLAKENEY AND his escort rode throughout the night, pausing only for a change of horses, and before seven o'clock on Thursday morning they had crossed the Buckinghamshire border beyond the village of Eakley Lanes and were within four miles of Northampton. As they trotted between a wood and the park walls of Lord Halifax's estate Major Ruisshe Hassell saw four Highlanders at the edge of the trees, but the glimpse of scarlet was gone before he could point them out to the General. Believing that what he called the "grand party" of the deserters must therefore be in the wood, Blakeney wisely rode on to Northampton as if nothing had been seen. There he was told that five men of the 43rd had recently appeared in Eakley Lanes, standing before the door of the Bull's Head and boldly asking for food. Though he may have wished to knock the villagers' heads together for their failure to arrest the impudent rascals, or at least tell him about them as he rode through, Blakeney took the news as confirmation of his belief that the Highlanders were in the woods to the immediate south of the city, and he ordered John Ball's squadron to ride there and report.

The men whom Hassell had seen and those reported in Eakley Lanes were probably the same, scouts only and ranging wide, for the main body of the mutineers was at this moment twenty miles to the south and east below Bedford, climbing a spur of the Chilterns to find sleep and shelter for the day among its trees. Some hours behind them on the Luton road were Anthony Renkine's troopers, advancing cautiously at the walk and with carbines across the saddle, expecting every bend to splutter with the sudden musketry of an ambuscade. But the Highlanders had no wish for a fight, unless it were forced upon them. Under their own discipline or the control exercised by the Macphersons they had molested no one, and although they had forcibly taken bacon and cheese when it was refused them in a village north of St. Albans they had done so with no more violence than was needed to break open a stubborn door. At dusk that day, when they were rising and belting their plaids, Renkine admitted to himself that he had no idea where they might be, and he rode westward to Newport Pagnell, joining Major Otway and two other sweat-lathered troops of Montagu's Dragoons.

At nightfall too, Captain Ball returned to Northampton with nothing to report. Before Blakeney had finished his supper a message from Bedford said that the Highlanders had been seen at sunset, slipping down North Hill toward the River Ouse, and he decided that they must be moving toward the dense Forest of Rockingham where it would be difficult for his horsemen to search and fight. He sent a galloper to Otway with orders to put his squadron on the march to Kettering at once, and Ball was told to take his command eastward to Huntingdon, there to gather four troops of Wade's Horse and lead them all to Stamford on the northern edge of the forest. At noon on Friday, May 20, the General rode at a gallop to Wellingborough where he was irritated to discover that the Highlanders had outpaced him. Travelling thirty miles in the short night, running like deer over unfamiliar hills and fields, they had crossed the River Nene four miles to the east of the town and had once more disappeared. Three Scottish residents were said to have gone to them and told them all that was publicly known about the strength and disposition of the dragoons. Whatever rage Blakeney felt at this he later stifled by a confident letter to London in which he said he hoped soon to give a good account of the Highlanders. "I have now several persons to watch them and their motions, and have ordered each commanding officer to spare no cost for good intelligence." More practically, he sent the new information to Ball at Huntingdon, and it was at this point that the eager captain

decided to block the escape into Rutland. For all Blakeney's
chagrin as he rode northward, to Stamford now, he had deployed
his squadrons well, and in a manner that would have pleased his
friend Humphrey Bland, brutal trooper and cavalry theorist.
From Huntingdon through Stamford, and Kettering to Northampton, they formed the wide mouth of a net which the Highlanders must now enter, and which he could shortly close.
Should any evade the mesh there were further squadrons beyond
it, across the roads to Newark and the Fens.

It was seventy-two hours since the deserters had left Finchley
Common, and in that time they had travelled as many miles or
more, much of them in darkness and by field, trees and high
ground. No troop of dragoons had seen them upon the march,
or where they briefly slept in the dappled shade of remote woods.
They had used the open English countryside as if it were a dark
room, but this miracle was now ended. If the information
brought him by the Wellingborough Scots was accurate, Samuel
Macpherson must have known that he and his companions had
come as far as reason could hope. They must now surrender or
fight. That Friday night, as they moved once more, they abandoned the northward route of the roads and followed the crooked
course of the Nene to the north-east, a shallow valley with dark
hilltop hamlets and the silent wheels of a dozen water-mills.
Before first light on Saturday they had come no more than ten
miles and were less than three to the east of Sudborough, on
meadowland that had once belonged to John Creed's mother.
They saw high ground to their left, blanketed with thick trees,
and they climbed to it. As their rearguard looked back at the edge
of the wood, John Ball's troopers galloped along the Brigstock
road below.

The spine of the hill stretched for three miles between Sudborough and Oundle, cloaked in oak, elm, ash and thorn. The
densest part was known as Ladywood and its north-eastern fringe
covered the Jacobean shell of Lyveden New Bield, a cruciform
manor house planned in love and piety by the Catholic Sir
Thomas Tresham. He had died before its completion, and in the

same year his son died too, hapless betrayer of the Gunpowder Plot and a probable victim of prison fever. The New Bield was never finished. Cromwellians took its floor timbers, and finally the compassionate arms of Ladywood embraced its empty grief. Once they had walked about it and seen the symbols of the Passion on its moss-grown entablature – the nails, the sponge and spear, the wreath of thorns and the heart of Christ – the devoutly Protestant Highlanders would have avoided its idolatrous stones. It meant little to them, and they would have cared less had they known that eight miles away was Fotheringhay, where a Catholic Queen of Scots had been judicially parted from her head.

The ruins of Tresham's interrupted dream included an overgrown water-orchard a hundred yards from the Bield. This large square was surrounded by a moat that was to have been filled by some natural or contrived spring but was now dry. There was a rusted gate and perhaps the remains of a railing fence that may once have enclosed the orchard, and at three corners were dimpled mounds like the ravelins of a fort. The whole enclave was thick with trees and brush that marched over moat and ramparts at some points and down the slope to the north. The Highlanders made their camp within this unexpected defence work, lighting no fires, sleeping when they could under the cool green of spring leaves. Their earlier joy had now become a defiant despair. Beyond the trees to the north, to the east and the west, they occasionally saw the sparkling glint of metal, heard the sound of hooves, a trumpet call. Most of them accepted Samuel Macpherson's sober advice. Since they could go no further, here in this strange earthwork they were able to demand a free pardon or die where they stood. It was in this mood late on Saturday that they sent a message to a Justice of the Peace, and on Sunday morning accepted John Creed's word that they would be treated fairly and with honour. It was Pentecost, the day when the Holy Ghost brought wisdom to the disciples of Christ.

The Highlanders had not expected a man like Captain Ball. He and his quartermaster were allowed no further than the edge

of the wood where he spoke to the Macphersons and a Clan
Gregor man, Donald MacAlpin of the grenadiers. His brisk
demand for an immediate and unconditional surrender was
rejected, and he wheeled his horse about, shouting that he would
now bring his dragoons against them, sword in hand. But when
he returned to his squadron it did not move, since he probably
decided that he should have Blakeney's approval before he led it
in a glory-charge, uphill and against concealed muskets. The
Highlanders were alarmed by his threats however, and by some
means they sent a brief and melancholy appeal to Creed, asking
him to restrain Ball's dragoons.

Throughout that afternoon the roads about Ladywood were
full of red horsemen, riding from Stamford and Uppingham,
from Kettering and Oundle. They deployed on the fields, on the
slopes to the Benefield road, in the meadow-grass about Sudborough and Wadenhoe, their pickets standing in close to the
wood and just beyond range. The noise was unbroken, voices
and the whinny of horses, the sweet music of bridle-chains and
again the urgent calling of trumpets. At seven in the darkening
light another body of horsemen arrived on the Sudborough
slope, no troopers but men in fine geranium coats with gold and
blue cuffs, brocaded tricornes and glittering aiguilettes. William
Blakeney had come with his staff. About this hour the mutineers
received a reply from Creed. It gave them little comfort, and its
tone was that of a pedagogue lecturing wilful pupils. It also
indicated that the Major, robbed of the distinction of bringing
the mutineers to surrender, was now disengaging himself from
the whole affair.

I do not know what orders the King's troops may have had
since I saw you. You see now what situation you are in. I
think it proper you should surrender yourselves and return to
your duty. As I have already intended to do you the best
service I could by applying to the Duke of Montagu in your
behalf, in case you surrender'd, I will still continue to do so,
if you think to surrender. I will see you to-morrow morning

early, if you desire it, which is all I can say till I have an answer from the Duke of Montagu.

He must have known that by the next morning the miserable business would have been settled one way or the other by Blakeney. He did not come to Ladywood again, and the mutineers did not ask for his further help, but the loss of his presumed friendship was another blow to their spirits. Some time during that day they had buried a man who had died of exhaustion or sickness, and his grave was a fresh mound of loam among the leaves of past autumns. Farquhar Shaw was also ill, but he was one of a few who had stubbornly declared that they should die sword in hand. Samuel Macpherson knew that surrender was inevitable, but he was determined that it should be made upon terms that gave them all a hope of life or freedom.

At nine o'clock Blakeney sent Ball to the wood again, and this time the captain spoke civilly, asking to be taken before the whole body of the mutineers. He did this, he said in a report he later sent to the *Evening Post* in London, because he wished "to observe in what manner they encamped themselves". What he saw in the fading light may have made him thankful that he had not carried out his threat to take the position by storm. The Highlanders

> . . . were drawn up with a very thick wood on the rear, a large ditch about four or five feet high, with a forest hedge thereon, in manner as near could be like an half moon; before them was a small path about four feet wide, with a strong and thick wood behind that; and on each end of the half moon they had planted 20 men to secure the path, and in the body about 70; the rest were to guard the high gate that led to the path.

When Macpherson repeated the terms he had given Creed, Ball said he had no power to grant them, but would tell his General, and he was allowed to leave. Blakeney was impressed by what Ball had to report about the mutineers' defences, and he

sent the captain back to talk them into surrender. This time the
dragoon ignored the Macphersons and MacAlpin, and appealed
to the others who may or may not have understood him.
Suddenly uneasy, Samuel Macpherson brought his musket to
the charge, resting the point of the bayonet on Ball's chest and
threatening to kill him if he attempted to treat with them
separately. Three others also charged their muskets, but Ball
was unafraid. In a loud voice he said that if they all laid down
their arms now he would personally recommend them to the
favour of the Lords Justices. Some who understood him shouted
that they would rather die than surrender on any terms but their
own. Their defiance lacked the strength of the words, and he
knew it. "I am your friend," he said, or later claimed he said,
"and would do all in my power to serve you, but if you continue
obstinate another hour every man will be cut to pieces, and I'll
grant quarter to none!"

No man spoke. Putting an end to the dramatic silence, Ball
asked to be conducted from the darkness of the wood. He was
taken by two men who he thought were brothers, but who were
undoubtedly the Macphersons. He talked to them persuasively
and pleasantly, as gentlemen and his equals, sensing that their
unease was as great as their influence. With no power at all to
make the offer, he promised them both a free pardon if they
submitted. They may have believed that it was offered to all,
and if they knew it was for themselves alone their acceptance
was a bitter indication of their weariness and irresolution, and
this betrayal – almost the last in the miserable affair – was perhaps
the most excusable. Having got their agreement Ball suggested
that one returned to the water-orchard to "try whether fair
words etc., would prevail with the rest". It was probably Malcolm
who went, and he returned quickly with thirteen others including
Donald MacAlpin. Ball marched them halfway down the slope
and then, as if realising that he was leaving the game before it was
won, he halted and sent another man back into the wood. This
time there was no immediate response, and the dragoon waited
anxiously for thirty minutes until seventeen more men came

down in the moonlight, blowing powder from the pans of their muskets. Ball marched them proudly to Blakeney's bivouac where Donald MacAlpin and Patrick MacNicol were the first to lay their swords and firelocks at the General's booted feet.

The little erosion once begun, the surrender became a landfall. Black figures came from the trees, singly or in groups, their plaids flowing from their shoulders like dark wings. There was no sound at first but the soft slip of brogues on the grass, and then the clatter of weapons dropped before Blakeney. Major Hassell counted the muskets, and the pipes of Donald MacDonnell, and by that numbering told the General that ninety-eight men had surrendered upon his mercy. Fourteen were thus still missing, but the picket lines of dragoons who slowly entered the wood found only the dead man's grave. Some of the absent men were away on scout, but others had refused to surrender and were long since gone. One of these was Farquhar Shaw, who arose from his sickness and declared that he would die fighting if he could not find his way home to his hills.

Without the leadership of the Macphersons and MacAlpin, the surrender of the Highlanders was inevitable. The author of the *Short History* said that more courage had been expected of them, but he thought their submission indicated their good sense. "Some shadow they had of escaping by a surrender, whereas the death of one of the King's troops had been the death of them all." In charity it may be believed that this was the Macphersons' opinion also.

As a reward for his noble part in the affair, Captain Ball was given the honour of escorting the prisoners. He marched them that night to Thrapston on the Nene where they were herded in the churchyard, its walls patrolled by his dragoons. At two o'clock on Monday afternoon they were taken to Oundle and were the objects of emotional curiosity, but there is no record that John Creed saw them or spoke to them when they passed his door. From Oundle they were led to Kettering, and by noon on Tuesday they entered Northampton. At that same hour, seventy miles to the south at Gravesend, the last of their companions went aboard the transports, watched by nine hundred armed men of Wolfe's Marines.

They were held in Northampton for two days, that the dragoons' horses might recover their strength rather than the prisoners regain theirs, and then Ball put them on the road for London and the Tower. Within twenty-four hours his riders captured three of the men who had slipped away from Ladywood, and who had lost themselves in confusion or fear. The bitter, weary journey took five days, and the Highlanders' quarters at night were empty barns or cold graveyards, but it was said that they "kept up their spirits and marched very cheerfully". The news of their coming had reached London on Monday when Major Hassell brought word of the surrender to the Regents. Society was romantically excited, and the *Short History* said that some Scots in the capital compared the desertion "to the retreat of the 10,000 Greeks through Persia, by which, for the honour of the ancient kingdom of Scotland, Corporal Macpherson was erected into a Xenophon". Less classically minded, the Lords Justices prepared for the reception of a hundred dangerous criminals. William Douglas' Scots Guards were the garrison troops at the Tower and he was told to issue each man with ten rounds of ball cartridge. The Deputy-lieutenant of the fortress, Adam Williamson, was ordered to provide proper confinement for the deserters and a proper guard for their security. Since it was impossible to lodge so many men in the warders' houses, he cleared the three lower barracks of the Irish Mint. By Yonge's instructions every man was to have two trusses of straw and a daily ration of a pound and a half of bread, half a pound of cheese, and half a pint of oatmeal to be mixed with water according to their taste. To pay for this Williamson was authorised to draw fourpence from each soldier's subsistence pay.

In Highgate at nine o'clock on the overcast morning of Tuesday, May 31, Captain Ball was joined by a lieutenant and fifty men of the First Guards. Now the hands of the prisoners were tied behind their backs. They were divided into parties of twenty, each four ranks of five, with the dragoons flanking the spaces between them, and the mitred guardsmen marching in the van and rear. As the column passed through cheering or jeering crowds in Islington and Shoreditch the Highlanders were no longer in good spirits, and a writer to the *Westminster Journal*, with restrained understatement, said that they looked "much dejected". Early in the afternoon they passed by Eastcheap to Tower Hill, crossed the moat and entered their prison. That evening the Lords Justices decided, and so instructed, that Samuel Macpherson, Malcolm Macpherson, and the piper Donald MacDonnell should be immediately separated from their companions and kept "singly in a different place of confinement, and be not suffered to have any intercourse with any of the other prisoners". Williamson put each of them in the charge of a warder, and a sentinel stood day and night at the door of each stone cell.

Sick though he was, speaking no English, his identity betrayed by his red coat and green plaid, Farquhar Shaw travelled sixty miles and more from Ladywood in three days before he collapsed from exhaustion. He was found outside Lichfield by William Sneyd, a gentleman of the district, and was quickly lodged in Stafford Gaol. Mr. Sneyd was thanked for his devotion to the King's service and was asked to draw upon the War Office for the usual reward and the forty shillings extra.

"But my blood, I hope, will contribute to your liberty"

WHEN HE HAD counted the last musket laid at his General's feet, Major Hassell was ordered to London with the joyous news of the mutineers' surrender. On Monday evening, weary and travel-stained, he made a full report to an extraordinary meeting of the Lords Justices who at once sent the information to the King in Hanover. Their Lordships properly delayed the ordering of a court-martial until His Majesty's pleasure was known, although this formality need not have been so precise. Without full knowledge of the causes of the mutiny, the bitterness and the grievances, the King replied that his mercy could be extended in general "but for the good of his service an example of severity should be made on some of the most guilty". This instruction was received on June 2, and on that day the Regents also read a brief petition from the unhappy men in the Tower. It asked for compassion. The petitioners had feared they were to be sent to the West Indies "where everyone would die of the severe heat of the climate". They had explained this to Major Creed who had promised to ask the Duke of Montagu for a pardon, and now they wished only to join their comrades in Flanders and to serve the King to the last drop of their blood. The petition was set aside, and the Judge-Advocate-General was instructed to call a court-martial forthwith.

Before the arrival of the King's letter the Lords Justices had already decided upon those who might be considered "most guilty". There was enough evidence in the letters of Creed and Renkine, and in Hassell's report perhaps, to damn the Macphersons, although none of it would be heard at their trial. They were also non-commissioned officers, and therefore more culpable. No explanation can be found for the selection of the piper Donald MacDonnell. Yet it is possible to understand the reasoning of the Regents who may have been guided to the decision by the one member of their council who was Highland, Archibald Campbell, Earl of Islay and Keeper of the Seal of Scotland. He could have explained the exclusive and honoured status of a piper in a clan society, that the man's music was inspirational and his presence a rallying-point. Three years later English courts would understand this, and grant little mercy to the Jacobite pipers brought before them. The pipes, it would be said, were weapons of war. MacDonnell's dangerous distinction, however, did not last long and his place among the "most guilty" was shortly taken by Farquhar Shaw whose instinctive and violent reaction to Sergeant MacBean's grasp had made this inevitable.

One hundred and twenty men were involved in the desertion and mutiny, of whom one hundred and seven were brought to trial – the men who surrendered in Ladywood and others whom the dragoons flushed from ditch and field between Northampton and London. Of the others, one lay unnamed in the earth of the water-orchard, three were never heard of again, and nine walked four hundred miles to the safety of their own glens. Among these nine was Peter Farquharson, whom Lieutenant Fraser had taken prisoner and lost in the darkness of Finchley Common.

The officers of the court-martial sat in Adam Williamson's house at the Tower, a bank of scarlet, gold, and white lace against brown panels and grey stone. They began their business on Wednesday, June 8, and concluded it in a week, during which they tried and sentenced one hundred and four men, the other three being tried two weeks later in the Great Room of the Horse Guards. The President of the Court was Major-general John Folliot, Colonel of the First Foot Guards, and with three exceptions the twelve colonels and lieutenant-colonels who sat with him were also officers of the Guards. They tried fifteen and sometimes twenty men a day, and did so briskly even though much of what was said had to be translated into Gaelic by the Reverend Mr. Campbell, that the prisoner might know what was being said for and against him. Many of the Highlanders were sick, weakened by poor rations and the foetid riverside atmosphere of their prison. A surgeon's mate of the Scots Guards had successfully asked for a small increase in the cheese or oatmeal, and Williamson had been given permission to exercise them in groups of eight or ten, but none was strong in body or spirit.

There had been rumours in the city – which would persist in romantic myth for two centuries – that Jacobite agents had provoked the mutiny, but the Court did not take this seriously. Twice the prisoners were asked if they knew of certain papers believed to have been circulated at Barnet, but when all knowledge of this was denied no further reference to the subject was made. The same questions were asked of each man: Had he been properly enlisted and attested? Had the Articles of War been read to him? What was his religion? Had he received his proper pay and clothing? What caused him to desert? Who had been the leader among them? The Court heard of improper enlistments, of oaths untaken and the Articles unread, poor clothing and pay in arrears, the common fear of the West Indies, but no leader was named. To that question the same answer was recorded: *Denies their having any chief or commander among them.* No prisoner made any complaint against the officers of the regiment, and the reason for this was more sinister than their obstinate loyalty to the Macphersons. Campbell and his colleague Paterson, another Scots minister, constantly attended the prisoners, and one of them may have witnessed this incident or heard of it soon after. Campbell wrote that early on Wednesday morning, before the Court first sat

. . . a person, a stranger to all the prisoners, came to the grate, and pretending a great deal of concern for their misfortune, advised them not to mention on their trial any complaint they might have against their officers, intimating that he was certain such a plea would not avail them, and without serving them would expose their officers. . . . One of their officers came next day to the Tower and inculcated the same doctrine unto the prisoners that the stranger had done before, assuring them that they would all be liberate in a short time when all justice should be done them.

The mysterious stranger advised the Highlanders that their safety depended upon an honest admission of guilt and a plea for mercy. He gave them a petition which he said he had composed, and which would "effectually work their deliverance". The paper begged the Court to believe that the prisoners were deeply conscious of their infamous crime and that no injury had been done them by their officers. "Our unhappy conduct," it said, "was owing solely to our ignorance and credulity." Such was the persuasive rank and manner of the stranger, accompanied by a recommendation from one whom the Highlanders knew and trusted, that the prisoners accepted the petition. It was signed "with consent of the whole" by two MacDonalds, two Macphersons, two MacGregors and a Grant. These seven men were perhaps literate enough to understand the paper and had signed it for that reason, after reading it to the others. There is no evidence that it was seen by Farquhar Shaw and the Macpherson corporals, but they too made no complaint against the officers.

The petition was presented by the first man charged, William Gordon of the grenadiers. It was read and not referred to again, but by its admission of a heinous and infamous breach of duty, a crime too gross to be excused, an acknowledgement that the King could send them wherever he pleased, the prisoners had destroyed any legal or moral justification they might have had for their actions. They had also totally exonerated the officers from whom they had turned in anger and bitterness. Captain Munro of Newmore, with Lieutenant Fraser and half a dozen sergeants, had remained in London to give evidence, and they did speak in favour of some men, not condoning their crime but stating that they had always behaved well until the mutiny. Thus

Newmore said that he had never heard ill of Malcolm Macpherson before he went off from Finchley Common, and that Samuel Macpherson "bore an exceeding good character". Sergeant Donald Grant spoke well of many men, most of them from his own country, but neither of the officers and none of the sergeants spoke up for Farquhar Shaw, the resolute drover from Rothie-murchus.

John Folliot and his colleagues were no doubt grateful for the petition, since it enabled them to conduct the trials without dispute and with the utmost speed. Every prisoner who came before them in that small, hot room of Williamson's house received the same sentence: *"The Court-martial is of opinion that he is guilty of mutiny and desertion and adjudges him to suffer death."*

The daily trials and sickening repetition of the sentence had an inevitable effect on the sentimental emotions of mob and society. Men who had been objects of ridicule or barbaric curiosity were now seen as helpless victims. Before the court-martial was over a London correspondent to the *Caledonian Mercury* reported that "great intercession is making here by people of all ranks and sexes in favour of the unfortunate Highlanders". From early morning until dusk Tower Hill was crowded with coaches, chairs, and pedestrians, and since this was an age before imperial responsibility placed British emotions in a strait-jacket of reserve there were tears and lamentations, the crying of unheard sympathy to the moated walls. The broadsheet which had earlier described the mutineers as leprous Israelites was answered by another execrable doggerel, written in quasi-Scots and printed below an illustration showing the Highlanders' entry into the Tower. It compared them to caged robins, pecking at English crumbs and longing to be free, be it alive or dead. The author of the *Short History* dispensed with the dramatic climax the executions would have given his narrative, and rushed the manuscript through the press while interest was still strong. In a splutter of italics, and recognising his need of both public sales and official tolerance, he appealed for mercy and recommended an alternative severity.

What now remains, but that we wish them as men, as unfortunate men, as strangers, as people bewitched with the love of bleak heaths and barren mountains, and yet our fellow-creatures and fellow-subjects, *a good deliverance*. If what shall be offered in their favour, to those in whose hands their lives now lie, shall be thought *weighty* enough to bear down the *load* of *reproach* this foolish action has brought upon them, let them *receive mercy*. If the present situation of things, and the necessity of preserving military discipline in a time of war, render this inexpedient, *let them feel the severity of justice*. But if on a strict examination any circumstances have been found which *exaggerate* their *crimes*, to a degree unworthy of all *pity*, let their *fears* pronounce their *sentence*, let them not be shot like *soldiers*, *let them be transported to the WEST INDIES*.

The Lords Justices were not influenced by the emotions of the mob or the intercessions of fashionable ladies and political opportunists, but they were concerned with what effect the matter might have upon the Highlands. They were soon reassured. Old Joshua Guest told the Secretary at War that he had spies among the clans, that he had marched his best regiment into the mountains and "posted men at all the passes to hinder depredations and secure the peace". He would shortly travel to the forts in the Great Glen and would keep all quiet. No one knows what the ordinary clansman thought or felt at this time, but many of the chiefs may have agreed with the time-serving Simon Fraser of Lovat. Writing to his cousin Cluny, and expressing sympathy that so many of the mutineers were Macphersons, he said, "It grieves me to the heart that the unhappy desertion brings such disaster and disgrace upon our country." His concern for that country and his professed loyalty to its present Government would not prevent him from committing his clan to the Jacobite Rebellion two years later, and thus to the greater disaster which followed it.

The necessary and agonisingly slow ritual of a military execution made the shooting of more than a hundred men absurd and impossible, and the Regents had no intention of ordering such a hecatomb. The sentence of death was obligatory, and the inevitable pardon granted to most of the condemned was thereby a greater demonstration of clemency. The King's pleasure had again been made known by a letter from his secretary in Hanover. A public example must be made of some, and the rest "His Majesty would have pardoned on condition of their being sent to our several Colonies in America." None of those reprieved should be allowed to return to Scotland, and none should be sent to any regiment now on the march in Flanders. The Regents received these instructions when they were voting grateful bounties of £200 and £50 to General Blakeney and Major Hassell, and since it was late in the afternoon they postponed any decision until their next meeting. Two days later, on July 7, they agreed that twenty-six prisoners, being young and inexperienced, should be sent to garrisons at Gibraltar and Port Mahon on Minorca. The rest were to be sent to regiments in the Americas, and thus did indeed have their sentences pronounced by their fears.

There were four exceptions. The first was Patrick MacGregor *alias* MacAlpine *alias* Campbell, the Breadalbane soldier of the colonel's company who had exchanged his plaid for a villager's small-clothes and gone northward a week before the review. For this individual effort at desertion, by which he had certainly escaped a charge of mutiny, he was awarded "one thousand lashes with a cat-of-nine-tails upon his bare back at five different times, videlicet 200 each time". Samuel Macpherson, Malcolm Macpherson, and Farquhar Shaw were to be shot.

On Tuesday, July 12, the warders of the houses in which the three men were separately confined went to their prisoners, each accompanied by two private soldiers of the Third Scots Guards lest there be some violent reaction to the news they brought. When told that he would die on the following Monday, Samuel Macpherson was shaken. Campbell said the corporal had not expected this, which indicates that like the others he had believed the stranger at the grate. In an emotional voice he asked how he was to die. "You are to be shot, sir," said the warder, and after a moment's silence Macpherson nodded. "God's will be done," he said, "I have brought this upon myself." Controlling his feelings he asked if he might have pen and ink, and when the post went for Scotland. The warder said it left that night, and in what may have been a charitable if clumsy attempt to be helpful he added that Macpherson would be dead before an answer could come. The Corporal said he did not want a reply. Upon request, he then surrendered his razor and a small penknife, that he might not anticipate the taking of his life.

The Gaelic minister Campbell, with his colleague Paterson, spent much of the remaining days with the condemned, and Campbell said that the three men "were reconciled so much to their circumstances as to be able to bear the thoughts of death with great decency and Christian resignation". There were times, however, when Samuel Macpherson was more bitter than resigned. He admitted that he had been active at the beginning of the mutiny, but argued that by advising others to return to their duty later he had surely alleviated that crime. To the end, Malcolm Macpherson declared that he had persuaded no one to desert, and had not intended to do so himself until he went to Finchley Common. Rougher-hewn and lower-born than his comrades, Farquhar Shaw made no complaint. He had turned to soldiering when droving ceased to be profitable, and since he had probably driven more cattle against their owners' will than he had by honest business, his sturdy defiance was in character. The *Caledonian Mercury* said that he "regretted to the last their having surrendered, and that they had not rather resolved to die sword in hand". He had no grudge against Alexander MacBean. The Sergeant had been too ill to give evidence against him at the court-martial, but an account of their struggle on the Common had been related by another. Now Shaw was concerned that his death might trouble MacBean's conscience, and asked to see him. The meeting was emotional. They talked as equals, men of the same race and of Clan Chattan, each conscious of the other's pain. The Sergeant bitterly regretted that he had brought Shaw to such an end, but the private begged him not to be distressed. He had no spite, no ill-will, he said, but wished to die in love and friendship with MacBean. During the following days, said Campbell, Shaw "frequently expressed to me his concern for the Sergeant, lest his reflections on himself should prejudice him or make him uneasy". The minister thought that such a generous disposition of mind was remarkable, and seldom found among men in more elevated stations of life than Private Farquhar Shaw.

Before the end of the week the Highlanders twice petitioned for their lives. They first addressed the Lords Justices, and then asked for the intercession of the Duchess of Richmond. Neither appeal was of course successful. The Duke of Richmond was a member of the Council of Regents, but since he was never present when it debated the mutiny his wife's influence over it and him can have been minimal only.

At four o'clock, shortly before sunrise on Monday, July 18, the three men were brought together in the Master Gunner's House, meeting for the first time. They were grotesquely dressed, each wearing a shroud beneath his belted plaid, but they embraced with dignity and encouraged one another to be of good heart. Samuel Macpherson said that he had ordered and paid for three coffins at fifteen shillings each, and Malcolm asked to see three members of his clan that he might entrust them with his will. They then knelt in fervent prayer with Campbell and Paterson until six o'clock, when Adam Williamson came to take them to their deaths.

The gates of the Tower had been closed, to keep out the mob and any ladies and gentlemen with a taste for executions civil or military. The Scots Guards were on duty in the garrison, and would thus find the firing-party to shoot their Highland country-men. Three hundred men of the regiment were already assembling when Williamson came to the Master Gunner's house, and upon his compassionate order they paraded without beat of drum. They formed two half-moons before the south-eastern corner of the Chapel, three paces apart, and between them were the other Highland prisoners. Graves had already been dug beneath stunted trees by the tower of the chapel, the fifteen-shilling coffins waiting nearby. The Third Guards made no sound as they paraded, moving at the motion of an officer's hand or a sergeant's halberd, but the men of the 43rd were already keening with grief, a sighing wave of melancholy.

The condemned men came out of the Gunner's house into a little forecourt where their arms were pinioned, and then they walked to the chapel behind the ministers, Campbell in a flowing gown of black and Paterson in sombre small-clothes. Before a blank wall of the Chapel, which was to take the shot that passed by or through the bodies, was a raised plank upon which the condemned were to kneel again in prayer, but Samuel Macpherson stepped upon it and addressed his comrades in the half-moon, their faces scarcely seen behind the tall scarlet of the Guards. He said he hoped that the anguish of the executions would be their last punishment, "for I am convinced you must think it a punishment to see us bleed, but my blood, I hope, will contribute to your liberty". He told them to do their duty to God and the King, to wipe out all reproach by respectful and loyal obedience. Then he knelt on the plank with Malcolm and Shaw, the ministers in the dust beside them. Though pinioned above the elbow, the condemned could move their fore-arms freely, and they closed their hands before them. Williamson called softly to the watching Highlanders, telling them to pray if they wished, and the order released a great emotion. They fell upon their knees, lowering their heads to the stones. They asked for God's mercy in their own tongue and in the bleak words of Protestant prayer. They covered their faces with their bonnets or their plaids, hiding their tears, muffling the crying cadence of their grief, and their bent bodies moved like a green river between the red ranks of the Guards, many of whom were also weeping.

The prayers lasted for nine minutes until the three men rose together. Samuel Macpherson was the bravest, said Williamson, and he cried boldly, "What, are we not to be shot? Where are the men who are to shoot us?" Williamson asked them to kneel again, to draw down their caps and they would soon be dispatched. The Macphersons bowed to their comrades, a stiff movement of farewell, but Shaw kissed his hand and extended it as far as he could, as if he wished his lips to touch the wet faces before him. The ministers moved away and the condemned knelt again, pulling their bonnets over their faces. On the left and right Samuel Macpherson and Shaw put their hands behind them, and in the centre Malcolm crossed his on his chest. Eighteen Guardsmen who had been waiting behind the Chapel now came to the centre of the half-moon, on tip-toes said Campbell, their muskets already loaded, primed and cocked so that there might be no unnerving noise. Their orders were given by a handkerchief held in the air by Sergeant-major Ellison, and they formed three ranks of six some paces from the kneeling men. At the fluttering command of *Make Ready!* the first rank knelt upon the right knee, the second took a pace to the rear with the right foot, and the third remained at the shoulder in reserve. At *Present!* the first and second ranks brought their muskets to the aim, and upon the fall of Ellison's handkerchief they fired.

The three men were thrown backward by the close volley, but when the white smoke cleared Williamson saw that one of Shaw's hands still moved in the dust and that Samuel's body was trembling. He called upon two men of the reserve and they went forward and shot the Highlanders, Shaw in the forehead and Macpherson through the ear. The bodies were carried to the graves by men of their own name and were quickly buried. "There was not much blood spilt," said Williamson, "but what was, I ordered immediately to be covered with earth and their graves levelled, so that no remains of their execution might be perceived." The gates were kept locked for another day.

It was autumn before the prisoners left the Tower. Although short-lived, public reaction to the executions had been intense and angry, and it may have persuaded the Lords Justices to set aside Patrick MacGregor's flogging. He was ordered to Georgia, but he successfully petitioned against this and was sent to Gibraltar instead. Before the end of July agents of regiments in the Medi-

terranean and the Americas were eagerly asking for the prisoners
to be drafted into their battalions. Beyond the enduring need to
fill the gaps made by sickness, there was also the fact that the
Government intended to pay commanding officers £5 for every
Highlander sent to Gibraltar or Minorca, and £6 for each of
those sent to Georgia and the Indies. The money was to meet the
expenses of transportation, but it was an agent's business to make
what profit he could for his Colonel in such transactions. The
resulting correspondence built a little mountain-range of paper
on Sir William Yonge's desk, and not the least of his many
irritations was the Highlanders' bold demand that they should be
paid for the surrender of their own pistols, dirks, and broadswords. The Secretary at War ordered their new colonels to
sell the weapons, and to credit each man's pay with the sum
realised.

The Reverend Mr. Campbell remained with the prisoners until
they were all gone. He married some of them when the Government announced that a certain number could take their wives to
Georgia. The concession was less compassionate than it may
seem. Brigadier-general James Oglethorpe, to whose regiment
thirty-eight of the men were drafted, was the founder of the
colony of Georgia. He acted upon strict moral principles, for-
bidding the sale or consumption of rum, the employment of free
or slave Negroes. These admirable restrictions, added to the
unhealthy climate and the General's taste for Wesleyan sermons,
had reduced his colony's population from five thousand to five
hundred. He needed the Highlanders to complete his regiment
and to restrain unsympathetic Indians, but he also needed them,
it can be assumed, to breed him native-born Georgians. The
Highland women walked from their mountains to join their
husbands or lovers, selling a cow or a sheep to pay for the journey.
The marriages were performed on a low platform and in the
open, watched by officers of the Guards, and Williamson set
aside a barrack-room where husbands and wives might have
some privacy, their cots separated by blanket walls.

There were many sick men now, and two died in the stifling

heat, one of them dramatically enough to make an ironic if
unintended comment on the whole affair. Late at night on
Friday, August 5, John Campbell rose naked from his straw in
the Infirmary and threw himself from a window above Traitor's
Gate. He was found at dawn, face down in the tidal mud.

The first drafts left the Tower on Tuesday, September 6.
Twenty-six men, many of them nineteen years of age and
younger, were taken to Portsmouth and there put aboard ship
for the Mediterranean. A second draft of thirty-eight crossed the
Thames to Gravesend where a naval transport was waiting to
deliver them to Lieutenant-general Robert Dalzell's Regiment
in the West Indies. At eleven o'clock on the morning of
September 19 the remaining thirty-eight, who had been allotted
to Oglethorpe, marched to Tower Wharf with their women and
behind Piper MacDonnell's brave music. They believed that
though they might never again wear the belted plaid they were
at least to serve with men of their own race and tongue, for they
had been told that there was a Highland company in the
Brigadier's battalion. This had originally consisted of one hundred
and sixty young men of Clan Mackintosh, captained by their
chief's brother, but after eight years of war against Indians and
Spaniards, rotting fever and killing despair, no man could be
sure that any were still alive. Captain Aeneas Mackintosh had
long since come home, to succeed his brother, and was now
purchasing a commission in the 43rd. Perhaps it was he who sent
an encouraging message to the departing Highlanders, assuring
them that the climate of Georgia was "wholesome and that they
would meet with a kind and generous reception from all who
had any power there".

Samuel Macpherson had been wrong when he said that his
death would be his companions' last punishment. None of these
men can have returned from Georgia or the West Indies. Oglethorpe abandoned his miserable colony before the Highlanders
were disembarked, and some years later what was left of it and
his battalion, if anything, was transferred to the authority of the
Crown. Under one absent colonel or another, Dalzell's regiment

had been the permanent garrison of the Leeward Islands for thirty years, and would still be there for another thirty. The Highlanders were like the doomed drafts who had preceded them and who would follow them – another small transfusion of blood, soon expended, soon forgotten.

2

IMMOVABLE AS A ROCK

78th Lord Seaforth's Highlanders
Edinburgh, September 1778

76th Lord Macdonald's Highlanders
Burntisland, March 1779

42nd and 71st (Fraser's) Highlanders
Leith, April 1779

The Argyll (Western) Fencibles
Edinburgh, October 1779

77th Duke of Atholl's Highlanders
Portsmouth, January 1783

"Not only by affection and the enthusiasm of clanship"

GENERAL OUGHTON COULD see the mutineers' night-fires from his windows at Caroline Park. Five miles to the south-east, their red glow was an unnatural dawn above the volcanic cone of Arthur's Seat. He shared none of the modish excitement in Edinburgh and was irritated by those who were saying, like the sentimental laird of Cultibraggan, that olden times were come again. More than thirty years ago the Young Pretender's clansmen had built their fires on the southern slopes of the great rock, not many feet below the spot where Lord Seaforth's Highlanders were now standing in defiance of their chief and their King. The General did not refer to this coincidence in his dispatches to Lord Amherst, the situation was troublesome enough without such tactless reminders. Had he known that the mutiny was the first of four he would have to endure in the coming year, and that they would undoubtedly cause his premature death, he would have borne the knowledge with a soldier's fortitude.

Lieutenant-general Sir James Adolphus Oughton had become the Commander-in-Chief of North Britain three months before, in June 1778 and upon the resignation of the Duke of Argyll. He had accepted the appointment with enthusiasm, pleased that the office was once again filled by an Englishman, as custom and good sense required. He was fifty-eight, double-chinned and well-fleshed, with a sweet temper, an amiable face, and bright inquisitive eyes. The bastard son of a Warwickshire soldier-squire, he proudly treasured a pair of pistols that had been given to his father by the Duke of Marlborough. Except for some service in Flanders, and a period as a lieutenant-governor of Antigua, he had lived and soldiered in Scotland, and he liked the

land and its people. He was married to the widow of a Dalrymple
of North Berwick, and although they had no children of their
own he loved her son as his, an affection which the young man
returned, as much out of good heart as from the sensible realisation that military preferment depended on his step-father's
favour. At twenty-six James Oughton had commanded a battalion
company of Munro's 37th Foot, had seen it run at Falkirk and
then stand its ground on Culloden Moor against the desperate
charge of the Appin Stewarts. His honest respect for Highlanders
was probably grounded in this bloody experience, but his attitude
toward them was always sternly paternal. He was the only
general officer and one of the few Englishmen of his time, or
indeed any other, who learnt Gaelic. Some of his interest in the
language was due to the fashionable popularity of James Macpherson's spurious translations from Ossian, but he also resembled
the British officer of the next century who thought himself
obliged to learn the tongue of his sepoy children, the better to
be their father and guardian.

He was a scholarly man with a taste for philosophical and
moralising debate. He argued gently with the great jurist Lord
Kames on whether or not respect for the Law could tolerate a
Court of Honour, by which the barbaric practice of duelling could
be subject to humane principles. He was a patron of that contentious professor of moral philosophy, James Beattie, and urged
his titled friends to exert themselves on the unhappy man's
behalf. Dining at Boswell's house in James's Court, he angered
Johnson by his belief in Macpherson's *Fingal*, and then courteously
and wittily defused the doctor's ill-temper. Johnson said later that
there could be few men more learned. "Sir Adolphus is a very
extraordinary man, a man of boundless curiosity and unwearied
diligence."

When he became Commander of the King's Forces in North
Britain the rank was more impressive in words than substance,
for he had less than two thousand men under his orders. The war
with the American colonists, already in its fourth year, had once
been far enough away not to endanger the security of the

kingdom, but now it had come unpleasantly close. John Paul Jones, first hero of the new republic's makeshift navy, was cruising off the northern coasts, an impudence more damnable because the fellow was a native-born Scot. France had recognised the United States and become their ally, not from love of life, liberty and the pursuit of happiness but for the humiliation of Britain. The need for extra battalions, to fight overseas campaigns and resist invasion at home, naturally turned the minds of governing men to the King's Highland people. The Great Commoner had set a precedent, or so he claimed. In 1766, when the long quarrel with the colonists was beginning, William Pitt reminded the Lower House of the work he had given the broken clans in the Continental war just ended.

> I sought for merit wherever it was to be found, it is my boast that I was the first minister who looked for it and found it in the mountains of the north. I called it forth and drew into your service a hardy and intrepid race of men, who when left by your jealousy became a prey to the artifice of your enemies, and had gone nigh to have overturned the State in the war before the last. These men in the last war were brought to combat on your side; they served with fidelity as they fought with valour and conquered for you in every part of the world.

Beneath his patronising conceit, and apart from his inaccurate claim to have been the first to make regular soldiers of the clansmen, what Pitt said was true. In the years following the last Jacobite rebellion the Government had raised ten marching-regiments in the mountains, twelve thousand men, and had deployed them bloodily in Europe, India and North America. Between 1757 and 1763 more Highlanders wore the King's red coat and the King's black tartan than ever followed the last Stuart prince. This early exercise in the military use of a subjected people, to be consciously or unconsciously copied later in the similar employment of defeated Sikhs or Baluchis, had diverted the warrior zeal of the clans into the service of an authority they had instinctively resisted for centuries, and while their spirits were still numb with despair. The young men of these regiments, as Duncan Forbes had foreseen, were also hostages for the good behaviour of their kinsmen, and their valour on distant battle-fields had solaced their fathers' bitterness.

The use that might be made of Highlanders in the King's wars had been recognised by some English officers who faced their furious charge at Falkirk or Culloden. Soldiers must die in battles, and where else in the kingdom were there men whose courage could be better employed and whose death would be the least regretted? An early enthusiast was Major James Wolfe who at the age of twenty-four was commanding the 20th Foot in the Army of Occupation. Jacobite romance remembers him for his chivalry at Culloden, his refusal to pistol a wounded Fraser, although there is no record of what he said or did when the order was carried out by a private soldier. His opinion of the High-landers – who would later help him to secure a theatrical im-mortality on the Heights of Abraham – was a mixture of respect for their bravery and contempt for their way of life. When stationed with his battalion at Fort Augustus in 1751 he believed that lingering resistance among the clans might be finally crushed by a contrived massacre, that the deliberate sacrifice of one of his patrols in the killing of the Macphersons' chief would justify the extirpation of the whole clan in reprisal. "Wou'd you believe that I am so bloody?" he asked his friend William Rickson. The proposal remained a thought only, but he was ever amazed by his bloodthirsty dislike of the clans. In an earlier letter to Rickson, then in America, he suggested that Highland companies should do the fighting in that inhospitable land. Using adjectives that Pitt would also choose, he said, "They are hardy, intrepid, accustom'd to a rough Country, and no great mischief if they fall. How can you better employ a secret enemy than by making his end conducive to the common good?" He admitted that if this scheme became public he would be thought "execrable and bloody", but his feelings were natural in a man surrounded on every side by Jacobites and Papists, all suffering from the itch.

William Pitt's boast, still quoted by panegyrists of Highland regiments, does not explain how or why it was possible to make such use of that hardy and intrepid race. Certainly it was not his voice alone, calling from the Palace of Westminster. The clan system, already under stress and decay since the beginning of the century, had received a killing blow at Culloden. Though a minority only of the clans had taken part in the Rebellion, all had felt the savage effect of the reprisals that followed. Their society was torn from its past by the use of rope, musket and bayonet, by prison and transportation, by the burning of glens, the driving of cattle, the harrying of homeless men, women and children. The Jacobite clans were left leaderless by the death or exile of their chiefs, and the house of the *ceann-cinnidh* was occupied by a kinsman who had prudently remained at home during the Rising, or by an alien and bewildered factor of the Commissioners for the Forfeited Estates. No chief, loyal or rebel, was left with his ancient authority. Admirable though it was in civilised terms, the abolition of his heritable jurisdictions, his power of pit and gallows, struck off the head of the clan and left the body still living. It would continue to move for half a century, while chief and Government employed the strength of its weakening muscles. Legally relieved of his ancient obligations to his children, while retaining some of his vestigial rights over them, the chief was now eager for the more rewarding status of a Lowland or English gentleman, driven to it by preference or by the crippling need of rents that must now be counted in coin not kind. One of the rights he stubbornly retained, even when it had become a social and economic absurdity, was to treat his tenants and sub-tenants as if they were still the warrior rent-roll of his grandfather. Since they held their land upon his yearly pleasure, and were as much subject to threat and persuasion as their ancestors had been, their sons could be gathered into a platoon, a company, or a battalion and placed at the service of the Crown.

In the beginning, in the years immediately following the battle of Culloden, the young men had been eager enough to serve in the regiments. The greatest blow to the dignity and self-respect of the Highlander, to the mystic link between the present and a heroic past, to his deep and passionate pride in the *Gaidhealtachd*, had been the ruthless imposition of a new Disarming Act and a further statute that denied him the right to wear tartan and plaid. "From and after the 1st of August 1747," it was declared, "no man or boy within Scotland, other than such as shall be employed as officers and soldiers in the King's forces, shall on any pretence whatsoever, wear or put on the cloaths commonly called highland cloaths. . . .' For the first offence against this inexorable edict he could be imprisoned for six months, and if he offended again he could be transported for seven years. Wherever possible he was made to swear upon the holy iron of a dirk, and as he would answer to God on the Day of Judgement, that he had no gun, sword or pistol and that he would never again wear his ancient dress. In final humiliation, for want of other clothes, he dyed his tartan plaid in a tub of mud and cut the cloth to make himself a pair of breeches. "Everything has gone that would please a youth," lamented a Badenoch poet,

> . . . since the coming of the great coat,
> long stockings and a cocked hat.
> A bad exchange for
> kilt, hose, and scarlet garters,
> and the kilt worn high above the knee,
> and the sword belt on shoulder,
> and the slim, sharp broadsword
> with its three flutings.
>
> Fashioned straight
> of the best pure steel,
> although it would bend it would not break,
> it was new and sharp, steel blue.
> A pair of pistols
> reliable in the time of conflict,
> A slender dirk with carved hilt,

these were the arms of a youth.
I saw each one of them
when I was a boy,
worn by the champions of Scotland before
her spirit was wounded.

Other than such as shall be employed as officers and soldiers in the King's forces. . . . Though the Act was designed to break the obstinately aggressive spirit of the clans it is possible to believe in hindsight that, like the broadsword itself, it was double-edged, that it took with one hand and returned with the other upon conditions useful to the Government. For dreaming youths like the elegiast of Badenoch, for older men whose world had seemingly ended in the sleet and musketry of Culloden, that excepting clause was an opportunity to discover or recover a lost identity. The Disarming Act and the prohibition of tartan and kilt made it easy to raise those ten marching-regiments for the Seven Years' War, but had it been suggested that they should wear the great coat, long stockings, and cocked hat, that they should abandon the broadsword and dirk, both chiefs and clansmen would have turned their backs upon William Pitt's patriotic appeal. The enlistment of the battalions was left to the Highland gentry and they raised them as clan levies, by threat and persuasion, by enticement and appeal to traditional loyalties, calling upon men of their own name and from their own districts. Once mustered and embodied they were quickly sent overseas, for one lesson at least had been learnt from Ladywood – that the regular Highland soldier should not be kept long at home. For the same reason, all but the 42nd were disbanded when peace came in 1763.

Pre-eminent among the regiments was the battalion raised by Simon Fraser, lawyer son of the old fox Lovat who had finally lost his head on Tower Hill. Fraser had taken his father's clan to the Stuart standard in the Rebellion, and the offer of fourteen hundred men to the Government was part of his long and ultimately successful efforts to re-establish his family's influence and recover his forfeited estates. Like their Colonel, many of the officers and men of the 78th Highlanders* had fought for the Pretender. More than half of the thirteen companies were raised in Fraser country and the rest from MacDonalds and Camerons, Stewarts, MacNeills and Campbells of Glenlyon. Their drill-sergeant was Donald MacLeod from Ulinish, now in his seventieth year according to his *Memoirs*. Carrying their ancient weapons and wearing coats of red and tartan green, sporrans of badger's or otter's skin, bonnets trimmed with black feathers, diced hose of red and white, they fought with spectacular courage at Louisbourg and upon the Plains of Abraham. There, before Quebec, Sergeant MacLeod ignored a shattered shin-bone and a musket wound in his arm, and gave his plaid to the dying Wolfe, a charitable act which no one but he thought worthy of record. At their own request, and as if they had seen the future and wished no part of it, many of the officers and men were discharged in Canada, taking grants of land that had been offered. "Thanks to our generous chief," said one in valediction to the regiment, and in unconscious comment on the bitterness that had made it possible, "we were allowed to wear the garb of our fathers. . . ."

They had all been remarkable regiments, and unlike any English battalion. They had a horror of the lash, and rarely committed an offence that merited it. Where other men boasted of the bloody coat they wore at the halberds, a Highlander's spirit broke under the punishment and he rarely returned to his home afterwards. They were religious to an excessive degree, disciplined by the harsh precepts of the Church of Scotland, and they were inured to hardships that destroyed the morale of other regiments of Foot. English officers attributed these qualities to an animal savagery or a childish simplicity, but a wiser explanation was given later in the century by Lord Selkirk. He was a compassionate and conscientious man who admired the Highlanders and who rescued some of them from their evicting landlords, settling them in Canada. These soldiers, he said, were respectable men,

* The number was later given to Lord Seaforth's Highlanders. See the explanatory footnote on p. 35.

. . . for whose fidelity and good conduct there was a solid pledge, in the families they left at home, and in the motives that induced them to enter into the service; men who had much stronger motives of obedience to their officers than the lash can enforce; who were previously accustomed from their infancy, to respect and obey the same superiors who led them into the field; who looked on them as their protectors, not less than their commanders; men in whose minds the attachment of clanship still retained a large portion of its ancient enthusiasm.

By 1778 that ancient enthusiasm was becoming strained, and much had changed. The Act against the wearing of Highland dress had fallen into desuetude, and the little kilt or belted plaid was again the clothing of man and boy in the Rough Bounds and farther north. But this was a reminder of the past, not a return to it. New economies, new moods and manners were weathering the fabric of Highland life and destroying the *Gaidhealtachd* far more subtly and effectively than proscriptions on the kilt or the carrying of arms. The purse-bare chiefs, anxious to enter southern society, hungry for town houses, for equality in wealth with southern gentry, had seen their possible future in the work of the Commissioners for the Forfeited Estates. The lands of attainted Jacobites had been annexed to the Crown by statute in 1752, and later the Commissioners were appointed "for the purposes of civilising the Inhabitants . . . promoting amongst them the Protestant religion, good Government, Industry and Manufactures". They encouraged forestry and fishing, introduced linen and flax mills, built roads, bridges and villages, established small schools where instruction was to be given in English only. All this was intended to bring the three hundred thousand people of the Highlands within the economy and culture of the rest of Britain, to reclaim them from their love of sloth and to reconcile them to the love of labour. But the society upon which these diligent experiments were being practised was still semi-feudal and patriarchal, its people still believed in talking stones, water monsters and the evil eye, in the power to read the future from the jaw-bone of a sheep, and in their ancestry of warrior giants. Their miserable homes, said an English visitor, were shocking to humanity, black mole-hills on their braes from which they came naked in the mornings to squat like animals on the dung-hill. Yet such people also believed that their hearts pulsed with the blood of kings, and they sang their sorrows in words that closed their ears to all but the sounds of the past.

Before the Rebellion chief and clansmen had been inter-dependent, father and family, and although this spirit was still maintained by the people its nature had changed. He no longer depended upon them for his safety and self-importance, but they were still his tenants-at-will, tied to his indulgence as their ancestors had been. Until the American Revolution some of the lesser gentry, angered and embittered by the rack-renting of the chiefs, had taken their families and sub-tenants across the Atlantic in the belief that they could maintain their ancient way of life in the new lands of the Carolinas, the woods of Upper Canada, or the littoral of Nova Scotia. Those who remained still thought of themselves as the chief's children, though their faith in his love and their trust in his protection were weakening in the confusion of a changing world. As it slowly became apparent that he saw himself as their landlord only, and one who was increasingly absent from them, their filial loyalty became stronger. They were more anxious than formerly, said Selkirk, to merit his favour.

> The only opportunity they had of rendering him any important obligation, was when he undertook to raise men for the army. The zeal with which the followers of any chieftain then came forward to inlist, was prompted not only by affection and the enthusiasm of clanship, but likewise by obvious views of private interest. The tenant who, on such an occasion, should have refused to comply with the wishes of his landlord, was sensible that he could expect no further favour, and would be turned out of his farm. . . . The most respectable of the tenantry would therefore, be among the

first to bring forward their sons; the landlord might, with an authority almost despotic, select from among the youth upon his estate, all who appeared most suitable for recruits.

The tribal ties still held, stretched taut by doubt and suspicion, and they could snap at the thought of betrayal.

When it became known that the Government once more intended to raise regiments of Highlanders there was an eager and immediate response from chiefs and tacksmen, and the wordy letters they wrote fell upon the desk of Lord Barrington, Secretary at War, who wearily passed them to his clerks. Anxious to secure field rank for themselves, captaincies, lieutenancies or colours for their sons, they confidently offered to raise companies or battalions from their tenants, and sometimes from each other's lands. Ranald MacDonell of Keppoch was the chief of a once powerful clan renowned for its raiding, thieving, and adherence to the Stuart cause. His father had died at Culloden, many paces before the hesitant Clan Donald line, crying that his children had deserted him. Ranald had commanded a company of Simon Fraser's 78th and had been wounded in the knee on the Plains of Abraham. He was then offered a captaincy with an English regiment in Jamaica, provided he raised a company which he did without difficulty from his tenants. Weakened by inevitable fever, he returned to the cooler air of Keppoch, having sold his commission to another officer and therewith his breeched and abandoned children. Now, he told Barrington, his health was entirely established and he earnestly desired to contribute his mite to reduce the rebellious Americans. "Lochaber, where I now reside, can furnish the best soldiers in the Highlands of Scotland, and I dare venture to assure your Lordship that the country could muster up a regiment of as good troops as serve His Majesty." He did not ask for a regimental commission, a captaincy would suffice, and in return his mite would be a company or two of his clansmen. "I flatter myself I have so much the command of men."

On the Isle of Mull, Sir Allan Maclean of Duart told Barrington that from the complexion of the times and the situation of affairs he thought it his duty to raise a regiment from his people. He had come circuitously to the leadership of Clan Gillean a quarter of a century before, by marriage and by the death of his childless third cousin, then in Roman exile for his part in the Rebellion. The Macleans had sacrificed themselves to Colonel Belford's grapeshot at Culloden, crying *"Another for Hector!"* in loyalty to their chief, but they had presumably recovered in the passing years and could now supply the thousand men whom Duart was offering to the Government, six times as many as those who had joined the Jacobite Army. As if he feared the indignity of a refusal, and had stomached enough bureaucratic stupidity, Duart arrogantly told the Secretary that were his application for a regiment not successful "I shall not for the future give any further trouble, as my usage has been rather hard".

Major Duncan Macpherson of Cluny, chief of his clan and cousin of Samuel long buried by the wall of the Tower Chapel, was at that moment in America and may not have thought it possible or practicable to offer his people to the Crown. The Cluny estates were still forfeit as a result of his father's support of the Stuarts, and the hope of recovering them perhaps persuaded James Macpherson to write to Barrington. The translator of Ossian, now enduring increasing public scepticism, was earning a living as a Government hack in London, but he reminded the Secretary of their past acquaintance and presumed upon it to recommend a regiment for the distant leader of *Sliochd Choinnich*. "May I suggest the propriety and even justice of giving a step to a Highland Chieftain, now absent in the service of his Country; and whose clan are ready to follow him to the Field?" William Mackintosh of Dunachton was not a chief, but he was a kinsman of *Mac-an-Toiseach*, a gentleman of estate and a brevet-major in a Welsh regiment. He asked Barrington for the lieutenant-colonelcy of any Highland battalion then being raised, offering to bring in a sufficient quota of men without costing the Government a farthing in levy money.

Sometimes this begging correspondence persisted for months,

and in one case for years. Allan MacDonald of Knock, on the Isle of Skye, badgered the War Office throughout the whole of the Revolutionary War. He wanted nothing for himself, of course, except justice. This he had failed to receive from his own country-men, he said, although their lack of charity seems to have had good cause. During the Rebellion he had been a captain of an independent company and a merciless servant of the Crown, vindictively harrying Jacobites, even his own kinsmen, carrying them to prison and pursing the coins he found in their pockets. Now worn out and old, living miserably in Ayr, all his sons dead but one, he appealed again and again for the young man's preferment. "If he obtains a company I bid adieu to the world and all its false glitterings." He resented the rejection of a scheme he had proposed to a previous Secretary, "a plan for raising 16,000 Highlanders, without hurting agriculture or grazings, and without forcing a man from the arms of his wife and children, and without taking an Irish refugee to the lot". This plan had been set aside in favour of another's, he said, but if it could be reconsidered he would go in peace to his grave, praying for his poor country.

All of these letters, and many more, were passed to Barrington's clerks with a curt endorsement: "*Acknowledge etc. I understand that there is no intention at present of raising more new Corps than those already ordered, the officers for which are all recommended by the Noble Persons who have undertaken to raise them.*" With one exception these noble persons were the titled chiefs of Clan Campbell and MacDonald, Murray, Mackenzie and Gordon, anglicised gentle-men of power and influence and therefore more reliable and useful than an aggrieved Maclean, an absent Macpherson, or a doubtful MacDonell. To them went the profit to be had from selling commissions, clipping clothing contracts, and milking levy money. The exception was Simon Fraser of Lovat. He was now a major-general, and upon payment of a fine had been restored at last to his estates. In 1775, a year after this good fortune and two before the Government decided to embody more Highland units, he retired from the Portuguese service and offered to raise the clans as he had twenty years before. In a few months he mustered two battalions of the new 71st Regiment on Glasgow Green, two thousand three hundred men, and delivered an inspiring valediction in Gaelic before they sailed down the Clyde for Boston. "The completion of this numerous corps," said Garth, "must no doubt have been accelerated by the exertions of his officers, of whom six besides himself were chiefs of clans." Lovat did not accompany them. He lived for much of the time in London, and it was from Hanover Square, his temper worsened by a malevolent cold and a sore throat, that he wrote to Barrington, ridiculing the Highland gentlemen who were making such ambitious offers of men. "I have heard persons named as having offered your Lordship to raise Highlanders, who have pretty near the same pretensions to raise Laplanders." Money alone would not recruit in the mountains. "Such a number of men as I raised in the year 1757 in four weeks could not have been procurred so speedily by any sum of money, without the concurrence and aid of friends, Gentlemen of the country with proper connections." Though he did not explain it, those connections meant the power of such chiefs as Cameron of Lochiel, Chisholm of Chisholm, and MacLeod of MacLeod to bring their children to his muster. Lest it be thought he hoped to make a profit from the 71st, he testily reminded the Secretary that he had lost £6,000 by retiring from the Portuguese Army.

Fraser alone found it easy to raise a regiment. The Noble Persons were less successful, and were forced to bid for men in other districts than those occupied by their own clansmen. The market in human cattle was conducted with energy, cunning, and duplicity by captains and lieutenants whose commissions depended upon the prompt delivery of the required quota of men. Those who failed to gather the number from their own tenants – because the young men could not be spared from labour, or were unwilling to wear the red coat despite their parents' entreaties – offered higher bounties to attract others from a neighbour's land. This put them into debt, and their recruits in a sullen humour when the promised money was not paid. The young laird of

Gruinard in Wester Ross had difficulty in raising sixty men who would bring him a captaincy in Lord Seaforth's regiment. According to stories still told in the area a century later, his resolute mother solved the problem. She had the tenants' sons taken up at night and imprisoned in the penal hole beneath the great house. Their feet were then greased with butter and scorched with a candle, so that they might not walk until they were required to march behind her son. Some small lairds, with no military ambitions themselves, found the men that others needed, first among their own people and then further afield, pursing an agreed portion of the levy money. Until old age mellowed his reputation, John Macpherson of Ballachroan was feared as *Othaichear Dubh*, the Black Officer who gathered men by cajolery, threat or violence, even a minister who he said would be a more handsome fellow in red than black. When an avalanche removed him in his seventy-seventh year it was agreed that the Devil had at last claimed his own.

Once he had enlisted his quota, an officer would sometimes offer them to a colonel of another regiment, hoping for higher rank, or less greedily for an opportunity to serve under the lord of his name. Kenneth Mackenzie, an officer from the Dutch service, raised a company for Lord Macdonald's 76th Regiment, gathering men from his own people and from Clan Donald, but when he heard that his chief Seaforth was mustering a battalion of Mackenzies he asked to be transferred to it with his recruits. The request was granted by Barrington, and it was only after hot protests from Lord Macdonald that the captain was ordered to return the men to the 76th. He marched them through February snows from Ross to Fort George where, upon some notion of honour or a dislike of their appearance, they were rejected by Major Alexander Donaldson of the 76th. Mackenzie delightedly took them back to Castle Brahan and the gathering of the 78th. The feelings of the Clan Donald men thus abandoned among strangers, and the Mackenzies who would have been surrendered by their chief to another, were not recorded in the acrimonious correspondence that passed between the Highlands and the War

Office. Another adroit trader in men was George Munro, younger of Culcairn. When he was offered a captaincy in Fraser's second battalion he made up his quota with thirteen men he had already enlisted for a lieutenant's commission in the 70th. He was in America before it was realised that he had thus received more than £110 from each of the commanding officers, for the levy money and subsistence of his thirteen men. It was two years before the Lieutenant-colonel of the 70th was able to recover his loss from Simon Fraser.

In addition to new marching-regiments the Government also issued letters of service for the raising of Highland Fencible battalions, to serve within Scotland only, for the resistance of invasion and the suppression of civil disorder. The gentlemen who were granted these letters soon discovered that the best of their tenants had already been attracted, coerced, suborned or sold into regular units. William Wemyss hoped to raise his Fencibles from the Sutherlands, Gunns, Bannermans and Mackays who were the subjects of his young cousin Elizabeth, Countess of Sutherland. He complained bitterly to London that the Mackenzie recruiters had been at work before him in the far north, that "Lord Seaforth and Lord MacLeod★ have drained that part of the country much". Willing though young Highlanders may have been to render that "important obligation" and save their parents from eviction, they were bewildered by the fierce competition for their enlistment oaths, by the indifference to clan or district loyalties, the breaking of promises and the withholding of money due. Below the wave of emotion upon which they came to the muster, pleased to be armed and kilted like their ancestors, there was already a deep undertow of doubt and suspicion. In the

★ Despite his title, Lord MacLeod was a Mackenzie, son of the 3rd Earl of Cromartie. Convicted of high treason for his part in the Rebellion, he was later pardoned and went into exile. He returned in 1777 and, like Simon Fraser, worked for the recovery of his estates by raising the 73rd, Lord MacLeod's Highland Regiment. War Office clerks were as confused by his title as later generations, asking who and what he was, MacLeod or Mackenzie, peer or gentleman.

villages they left there was little enthusiasm for what they were doing, their military service was a price that must be paid for the security of those who remained. In Strathspey an old song was recalled. It had been composed during the Rebellion, a protest against those Highlanders who were serving in the independent companies and not with the Jacobite Army. The present times made its regret more astringent. *Tha na caileagan fo mhulad . . .*

> The young girls are full of sadness
> and very melancholy,
> for many a comely redcoat soldier
> is now in King George's army.

The recruitment of the new battalions, with others it was hoped to raise in the Lowlands, was the ultimate responsibility of James Adolphus Oughton. Outside the Highland counties his efforts were sourly disappointing. With powers given by Act of Parliament he proposed a second levy of Lowlanders to fill the incomplete ranks of volunteer regiments, line and fencible, each parish to find three recruits of suitable age and fitness. He was bluntly told by the Lord Advocate that according to reports from the Sheriffs the response would be poor, that there would be no end to the excuses landowners would give for their inability to provide one or two of their tenants' sons. The most he could hope for was that the fear of being impressed might persuade some men to volunteer. In the towns the aggressive spirit of the people was more active in mobbing an inoffensive Catholic minority than in answering a call to suppress the insidious principles of American revolt. Even the lurking presence of John Paul Jones did not inspire military ardour, though it did provoke hysterical provosts into demands for muskets and guns, which would presumably discharge themselves against the pirate. Oughton decided that a levy was incompatible with the temper of the Scottish nation. "The Lord Advocate tells me," he wrote to the Secretary at War, "that after the multitudes which have gone out of this country within these two years, the Gentlemen will not be disposed to make any exertions beyond what the Law requires them to do, and that no effectual service can arise from the Act in this country."

When he wrote that, the watchfires of Lord Seaforth's mutinous Highlanders no longer burned on the escarpment above Holyroodhouse, and the killing drain on his health had begun. "It grieves me much," he told Barrington, "that my powers so ill correspond with my zeal."

"A parcel of deer on a mountain top . . ."

LORD SEAFORTH'S HIGHLAND REGIMENT was also payment for rank and property restored, but unlike Fraser's or MacLeod's it was gratitude for benefits received rather than an advance on those expected. His Lordship's immediate forebears had been lamentably unfortunate in their religion and their loyalties. The fourth earl had supported the last Stuart king in 1689, receiving an empty Jacobite marquisate in acknowledgement and five years in a Williamite prison as punishment, which he stoically endured until flesh and spirit weakened and he appealed for mercy. The fifth earl, another staunch Catholic and a man of melancholy beauty, gathered the Mackenzie fighting-men for the Rebellion of 1715, and thereby lost many their lives and himself his estates and titles. He attempted to recover two-thirds of this loss in another rising four years later, but on a June morning in the gorge of Glenshiel, as mortar-shells trailed smoke from the river bend below, his children ran and he was left alone with a bloody arm and a broken heart. He was pardoned in 1726, after he had persuaded his obstinate clansmen to pay their rents to the Government and not to him in exile. He then came home and died in the far Hebrides, where he was interred among the tombs of the MacLeod chiefs his ancestors had subdued or dispossessed. His Protestant son kept the Seaforth Mackenzies out of the Rebellion of 1745, but this pragmatic departure from family tradition did not immediately recover the attainted titles. When he died in 1761 at Grosvenor Square he was no more than the Member of Parliament for Ross, although he was buried in Westminster Abbey. Most of the forfeited lands had been returned to him and he leased some to ruthless factors, gentlemen of his own name. An English captain of the Buffs, of a class and race not usually in sympathy with Highland misery, said that the tenants of these men were "poor wretched people, mere slaves to violence and oppression".

The last of the line, Kenneth Mackenzie, worked as diligently as his father to earn the goodwill of the Crown and was finally rewarded with the earldom of Seaforth, albeit in the Irish peerage only. "In gratitude for these favours," said Garth, always pleased when a Jacobite family secured a safe transition to the winning side with power and prestige restored, "he made an offer to His Majesty, in the year 1778, to raise a regiment on his estate, which in former times had been able to furnish 1,000 men in arms whenever the Chief required their services". Seaforth was a dull and colourless man with little of his father's political intelligence or his grandfather's good looks, so small in stature that his people called him The Little Lord. His marriage was as luckless as his predecessors' loyalties, and the sorrow of it darkened his short life. His English wife, a Stanhope, died of consumption when she was twenty and their only child became the mistress of an exiled Jacobite, living alone into the Age of Steam, buried at last in the grime of a St. Pancras cemetery.

The home of Clan Kenneth was beyond the Great Glen, across the Highlands from Easter Ross to Gairloch, and the estates of its chief extended further to the Isle of Lewis. Long after Glenshiel the Mackenzies had been fiercely attached to their *ceann-cinnidh*, to Uilleam Dubh of dark and beguiling beauty, and four hundred of them once walked from the far hills to Inverness, in defiance of George Wade and to pay their rents to an agent of the exiled chief. Confident that such attachment to his name was still strong, Seaforth decided to be his own recruiter, to raise half the men of the 78th by personal appeal and from his own immediate estates. He travelled by horse and foot and in heavy snows to the white mountains of Kintail. There on the shores of Loch Duich and the soft shoulders of the Five Sisters lived the Macraes, the children of grace, subjects of the House of Seaforth and its bodyguard in war, calling themselves Mackenzie's Shirt of Mail. It was a title bloodily earned. All but a few of those who had followed the Fifth Earl in the Rebellion of 1715 had died in the November fight of Sheriffmuir, beneath his stag's-head banner if not about his person. On that day Black William stayed in the rear, with a guard of mounted servants. Five years before Lord Seaforth came recruiting, Johnson and Boswell had stopped at Achnashiel in the Macrae country, drinking frothed milk from wooden bowls, giving tobacco and unfamiliar wheatbread to the cottagers, pennies to the children. Boswell said the people were as dark and wild as American savages, although one woman had the face and figure of Sappho. "Were I a chief," said Johnson, "I would dress my servants better than myself. I would not treat them as brutes."

When he had secured a commission for his son Kenneth, the chief of the Macraes responded willingly to his lord's appeal and among the young men he called out to follow the boy was Christopher Macrae, a poet and later a sergeant of the company. After the bitterness that was to come in Edinburgh and India, the betrayal, the dead and the abandoned, Sergeant Macrae remembered the pride there had been in "the regiment of Kintail with its weaving antlers". *Bha mo chinneadh dileas. . . .*

> My kinsmen were faithful
> to the family of the great Seaforth.
> When there was to be strife in the land
> the Macraes would not shirk their duty.

Reassured that Mackenzie's Shirt of Mail was as bright as ever, the Little Lord sailed across the winter-grey Minch to enlist more men on the island of Lewis. Though bound to him in law and custom, his tenants there were not all men of his own clan, and for years they had suffered under the harsh factors he and his father had placed over them. The present extortionate holder of this office was George Gillanders whose lease gave him a monopoly in the black cattle trade, in white fish, grain and meal, and he added £40 a year to an already handsome income by selling back to the people any surplus of the firing they were obliged to collect for his use. Such careful husbandry enabled him to save £20,000, more than enough to buy a fine estate in Easter Ross, and when he retired to it he was succeeded in the factorship by his son Alexander who, it was said, profited so well from his father's example and at the islanders' expense that he became richer than many Highland proprietors.* As if tyrannical factors were not curse enough upon them, the people of Lewis also endured epidemic fevers and recurrent crop-failures, and in their despair they were easily preyed upon by emigration agents. Seven ships once waited in the Minch like carrion crows about a carcass, one named in honour of the city of brotherly love, and their captains used persuasion, threat, and even kidnapping to fill their holds with men and women who could be profitably disembarked as indentured servants or frontier settlers in the Americas. In the hard spring of 1773 more than eight hundred people sailed from Stornoway to Carolina, so alarming Seaforth that he left his comfortable house in London and came to the Long Isle, asking his tenants what their constant loyalty and continued labour required of him. They wanted the dismissal of Gillanders, the restoration of their old rents, and a return of the increases extorted from them. The factor remained, but whether the other requests were granted is not known. Like many proprietors faced with the same challenge to their purse and their conceit, Seaforth may have reduced the rents for a while. Certainly he now felt confident enough of the islanders' obedience to ask for their sons, that he might pay his redcoat debt of gratitude to the Crown.

While he was in the Isles he delegated the enlistment of men from his mainland estates to fierce and energetic recruiters like Big Alastair Mackenzie, the bastard son of the laird of Hilton in Easter Ross. He was married to a daughter of that Gruinard chatelaine who had her own irresistible method of securing her

---

* In the next century Alexander's grandson James, factor and son-in-law of Robertson of Kindeace, evicted the people of Glencalvie and Strathcarron to make room for sheep, provoking the bloody "Massacre of the Rosses" in which twenty women and girls were seriously wounded, one of them fatally.

son's quota, and if he were indeed affectionately respected in his old age, as a clan historian claimed, it cannot have been for his "successful efforts to procure willing and sometimes hesitating recruits for the regiment of his Chief". The raising of the other companies, five hundred men in all and half the proposed regiment, was undertaken by the Mackenzie lairds of Scatwell and Kilcoy, of Redcastle, Applecross, Gairloch, Torridon, Gruinard and Lochend. Their blood-lines were tightly meshed by inter-marriage and all claimed the same descent as Seaforth, from a 14th-century Lord of Kintail whose lands had been the grateful gift of a king he rescued from the antlers of a wounded stag. Though they were eager enough to enlist the sons of their tenants and sub-tenants, few of them took up the commissions these quotas brought, preferring the profit to be got by selling them. Of thirty-seven officers gazetted, eight only were from Clan Kenneth. One of these was Captain George Mackenzie, younger son of Scatwell, who came to the 78th from an English regiment. He brought with him a belief in hard discipline and a contempt for the private soldier, and his methods of imposing the one and expressing the other were so much a contradiction of Highland custom that he was murderously hated by his company. Another was Lieutenant Kenneth Mackenzie of Redcastle who would demonstrate his notions of maintaining discipline, in a later year and another regiment, by blowing a man of his own clan from the mouth of a cannon. A hot-tempered and purse-poor bravo, he considered himself an invincible duellist and within a week of joining the regiment he fought three contests with its officers. He would have engaged in a fourth some months later, declaring his dignity outraged by a mustard-pot hurled across the mess table, had not his weary colleagues demanded his court-martial. His taste for duelling ultimately brought him to a dawn encounter with a superior antagonist who shot him to death outside the walls of Constantinople.

One of the officers with whom Redcastle fought, until honour was purified by the letting of blood from an arm or a thigh, was the senior captain, Seaforth's second cousin Thomas Mackenzie Humberston, who had taken his mother's surname when he inherited her family's estates in Lincolnshire. A handsome, anglicised gallant, he too was dedicated to the harsh methods of discipline he had learnt in an English regiment of dragoons, but although he was not yet twenty-five he had more skill and intelligence than might be inferred from his frequently expressed hope that the Secretary at War would forgive his youth and inexperience. In the spring of 1778, by the continued absence of the Little Lord in Lewis and the Battalion-major in America, he was in command of the slowly assembling companies. They were mustered in Easter Ross, where the green plain between Strath Conon and the Black Isle was studded with the decaying stumps of Mackenzie strongholds. The regiment's headquarters were at Seaforth's castellated home at Brahan, held in a woodland palm of oak and chestnut, its walled garden rich with the promise of apricots and greengages. The officers lived and dined in the great house, below the candle-smoked portraits of dead chiefs, the melancholy face of Mary Stuart and the vacuous smirk of her husband Darnley. The men existed as best they could, in cupboard beds of cottage quarters if they were fortunate, more often on trusses of straw in the open bivouacs of wet fields.

Many of the senior officers came from English regiments, from the Dutch or Austrian service, and their hard ways were imitated by the young Highland gentlemen who held junior commissions. Their treatment of the private soldier, the discipline they imposed upon him, was no worse than that experienced by southern marching-regiments, but its inhuman brutality was an affront to the racial pride of Highlandmen who, however reluctantly, had put on the red coat in obedience to their father the chief, and who innocently believed themselves entitled to the familiar protection of his commissioned kinsmen. Many of the more savage punishments intended to break the wilful spirit of a soldier – tongue-boring, the slitting of ears and nose, the branding of cheek or forehead – had now been abandoned by the Army, but those that remained were still obscenely degrading and could some-

times be imposed upon an officer's whim and without sentence
of a court-martial. A hapless victim of his captain's ill-temper, or
his own indiscipline, might be thrust upon the ground with his
chin on his knees. A musket was then passed under his hams and
another laid upon his neck, both drawn together by tightened
belts, and thus he remained until his officer relented or until he
bled from mouth, nose and ears. The lash, laid on by relays of
muscular drummers, the strokes numbered in scores, hundreds,
or thousands according to the offence, was the principal and
persisting means of enforcing discipline, it being argued that a
soldier should fear his officers more than he might the enemy.
The manuals which described the proper use of the lash advised
officers to make sure that the condemned men were not drunk
when they were tied to the halberds, lest they died from the
effect of the spirits and "evil and designing persons impute their
death to the flogging". Whereas English soldiers were said to
endure the lash with philosophical resignation, and sometimes
with perverse pride, the thought of it horrified a Highlander,
and the experience flayed his self-respect as much as it lacerated
his flesh.

Highland soldiers, by definition almost, were usually docile in
behaviour, and were thus rarely subjected to bloody punishment,
but within a few days of his enlistment in the 78th a young
recruit from Kintail or the blue Hebrides would have been told
that the coarser seed of Kenneth was not exempt from a flogging
should he deserve it, and the consequent shock to his spirit must
have been deep. Docility did not save him from the Black Hole,
into which he could be flung for the least transgression. All
battalions were obliged to have such an oubliette, be it a small
and airless cell or literally a hole in the earth. Captain Thomas
Simes' *Military Medley*, a handbook carried in the valise of every
ambitious officer, recommended that the Hole should be "free
from damp, as dark and dismal as possible, where clean straw is
to be put every week". A soldier who was absent or late for drill
was sent to the Hole for forty-eight hours upon a low diet, and if
he repeated the offence he spent a week in its cramped and

suffocating darkness. If he did not return at once to quarters when civilians were entertaining themselves with mobbing, football, or bull-baiting, he could expect a similar sentence. Should he lose his temper and threaten another soldier in front of an officer he went into the Hole for two weeks on bread and water, and was released only when he had agreed to ask his commander's pardon in public. The loss of his own equipment, or that of a comrade placed in his charge, was rewarded with three weeks. If he cut his hair without permission he was given fourteen days, and a wise soldier thus sentenced preserved what he could of his strength, for when he emerged, white-fleshed and blinking, he would have to endure sixteen more days of hard drill in marching-order.

It would appear from the bitter complaints made by the men of the 78th, when they parleyed with Oughton's representatives on the slopes of Arthur's Seat, that their officers made frequent use of the Black Hole. They also complained of the humiliating and hurtful abuse to which they were constantly subjected and which outraged their traditional belief in what was proper between Highlandmen. This abuse, physical and verbal, was part of the normal life of any battalion and went on from reveille to taptoo. English soldiers, accustomed to more sophisticated class divisions and hatreds, expected it and endured it, but nothing in a High-lander's history had prepared him for an insult he could not openly resent or a blow he must not return. That he now received both from gentlemen of his own race, and sometimes of his own clan, was bewildering.

Most officers of the Army accompanied their orders with blasphemy and obscenity which they apparently regarded as the necessary language of communication with inferiors, although any soldier found guilty of swearing lost a day's pay. Hectoring and verbal bullying were the carrier-wave of an officer's parade-ground orders, and "I'll flog your guts out, you rascal!" or "I'll cut the flesh from your bloody back!" was shouted at any scarlet figure too slow in recovering his musket or closing upon his right-hand marker. Soldiers were never allowed to forget that the authority of their officers was backed by the power to inflict pain

upon body and spirit. Recruiting speeches, as suggested by
Captain Simes, were addressed to "all aspiring Heroes bold who
have spirits above slavery and trade, and inclinations to become
Gentlemen by bearing arms", but the reality of the profession the
heroes had chosen was more accurately expressed in the single
sentence by which one new commander introduced himself to
his regiment. "If you'll furnish the backs, I'll provide the cats for
'em!" At its questionable best, the physical abuse of a soldier
consisted of pushing and prodding him at all times, the rough
manhandling of his body. At its worst he could be struck on the
face by the flat of an officer's hand, or beaten on the back with a
rattan cane. A general officer, who had probably forgotten his
own youthful behaviour once interrupted a boyish ensign who
was caning a private of the guard. "Well done, sir! Beat the dog!
Thrash him! For you know he dare not strike you!" The manuals
written by old soldiers urged young officers not to beat their men,
but the constant repetition of this advice suggests that it was
rarely followed.

In March 1778, Oughton sent a rider to Brahan with orders
that five hundred men of the 78th were to be ready to sail for
America within two weeks. Humberston's unhappy reply
revealed that Seaforth's gratitude was far short of his hopes. The
Little Lord was still storm-bound on the Long Isle, and many of
the Highlanders he had enlisted had not yet come in from
Kintail. The men already mustered, living and drilling on the wet
aird below Brahan or the late snows of Strath Conon, were
without complete uniforms, without pay, and without the
bounty money they had been promised. So great had been the
demand for the Government's black tartan by all the Highland
regiments then recruiting, that Humberston had found one
manufacturer only who could supply him with plaids, and that
not before May. He told Oughton that if this Stirling weaver
could be persuaded to apply himself to his contract, five companies might be ready for embarkation in late April, and by then
his cousin would have returned from the west with the remainder
of the companies. When Seaforth did come to Brahan, weary and

disheartened, it was with no more than half the five hundred men he had promised. He did not tell Lord Barrington that his tenants on Lewis were lacklustre in enthusiasm. He blamed the delay upon the wild country and the bad weather through which he had travelled, and he promised to set out again once he was rested and the glens were opened, shortly to return with one hundred and fifty more men. "I may be allowed, I hope, without vanity, to say that few of His Majesty's subjects could do the same, as not one of those men could have been got by anybody but myself." This was certainly true, although his dreams at Brahan may have been disturbed by the memory of the fifteen hundred young Mackenzies who once responded willingly to the summons of his grandfather. He was relieved when Oughton told him that the 78th was no longer required in America at this moment, and he gave his officers leave to make up their companies with Lowlanders, Irishmen and English, always obtainable through crimps and agents in the south.

When early summer came the regiment was at last complete, and the companies moved south to Elgin to be inspected by Oughton's deputy, Major-general Robert Skene, who reported favourably on their fine and robust build, their dutiful attention to drill. He judged them upon their appearance, the steadiness of their scarlet and green files, their automatic response to the ruffle or flam of the company drums, and he said little of their morale. He knew nothing, perhaps, of the sullen discontent behind their impassive faces as he rode along the ranks. Their pay was now long in arrears, the promised bounty money still awaited. Arrogantly proud of their ancient service to the house of Seaforth, and not unnaturally expecting to be treated with respect therefore, Mackenzie's Shirt of Mail angrily resented the humiliating and abusive behaviour of officers like Scatwell and Redcastle. 'S iomadh diuc agus àrmunn, was Christopher Macrae's boast, "Many a duke and warrior is drinking our health at the table!" Men who had such a fierce conceit of themselves could not stomach foul-mouthed bullying, the pummelling of young lieutenants, the Black Hole and the whistling song of a threatening cane, the failure to pay what was honourably due. The Lewis men, hostages for their fathers' security of tenure, had taken the red coat in bitter hatred of Seaforth's factors and now felt themselves doubly betrayed by him. The Little Lord was unhappily aware of the sullen and dangerous mood of his command, and believed that it might be neutralised by isolation. When the companies had come south to the Stirling plain Barrington told Amherst that "Lord Seaforth wishes very much to be sent on foreign service and thinks his regiment will suffer by remaining in England."

The War Office did not dispute this, nor did it want the 78th in England. Since the mutiny of the Watch it had been realised that once embodied a Highland marching-regiment should be sent away as soon as possible, if not to campaign at least to an overseas station. Oughton was told that he could expect transports as soon as the North Sea was safe from the pirate Jones, and that once embarked the regiment would be taken to the Channel Islands, there to replace Lord MacLeod's 73rd Highlanders who were under orders for the East Indies. Seaforth's men learnt of this in August when they were garrisoned in Edinburgh Castle, wearily suffering the drill-parades which their officers called every morning and afternoon for the entertainment of fashionable society. When taken from their glens the young men had been told that they were needed to chastise the King's enemies in America, and they innocently believed that they could not be required to do anything else. The Islesmen had perhaps welcomed the duty, however distasteful the service. They remembered their many kinsmen who had crossed the Atlantic to escape the rapacity of Gillanders, and hoped that once discharged they might be allowed to remain in the colonies. They knew nothing of the Channel Islands. Distance to a Highlander was measured in emotion not miles, and North Carolina and Georgia were thus closer than Guernsey or Jersey. They also suspected that if their fellow-clansmen of the 73rd could be sent from these islands to India, then the same might be planned for them. This suspicion grew upon gossip and flowered in a bitter fear of betrayal, encouraged by the citizens of Edinburgh who were always ready to

embarrass authority, and who told the Highlanders that Lord
Seaforth had sold them to the East India Company. There was
some substance to the British soldier's obstinate belief that he
could be disposed of in this way, for if the Company did not buy
Crown regiments like cattle it did pay for the use of them, to
defend its profitable holdings, to fight its little wars.

At dawn one glittering September morning the last Mackenzie
sentinel of the night looked northward to the firth from the
ramparts of the Argyle Battery, across the grey stone and scaffolding of the growing New Town. What he saw was soon known
by all the companies. Six black transports were anchored off
Leith, with a hospital-ship sweetly named *The Brothers*. Still under
sail, and standing out in the firth was their escort H.M.S.
Jason.

Oughton signed the orders for embarkation, but it was some
days before they could be executed. Captain Jones's piratical
vessel *Bonhomme Richard*, or one of his French allies, had been
sighted hull down to the east of the Isle of May, and it was
necessary for the *Jason* to make sail and draw the threat away.
During this time the increasing alarm of Seaforth's Highlanders
went unrecorded by their officers or the Commander-in-Chief,
although newspapers later spoke of it as if it had been common
knowledge. It is probable that Oughton knew nothing of the
men's grievances and their sullen temper, for his good nature and
sense of justice would have compelled him to settle one and soften
the other. He was tired by the exertions and the pressures of the
past weeks, by London's repeated insistence that the 78th be
dispatched as soon as possible, by the problems of dispersing his
meagre command as widely as possible between the eastern and
western coasts, the need for a defensive fort at Greenock, and the
delay in obtaining guns from the foundry at Carron. He was also
harassed by the fear of anti-Catholic riots, by hysterical provosts
who wanted arms for the protection of their towns, and by
indignant citizens who accused him of too compassionate a concern for French prisoners in the Castle. But when he went late to
bed at Caroline Park on Monday, September 21, having sent

Seaforth his orders to march, he could at least feel that the most urgent of his duties had now been done.

Early on Tuesday the drums beat Assembly above Castle Hill and the Highlanders fell in by companies, the wind teasing plaid and kilt, the ranks rippling and steadying as the sergeants straightened them with fist and halbert. Standing among his senior officers, Seaforth watched with approval, a tiny figure in a cocked bonnet, cut-away coat and white breeches. He may have been proud of what he saw, happy that his debt was paid, but when his order to march was transmitted by the short beat of a grenadier drum on the left flank, there was an unexpected and violent reaction. A hundred men of the Macrae company broke ranks, shouting that they would not be sold to the Indies, they would not march until they had been paid, until they had seen justice done against their officers. They ignored the anguished appeals of their chief's son, Lieutenant Kenneth, and they shook their fists and muskets at Seaforth, for whose ancestors theirs had once died without protest. Their anger was a fuse that exploded a mine of fury, and Seaforth stared in astonishment as three hundred more men surged from the line toward him.

He stood his ground, more in stupefaction than courage at this moment, but before the black-topped wave reached him it stopped and broke into swirling eddies. Some men loaded their muskets and pistols, ramming the charges home in desperate haste. Others fixed their bayonets, and more drew their broadswords in a bright gleam of metal. When the first shock was over, officers and sergeants plunged boldly into the mob, shouting useless orders, wrestling with the flourished weapons, striking the breasts and shoulders of the angry men. Some muskets were fired, by accident perhaps, but Mackenzie of Scatwell, who had heard his name among the oaths and the threats, wisely ran toward the Outer Barrier of the Castle, ducking his head to avoid the more deliberate shots that were fired at his back. And then, as if a plan had been agreed, the four hundred mutineers formed an orderly column, behind a piper, behind two uplifted pikes from which hung the dark green plaid that was to be their standard of revolt. Led by Mackenzie's Shirt of Mail, and followed for a few yards by the more resolute officers, they strutted eastward below the leaning astonishment of the tenements, past the traders' stalls in the Lawnmarket, the lantern tower of Saint Giles. Aroused by the pipes and the defiant discharge of firelocks, or by some pre-knowledge of the mutiny, the mob came out of the wynds, baying behind its customary leader, a pope-hating, judge-hating cobbler from the Cowgate. At the Tron Church, seven hundred yards from Castle Hill, the column was halted, held by the press of the cheering crowd.

There was silence on the earthen slope before the castle. Five hundred men of the 78th still remained where they had assembled, their ranks unclosed, their heads turned to the distant shouting and the echoing explosion of musketry. Officers stood in speechless rage before their depleted companies, some with torn coats and bloodied faces, cropped heads bare from the loss of bonnets and wigs. The Little Lord did not know what terrible things might be happening below the drop of the Lawnmarket, or what could take place here on Castle Hill if he delayed longer, and with courage or foolhardiness, but in stubborn determination to obey his instructions, he ordered the drummers to beat the march again. The files closed without protest and turned to the left in column of companies. As they moved off Seaforth took his place in the van, a small figure with twinkling white legs, his chin up and his hand holding the hilt of his small-sword to his side.

Once through the Lawnmarket he could see what lay ahead, for the jeering mob parted to let him through, as if inviting him to engage the mutineers. They turned to face him, a wall of red from tenement to tenement, the uplifted plaid above their black bonnets and the autumn light on their broadswords. Seaforth halted his command within a few paces of this hostile line and went forward alone, his arms wide and his voice lifted in passionate appeal. The Macraes shouted him down and called upon his men to join them. Some did break ranks, but as they moved forward the closing fist of the mob drew mutineers and loyalists together in struggling confusion. Seaforth stumbled to his knees, falling upon them in supplication it was said by those who watched from the windows above. A blow from a musket knocked him on his back, and he would have been killed by the stamping feet had not two of his captains dragged him into the opening of a wynd. The air was full of the smoke and smell of powder, of stones thrown by town-boys at the back of the mob, and two or three officers who boldly wrestled with the mutineers were soon bleeding from sword-cuts or bayonet-thrusts. Then, suddenly, the mutineers turned about, swinging their weapons to clear a lane to the east. As they marched down the Canongate nothing could be seen of them but their bonnets and the waving of their tartan standard above the heads of the following mob. Seaforth came unsteadily from the wynd, ordered his companies to the march again and wheeled them to the left, over North Bridge and on to the Leith road.

The mutineers halted at the regimental guard-house in the Canongate Tolbooth, shouting for the release of comrades held there. Men and women whom newspapers later described as respectable, to distinguish them from the Cowgate mob, came from the tenements to press food and drink upon the Highlanders, calling them brave fellows and praising their refusal to be sold as slaves to the Indies. The Tolbooth was a narrow, eyeless gaol, straddling the entrance to a close and glowering with corbelled turrets. Fifteen steps of the forestair led to a nail-studded door and before this now was the officer of the guard, Kenneth Mackenzie of Redcastle, defiantly posed and intoxicated by his own heroism. He refused to stand aside, and when bayonets were charged at his breast he pulled open his coat and shirt, daring the mutineers to thrust home, for he would surrender no man placed in his care. They cheered his courage ironically, threw him down the steps and opened the door. When they had liberated the prisoners they fired their muskets at the obdurate face of the prison and marched down the hill toward Holyroodhouse.

Leading his sullen companies along the Wester Road to Leith, his breeches and hose black with the filth of the Royal Mile, the Little Lord had one desperate hope only, that he could put these men aboard the transports before more of them deserted. To his astonishment, as his column came by the bowling-green and on to the links outside the port, he saw that the mutineers had arrived before him. They had left Edinburgh at the foot of the Canongate and taken the Easter Road about Abbeyhill, their natural swiftness outpacing the slow infantry march of the loyalists. Now they stood in line on the dunes, their backs to the waiting ships and the white-tipped firth, once more calling upon Seaforth's men to join their just cause. This time he did not halt. When the two forces met there was again a fierce and bitter struggle, a shower of stones and scattered shots before the breath-denying impact of body against body. The little battle was brief, breaking into bizarre debate. Officers stood before small groups of mutineers, protesting that the regiment was ordered to Guernsey and nowhere else, that upon their honour no man would be sold to the Company. Seaforth called for obedience, in the name of Clan Kenneth and the King, promising that all grievances would be met and all money paid once the regiment was embarked. He was roughly told that he could not be trusted, that he had betrayed his clansmen, and that if they were fools enough to go aboard they would become the King's prisoners, to be sent wherever he wished. There was now a great crowd gathering, pouring across Constitution Road from Leith and down the slopes to the dunes. At this the mutineers drew back, presented their muskets and fired a contemptuous volley over the heads of the civilians. When the smoke lifted, and while the thunder of the discharge was still rolling along the sands, they were seen to be marching away in good order behind their piper, back down the Easter Road toward the surging rock of Arthur's Seat.

They took with them nearly two hundred of Seaforth's men whose weakening loyalty had at last been destroyed by a closer sight of the transports. Those who remained were put aboard in haste, but at dusk the boats that ferried them were still bouncing between shore and ships. Long before then the mutineers had passed by Holyroodhouse and advanced up the Dry Dam, scattering its grazing sheep. The sloping trough rose southward to the cone of the Seat and there, on an eastward ledge below the summit and among the hawk and raven, they halted and lit their fires, building ramparts of stone against the wind. Before sunset they had posted sentinels along the escarpment of Salisbury Crags, facing the darkening city.

The glow of their fires was seen by Oughton as he worked late into the night at Caroline Park, writing dispatches to London and to the commanding officers of those regiments of Horse and Foot who were within a day's march of Edinburgh. Thigh-booted gallopers waited to carry his letters, and with them were two or three weary officers of the 78th who had come to report the failure of Seaforth's last attempt to bring his men back to their duty. At nightfall these captains had climbed Arthur's Seat in the hope of persuading the men to surrender but had been turned back by the flash of muskets and the warning sigh of shots above their heads. Despite a compassionate desire to settle this miserable affair without bloodshed, Oughton knew what his conscience and his duty demanded. "Treating with rebels while they have arms in their hands," he had once written on the American War, "would demonstrate a weakness which no victory would compensate for." The need of force to compel submission prompted him to call upon the 11th Dragoons, the Duke of Buccleuch's South Fencibles, and the Glasgow Volunteers to march at once from their country quarters, but he hoped that their arrival alone would be enough to bring the Highlanders down from the rock. There was also, as always, the fear of the mob, the knowledge of what it could and might do now that the city was without protection.

Oughton was not only worried by the behaviour of the lower orders. Society and the respectable classes had demonstrated an unhealthy and disloyal sympathy for the Highlanders, and he had been told that as well as carrying food and drink to Arthur's Seat some foolish persons had given the mutineers powder and ball. As he wrote now, carefully phrased letters in a crabbed and childish hand, he knew that ladies and gentlemen were taking the night air about Holyroodhouse, listening to the sound of the pipes, the calling of the sentinels above, and remembering the days of excitement thirty years before when the Pretender's handsome Highlanders had lit their fires upon the hill. One of the gentlemen who walked in the park that night was Captain John Macpherson, an officer of the 17th Foot recovering from wounds and anxious to be away south to marry his English bride. In the Canongate earlier that day it had seemed to him that the mutineers were behaving like a mad drove of black cattle, but now, pleasantly enjoying an evening warm enough for a man to put on linen waistcoat and breeches, he felt more sympathetic. "How the affair will end," he wrote to his brother of Invershie, "is more than I can pretend to say. They put me in mind of a parcel of deer on a mountain top. Poor devils. . . ."

"This unlucky business has been rather badly managed"

THE DRAGOONS ARRIVED before dusk on Wednesday. They tethered their black horses by the washing-house at the northern spur of the Crags, and by nightfall their dismounted picquets were posted at the mouth of the Dry Dam and on the marshy ground below Dunsapie Rock. Throughout the night two companies of Buccleuch's Borderers and four of the Glasgow Volunteers came into the city, their drums rattling as they encamped on Saint Ann's Yards to the east of Holyroodhouse. Such a force, thought Oughton sadly, could certainly storm the mutineers' position but he still hoped that the threat would be enough. He did not know what reaction there might be in London to the bloody use of bayonet and sabre, and a seaborne reply to his first dispatch could not come within seventy-two hours. He did know that before those three days were past he was morally and professionally obliged to bring an end to what the delighted people of Edinburgh were now calling The Affair of the Macraes.

Strong winds had blown away the mild weather during Tuesday night and by morning they were ploughing the firth beyond his northern windows, rocking the transports and creating a vomiting hell for the loyalists below decks. Civilians who visited Arthur's Seat early on Wednesday told Oughton that the Highlanders were unaffected by the sudden cold and the stinging flurries of bitter rain. They had elected officers whom they cheerfully obeyed, although their spirits had been saddened by the loss of one of the sentinels, plucked from the escarpment in the night wind and thrown to his death below. They believed that force would be used against them but were determined to make a stand until their demands were met or the last man was dead. They remained stubbornly convinced that they had been sold to the Indies, and in proof of this they asked why else had *Mac-Coinnich* their chief not given them a King's or regimental colour? Was the expense thought unnecessary, because their battle-flag was to be the standard of the East India Company? This concern for their colours, if Oughton thought of it at all, may have explained that green plaid snapping on a pike above the ramparts of stone.

Other visitors, less sympathetic and more derisive, said that the mutineers were as mad with drink as with enthusiasm, and that they foolishly talked of going home to the Highlands as soon as they could.

Before the arrival of the 11th Dragoons, and as if he felt compelled to observe the punctilio of a siege, Oughton had opened a parley with the mutineers. He sent Robert Skene up the wet glissade of heather and grass with a Gaelic interpreter, and either at his request or upon their own desire the Major-general was also accompanied by four noble gentlemen well-wrapped in capes. The first was of course the unhappy Seaforth, another the Duke of Buccleuch, and a third the Earl of Dunmore, an officious kinsman of the Atholl family whose previous experience of reasonable conciliation had been the burning of American houses and a consequent hasty retreat from the governorship of Virginia. He now lodged in Holyroodhouse and may therefore have thought it his business to settle any improper behaviour on its policies. The fourth member of this distinguished party was Lord Macdonald, the anglicised chief of Clan Donald who had little or no Gaelic and who was so rarely in the Highlands that it is improbable that he would have been recognised by any mutineers who were men of his own name. Nor might he have been welcomed by them, for they had faithfully enlisted in his regiment and been carried unwillingly into the 78th by their ambitious recruiter.

The windswept parley was brief. The mutineers would not

listen to Seaforth, but he was forced to endure what one civilian, standing closer to hear, called a "very pathetic harangue on his vices and bad qualities". Before they came down to their duty, said the Highlanders, they would have a written assurance that every man would be freely pardoned, that they were not to be sold to the Company, that the money owing them would be paid, and that the officers who had so brutally abused them would be punished. As the General and his noble companions slipped and stumbled down the slope it gave them no comfort to pass small groups of smiling citizens, climbing the hill to visit the mutineers. One of these was a correspondent to the *Aberdeen Journal*.

> I had the pleasure of patrolling this morning round the encampment, for though without tents, and not so much as a sergeant among them, they preserve the best discipline, and of a most desolate place make a most elegant summit to Arthur's Seat. It puts one in mind of the warriors of Ossian, seen from afar, with their glittering arms on the tops of the mountains.

Despite his own enthusiasm for the brave followers of Fingal, James Oughton saw no resemblance between them and the mutinous men who were holding authority at defiance eight hundred feet above sea level. He spent the day directing the dispersal of his troops about the hill, and much of the night at his London correspondence. The winds became stronger, the falls of rain heavy and prolonged, and some time during the darkness another sentinel was severely wounded by the accidental discharge of a comrade's musket. He was taken to the Infirmary by two of the many Highland citizens of Edinburgh who came night and day to encourage the mutineers. At dawn there were dragoon trumpets singing below the mount, red and white figures moving in the rippling rain. An hour or so later Robert Skene and their lordships arrived once more, climbing past the grazing sheep to parley at the tartan banner. They were accompanied by ministers who called upon the wrath of God to compel the mutineers to submit, but this was no more successful than the well-intentioned appeals of Skene. Oughton had now to decide whether to accept the Highlanders' terms or to order his regiments to violent assault. That afternoon, as he sat alone with his troubled thoughts, a report spread that the mutineers were coming down to loot the city. No sensible man believed this, for as the *Scots Magazine* said "they would not have done the least hurt to the inhabitants by whom they had been liberally supplied with provisions". But the Provost and Magistrates, already terrified by the thought of the unrestrained Cowgate mob, readily accepted the story. By tuck of drum, and by posters from Castle Hill to the Water Gate, they announced that a fire-bell would be rung when the first Highlanders were seen, and that upon its alarm all citizens were to retire to their houses.

That evening Oughton decided that he must accept the mutineers' demands without qualification. The letter in which he explained his reasons to London has been lost, and they can only be seen in the light of his character. He was not a weak man, nor too squeamish a commander to issue orders that would rob men of their lives, but as with the best of soldiers the nature of his profession urged him to avoid useless bloodshed. He also understood the Highlanders' uncomplicated notion of honour, and while he would not place this above their duty he could not outrage its affecting simplicity. More practically, the Crown could not afford the loss of a regiment in this unprofitable way, or the terrible effect its destruction would have upon other Highland battalions. Once he had set aside, with difficulty, his instinctive reluctance to agree to any mutinous demand, the matter of the alleged grievances was easily solved. The belief that the 78th had been sold to the East India Company could be honestly denied, and he hoped London would honour his assurance that the battalion would never be sent to the Indies. If there were indeed arrears of pay and levy money, these could and should be paid at once. If officers had abused their men, they must be held to account. The most difficult matter of all was the demand for a free pardon. Military law did not permit this without proper trial and sentence, yet to avoid a savage slaughter Oughton had no alternative but to grant it. He asked for Seaforth to come at once from Leith, and while he waited he wrote an order for the arrest of Captain George Mackenzie of Scatwell, believing this justified by the mutineers' accusations and by the need to convince them of his sincerity.

The news of their victory was taken to the Highlanders late that night by Seaforth and the chief of Clan Grant who, because he was known as "The Good Sir James", was perhaps thought to be a man who would be received in trust. They carried a letter signed by Oughton and Skene, by Buccleuch and Dunmore. The officers of the 78th later referred to its three major clauses as a compromise, salving their scalded pride with the fiction that mutual concessions had been made, but the letter was in fact a total surrender to the mutineers' demands. There would be a free pardon for all past offences. Levy money and arrears would be paid before embarkation, and no man would be sent to the East Indies. The Highlanders were further assured that they would soon receive their colours, and that any officers who had ill-used them would be punished. This last promise, as he faced his relentless Shirt of Mail in the firelight, must have burnt like gall on Seaforth's tongue.

Lord Dunmore brought the six hundred mutineers down from their encampment at eleven o'clock on Friday morning. Why his lordship was given this duty is not known, if indeed he were not play-acting the part of a Murray chief, escorting his departing guests to the boundary of his land. From what the officers of the regiment said later it would appear that the Highlanders had agreeably accepted his assumption of authority and trusted his professions of friendship and understanding. A great crowd had come to watch the victorious surrender, standing on Whinny Mill or held back by dragoons and foot-soldiers in Saint Ann's Yards. The weather had once more changed, and a golden sunlight shone on burnished metal and polished wood, on the white facings of the troopers' coats, on brocade, boot-leather and horseflesh where Skene waited with his staff. There was a sustained roar of cheering when the Highlanders first appeared, six orderly companies marching from the narrow throat of the Dry Dam behind Dunmore, their piper strutting beside the green plaid. As they came on to the Yards they halted, faced into line, raised their bonnets on their muskets, and saluted Skene with skirling cheers until they were brought to silence by the vibrating ruffle of a Fencible drum. Upon an order from one of Buccleuch's officers, and marching to a long roll from the same drummer, they formed hollow square, the two centre companies standing fast and the flanks wheeling through forty-five degrees to the right and the left. Skene rode to the centre of the open side with his officers, and there one of them read the articles of surrender, waiting while each sentence was translated into Gaelic. When the General spoke to the Highlanders he urged them to behave as loyal and devoted soldiers now that they had returned to their duty. He said that a Court of Inquiry into the behaviour of their officers would be held the following morning in the Canongate Council-house, "which every man who thinks himself aggrieved may attend, and justice will be done him". He then saluted them respectfully and rode away.

The emotional Highlanders were deeply affected by the ceremony. When they broke ranks to eat the bread and cheese that had been brought them, they moved to the stiff and lonely figure of their chief, childishly assuring him that they would now follow him wherever he went. In this mood of contradictory forgiveness they cheered him and every field-officer upon the ground. They were still cheering when they marched away to quarters in the suburbs, there to await embarkation. That evening, now that the theatrical excitement was over and realising how close the city had come to mob-rule, many respectable people wondered if Oughton had been wise to be so lenient with the mutineers. "I am happy on their account the affair is made up," Captain Macpherson told his brother, "though at the same time some of them deserve to be made an example of."

Seaforth's officers were of the same mind, bitterly angered by the success of the mutiny and by the manner in which the newspapers had reported it. They had been libelled as rogues who defrauded and abused their men, and those captains who had attempted to parley with the mutineers on the mount were said to have "had the pleasure of running full speed down the hill with bullets flying after them". Worse than public ridicule was the fact that Scatwell was under arrest without explanation and that the rest of them were to justify their behaviour before a Court of Inquiry. All this without one word in their defence being sent to London. That Friday evening, and probably on Humberston's advice, they met at Lawson's Coffee-house in Leith, arguing in the smoke and candle-light, swearing that they would have redress for Oughton's betrayal. Good sense or a cautious concern for their careers persuaded them to abandon their original intention of sending an angry protest to Lord Amherst, and instead they composed a letter which was taken that night to the printer of the *Edinburgh Advertiser*.

As we conceive the terms granted this day to the mutineers of the 78th regiment to be totally inconsistent with the future discipline of the regiment, and highly injurious to our characters as officers, we think ourselves bound to take this first opportunity of publicly declaring, that it was transacted without our advice, and against our opinion. We understand Lord Dunmore was the principal agent on this occasion; we therefore think it necessary also to declare that he was never desired to interfere by any officer in the regiment, and, we believe, acted without any authority whatever.

The letter cannot have been written without Seaforth's knowledge, and may have had his approval. He too had been grievously injured, as a commanding officer humiliated by his regiment and a chief rejected by his clan. No newspaper had said a word in his favour, but many had boldly printed the mutineers' scurrilous references to his "vices and bad qualities". He was particularly hurt by the report that during the affray on the Royal Mile he had fallen to his knees in terror, pleading for his

life, and some days after his officers' protest he wrote his own to
the *Weekly Mercury*.

> I beg you will publish this to let the world know it is an
> infamous falsehood; nor would the certainty of immediate
> death have procured from me so humiliating a concession.
> At the same time I must add I never had any apprehension
> for my personal safety during the whole time the mutiny
> lasted.

The Court of Inquiry met early on Saturday morning, four
officers of the Volunteers and Fencibles under the presidency of
Colonel George Scott of the Glasgow Regiment. The officers of
the 78th came from Leith, pushing their way through a jeering
crowd outside the Council-house, and their evidence was briefly
given. They denied that they had withheld any money owing,
that they had abused or ill-treated their men. They blamed the
mutiny upon "an idle and ill-founded report that the regiment
was sold to the East India Company", which had been put about
by the people of Edinburgh, particularly those of the Highland
race. Although Skene had honestly promised the mutineers that
they would be fairly heard by the Court, no man appeared to
make charges of personal grievances. Those who did attend,
either willingly or at the prompting of others, gave evidence
upon hearsay which was disregarded. Throughout the mutiny
the Highlanders had taken particular care that none of them
should appear to be ringleaders, and none was so named in either
the press or the official reports. It is not surprising, therefore, that
with their victory won they were now reluctant to expose themselves to future reprisals. Inevitably, too, the Court decided "that
there is not the smallest degree for complaints against any officer
in the regiment, in regard to their pay and arrears". Nothing was
said of brutality or abuse, nor might any of the Lowland officers
of the court have thought such behaviour exceptional or unnecessary. Oughton received their laconic report on Saturday
evening, and was perhaps thankful that it restored some of the
Army's self-respect. He signed his approving signature below

Scott's, put it in the London bag for the morning packet, and told his clerk to send a copy to the newspapers. He also ordered the release of George Mackenzie of Scatwell.

On the following Tuesday morning the Highlanders were called from their quarters by the beating of the General. They paraded in Abbey Close before Holyroodhouse, and with Seaforth and Robert Skene at their head they marched cheerfully down the Easter Road to Leith. Behind the last files walked seventy-two women and twenty-three children, wives and families whose presence had been unrecorded in press or dispatch until now, but who had shared the three defiant nights on Arthur's Seat or waited in the rain of the park below. By dusk the regiment was aboard the transports and Oughton had signed Seaforth's last return of its strength. Apart from the man killed on the escarpment, and the other wounded by gunshot, sixty-six men only were absent. One of these was a prisoner in Glasgow, a second was sick at Dunbar, and twenty-four had been discharged as unfit. The remaining forty were entered as *Missing since the Mutiny/deserted*. Almost all of these were reluctant Irishmen, enlisted by crimps or by coercion, in a moment of vainglory or drunken despair. Some time during those three nights on Arthur's Seat they had thanked God for his merciful intervention and disappeared for ever.

In the first week of October the London packet brought a chilling letter from the Commander-in-Chief of the King's Forces. "I cannot help observing," wrote Lord Amherst, as if he were a grenadier biting open a cartridge before a despised enemy, "that this unlucky business has been rather badly managed." The tone of distant distaste continued throughout the letter and must have wounded Oughton, for he shared his profession's admiration for the writer. Jeffrey Amherst was a brilliant soldier whose year of hard campaigning had turned the triumph on the Plains of Abraham into decisive victory. Posthumous laurels and public laudation had gone to that sickly and bloodthirsty hero James Wolfe, but the Army was in no doubt about the true conqueror of Canada. In his sixty-first year Amherst's body was now turning to fat, his red hair fading to autumn snow, but his dragoon's back was as straight as ever, and his famous long nose and determined chin could still come together like the jaws of a pike in moments of controlled anger. It was said that he had once suggested that the vexatious problem of the American Indian could be solved by distributing the blankets of small-pox victims among the tribes, and if not true in fact the story illustrated his preference for relentless and conclusive action. He believed that no war should be begun without the will to triumph, and although he had at first been saddened by the thought of fighting Americans with whom he had once campaigned, he was now determined upon their total defeat. Equally he knew that victory depended on the private soldier's courage in the line, and if this must be sustained by the noose and the lash both should be used without hesitation. Only his closest friends knew that he would rather drive a plough on his Kentish estates than spend one more day than was necessary on a campaign. His present duties included the prompt and speedy dispatch of regiments to battle, and he could tolerate nothing that might persuade them that they were stronger in will and spirit than their superiors.

> The granting of terms to mutineers, and engaging with them in their present state of disorder, that they should not be sent to India, must have a bad effect, and tend to encourage young regiments to a like conduct. Major-general Skene went too far in the beginning of this defection in promising them a full redress of their grievances, a plenary pardon, and that they should not be sent to the Indies. . . . It was more than anyone should promise, that a regiment should not be sent to India, or to any other place, for tho' there was no such intention in this present case, such promises must tend to the ruin of the King's Service.

Although his deputy was thus to carry the disgrace, Oughton knew that the implied responsibility was his, as he also knew that he was held to blame for the unregimental behaviour in Lawson's Coffee-house. "The Advertisement of the officers is big with mischief," Amherst told him, "for after the men have gone such lengths there can be no wonder if they should avail themselves on some other occasion of the substance of the paper."

Most of the company commanders and their lieutenants were now aboard the transports, but the hostility between them and their men was suspended in common misery. Continued storms delayed the ships for a week, damaging yards and rigging, and no soldiers were allowed above deck. They lay below in semi-darkness, enduring the endless pitch and roll of complaining timbers, and living without hope in the filth of vomit and the stench of brine and vinegar. Seaforth was ashore, weakened by a cold and dispirited by shock, and although his baggage was aboard the *Triumverate* he decided to make the southward journey by coach. Captain Humberston was also lodged in Leith, having applied for leave of absence in London. James Oughton granted it, telling Amherst that the captain had suffered a dangerous fit of sickness and feared a relapse at sea, but he cannot have been unaware of the young man's real design. By mid-October the damaged transports had been repaired and they made a fair voyage to Deal. Seaforth was already in the town and he came out by boat to talk to some of his men. He told the Secretary at War that "they seem in a great measure to have forgot the unlucky spirit of mutiny, and I am still confident that they will keep up that character I always gave them". This hopeful optimism was contradicted by Humberston, who had also visited Deal and was in correspondence with the officers. From his lodgings in King Street, St. James's, he sent Amherst the angry protest that was the true purpose of his presence in London.

I am desired by the officers of the 78th Regiment to inform your Lordship that the soldiers of that Corps who were engaged in the late Mutiny at Edinburgh, have since their embarkation continued to conduct themselves in ye most insolent, disrespectful and unsoldierlike manner; and they apprehend that unless a proper example be made of the

Ringleaders, or such other measures taken as your Lordship shall think proper, consequences may ensue prejudicial to his Majesty's Service. The officers of the 78th were always of opinion that the manner in which the Mutineers were treated and the compromise made with them would be attended with the worst consequences.

Amherst undoubtedly agreed with the spirit of this protest, and was as angry as the Mackenzie subalterns who complained that when the Highlanders were rowed out to the transport they had exulted in the public humiliation of their officers. But the Commander-in-Chief had heard enough of the disgraceful affair and saw no profit in pursuing it further. He refused Humberston's passionate request for another inquiry, for evidence to be taken from the officers of the Dragoons, Fencibles and Volunteers. He did, however, take the sensible precautions the situation required, realising that the men of the 78th were of the same race and largely of the same clan as the regiment they were to replace in the Channel Islands. Lord MacLeod was told that his battalion was to be embarked before one man of Seaforth's was allowed ashore, and that there was to be no communication between them.

The 78th remained in the Islands for two and a half years, during which time the officers followed the harsh example of Humberston, now promoted to the second majority of the regiment and determined that the Highlanders should not escape the least penalty for the slightest indiscipline. When reports reached Amherst that the battalion was again insubordinate, Humberston quickly denied them. "I can safely assure your Lordship that the men are heartily ashamed of their former ill-conduct, and that every irregularity has been as constantly and as severely punished as in other regiments." The Little Lord's poor health and low spirits never recovered from the shame of the mutiny, and he was rarely with his men, preferring the more agreeable environment of Westminster, but when he was told that they were to leave the Islands for more active service he was eager to share their triumphs and misfortunes. He joined them on the transports at Portsmouth, going aboard with the news of their destination.

The promise that had been given on Arthur's Seat was broken. They were to sail for India.

It is difficult to believe that this betrayal was accepted without protest, but none was recorded, and Garth's claim that the men were "in high health and well-disciplined" reveals nothing except his constant wish to believe the best of all Highland regiments. The voyage was long and hard, and it was eleven months before the battalion reached Madras. While the ships were still in the southern Atlantic the Little Lord died of a fever, suddenly and in the night, his body slipped into the morning sea. His death was emotionally lamented. "It is bitter news to tell," said Sergeant Christopher. "Who will now assume the honour of Mackenzie of Kintail of the Cows?" The question was answered by Major Humberston. If he could not inherit his cousin's earldom he was entitled by birth to the leadership of Clan Kenneth, and rich enough by his English inheritance to acquire its landed power. At Saint Helena he sent instructions to his agents, empowering them to purchase the Seaforth estates.

Garth said that grief and homesickness, a fear of the future, made the soldiers easily susceptible to disease on the voyage, but their resistance was more probably lowered by their lingering sense of betrayal, by eleven months of salt rations and long hours below decks. Before the Coromandel Coast was sighted, the white walls of Madras, two hundred and fifty men had died of scurvy and had joined *Mac-Coinnich* in the great embrace of the ocean. Of the remainder only half had the strength to stand once they were ashore. Heat and fever, the weight of bonnet, plaid and equipment, killed or sickened more, and the few who could still march were drafted into MacLeod's regiment. When the invalids recovered, the battalion was reformed and committed to a bloody assault on Cuddalore, a long day's fight between the sea and the dunes, a useless, wasting battle that was remembered with para-doxical pride. "Notwithstanding the might of Hyder Ali," boasted Christopher Macrae, "a tribute was exacted from him by the regiment of Kintail with its weaving antlers!"

At the end of the American Revolution the men of the 78th were entitled to their discharge, having enlisted for three years or the duration of the war. Two-thirds of them asked for their release, rejecting the ten guineas that were offered to any man who stayed with the colours. Six years before, Seaforth's letter of service* had declared "His Majesty's consent that, on a reduction, the Corps shall be disbanded in Ross-shire," and Garth said that the discharged men were embarked for Britain. The truth is in the sorrowing lament of Sergeant Macrae.

> When we got the order
> from the Consul we were not pleased.
> Our discharge put in our hands,
> free to go where we wished but without a bounty.
> And told everywhere
> that there was no ship, no boat nor sail.

They were disbanded where they were and no more was done for them. This last squalid betrayal of trust was perhaps explained – if the War Office were ever asked for an explanation – by the fact that all engagements were at the option of the King, that the regiment was not reduced but embodied still in the men who had not taken their discharge, although they had been re-enlisted and re-mustered under another numeral. Ten thousand sea-miles from their cool blue Highlands, with little money and speaking Gaelic only for the most part, it is astonishing that any of the disbanded men found their way home. What was left of Mackenzie's Shirt of Mail was brought back to Loch Duich by Sergeant Christopher Macrae, "only an odd one surviving of the hundred of us". In his memory and in his verse he sometimes believed that he was abandoned still, on the far Coast of Coromandel, and wondering if he would ever see Kintail again. 'S truagh nach robh mi cho aotrom ris an t-seabhaig theid caol anns a' speur. . . .

* See Appendix, p. 493.

It is a pity that I am not as light
as the hawk, slim flying in the sky.
I would take the desert road
and I would not rest in the tree-tops.
In spite of the violence of Turkey
I would pass it by like a lark in the sun.
And I would make a complaint in London
that would bring us all home.

"Call together every respectable man of your name"

WHEN HE STOOD with the other wind-blown gentlemen on Arthur's Seat the chief of Clan Donald could not have believed that six months later he would again be involved in a hill-top dispute, this time with mutinous men of his own name and regiment.

Alexander, Lord Macdonald of Macdonald and Sleat, ninth baronet of the same, heir-male of *Clann Uisdein*, descendant of Conn the High King of Ireland, of Somerled the Regulus of Argyll, and of Iain the first Lord of the Isles, had been educated at Eton. He was an ineffectual man of taste and delicacy, with a round and chinless head from which jutted a hawk's nose of bizarre incongruity, the only recognisable indication of an awesome ancestry. He was married to an Englishwoman, and his preference for life in London and Edinburgh was made the more agreeable by society's attachment to the romantic nonsense of Macpherson's Fingalians and its willingness to receive him as a representative of that mythical race of warriors and poets. He was a versifier himself, although not of course in Gaelic, and he composed an elegant Latin panegyric in honour of Samuel Johnson who greatly admired his lordship's late brother Sir James, a scholar renowned as the Scottish Marcellus.

Johnson's willingness to extend this admiration to Alexander Macdonald had withered by the time the verses were handed to him at Armadale House on Skye. Although he had been well-pleased by the man in London, he reached the island with entirely new opinions on the nature of Highland chiefs in general and *Mac-Dhomnuill nan Eilean* in particular. "My fellow-traveller and

I," said Boswell, "were now full of the old Highland spirit, and were dissatisfied at hearing of racked rents and emigration, and finding a chief not surrounded by his clan." In Johnson's view no chiefs should be allowed beyond Aberdeen, with the exception of the late Sir James, since it was clear that a southern education only tamed them into insignificance, and this "English-bred chieftain" whose hospitality he enjoyed was now a disappointing fellow indeed, despite the hereditary piper who strutted about the table. Winter was coming to the Isles, and Macdonald and his wife were departing the next morning for more comfortable residence in Edinburgh, leaving the management of his estates to his factors. There was time enough, however, for Johnson to lecture him upon his obligations and his failure to keep his clan about him. "Were I in your place, sir, in seven years I would make this place an independent island. I would roast an oxen whole and hang out a flag as a signal to the Macdonalds to come and get beef and whisky." When the chief foolishly protested that he would need arms to maintain such independence, and that they might rust in the magazine, Johnson brushed the objection aside: "Let there be men to keep them clean. Your ancestors did not use to let their arms rust."

Everything Johnson heard about the rack-renting of Macdonald and his factors filled him with disgust and provided him with a whetstone upon which to sharpen his clumsy wit. He and Boswell had come to Skye at the rising swell of a long wave of emigration. Less than three years before their arrival, two thousand of Macdonald's tenants had subscribed as many pounds to a fund that would take them to Canada. In the following autumn four hundred more left for North Carolina, and those who watched them sail from Portree then fell upon the ground in grief, biting at the grass. Boswell saw a dance which the people called *America*, its whirling, widening circles illustrating how the desire to be gone spread from one to another until a whole neighbourhood was free and afloat. The population of the island at this time was under fourteen thousand, and the Bishop of Ross believed that Macdonald would soon become a proprietor without tenants. "All, *all* this," he said sadly, "is owing to the exorbitant rents." The old influence of the Sleat chiefs had begun its decline earlier in the century, and even the dead were no longer recalled with regret. It was remembered that Alexander Macdonald's father had once sold a hundred of his people to the Americas, that he had been one of the Government's most ruthless supporters after the Rebellion. He had died in Glenelg while still at this harrying work, looking westward from the barracks at Bernera to the eternal beauty of his mountain isle. His departure inspired one of the best of Highland valedictions.

If Heaven is pleased when sinners cease to sin,
If Hell is pleased when sinners enter in,
If Earth is pleased, freed of a truckling knave,
Then all are pleased – Macdonald's in his grave!

Wherever Johnson went on Skye he amused his audiences with malicious ridicule of Alexander Macdonald. Told by Mrs. Mackinnon of Corriechatachin that she and her husband would emigrate rather than suffer the landlord's further oppression, he waited for the conversation to turn its flank before placing a sympathetic barb. Another guest said that Macdonald was afraid of the sea, which, if true, was an unhappy weakness in a man whose web-footed clan bore a galley on its arms. "He is frightened at sea," said Johnson, accepting the cue, "and his tenants are frightened when he comes to land." The people complained that their chief visited Skye in summer only, but the doctor reassured them. "That is out of tenderness to you. Bad weather and he at the same time would be too much." He left the Highlands with contempt for men who had degenerated from patriarchal rulers to rapacious landlords, and most particularly did he despise Alexander Macdonald of Macdonald. "He has no more the soul of a chief than an attorney who has twenty houses in a street, and considers how much he can make by them."

The contempt was justified if harsh, but nowhere in the Highlands would Johnson have found the soul of a chief. The last to possess this metaphysical quality had died before the redcoat line at Culloden, or in exile, supported by the rents of their abandoned clansmen. If Macdonald differed in any great degree from others of his class it was in his ambitious vanity and his penny-counting meanness. In December 1777 both these characteristics were excited by the Government's invitation to raise a regiment of a thousand Highlanders. He had recently been elevated to the Irish peerage and to refuse the request might have seemed churlishly ungrateful, but it was not this that made him accept. The proposal was first put to his London agent who assured him that it was an opportunity

> ... to distinguish yourself in the eyes of *Administration etc.* I was asked whether you would exert yourself *in person* to raise a regiment among the subordinate chieftains of your name. I am given to understand that the old proverb, a friend etc, will not be forgot. Call together every respectable man of your name, or of any other connected with you. Your family will for ever be benefitted and respected, and I have ventured to use your name as ready to go in person.

Macdonald was not pleased that he should be thus committed to leave Edinburgh in winter, to put to sea in the worst of weather, to stay in the mean houses of his lesser kinsmen, sharing these lodgings with their livestock. But the promise of preferment was irresistible, and his natural concern for his purse was comforted by the last sentence of the agent's letter. "If you cannot, with your friends, complete a regiment, you will lose nothing as Government will buy your men from you."

It was to be the sorriest and most unprofitable venture he undertook, for it brought him no rank, no credit and no coin. He was already on Skye, using cajolery or threat to persuade his tenants to surrender their sons, when he heard a rumour from his agent in Edinburgh that he was not to receive the command of the regiment, that Major John MacDonell of Lochgarry, now with Fraser's battalion in America, was to be its Lieutenant-colonel commandant. The astonished agent had taken the coach at once to London and in the British Coffee-house on Cockspur

Street, close to Whitehall, he was told that the news was unhappily true, Lochgarry's letter of service had been signed on Christmas Day. To add to Macdonald's dismay, he said that contractors were now asking twelve per cent more for their plaids. "God knows how much your lordship is perplexed and embarrassed." To be used as a recruiter only was galling enough to Macdonald's pride, but the appointment of Lochgarry was insufferable. The families of both men were separated by historical hostility and by rival claims to the leadership of Clan Donald. Macdonald had understood that the command was in his option, and had been so assured by General Simon Fraser of Lovat, and he had taken it to be a recognition of his father's loyalty to the Crown in the late Rebellion. Now he was to be passed over by a man whose turncoat parent had commanded a regiment in the service of the Pretender. When he received this humiliating news his work was almost done, in seven weeks he had raised a thousand men, or had been promised them by the gentlemen of the west, and the cost of all this so far coming from his pocket only. For the moment, if he were not to lose what he had expended in time and money, and what he hoped for in preferment, he must choke on his resentment and continue as the Crown's noble recruiter.

He had been responsible for a small miracle. This was the first time, and would be the last, that MacDonald gentlemen were willing to supply the Government with a marching-regiment of their own name. Clan Donald had once been the mightiest in the Highlands, proud of its claim to be the leader of Gaeldom, and always in opposition to established authority if it meant defending that claim against the rival houses of Argyll, Atholl or Seaforth. The MacDonalds, said one of their bards, were "as deadly as the eagle and as angry as lions, with devil a fault but loyalty". Most of the officers to whom Macdonald granted commissions had been bred in this tradition, and in the memory of blood bitterly spent on a lost cause. As a child, the father of Lieutenant Alexander MacDonald of Glencoe had been carried to safety from the massacre in his glen, and had later commanded a hundred of his clan at Culloden. On the same field the wounded grandfather of

Lieutenant Aeneas MacDonell of Scotus had been bayoneted by Cumberland's advancing infantry. The father of Ensign James MacDonald of Ashkernish had sheltered the Pretender during his wanderings in the Isles, and Allan MacDonald of Rammerscales treasured the sword his grandfather had used at Killiecrankie and his father at Falkirk and Culloden. Similar memories of the same hopeless past were shared by the lairds of Morar, Benbecula and Knoydart, the Mackinnons and Martins of Skye, who took Lord Macdonald's commissions and promised him their sons and tenants in return.

The enthusiasm with which they answered his appeal was not a violation of past loyalties, it sprang from the realistic belief that they might now regain something of what those attachments had lost. The little MacDonald chiefs were among the poorest in the Highlands. They had only their pretensions to superior gentility and an embarrassing profusion of followers to restore the position and fortunes their ancestors had squandered, but if they were eager to see red coats on the backs of their young men, their tenants were not. The people had no fanciful loyalty to the Jacobite cause, except in their melancholy songs. For a generation, during which they had been robbed of their national dress and denied the right to speak their language in the new schools, they had also been subjected to rack-renting and eviction, to the slow erosion of their laird's protection. Macdonald was now told that many were insisting upon "exorbitant terms" before they would part with their sons. Although tenants-at-will, they were learning how far they might go in resistance, striking a bargain before the point when the threat of eviction might be executed. Macdonald himself had been forced to treat with his people in glens where his father's will had once been obeyed without question. Thus Angus Matheson at Raigill in Skye would give up his son only after he had secured a written assurance that he and his children would have "a preference always to the lands which he now possesses". Among the mainland gentlemen whom Macdonald had canvassed was Charles Cameron, younger of Callart, whose father had died a Jacobite exile in Dunkirk. He had promised fifty men, and his brother another twenty-five, in return for a captain's commission, but now he said "Upon our coming into the country we found men was very difficult to be had, and none without a very high bounty".

Macdonald asked for time, but little was allowed him. At the end of February he was told that the 76th Regiment of Highlanders must be ready to embark for America in April. Few of the companies gathering at Inverness were complete, and in Edinburgh Quartermaster-lieutenant David Barclay complained that he had not four hours' sleep at one time, so busy was he haggling with clothing contractors, or writing letters to encourage the laggard gentlemen of Lochaber. There had been time, however, for the young man to take tea with Lady Macdonald who was happily in good health, and the thought of his wife, the warm comfort of her drawing-room, brought Macdonald back from the frost-hard valleys of Skye. He left the recruiting there to his factors and to Lieutenant Angus Martin of Beallach, and he asked leave to complete the companies with Irishmen, Lowlanders and scarred Invalids. In April he went reluctantly to Inverness, a hard journey for there was late snow on Drumochter, and after a week of the town's bleak hospitality he decided that he had suffered enough humiliation. He told Lord Barrington that he would now wash his hands of military employment. "I have blundered enough in your Lordship's eyes from first to last, which is additional proof that I am unfit for any military command, at least in this regiment." The complaint was childish and dishonest, for he also sent a memorial to his friend the Duke of Portland, protesting that after indefatigable labour and considerable expense he had been ill-used by the Government.

Notwithstanding he had signified his acceptance, the Memorialist was totally excluded not only from the command of a regiment chiefly raised upon his own estate and among the friends of his family, but an officer appointed, who however great his merit, had no claim whatever upon the Memorialist to induce him to undergo so toilsome an undertaking to his exclusion, and whose duty to his country in America at the time of his appointment, made it necessary for the Memorialist to raise his quota of men from his own property.

That Lochgarry should receive the lieutenant-colonelcy without giving a man or a guinea to the regiment filled Macdonald with "pungent concern", but he was not so blinded by anger that he forgot his agent's assurance that he need lose nothing, that he could sell his men to the Crown. He told Portland that he hoped the Government would pay him £2,000 in consideration of his labour and expenses.

Lochgarry was a prisoner, taken from his returning ship by a French privateer, and when the 76th was inspected by Skene in May it was commanded by Major Alexander Donaldson, an officer of the 42nd for twenty years and much weakened by the physical strain of them. Skene thought well of the regiment when he watched it at its exercises in the spring sun by Inverness Castle. It was composed, he said, of "good, strong-looking men in general, all fit for service and none under the age of sixteen". The grenadiers were not as tall as they might be, but all were sturdy and broad-shouldered, and the men of the light company also had good shoulders and strong legs. Even the poorer recruits, whom Donaldson had placed in the rear ranks, were "very fine little fellows". Three-quarters of them were Highland, remarkable men thought Skene, the rest Lowland and Irish of whom he said nothing. Lord Macdonald attended the inspection, wearing Highland dress but not the uniform of the Highland regiment he had raised, bitterly enduring the handsome compliments that were paid to Lieutenant-colonel MacDonell's company, men of his own estates, enlisted by himself or Angus Martin. More than £3,000 had been advanced in bounty money, but Skene did not say, nor was it his duty to say how much of this had finally reached the deer-skin sporrans of the private soldiers.

Once embodied the battalion was marched along the coast road to Fort George, a powerful stronghold on a spit of land, the head of a water-snake across the entrance to the Moray Firth. The men of the 76th had been told that they were needed immediately in America but here, within moat, ravelin and walls, they remained for ten months, their spirits rotting in idleness, eyes and thoughts turned toward the mouth of the Great Glen, to the beckoning valley that led to Lochaber and the Isles. Donaldson was a considerate officer, a Highlandman of their own clan, but as the months passed he was more and more troubled by a painful tumour on his back, and his duties passed to the battalion's second-major John Sinclair, Lord Berriedale, heir to the earldom of Caithness. In another place and at another time Berriedale's authority might not have been resented, but the MacDonald men were bewildered by the loss of familiar leadership. They had been enlisted by men of their own name, given to another who washed his hands of them, placed under the authority of a third whom they had yet to see, and were now commanded by an English-speaker for whose family and people they had a traditional contempt. Many of them were still awaiting their bounty money, their pay was in arrears, and like Seaforth's men they resented the abusive behaviour of their officers.

When they could, most of those bored and idle gentlemen secured leave of absence, returning to their glens and families or parading their tartan and scarlet in the drawing-rooms of Edinburgh. This too was resented by the men, who had no right to leave and could receive it for the most urgent reasons only, by a humble and convincing petition to their commanding officer. In January, 1779, James Oughton recalled the absent officers to their companies, fretting at their insolent and unregimental delay in responding. Amherst had told him that he must embark three marching-regiments for America in March, the 76th, the 80th Royal Edinburgh Volunteers, and Francis Maclean's 82nd. He was not happy to have these battalions taken from him. The *Bonhomme Richard* was still a comic or tragi-comic menace, and the risk of public disorder had increased. Outraged by the Government's intention to give Scots Catholics the same liberties that had been promised their co-religionists in England, the people of Scotland were expressing their Christian disgust in wordy petitions, declaring that they would not tolerate any surrender to the "intolerant and intolerable principles of Papism". Oughton knew that it was a matter of brief time only before the shoemakers, cordiners, weavers and wrights moved on from literary protest to the burning and mobbing of Catholic homes and chapels. He told Amherst that if the War Office also embarked the 83rd Glasgow Volunteers there would be no regular force in Scotland able to restrain the mob.

At the beginning of March, Alexander Donaldson rose weakly from his bed, called in his outposts from Banff, and put the 76th on the road south. Moved by unnatural sentiment, by resurgent vanity and a desire to let authority know that it would not have acquired this battalion but for him, Lord Macdonald was waiting for the Highlanders when they came out of the mountains to Perth. In tartan coat and trews, moon-faced beneath a feathered bonnet, he rode before them to Burntisland on the north shore of the Forth. There he left them, taking the ferry to Edinburgh and his wife.

The sight of Arthur's Seat, cobalt-blue across the water, the transports riding the ground-swell of dying gales, encouraged the MacDonalds to believe that they would be lost if they did not now follow the example of Seaforth's men. The people of the little port were as ready as Edinburgh's citizens had been to confirm a growing fear that the battalion was sold to the East India Company, and on the third day after the Highlanders' arrival, when the evening parade was dismissed, they gathered in excited groups before their quarters. No officer who saw them thought it his business to concern himself with their obvious discontent, and no word of it was taken to Donaldson. He was now prostrate, and his surgeons had told Oughton that since the tumour was ripe for operation the Major should not embark until it had been removed by their knives. Before taptoo, delegates from all the companies appeared at their captains' lodgings, standing silently in the light of lanterns while the astonished officers read their petitions. At morning parade, when they received no acknowledgement of their demands, no promise of bounty money and arrears of pay, no assurance that they were not sold to the Indies, they turned about and marched to the high ground of The Binn above the town. They would not obey the threats or appeals of the junior officers who followed them, although some of these angry gentlemen – like Glencoe, Scotus and Morar – were their little chiefs. They were as orderly and as disciplined as Seaforth's men had been, appointing leaders, mounting sentinels, and behaving with polite civility to all who came to their camp. Maclean's Regiment and the Edinburgh Volunteers were also quartered about the town, and Garth said that when some of their young soldiers came to join the mutiny, "perhaps as much for the sake of the frolic as anything else, the Highlanders ordered them back to their quarters, telling them that they had no cause for complaint, and no claims to be adjusted".

The mutineers remained on the hill for three days more, sending armed parties into the town for provisions, and paying what they could for what was given. From dawn until dusk on the second day they watched the small boats that embarked the men of the 80th and 82nd, crimson flowers floating seaward from the quay to the ships. Donaldson sent a message to Lord Macdonald, advising him that his presence and his influence would be welcome this side of the firth. He then ignored the protests of the surgeons and went to the crest of The Binn with David Barclay, standing painfully in the high wind and listening to every complaint, ordering the Lieutenant to make careful note of them. He gave his word of honour that the battalion was not sold to the Indies, and he was believed. When Macdonald came he was shown the list of money owing, and the paymaster's accounts to prove that the men's claims were indeed just. He had no responsibility for the regiment, but his reputation and self-respect were in jeopardy, and both would be destroyed if he allowed his clansmen to be driven to the boats by musketry or bayonet. He addressed the mutineers as *Mac-Dhomnuill nan Eilean*, histrionically appealing for their obedience, and he was told it would be gladly given when they had been paid. The chief of one of the greatest clans in the Highlands, whose bards had once called upon God's only Son to be the shield of their father in misfortune, was told that his children's loyalty must now be bought for a soldier's pay. Since they plainly required it immediately there was one source only from which it could be got. If Alexander Macdonald had ever received the £2,000 he had requested from the Government it passed this day into the hands of the 76th Regiment.

On the following morning, under Berriedale's command, the companies came down from The Binn to the harbour. Eighty women walked behind with the camp equipage. A correspondent to the *Caledonian Mercury*, who must have been otherwise occupied during the past few days, said that "They marched with great cheerfulness and repeated huzzas, and it is but justice to say the behaviour, sobriety, and good conduct of the regiment since they were raised reflects the highest honour on the officers and men." When the regiment finally reached America four hundred men were put into white ticken breeches, mounted upon unfamiliar horses and used as dragoons. They rejoined the battalion at Yorktown, and upon its miserable surrender all the companies were taken prisoner by the Americans.

James Oughton made no report of the mutiny that has survived. After the unhappy affair of Lord Seaforth's Regiment he was probably grateful that the matter had been more agreeably settled with no great injury suffered, except by Lord Macdonald's pride and Lord Macdonald's purse.

"I fear the Highlanders will not readily be prevailed on"

MR. WALTER SCOTT, a lawyer of modest substance, was entertaining officers of the Duke of Buccleuch's Regiment at his new house when the beating of drums called them abruptly from his table. His son Wattie, then a limping boy of seven, remembered the occasion many years later in a letter to Maria Edgeworth, not the excitement of seeing so many scarlet coats in George Square but the bloody event that took them away. The Scotts had been proud to receive these guests whose ducal colonel was the head of their Border family, and the officers may have been grateful for the hospitality, despite Mr. Scott's chill Calvinism and abstemious tastes. Since September, when Oughton brought them into Edinburgh to suppress the Seaforth mutiny, the South Fencibles had become increasingly unpopular with all classes, and were now regarded as the instrument of an authority determined upon the destruction of political liberty and the Protestant faith.

Oughton's fear of riots against the Catholic Emancipation Bill had been realised within a week of his letter to Amherst at the beginning of the year. For some months the Government had been cannonaded with protests from kirk sessions and trade societies, political, literary, scientific and philosophical clubs, the emotional absurdity of which was finally encapsuled in a resolution by the General Assembly of the Church of Scotland. While this hoped that a greater tolerance would be extended to Protestants of all denominations it also declared its "firm persuasion that a repeal of the penal laws against Papists would be highly inexpedient, dangerous, and prejudicial to the best interests of religion and civil society". Fear of the mob rather than a confused understanding of the Beatitudes was responsible for this resolution, and General Joseph was again the prevailing voice of true religion. Encouraged by the protests of respectable society, this deformed Cowgate cobbler and his fellows swarmed into the High Street behind their noisy drummer. For once the city council could not disperse them with a hogshead of ale, and there was nothing but three companies of the Duke of Buccleuch's Fencibles to prevent them from reinforcing Protestant argument with primitive club and torch. "Last night," Oughton wrote to Amherst on February 3, 1779, "a very numerous mob arose, burned down the Popish Meeting House and plundered that of the titular bishop. The Magistrates required the aid of the military, and supported by 250 of the South Fencibles prevented the mob from committing any further outrages at that time."

On the following night, despite a proclamation from the Provost that the Bill had been set aside, there was more disorder during which the Fencibles, supported by fifty black-horsed dragoons, advanced down the Cowgate with bayonets at the charge. The riot drained away into the darkness of the wynds, leaving a silt of insults and stones. The Magistrates ordered Major Sir James Johnstone to drive the rogues out, but he was naturally reluctant to send his men singly into narrow alleys where they would certainly be wounded and possibly killed. As a result of this the Borderers were now distrusted by the city council, detested by the mob, and despised by those citizens who believed that anti-Catholic violence should be restrained only when it failed to distinguish between the property of an honest Protestant and that of a Popish knave. Johnstone's sensible decision in the Cowgate led to acrimonious charge and counter-charge in press and pamphlet, the use of such words as "scoundrel" and "infamous liar". The mobs of Edinburgh and Leith, and many sober persons besides, were eager to see the humiliation of Buccleuch's country boys and their high-nosed officers. An opportunity for this came in April, on the day that Mr. Scott's guests left his house and marched with their companies to Leith. In that town a number of Highlandmen were standing with their backs against a wall, defying their officers and preparing to defend themselves with musket and bayonet.

This unhappy situation was the result of James Oughton's orders and he had expected trouble, although he could not have foreseen how desperate and gladiatorial it would become. In the last week of March a dispatch from London had told him that since the 83rd Glasgow Volunteers were now to be embarked for the Channel Islands he was to bring them up to strength with impressed men. The tired old man may have wondered if any of his reports were ever read by Amherst or by the new Secretary at War, Charles Jenkinson. A recent Impress Act, designed to raise two thousand men in Scotland, had been the farcical failure he had said it would be. Three men only had been surrendered by the parishes, and these had been taken by the 11th Dragoons. A more determined effort had produced another twenty-six reluctant warriors, and although they had been sent to the 83rd they had since deserted. There was, however, an alternative source. Recruiting officers of the 31st Foot, of which he was Colonel, had drafts of men in the suburbs of Edinburgh and he was willing to part with some of them. In Stirling Castle there were also four companies of recruits for Fraser's 71st and a fifth for the Black Watch, now known as the 42nd Royal Highland Regiment, all waiting to join their battalions in America. However strong the pressures brought upon them or their parents, the young men of these two regiments had accepted enlistment upon an understanding that they would serve in kilted battalions only, with men of their own race and tongue, and the belief that they would belong to an exclusive corps had been stimulated by the heady language of recruiting posters, pinned to the doors of parish churches in Argyll, Inverness and Ross.

O YE HIGHLANDERS. . . . You who, uncorrupted by the universal depravity of your southern countrymen, have withstood, immovable as a rock, all the assaults of surrounding luxury and dissipation, while others, effeminated by voluptuous refinements, and irrecoverably lost to honour, loll in the arms of pleasure. . . . You, O ye hardy race! ye HIGHLANDERS! who have yet arms unenervated by luxury, capable to defend your King and Country, to you BRITANNIA addresses herself. . . .!

Oughton told Amherst that there would be no way to find the men needed by the Glasgow Volunteers unless his lordship thought it proper to take them from the 31st and from the Highland regiments. Amherst's reply was prompt and curt, he acknowledged the proposal and said that he would be obliged if Sir James could carry it out as soon as possible, but Oughton wrote again on April 8, plainly giving his commander an opportunity to change his mind. The Volunteers were now being embarked at Leith, he said, and he would immediately send them the required drafts, but "I fear the Highlanders will not readily be prevailed upon to serve in a Lowland regiment, and it will hurt their further recruiting." Amherst accepted the point, though it was not in his nature to put the wishes of private soldiers before the King's public needs, and he moved a pace only to the rear. As few Highlanders as possible should be drafted, and he hoped they would have no material objection to their change of service.

Neither officer understood that a regiment from Glasgow, so recently deployed against the Seaforth mutineers, was the last into which the Highlanders would be willingly drafted, for if they did believe in the general depravity of their southern countrymen they knew it must be rife in that douce cathedral city. There was an historic hostility between the Gael and the Glasgow middle class, worsened in recent years by the slum ghetto into which the city was forcing its immigrant minority of evicted Highlanders. Within the memory of living men the town-gates had been closed against the winter forays of landless thieves from the hills. The sack of the city had been the hope of every clan army that had come south in war, and a refusal to gratify that desire had shaken the loyalty of Montrose's followers

in 1645 and the Young Pretender's a century later. The first
regiment of Glasgow Volunteers, rightly known as The Enthusiasts, had been raised to resist that last Rebellion, and the joyful
ferocity with which the Highlanders had fallen upon them at
Falkirk, and the losses that both had suffered, were bitterly
remembered. The present battalion had been formed in 1778,
upon a subscription of £10,000 freely given by rich trading
societies, by bonnetmakers and dyers, tailors, maltmen, bakers,
wrights and weavers. On the day of its embodiment, councillors
and gentry had walked behind its drums and fifes, casks of porter
had been broached in the street, and all the city's bells had rung
with pride. Despite this, and the willingness of nine hundred
young artisans to serve in its companies, it was still under
strength. To correct that default, but not without misgiving,
General Oughton sent his order of April 16 to Captain James
Innes, commanding the additional companies of Highlanders at
Stirling.

> You are to march with all the Officers, Non-Commissioned
> Officers and Private men of the 42nd and 71st Regiments
> under your Command in Stirling Castle, on Monday morning
> next the 19th instant (with the utmost expedition) to Leith,
> where they are to be quartered and remain till further orders.
>
> *N.B.* Lieutenant Stelfox to march with the Party to Leith.

The order said nothing of what was intended and if Innes read
it to his men, as he was obliged to do, they could assume that they
were to be quartered in Leith until they were embarked for their
regiments in America. Oughton may also have hoped that
Amherst would change his mind, but no such countermand
came. On Monday morning the five companies marched out of
the Castle behind their officers and followed by two wagons of
baggage. They were quartered that night in Linlithgow, twenty
miles away, and there in his tavern lodgings Innes was found by
Captain Ninian Imrie of General Skene's staff. The aide brought
another order from Oughton, and this time it was unequivocal.

You will please draught Fifty men from the four companies of the 71st Regiment and Fourteen men from the 42nd Regiment under your command, to be incorporated in the 83rd Regt. (or Royal Volunteers) and deliver them to the Honble. Major Ramsay of said Regiment who will give separate receipts for them, and their clothing, to be transmitted to the Agents of the different regiments.

When he received the first order at Stirling, Innes may have known or suspected that some of his men were to be drafted, but his behaviour after receipt of the second order suggests that he did not. He was an old soldier of the 71st, and his courage and obedience had never been questioned. He was also a Highlander and had come from Moray to command the additional companies and to sail with them to America. He knew of his countrymen's fierce attachment to their dress and language, and sympathetically admired it. Their innocent belief that they could not be called upon to serve in any regiment that was not Highland had also been confirmed, or seemingly confirmed by authority. Some months before, upon Oughton's orders, he had sent thirty of his men to Kent where they were then told they were to join a battalion of the 25th Regiment. Fourteen of them had stubbornly refused to accept the draft, declaring it a breach of their enlistment, and they had been returned to Stirling. Innes did not know what effect this attempted betrayal had had upon his command, or what might happen now when it was repeated, and some time during that unhappy night of indecision he lost his courage.

In the morning he gave Lieutenant Thomas Stelfox the names of the sixty-four men who were to join the Glasgow Volunteers, and with a crass stupidity that can only be explained by the failure of his self-control he included some of those who had refused to join the 25th. He also told Stelfox that Oughton's orders obliged the Lieutenant to march the drafts to Leith. In proof of this he showed both letters he had received, but in the first a significant alteration had been made, so blatantly that it is astonishing that the junior officer did not question it. Oughton's *nota bene* said that

Stelfox was "to march with the party to Leith", but the word *with* had now been scratched away by a pin, a fingernail or the point of a knife, and replaced by a curling line so that the sentence might appear unbroken. Months later, in a pathetic attempt to save his career and to prove that he had acted in honour and according to his instructions, Innes would send that order to Jenkinson, and would be told that the erasure was so obvious and outrageous that only a reluctance to revive an unpleasant business prevented the Secretary from reporting the Captain's behaviour to the King.

When the drafts left Linlithgow early on Tuesday morning Stelfox had not read their orders to the men, neglecting this obligatory duty because Innes said it would be improper to observe it. Ninian Imrie had told the Lieutenant that Skene expressly wished the drafts to arrive on the links of Leith not later than ten o'clock, but Stelfox did not hurry, even though the staff officer rode with him, repeating that wish at urgent intervals. He was an aging Englishman detached from the 55th to garrison duties at Stirling, still a junior officer after seventeen years in the service, and perhaps he resented the officious superiority of this gay young captain in the blue and scarlet of the Royal Scots. The little that is known of Stelfox says less for his intelligence. He had a low opinion of the men he commanded, and his ignorance of their language isolated him still further. He was also irritated by three men who rode on the baggage wagon at the rear, and he asked Sergeant William Ralston for their names, remembering them and their faces later. Archibald MacIver, an Argyll man of the 42nd, claimed that he was sick, but in the Lieutenant's opinion he was drunk or malingering. The second man, Charles Mac-William or Williamson from western Inverness and also of the 42nd, was certainly drunk and very noisy. The third was Robert Budge, a Caithness soldier of the 71st, and Stelfox did not know whether he was drunk, sick, or lazy, or why indeed he was with his friends on the wagon.

The party entered North Leith by the Queensferry road shortly after eleven o'clock and crossed the arched mediaeval bridge to the south bank of Leith Water. There, to the Lieutenant's relief, the baggage wagon and its happy soldiers three could be left behind. He took the rest of the men down the crowded Tolbooth Wynd and then by Charlotte Street to the dunes where Major Malcolm Ramsay waited with other officers of the 83rd, short of temper and their capes blowing in the wind. Upon a call from Ralston the Highlanders halted, turned into line and ordered their arms, watching with growing unease as Stelfox exchanged civilities and receipts with the Glasgow officers.

Though he had surrendered command and responsibility to his lieutenant, Innes did not remain at Linlithgow with the rest of his command. He followed the drafts at some distance, but keeping them in sight until he reached the gates of Caroline Park, two and a half miles from Leith. There, he said later, he reported to James Oughton, asking for orders, though what he expected them to be he did not say. It would be charitable to believe that he went to protest against the drafting, to declare that the Highlanders should at least have been asked to volunteer for the 83rd, a privilege Oughton had given to his own men of the 31st. Or it may be that one deceit demanded another, that he needed a valid reason for being absent from his duty at this time. Whatever his purpose, nothing came of it, except perhaps Oughton's angry order that he rejoin the drafts at once, for that is what he did. He came to the dunes at noon, when the Highlanders were leaning on their muskets, listening to Corporal Buchanan's translation of Ramsay's address of welcome. They were now soldiers of the Royal Glasgow Volunteers, the Major was saying, and he hoped they would be loyal and dutiful. In the sullen silence that followed, Innes recovered some of his courage. He suddenly spoke to the men in Gaelic, urging them to accept the officers of the 83rd as their own, to go down now to the boats for embarkation.

"Upon which they seemed to be concerned," said Stelfox, "but marched quietly to The Shore."

"For God's sake retire now, these men are desperate!"

THE HARBOUR WAS a crescent formed by the labour of man and the last seaward turn of the Water of Leith. A slender pier of stone and timber was its northern horn, curving into the firth for three hundred yards, a wide enough embrace to hold all the coastal vessels of the port and most of its ocean-going traders. The lower horn thrust westward into the town and created a deep basin fifty yards in width, a garden of masts, the folded flowers of red and yellow canvas. The Shore, toward which the Highlanders now marched, was the eastern side of the basin, a broad quayside between the water and an arcing terrace of flat houses with crow-step gables. For the last hundred yards to the north, between the opening of St. Bernard Street and the pier, the houses backed upon a timber yard and ended at the Signal Tower. This beacon was round and slit-eyed, like a Border peel, built on the site of an ancient earthwork, once a fortress, then a windmill for crushing rape-seed, and now a comfortable shelter wherein Leith merchants watched and waited for the arrival of their ships.

The Highlanders came from the links by St. Bernard Street, with the timber yard on their right, and when they had wheeled left on to The Shore they marched a hundred and fifty paces, halting by the boat-stairs. They faced the dry-docks and the carpenters' yards across the basin, smelling the scent of wood and tar, of wine casks, dried fish and tidal water. The good order they had kept on the march from the links was now broken, and although they held their line it rippled with anger. They shouted in protest, raising their muskets above their heads, and only five soldiers of the 42nd and two of the 71st obeyed Ramsay's order to go down the stairs to the waiting boats. Looking south toward the Coal Hill and the bridge, Stelfox saw MacIver approaching. The Highlander's bayonet was fixed, and when he reached the eddying line of tartan he began to shout. "I did not understand what he was saying," said Stelfox, "but from his gestures I supposed he was persuading the men not to embark." MacWilliam now came out of the Tolbooth Wynd, also shouting, and very drunk thought Stelfox. He was followed by Robert Budge, who locked his bayonet to his firelock as he ran behind his comrades. While they waited with the baggage-wagon the three soldiers had learnt what was intended, from the boat's-crews perhaps, the men of the 31st already embarking, or the sentinels of the 83rd who stood at the head of the stairs. Their anger and dismay had been encouraged by a gathering mob, the leader of which was Tinker Tom, a capering Highland porter from Edinburgh. He and another man, Timber Leg, were assumed later to have been the first to give powder and shot to the Highlanders.

Innes' behaviour at this moment is vaguely recorded, and depends entirely upon his own doubtful evidence. He said that he too heard MacIver and MacWilliam urging their comrades not to go aboard. Loyal to his own regiment, he believed that the embarkation would have gone quietly had it not been for the troublesome fellows of the 42nd. And then, contradicting this belief, he said that it was Budge, a soldier of the 71st, who was the first to unsheath his bayonet. In the growing confusion no one could see more than what was to his immediate front, and that not clearly, but all the Highlanders now had their bayonets fixed or their swords drawn. Innes alone could understand what they were shouting. They would never be put into long clothes and breeches. They would not serve with men who spoke no Gaelic. They would be soldiers of a Highland regiment, that was the promise given when they left their homes.

In the shock of this sudden uproar, nothing was done to suppress it. Ramsay and his officers remained at the edge of the quay, stiff-necked and blue-caped, looking to Innes. Thomas Stelfox was dumb with horror. Ralston and Buchanan also waited upon a word from their captain, although the sergeant's eyes marked those men who seemed most forward in protest, and one or two more who slipped away to an ale-house. The crowd was increasing, sailors from the ships, carpenters, glass-workers and rope-makers, shop-keepers and artisans, while Tinker Tom danced in glee before the Highlanders, calling them bold fellows, brave fellows. The mutineers were bewildered by the noise, by the cries and applause from the windows above their heads, and they moved sullenly northward toward the pier. Some of the seven men who had obediently gone down to the boats now changed their minds, leaping up the stairs to the quay and running after their friends.

By this time Innes was gone, back to Caroline Park. The speed with which he travelled suggests that he found a horse somewhere. Hot and excited, he broke into Oughton's business of the day, saying that his command was in a state of mutiny, and he was still stammering out the story when Imrie arrived, calmer and more informative. Once again Innes was told to rejoin his command, this time to restrain it if he could until assistance came. Pushing his way through the crowd, now greater in his hour's absence, he found the mutineers with their backs to the houses between St. Bernard Street and the Signal Tower, the men of the 42nd on the left, and the 71st on the right. In the darkening light of a clouding sky he saw the dull gleam of broadswords and bayonets, the stain of crimson and the flow of green along the grey walls. He silently thanked Providence that the men had no ammunition, but some of the cartouches that had been empty when he examined them at Linlithgow now contained spills of powder, loose balls and small shot, the gift of the mob. Innes said that they had also been given ale and whisky, and that many of the Highlanders were drunk, but there never was a mutiny which authority did not believe was largely the result of liquor.

He went bravely enough to the flank-men of the 42nd, appealing to them and to others beyond, saying that General Oughton was sending troops against them and that any who resisted would certainly be killed. A blur of angry faces turned toward him. Beyond them, the white anger of a rising sea was breaking against the eastern shoulder of the pier. Voices shouted that they would rather be killed than serve in the Glasgow Regiment, and then one man of the 71st, Hugh Muir, came running down the quay with his musket charged, stopping when the point of his bayonet was an inch from the captain's breast. "I would have gone aboard," he said in bitter passion, "had the gentlemen asked me to volunteer. But if we are to be put aboard like a parcel of sheep I will stand out to the last." Innes turned, and walked stiffly away.

When he had ordered the captain back to Leith, Oughton sent Ninian Imrie to Edinburgh with a hurried dispatch for the Duke of Buccleuch. "You will order two hundred men of the South Fencible Regiment under the command of a Field Officer, with some rounds of armed cartridges, to march immediately to Leith, seize the Mutineers and march them immediately to Edinburgh Castle." So the Border drums beat an assembly, and Mr. Scott's dinner party ended before it had truly begun. The command left the Citadel under Major Sir James Johnstone, and at the Tron Church he broke it into three divisions. The first went by Canongate and the Easter Road, across the links of Leith to the beach, coming through shallow water to the Signal Tower. The second and third divisions marched together by the Wester Road until they reached the edge of the town, and there one was sent up Constitution Street to come upon The Shore by the timber yard. The third, led by Johnstone and followed by an Edinburgh crowd eager to see the bloody humiliation of the Fencibles, marched by Kirk Gate and Tolbooth Wynd to the southern end of the harbour. The first division to reach its objective was that which came along the beach, but when its drummer, captain and first files appeared about the Tower they were faced by two men, MacIver and MacWilliam with bayonets charged and standing some paces beyond the right flank of the 71st. The Fencible captain halted his command, content to block that way of escape.

At its northern end The Shore widened, holding the tine of

the pier like the handle of a sickle, but it was no broad battlefield. When Johnstone led the second and third divisions up from the south, across the front of the Highlanders and turning them into line by the right, there were perhaps no more than twelve yards between the opposing ranks. Neither side could retreat, the mutineers stood against the walls of the houses, and behind the Fencibles was the water of the harbour. The mob pressed forward, breaking the single rank of Borderers that had been stretched across the street, and Tinker Tom danced excitedly before the left flank of the 42nd, calling upon the Highlanders to open fire, to advance with bayonet and broadsword. Innes said later that he went again to the mutineers at this point and begged them to submit, but once more they shouted him down. He turned away for the last time. "They are drunk," he said to a Fencible officer. "If you fire on them it will be horrid butchery." He was already pushing his way through the crowd when he heard the first shot.

James Johnstone of Westerhall was a middle-aged Dumfries baronet whose heavily laden genealogical tree included several kings of Scotland, England and France, but who would have been modestly satisfied if he could one day inherit the marquesate of Annandale. A brave if uninspired officer, he may have thought that the arrival of his men, their steadiness when he deployed them in this hazardous fashion, would be enough to bring the mutineers to submission, but he now knew that more was needed. Calmly facing his front, he ordered the Fencibles to prime and load. The crowd was suddenly still, an impatient audience silenced by the rising of the curtain. The only sounds heard were the rasp of cartouche flaps, a sibilant ripple as the Fencibles spat out their bitten cartridge-paper, the gentle click of closing pans, the rattle of brass-tipped rammers, and the final tap of muskets upon the cobbles. Thirty seconds after this first order, long enough for trained men to obey it, Johnstone called "*Make ready!*", and each Fencible man took a pace to the rear with his right foot, his thumb cocking his musket as he brought the butt to his hip. A moment's pause that soldiers know, a drying throat, a paralysing pain in the small of the back, a lonely, incredulous wonder, and the strong smell of one's own sweat. And then Johnstone walked toward the mutineers with Alexander Ross, a Gaelic-speaking sergeant of his regiment. "Use every gentle method," he said, "but tell them that if they refuse I have orders to force them to embark or carry them prisoners to Edinburgh."

At the order to prime and load MacWilliam and MacIver had come quickly from the right of the line, and now, before Ross could speak, MacWilliam brought his musket to the aim, the tip of its bayonet almost touching the lace at Johnstone's throat. He shouted one contemptuous word that sounded like *"Dunemore!"* which the Major was later told meant big man or great gentleman. MacIver pressed the weapon down, shaking his head in disapproval, but MacWilliam turned upon Ross, pushing the bayonet against the Sergeant's coat. Ross stood his ground, calling to the Highlanders beyond "You've seen us prime and load!" He was answered defiantly. "We have ammunition too!" said some, and others "We'll die before we wear breeches!" Tinker Tom screamed from the front of the crowd, asking why MacIver did not fire, but the Highlander shook his head. "I'll not be the first."

Other Fencible officers had also advanced upon the mutineers with appeal or threat, and all along the swaying line there were little knots of dispute. Close to the Signal Tower, Ebenezer Buchanan persuaded two men to unlock their bayonets, but Budge swore at them for cowards and they replaced the weapons. Johnstone now pushed MacWilliam aside and went among the Highlanders, advising them to submit before blood was spilt. He did not understand when they told him that if it came to a fight they would kill man for man, but Ross understood and was afraid. He pulled his Major's sleeve. "For God's sake retire now," he said, "these men are desperate!" After a moment's hesitation, Johnstone turned about and walked back to his own men. Before he followed the officer, Ross looked to his right and left. He saw two Fencible sergeants take hold of MacIver, and then three mutineers grapple with them. Almost immediately there was a shot, but he could not tell from which flank it came.

There was a second shot, and then a dropping volley like the tearing of stiff paper. He saw a musket raised beside the sergeants, the flash and breath of smoke from the pan as the hammer struck and then a feather of white from the barrel. At the same moment he felt the impact of a bullet in his side, no pain but a heavy blow as from a man's fist. He remembered no more of that day.

The first shot had killed Captain James Mansfield, the son of a banker and a gentle, popular man. He had gone forward with Private John Home, walking to the charged bayonets without fear, advising the mutineers not to resist for the men of his company were good soldiers and well-trained. An English-speaking Highlander shouted back with defiant pride. "We can prime and load as fast as any Fencible!" Others pressed so closely forward with their bayonets that Mansfield foolishly drew his sword, not to use it upon them but to hold down their weapons. He was forced back two or three paces until he turned about and walked away with Home. They had reached their company when the shot was fired. Mansfield coughed, fell on his knees and then on his face. With a cry of angry grief, Home shot the Highlander who had fired.

Without an order being given, the firing now became general. Useless at more than a hundred paces, and impossible to fire with expert aim, the infantryman's musket was murderous at this short distance of feet. An ounce or more of lead, discharged by eight grams of black powder, could pass through a man's body, tearing a bloody hole of bone and flesh at its exit. With the volley there was a great cloud of smoke, a compassionate pall masking the horror of what was happening. Once they had fired, the Fencibles and Highlanders did not re-load but advanced upon each other with bayonet and butt, their feet sliding on the blood-greased stones.

Although they had been given what they demanded, few in the crowd stayed to watch it, and at the first shot they moved like starlings rising from a tree, pressing down The Shore or fighting for the safety of the wynds. James Dempster, a jeweller from Edinburgh, had already gone into a friend's house and was watching from a window immediately above the men of the 42nd. He thought the first shot came from the right, whether from the mutineers or the Fencibles he did not know, and that Captain Mansfield was killed by a second. Then the black bonnets below him were hidden by smoke, and he closed the window quickly, hurrying to a back room. Thomas Anderson, a surgeon of Leith, had come from his house when the Fencibles marched by, and he followed them to The Shore. He was standing to their right and rear when the firing began and could not escape until "the Fencibles rushed in upon the Highlanders with their bayonets fixed". A shipmaster of Leith, Robert Mudie, had been sitting on the pier near the Tower, enjoying the spectacle for some time before he decided that there was perhaps a safer place to be. He ran along the rear of the Fencibles looking through their ranks as he passed. He saw Mansfield pressing down the bayonets with his sword and then, almost immediately it seemed, voices were shouting that the captain was killed, and the air was full of smoke.

The little battle was quickly over. An easterly wind lifted the white cloud, pulling it in strands through the ships' rigging and across the roofs of North Leith. Buccleuch's officers beat at the struggling men with their fists and the flat of their swords, shouting *"Recover . . ! Recover your arms!"* until both sides drew back and stared at each other in breathless shock. Of the sixty Highlanders who had taken a defiant stand against the wall less than half were still on their feet. Nine were dead or dying, and four of these were men who had once refused to be drafted into the 25th. Twenty-two were wounded, their bodies prone or bent, motionless or crawling in pain. One of them was Robert Budge and another was Hugh Muir. Five Fencibles were also dead – Mansfield, a sergeant, a corporal and two grenadiers – and a half dozen or more were wounded. After the savage noise of musketry, the shouts and cries, the silence was soundless, and the movement of the sea and the moans of the wounded were at first unheard. Upon a sudden impulse the Highlanders threw down their firelocks and their swords, opening their arms in surrender.

It was almost six o'clock before the dead and the wounded were taken to Edinburgh in seven carts, the rest marching behind. When they reached the North Bridge the long-promised rain fell in one sharp and bitter squall, washing the blood from the floor of the carts and staining the spokes of the turning wheels. Many people wept as the procession moved slowly into the Royal Mile. The carts were taken south by St. Mary's Wynd to the Royal Infirmary beyond the Cowgate, and the uninjured men marched on to the Castle, to the vaulted casemate below its Great Hall, there to share the darkness with French prisoners of war. Students and teachers of the College of Surgeons came to the chirurgical ward of the Infirmary to deal with the unfamiliar butchery of musket-ball and fluted bayonet, and as the carts were gently unloaded it was discovered that two Highlanders were now beyond such help, their deaths unnoticed on the slow journey from Leith. One more died in the night, and the surgeons had little hope for another whose leg they had removed.

Controlling his shock and pain, Oughton could do no more that night than write a brief letter to Amherst, enclosing copies of the orders he had given Innes and of a report he had received from Buccleuch. The bloody day had been a greater blow to his health than he realised at this moment. The oblique reprimand he had received for his handling of the Seaforth mutiny had obliged him to use immediate force, to set aside any thought of suppressing the mutiny by reasonable argument. He could make no comment on the affair, beyond saying that he greatly regretted the death of Mansfield, "a very good officer and a very worthy man". Two days later he was able to write more fully. Tinker Tom was lodged in gaol, and Oughton said that if the fellow could be hanged it would do infinite good, for the rebellious disposition of the mob strongly needed such correction. His sympathy for the Highlanders was under great strain, and he wrote as if he had been personally betrayed by them. He told Amherst that their attachment to their native dress and customs was undeniable, but there had been "too many instances of late of their proneness to mutiny".

Their invincible obstinacy on this occasion surpassed all belief. That fifty recruits without any ammunition but a few balls, slugs and small shot which they had picked up from the inhabitants, should dare to attack a regular detachment of two hundred men, and choose to throw away their lives rather than go into a Lowland regiment, or submit to be made prisoners, is I imagine without example.

That night he heard that a putrid fever had attacked the South Fencibles in the Castle. It had been contracted from the miserable French prisoners they were guarding.

"If they had offered a decent and humble representation"

WRAPPED IN THEIR bloody plaids the dead men lay in the shadows of Lady Yester's Church, a hundred yards from the italianate façade of the Infirmary. Young Walter Scott and his friends from the High School next door were attracted to this macabre mortuary, swarming like insects in their bright jackets of blue, scarlet or green. "The Sexton admitted us to see the quarry for a penny apiece, and never was a penny in my case so well laid out for I saw nothing for ten days after but the highlanders lying stiff and stark, and so had my penny worth for a whole week." These lifeless bundles of tartan awaiting an unmarked grave were the only clansmen he would see who had been killed in battle, although his imagination and his pen would be inspired by the warrior history of their race. Even in mature recollection he had no real understanding of the men who had given him that week of nightmares. When there was a conflict of loyalties, Border and Highland, his partisanship was never in doubt and he still thought of the dead as a huntsman's quarry. He told Miss Edgeworth that without their officers the men from the mountains were inferior to Lowlanders and had thus been shot and stabbed like deer in a *tinchel*, in a closing circle of pursuers. He remembered nothing of why they had chosen to die on The Shore, only that they had been "obstinate in refusing to embark".

Twenty-four hours after the affray James Oughton reviewed the South Fencibles on the links of Leith, in acknowledgement of their steadfast behaviour and to restore their self-respect. He told them that he was pleased by their discipline and their drill, and he saw no irony in the fact that they should now be discharging the blank volleys of a mock battle within a mile of where they had so recently loaded and fired with killing ball. But the spectacle restored some of the regiment's reputation with the public, as Oughton no doubt intended it should. The Duke of Buccleuch commanded the review, a splendid figure on a magnificent horse, indifferent to an impudent fall of rain, and the *Mercury* printed an adulatory verse in his honour.

> Persist, GREAT CHIEF! with your compeers
> And prove the saviour of the land.
> Your spirit has dispelled our fears,
> Your virtues may disarm the avenging hand.

At his lodgings in Edinburgh Innes was writing bitterly to the Secretary at War, anxious to be early in the defence of his honour and protesting that "there was never, never such a massacre in Britain before". He had been to the Infirmary that day and the experience had perhaps affected his judgement and his memory. He blamed the Fencibles for firing upon drunken men and also for the death of Mansfield, saying that the captain had been shot through the head by one of his own company. As his pen rushed on before the force of his fear, he said that when ordered to take the drafts to Leith he had gone to Oughton in protest, warning the commander that the Highlanders would not embark without an assurance that they were to join the 71st or the 42nd, and if he did indeed say this, on one of his anxious visits to Caroline Park, Oughton's reports make no reference to it. The long, high chirurgical ward of the Infirmary at this moment was enough to unhinge any man's reason. The surgeons had worked with desperate haste throughout Tuesday night and Wednesday, on bloody tables with probe, gouge, knife and needle, extracting obstinate shot, tying severed vessels, sewing ragged fissures of flesh and plugging seeping holes. Although the building was the pride of the city its merits would seem to have been more architectural than medical. There were not enough bandages to stop the prodigal flow of blood, and the *Mercury* said that "Any old linen sent by the humane and charitable will be gratefully

received by the mistress of the hospital." Before he left the
stinking ward Innes was told that the surgeons did not yet know
whether four of the mutilated men would live or die, and none
might be fit for service again.

On Saturday morning, an hour or so after the City Guard had
at last dragged Timber Leg from his hiding-hole and taken him
to the Tolbooth, the body of Captain Mansfield was brought
from Leith to be buried in the overcrowded graveyard of
Greyfriars. Public emotion, already heated by the carts of Highland wounded, the blood on the cobbles, was further excited by
the muffled drums of this solemn funeral, the slow march of its
stiff-legged escort. Mansfield had left a widow and five children,
two of whom now waited with their mother by the ugly hump
of Greyfriars Church. Mob and society wept openly for them,
although they would be better protected by the banker's shield
than would the unprovided kin of the Highland and Fencible
dead. Once across the North Bridge the cortège was halted and
the coffin was removed from its carriage. Now it was carried on
the shoulders of six Fencible men like the corpse of a classical
hero, the Duke himself supporting its head from the Tron
Church to the West Bow and down the hill to the Grassmarket
and the church. This theatrical departure from custom may have
been a spontaneous expression of grief or a contrived display to
influence public feeling, and if it were the latter it misfired.
Mansfield was certainly seen to be a tragic victim, but not of
insensate Highland fury alone, and a correspondent to the
Mercury voiced a popular belief that "The fruits of Arthur's Seat
have ripened on The Shore of Leith". Another proposed that a
public fund should erect a monument above the noble Captain's
grave, its inscription declaring that "he fell in the spirited exercise
of his duty by the desperate violence of misguided ferocity,
probably in consequence of a recent remission of Magisterial and
Military Power". James Oughton knew that he was held responsible for this remission, but if he felt the hurt he did not show it
publicly.

Most of the mutineers were illiterate and could compose no

letters to the press, but a sympathetic citizen wrote a memorial in their name to the Secretary at War. He may have been one of the lawyers who prepared the defence of the accused at the coming court-martial, and his simply phrased petition was signed by the men in the Infirmary, three only with their names and the rest with a trembling cross. Beside their signatures was a list of their dead. They asked for understanding, for it to be known that when they marched to Leith they believed that they would embark for their own battalions, that no one had told them that they were in fact to be drafted into a Lowland regiment, "notwithstanding it is constantly the practice of the Army to read such orders when a draft is proposed".

> This indignant treatment, joined to the insuperable inherent dislike and round aversion which we entertain for the dress of the 83rd Regt. and the attachment to our own Highland garb, fired our minds with violent indignation, which caused an absolute refusal in us to go on board to be incorporated with the Glasgow regiment, though we declared again and again in the presence of some hundreds of people at Leith, that we were willing to be incorporated with any Highland regimt. let its destination be wheresoever it might happen, would any officer of sufficient authority assure us that we should not be forced to serve in any regimt. but a Highland one; but none could be found.

No reply was sent to the petition, nor was it read at the court-martial. This began its hearing in the Castle on Thursday, May 6, at the officers' quarters on the west side of Palace Yard. Three men only were brought to trial, charged with mutiny and incitement to mutiny under the Articles of War. Inevitably, perhaps, they were Archibald MacIver, Charles MacWilliam and Robert Budge, the last heavily bandaged and weak from his unhealed wounds. They were as much the victims of their happy malingering on the baggage-wagon as they were of mutiny, first marked down as trouble-makers by Stelfox, then held entirely to blame in his evidence, and further condemned by that of Innes, Ralston and Buchanan. The court sat for three days under the presidency of Lieutenant-colonel Ralph Dundas of the 11th Dragoons, and most of its members were junior officers, five of them Highland gentlemen from the Argyll and the Gordon Fencibles. The prisoners were not without friends although none of these was a soldier. Three young lawyers, one of them a Gaelic-speaker, freely offered their services in the preparation of a defence. Although it was not customary for the accused to be represented by counsel at a court-martial, an unexplained exception was made, perhaps upon the earnest appeal of the advocate himself, Andrew Crosbie. He was a spirited, good-humoured man with a taste for military play-acting in the blue and buff uniform of the Edinburgh Volunteer Defence Band, and Walter Scott would later use him as the model for Councillor Pleydell in *Guy Mannering*. He had been present at the dinner party in James's Court when Johnson met Oughton, delighting both patriotic Englishmen with his possibly ironic suggestion that their countrymen were better animals than Scots, being closer to the sun and thus with blood more rich and mellow. The interpreter in the court was a MacGregor from Perthshire, once an upholsterer's clerk and now the minister of the Gaelic Chapel-of-Ease in Castle Wynd. His family had taken the name of Robertson to avoid the proscription upon Clan Gregor, and although this moribund penal law was still on the statute book he declared his racial sympathy with the accused by giving his name as Joseph Robertson MacGregor, and was so accepted by the court.

Crosbie defended the men with charity and sympathy, not denying the body of the charges against them, but calling upon the particular and peculiar circumstances in an appeal for mercy. He said that MacIver and MacWilliam had spoken nothing but Gaelic from their birth, coming from those parts of the north where it was the only language.

They have always been accustomed to the Highland habit, so far as never to have worn breeches, a thing so inconvenient and even so impossible for a native Highlander to do, that when the Highland dress was prohibited by the Act of Parliament, tho' the philabeg was one of the forbidden parts of the dress, yet it was found necessary to connive at the use of it, provided only it was made of a stuff of one colour and not of tartan. These circumstances made it necessary for them to enlist and serve in a Highland Regiment only as they neither could have understood the language, nor have used their arms, or marched in the dress of any other regiment.

He used the same plea on behalf of Budge, adding that although the Caithness man had acquired some knowledge in his droving "to enable him to buy or sell to one who spoke English in the common articles of commerce", he could not speak the language himself. He had also dressed in the little kilt since childhood and had not wished to soldier in a regiment that did not wear it. Crosbie referred the court to section six of the Articles of War, sub-section three, which declared that no soldier could be enlisted in another regiment without a proper discharge from that in which he was presently serving, and he claimed that no such discharge had been given to any Highlander on the links of Leith. MacIver had committed no act of violence, MacWilliam had been drunk, and Budge had surrendered without protest, although the advocate did not say that a grievously wounded man could scarce do more than submit. Denying allegations made by the prosecution, Crosbie further said that none of the three men had any ammunition on The Shore, and no premeditated intent to mutiny since the cause of it had been "intimated to them of a sudden so as to leave no room for deliberation".

Able and impassioned though the defence was, it was unsuccessful. When the trial ended on Saturday, while the belltongues of St. Giles were calling noon, the three men were found guilty and were sentenced to death by shooting.

They were returned to the dark casemate among the fever-sick French prisoners, and there they waited for three weeks. Mr. MacGregor came to see them every day, climbing the grassy footpath from his chapel to Castle Hill, bringing the comfort of his compassion and the encouragement of his prayers. He was with them early on Friday, May 28, when they were brought up to the chamber of the Great Hall and out into the sunlight of Palace Yard, their heads bare and their hands tied behind them. Preceded by muffled drums and escorted by a platoon of the Argyll Fencibles, now the garrison regiment and soon to be in revolt itself, they were slow-marched from the citadel under the narrow arch of Foog's Gate, northward past the foot of the Lang Stairs to the Portcullis and Inner Barrier until they crossed the drawbridge to the mound of Castle Hill. Here five companies of the Argyll Fencibles were drawn up in hollow square facing the fortress, and three ranks of red dragoons held back the press of the crowd from the Royal Mile. The sun was strong, but a brisk wind moved across the high ground, pulling at the belted plaids of the Argylls and of the other Highland prisoners who had been brought out to watch the death of their friends. By the wall of the dry ditch and below the Half Moon Battery were three open coffins to which the condemned men were led. Each man knelt beside the plain box allotted to him, MacGregor with them, but as the minister began to pray he was stopped by Major Hugh Montgomerie of the Argylls. Before the condemned men could submit their souls to God they must listen to the General Orders issued two days before by Robert Skene.

Although these orders were brief the reading took some minutes, for the Major frequently paused, awaiting MacGregor's whispered translation. The court having found the accused guilty of mutiny and a breach of the second, third, fourth and fifth Articles of War, and having duly considered the evil tendency to mutiny and sedition, especially when carried to such enormous lengths in the present case, did adjudge Charles Williamson, Archibald MacIver and Robert Budge to be shot to death. Which sentence had been transmitted to the King, and His Majesty had been pleased to signify his pleasure. Having regard to the former commendable behaviour of the 42nd Regiment, and that Robert Budge, only now recovering from the wounds he had received in the affray, did not appear to have any forward part in the mutiny, His Majesty was most graciously pleased to grant the condemned a free pardon "in full consideration that they will endeavour upon every future occasion, by a prompt obedience and orderly demeanour, to atone for this unpremeditated but atrocious offence".

Quickly stripped of their muffling crêpe, the Argyll drums now beat a spirited march, the companies turning and wheeling toward the Royal Mile in a river of green tartan. The bewildered prisoners rose from their knees. Their hands were untied and they stumbled from the coffins to the waiting, weeping embrace of their comrades.

Their lives had been saved by Oughton's intercession and by the Government's realisation that after so wanton a waste of blood a judicial demand for more might harm recruitment in the Highlands. A report of the court-martial, with Oughton's plea for reasonable clemency, reached the Judge-Advocate-General, Sir Charles Gould, on May 15, sent to him by Lord Weymouth the principal Secretary of State. Recently knighted and enjoying the King's friendship and favour, Gould was as able a jurist as he was an amateur agriculturalist, and was as disinclined to bend the law as he was to misuse an acre of fertile soil. He was convinced that the charges were proved and the sentence just, and he thought little of a defence that depended upon the Highlanders' attachment to their dress and language. This argument might have merited consideration "if instead of opposing the measure by tumult they had offered a decent and humble representation of what appeared to them a grievance". He did not say how such a humble representation could have been made to, or a favourable answer received from a Lowland officer determined to use force against them if they did not obey his orders. Gould told the King that the peculiar circumstances of the affair, the fact that the mutiny was not premeditated, that the accused had been no more active than others, *might* justify mercy if the maintenance of good order was not thereby impaired. He invited George III to answer that question himself. "Whether strict discipline so salutary and even essential to Your Majesty's service can be enforced and upheld without some instance of exemplary punishment, is in all humility submitted to Your Majesty's wishes."

His Majesty's wishes, prompted by the advice of his ministers, decided upon a reprieve, but the need for exemplary punishment, even in the form of a grim charade, kept the knowledge of that mercy from the condemned men until they knelt beside their coffins in what they believed to be the last moments of their lives.

The War Office was deeply disturbed by the miserable affair, not in moral concern but uneasy that the nation might now lose its mountain reservoir of warriors. Jenkinson ordered his staff to find the answers to a number of relevant questions, with particular reference to the privileges, if any, of Highland regiments. It was some weeks before he received a reply. The report stated that men of the 42nd and the 71st had never before been drafted into a Lowland regiment against their will, that those taken into the 25th Foot had been volunteers, the objectors being returned to Stirling upon Amherst's instructions. "There is nothing *expressly* particular in the manner of recruiting Highland corps, but the circumstances of *clanship*, *dress*, and *language* (circumstances under which no other regiment can fall) have always entitled Highland corps to an exemption from drafting." It was clear that the mutineers would have embarked at Leith had they been given an assurance that they were to serve in their own regiments, "but as this calling for security so precisely followed the example of Lord Seaforth's Regiment it is not to be wondered at that Sir Adolphus Oughton, who had been so much blamed for giving way *then*, did not yield to the present request". In this indecisive way the report acknowledged the privileges previously granted to Highland recruits but did not demonstrate that they were supported in law, and it made no proposals for abolishing them or confirming them. The Government also failed to determine this, realising perhaps that further recruitment in the Highlands depended upon the soldiers' simple belief that they could not be called upon to serve in any corps but a kilted regiment of their own race. The cynical evasion of responsibility, which permitted recruiters to repeat this dishonest promise to the men they enlisted, would continue to have disastrous results.

Although the report exonerated Oughton, in the eyes of authority if not the public, he was past the moment when it might have given him comfort. He had defended his actions as best he could as soon as he recovered from the shock of the mutiny and the court-martial was over, telling Amherst that the bloody affair would check any future disobedience and obstinacy of Highland soldiers. He spoke of them as if they were ingrate children, and although he had once believed in the value of clan regiments he now thought that they would make better soldiers when dispersed among other corps. He knew that their attachment to their native dress was a strong encouragement to enlist, but in foolish spite he now said that "the love of gain is still more powerful". His bitterness can be understood. These wild and intransigent men, prepared to die rather than abandon kilt and tartan, were not the Fingalian warriors who peopled his imagination and inspired such delightful conversations in the drawing-rooms of Edinburgh and London. He agreed with Amherst that never again should Highland soldiers be promised that they would not be drafted, and with more insight than he perhaps knew he blamed the chiefs who gave this assurance to their clansmen and "who had profitted so much by the late levies". But however cogent the reasons might be for such a privilege, he was sure that his lordship would never consent to it being extorted by mutiny and murder. His admiration for the Highlanders, first aroused when he saw them coming through the smoke upon his battalion at Culloden, could not prevail over his loyalty to the Army that had defeated them and which must, by definition, be therefore superior to their obsolescent way of life. Within a week of the obscene farce on Castle Hill he suffered a stroke. Semi-paralysed, broken in heart and body, he returned to his duty as soon as he could, but with no strength to resist the further blow that was to come in the autumn.

When the prisoners were returned to the casemate below the Great Hall of the Castle they were kept in its fever-stinking gloom throughout the early summer and until they could be dispersed among other regiments and forgotten. In November there were still eight wounded men in the Infirmary, and although Innes had gone back to his duties at Stirling he did what he could for them. He was still trying to restore his reputation, writing desperate letters to Charles Jenkinson, making claims and affirmations that should more properly have been heard at the court-martial. He foolishly sent the order he had mutilated, declaring that it cleared him of all responsibility. He blamed Stelfox for not informing the men that they were to be drafted into the 83rd before they reached the links. Had he known that force was to be sent against the Highlanders he would have ordered them to lay down their weapons, to go with him to Caroline Park and there fall upon their knees before Oughton. "Which I verily believe from His Excellency's humanity would have had a good effect to prevent their embarking, and I dare say Government would not have reprimanded me." Jenkinson's final response was to tell the unhappy man that the matter was now closed, implying that if the tiresome correspondence were continued the King would hear of his extraordinary behaviour.

His own career ruined, James Innes was able to win one concession for some of the men whose lives had been destroyed with it. He told the Secretary that the maimed Highlanders should not be discharged from the Infirmary until they were accepted as out-pensioners of Chelsea Hospital, and could thus return home with some money in their purses. Jenkinson secured this small favour from George III over whom, like Gould, he was supposed to have great influence. King and minister were perhaps less moved by compassion than by a realistic understanding of the captain's warning that if the men were sent penniless to their mountains "they would be looked upon as beggars and be of great disservice in recruiting His Majesty's forces in those parts".

"Thousands of dollars, with purses to contain them"

"AND NOW, MY LORD, I must entreat you," James Oughton
wrote to Amherst, "send me down an English regiment, for
though the Highlanders are brave, I have too much experience
of them to put any confidence in them, their mutinous and
obstinate disposition making them very unsafe." It was late on
an autumn afternoon, the end of a perilous day that had taken
him from Caroline Park to Leith and now to the Governor's
House in the Castle. Three hours before, this fortress had been
in the desperate hands of such mutinous men, and only the
resolute courage of Colonel Mordaunt's dragoons had compelled
them to surrender. Earlier still, harsh and brutal action had been
necessary to break the obstinate disposition of other Highlanders
on the links of Leith. Oughton was angry and bitter and ill. That
this humane and sympathetic man could condone a dishonourable
deception to restore order, could authorise summary punishment
of doubtful legality, was an indication of how close he was to
physical and mental collapse.

Buccleuch's Borderers had been ordered north in May, four
days before the *coup de théâtre* on Castle Hill, happy to be gone
from a city that bore them so much ill-will. They were replaced
by five companies of the Argyll Fencibles, Highlanders from the
great shores of the sea-lochs between Linnhe and Kintyre who
had waited a week or more in the suburbs until the fever-rotten
barracks were properly disinfected. This was the second fencible
regiment raised by Campbell gentry, the first having been
mustered in 1759 for the internal defence of the northern kingdom
during the Seven Years' War. It had been difficult even then to

find the men required. The exhortations of their chief *Mac-Cailein-Mór*, General John the fourth Duke of Argyll, had inspired no great enthusiasm, and unwilling to admit the loss of their old influence the little lairds had explained that their people preferred service in the Navy. The present battalion, approved if not personally called to arms by the fifth Duke, was raised by his brother Lord Frederick Campbell, whose qualifications for the colonelcy of a regiment were all that might be expected in a man whose active hours were spent at Court or in the Commons. He was in his fiftieth year, a Privy Councillor, onetime Keeper of the Seal of Scotland, and the only man to have been confirmed for life in the ancient office of Lord Clerk Register. As the member for Glasgow, an astute political animal and an ebullient dinner companion, he had intimate and conspiratorial connections with Government and Opposition. Stewart of Garth was usually able to discover martial talents in the most peaceful of Highland gentlemen, but he could give no explanation for this middle-aged leap into scarlet and gold. Campbell may have been envious of his father General John, or his ducal brother the gallant Colonel John of the '45, but more probably he shrewdly realised that the offer of a thousand fighting men at this time must further a career still short of his hopes.

Commissions to raise the companies were given to twenty-two gentlemen of Argyll whose people once more showed a lack of zeal for the boar's-head banner of Clan Diarmid. Part of their reluctance was due to a dispirited despair throughout all the Highlands, and part to the fact that Lord Frederick's stirring appeal was made in glens now well-trodden by lying recruiters. Many of the young men of Lorne, Cowal and Kilbride were already enlisted in a marching-regiment, the 74th raised by John Campbell of Barbreck, and even he had found it necessary to complete his numbers with three hundred Lowlanders. Those who escaped the cast of his net, or were willing to go for a soldier provided they need not serve beyond Scotland, were being gathered up by the Earl of Eglinton. As Archibald Montgomerie this veteran officer had taken a regiment of Highlanders to the Canadian wars twenty years before, from whence few had returned, being either dead or determined upon staying in a land where there were no oppressive tacksmen. He had now been given a letter of service to raise a fencible corps in the western Highlands, and the men and boys he was reluctantly leaving in their fathers' cottages were all that Lord Frederick's officers could hope to enlist. Clan Campbell had once boasted of its ten thousand warrior men, and the people's present hostility was a shock to the lairds of Argyll. In their efforts to fulfil their quotas they were as harsh as the MacDonald and Mackenzie gentry of the north, but tenants who stubbornly resisted persuasion or threat, and who could not be removed for one reason or another, put a crippling price upon the manhood of their sons. The minister of Strachur, writing for the *Statistical Account*, later said that when the gentry of his parish had recruited for the Earl of Loudon's Regiment in 1745 there had been no difficulty in finding volunteers, but "How different the sentiments of the people in 1778! Though they had an express promise from the government that they should not be called out of the kingdom, not even into England, except in the case of invasion, the heritors were obliged to bribe them high."

Lord Frederick had little personal influence to alter this situation, and like Lord Macdonald was but infrequently seen by the people of his name. His political power was strong, however, and it was probably he who persuaded the Government to withdraw Lord Eglinton's letter of service and to give him the men whom the earl had already enlisted. They came to him under the command of Major Hugh Montgomerie of Coilsfield, Eglinton's kinsman and heir, an able soldier who took the recruiting out of Lord Frederick's fumbling control and with the assistance of the second-major, John Campbell of Melfort, soon mustered seven hundred men. His reputation thus saved, and his regiment in professional hands, Lord Frederick returned to the business of his constituency and the challenging call of Westminster. His Lieutenant-colonel, the lawyer laird of Ardkinglas, demonstrated his family's traditional loyalty to the house of

Argyll by following his lordship's example, and was rarely if ever seen in quarters or upon the field of exercise.

At the beginning of 1779 Montgomerie brought the regiment to Glasgow, where it was understandably believed that the presence of Highland soldiers was the best corrective to civil disorder. This opinion was justified when the Argyll men were called out with bayonet and clubbed musket to disperse a mob intent on burning the warehouse, shop, dwelling and person of a Mr. Bagnal, who being English and a Papist was held to be a proper object for such an *auto-da-fe*. Oughton was pleased by the resolution shown by the Fencibles upon this occasion, although he was uneasy when circumstances compelled him to bring five companies of the battalion into Edinburgh, to use them in that mock execution on Castle Hill. Had he known of the increasing discontent in the regiment he would have considered its cause both trivial and impertinent, but he might well have thought it wise to disperse the companies beyond the city.

There was of course the usual bitterness caused by arrears of pay and unpaid bounties, and it had been sharpened by a new offence to Highland self-respect. The Argyll men strongly objected to part of their equipment. When first mustered they had been given cartridge-pouches discarded by the Glasgow Volunteers. This lack of tact had been insulting to their self-conceit, but when the box was replaced the new issue was more troubling. Like all others it was made of wood or tin, covered with lacquered leather and deep enough to contain thirty paper rounds of powder and ball. It was larger than the first pouch, however, and the wide belt upon which it hung made it uncomfortable and impracticable beneath a flowing plaid. Some of the more simple Highlanders, when told by the recruiters that they would wear their national dress in Lord Frederick's brave regiment, had believed that they would carry the powder-horn and shot-bag of their ancestors, and they now felt they had been deceived. They also detested their goat-skin sporrans, an absurd military adaptation of the plain deerskin purse that had once been an essential part of Highland dress. Their objection to pouch and sporran was further soured by the fact that the cost of both was deducted from their pay. They wore them under protest, innocently believing that their clothing could not be altered in a manner insulting to their race. This resentment was not peculiar to the five companies in Edinburgh, it was also felt by the two that had been sent on detachment to Dundee. In both cities some junior officers listened sympathetically to the complaints but nothing was done to remedy them, and the Highlanders' pride was more hurt by this indifference than by the equipment itself.

There was no outward sign of unrest when the regiment came to Edinburgh, parading in grand review before Oughton on the links of Leith. He thanked it and complimented it and was made happy by its seeming obedience and enthusiasm. He may have believed that he would endure no more from the rebellious nature of the Highlanders and in this gentle mood he released the prisoners of the 42nd and the 71st from the casemate of the Castle. "It is my duty," he had said, when defending himself against charges of too much compassion for French prisoners, "to take care that they are treated with justice and humanity." He felt the same concern for the mutineers, and was so touched by their emotional gratitude that he asked Amherst to send them back to service without any stigma, supporting the appeal with more practical advice. If the prisoners suffered further disgrace it might "alarm others and tend to lessen the high idea entertained of His Majesty's great lenity and goodness".

The Argylls' discontent smouldered throughout the summer, and the boredom of garrison life on the high rock lowered their morale still more. Their morning and afternoon parades on the Hill were a popular spectacle, and Duncan Ban Macintyre was salaciously amused by the quivering feminine reaction to their broad shoulders and white thighs. There were many smart ladies, he said, he would ask no more than to share the Argyll men's quarters, to give them sweet sugar kisses and "thousands of dollars with purses to contain them". The Glen Etive bard was now long past his youth and far from his homeland, carrying a Lochaber axe, wearing the cocked hat and shabby red coat of the City

Guard. He thought the Fencible regiment was the finest he had seen. "Lord how jubilant I am, my mind has been uplifted since my countrymen arrived!" *Tha iad leathan mu na broillichean* . . .

> Of great breadth across the chest,
> they are well-developed, stout men,
> with their trim and straight calves,
> bulging below the knees;
> variegated short hose
> is elegantly worn by them;
> red garters of the best quality
> the shops contain, become them.

He said nothing of their grievances, except perhaps that oblique reference to their purses. He was *Donnchadh bàn nan óran*, Fair-haired Duncan of the Songs, loyal to an obsolescent clan supremacy, to the gentlemen whose influence had secured him a post with the Guard, and he viewed the present through dreams of the past. He saw Lord Frederick as a *duine-uasal* should be, "a hero at the head of troops, marching with the regiment and directing them in person". The Colonel marched with no one and was directing nothing but his political affairs in a constituency where, he told Oughton, matters were now very critical. He was in Dunbartonshire on September 30 when Duncan Ban's trim and comely lads broke into mutiny.

The outbreak came as a surprise to the officers, who should have been aware by now of the serious discontent. Late that night, after taptoo and the setting of the sun, lamps were re-lit in the Back-Barracks above the southern escarpment of the rock, spilling their yellow light across Hawk Hill to the Governor's House. Almost immediately there was a great shouting, windows were opened and the offending cartridge-boxes and belts were flung onto the parade beyond. Nothing was done to stop the noise, and it lasted for some time until it died with the extinguished lamps. In the morning the companies dutifully answered the call of their assembling drums, parading on Hawk Hill and facing the litter of discarded equipment. For a while, as the ranks took their dressing, officers and men behaved as if the pouches were not there, but upon the first verbal order the soldiers tore their sporrans from their waists and threw them on the ground. At this the officers stepped forward from the wall of the Governor's House and were quickly surrounded by shouting men who said that the equipment would be worn no longer, that they had been overcharged for it, that it could not be kept clean on a soldier's pay, that their belt-buckles were too large, and the required cocking of their bonnets was unnatural to a Highlandman. When Hugh Montgomerie came from Foog's Gate to the open ground he could not be heard at first, and he drew his officers back, waiting until the passion of the men was exhausted. He then ordered the company commanders to make a written list of all complaints. At this the men cheered him and went obediently to their duties, believing that their grievances would be redressed.

For three days they answered all calls upon them, mounting guards and pickets, but they would not wear their sporrans, their belts and their cartridge-boxes. Every forenoon Montgomerie reported to Oughton, and the sick man let the days pass without action. Orderly though the soldiers' behaviour was, he did not know what turn their temper might take. At the first offensive sign they could raise the drawbridge and close the Portcullis Gate. "However necessary it was to quell this mutinous disposition and reduce them to obedience," he later told Amherst, "it was not advisable to employ force while they remained in possession of the Castle." It was not advisable because the fortress contained the largest supply of military stores and ammunition in the country, because the guns of the Half Moon Battery pointed down the Royal Mile, because there were more than a hundred French and Spanish prisoners in the casemate who might be released if the Highlanders were provoked. Although the Argyll men were perhaps unaware of it, desiring only the removal of their grievances, they were holding a primed and loaded pistol at Oughton's temple.

Lord Frederick was in Glasgow when he received an urgent express from Montgomerie on the morning of Sunday, October 3.

He set out immediately for the east, arriving at the Castle when a drum was beating its valediction to the day and lights were going out in all but the officers' quarters on Palace Yard. He was told that the men were quiet, neat and orderly, but obstinate in their refusal to wear the hated equipment. He dined well and slept well and came to the morning parade with confidence, pleased by the sturdy ranks and the absence of hostility. "I explained the nature of their crime," he told Amherst, "and with as much firmness as I could by *words* told them that they *should* put on their pouches, but having no force to support me it was useless to make use of the word *shall*." Since no man came forward in remorse, he told them that he had not heard of their complaints until this moment, but he would order a Court of Inquiry to sit the next day and if there were any just cause for the grievances they would be immediately redressed. This, he explained to the Commander-in-Chief, was a pretence, to save face and to gain time. He sat upon the Court himself, or so directed the officers who did that their report was in accordance with his wishes and intentions.

> Under pretence of this Report, which was meant to be as favourable as possible to the men's demands, I went far beyond the most sanguine expectations in redressing their complaints. I had some hopes that this relaxation, which could only affect myself, might have brought back the men to reason, and have induced them to petition me, to be permitted to put on their pouches again. But nothing of this sort happened, which put an end to every expedient but that of force.

The relaxation promised had been an assurance that he would return to them from his own pocket the money they had been overcharged for their sporrans, although he said that they had paid no more than the contractor's price. Having failed to bring them to order by this small compromise he had now to devise a way in which force could be used with minimal risk, and by which they could be drawn from the Castle. His politician's cunning, a pragmatist's belief in the virtue of justifiable means, produced a plan which he said should be carried out with "expedition, secrecy and success". It was approved by Oughton who promised armed support and the authority of his own silent attendance. This second pretence depended upon the men's faith in Campbell's honest intentions, their residual loyalty to a brother of their *ceann-cinnidh*, and it is impossible not to believe that he intended to exploit that ingenuous trust. General Orders given at the beating of Retreat on October 7 announced that the companies would parade on Hawk Hill the following morning, marching thence to the links of Leith for field exercises. This was a frequent occurrence, and since the men were willing to obey all orders except those concerning the rejected equipment, since they had no thought of remaining in the Castle and holding it by force, despite Oughton's fears, there was no protest against the order.

The companies left early on Friday with drums rolling and pipes playing, strutting down the Royal Mile behind the mounted figure of their Colonel, long-legged in the coat and trews of his unfamiliar uniform. The only men left behind were the sick and convalescent, the guard on the walls and gates, the non-commissioned officers and private men on orderly duty. Three wagons left the Castle five minutes after the companies were gone, and surprisingly the men remaining made no attempt to stop them. They carried the hated belts and cartridge-boxes.

When the Fencibles reached the links they wheeled to the right, halted and turned into line, opening their files by an extended right arm before ordering their muskets. Officers marched to the front of each company, sergeants to the rear, and twelve paces in front of the line stood five drummers, left knee bent and sticks at rest. It was a day like any other chosen for exercise, the sound of the sea and the taste of salt in the wind, white sails heeling below a skein of gulls. On the higher ground by Constitution Road there was the usual small crowd from Leith, idly enjoying the golden mist of the morning and the familiar sight of green tartan and black bonnets, but somewhere on the perimeters of the links, discreet and unobtrusive, Oughton also waited with his staff. For some minutes after the ordering of arms no further command was given. Unexplained inaction is the common experience of soldiers and the Highlanders were not alarmed, their eyes on the blue hills across the firth, or upon the two field-officers and an orderly-drummer who stood apart with their Colonel. Then the wagons rolled on to the soft sand, and above the creaking of their wheels another sound, the musical ring of bridle-chain and scabbard steel. Six troops of Thomas Mordaunt's 10th Dragoons came northward from the Musselburgh road, slowly at the walk, white metal buttons on their red and yellow coats, black tricornes pulled down over their foreheads in the menacing ferocity of all cavalrymen. Once past the bowling-green, and answering the call of a trumpet, they broke into three divisions, now moving at a plunging trot to the rear and the flanks of the Fencibles. There they halted and turned inward to face the Highlanders, each man unhooking his carbine from the ring and laying it across his saddle.

Montgomerie was already walking to the front of the line, the orderly-drummer stumbling behind and beating a warning on his bouncing instrument. The Major's order to ground firelocks was unexpected, but the response to it was a reflex. As the drummer struck a timing-roll the Highlanders bent in a green wave, rising at the last peremptory tap and leaving their muskets on the earth. Now they understood what was happening, but before they could react in anger or fear Montgomerie called again. *By files, left flank company leading, march off to collect pouches and belts.* There was no immediate obedience, nor was it perhaps expected, for within seconds Campbell shouted and was answered by the commanding cry of a dragoon officer. Four files broke away from the troop nearest the left flank company, cutting out the first six Highlanders and herding them forward until they stood before Lord Frederick. He looked at them briefly before riding across to Oughton. Their conversation was brief, its purpose and conclusion undoubtedly pre-arranged, although Oughton did not say this in his dispatch to Amherst later that day. "As Lord Frederick was of the opinion that an immediate punishment would produce a better effect than the slow proceedings of a General Court-Martial, I consented to their being tried and punished on the spot."

The six men, whom both Oughton and Campbell called ring-leaders, were tried at once by a regimental field court-martial, four subalterns and a captain standing behind a ritual altar of drums. The power of such a court was awesome, and troubling to many fair-minded men. It could hear evidence, pronounce sentence and inflict corporal punishment without placing itself or any witness on oath. It was not required to call upon a repre-sentative of the Judge-Advocate-General for its own guidance or for the protection of the accused's legal rights. Because there was no appeal against its decision, no record was kept of its proceed-ings. Frequent attempts had been made in Parliament to impose an obligatory oath at such trials, but had been rejected on the grounds that both judges and and witnesses could be trusted to act with honour. Field courts-martial were primarily intended for armies in the face of the enemy, when summary justice was believed necessary to maintain or restore discipline, and from that need they invariably brought in a verdict of guilty. Because they were fractionally less merciful than a soldier's risk in tomorrow's battle they were usually effective in purpose. It was generally admitted that they were also irregular, and few officers might have disagreed with Major Stephen Adye of the Royal Artillery, Deputy-Judge-Advocate to the King's forces in America and the respected author of *A Treatise on Courts Martial*.

On actual service, where immediate examples are often required, such irregularity (for in such cases it cannot be deemed injustice) may be deemed necessary, *inter arma silent leges*; but this will not hold good in times of profound peace, when the proceedings against offenders will admit of the legal and necessary delays. Custom may perhaps be urged on this occasion, but when a custom is even proved to exist, the next enquiry is into the legality of it; for if it is not a good and legal custom, it ought to be no longer used, *malum usus abolendum est*, is an established maxim of law.

It was true that these were not times of profound peace, but
the nearest enemy – if the omnipresent *Bonhomme Richard* were
ignored – was many hundreds of miles away. Sir James Dunbar,
Deputy-Judge-Advocate, was in Edinburgh and the Argyll men
had as much right to his protection as the inexperienced subalterns
of the court had need of his advice. Common humanity as well
as legal obligations should have compelled Oughton to resist
Lord Frederick's request and to confine the six men for a general
court-martial. He chose instead the custom which Adye questioned. He believed that the irregularity of this trial would be for
the best, that its sentence would be frightful enough to end all
disaffection in the Argyll regiment, and had he not been a sick
man he might have realised that it would in fact be the beginning
of the worst that could happen.

The trial was quickly over. Two of the six men were acquitted,
for no known reason except perhaps the need for an appearance
of reasonable justice. The remaining four were sentenced to an
immediate flogging.

Cowed by the slanting carbines of the dragoons, the nudging
horses, the Highlanders obeyed Montgomerie's order and formed
square, facing inward, silently watching the erection of a triangle.
This pyramidal scaffolding was made from four halberds, the
steel-bladed pikes carried by sergeants, each seven feet in length
and now lashed together to form the three legs and horizontal
cross-bar of the triangle. The hands of the first convicted man
were tied at the wrists and drawn upward above his head to the
crossed blades. His chest rested on the cross-bar, and his thighs
and ankles were belted to the straddling staffs of the pikes. He
was stripped naked to the waist, his plaid falling to his feet. All
this was done quickly and with careful concern for regulations,
the bonds not too tight to stop the circulation of blood but firm
enough to prevent the body from sagging, from bringing the
neck and throat within the curling sweep of the lash. A relay of
drummers moved to the triangle, the leading man pulling the
whip again and again through his left fist, to straighten the tails,
to moisten and soften the leather with his saline sweat.

Military flogging began upon the command of the senior officer present. "*Go on, drum-major!*" The lash then fell rhythmically, each stroke numbered and accompanied by drum-roll and tap. When the Major cried "*Stop twenty-five!*" or "*Stop fifty!*" the cat was handed to the next shirt-sleeved relay and the punishment continued. No drummer was exempt from this duty, though it came more often to those with muscle and phlegm. Some, moved by compassion or by bribe, would use the lash with the maximum of show and minimum of effect. Others boasted of their terrible skill in placing the blows where they wished, in the patterns they could cut on a man's flesh, in the squeezing of the tails through the left fist before each strike, to remove the thick blood that would cushion the pain. This last claim was a braggart myth, for its real purpose was to reduce the amount of blood that fell upon the drummer as he swung the whip. It was said that after a man first used the cat he was near-demented for days, scrubbing himself again and again, washing and re-washing his spattered shirt and breeches.

Few if any of the Argyll men can have seen a flogging before, and the brutal shock was worsened by their horror of any physical violation of a man's dignity. The first stroke of the nine-tailed cat broke the skin of the victim's back, drawing blood immediately and dramatically changing the appearance of the white flesh. "As if," said one witness, "it were thickly sprinkled with black coffee." By the third relay the back was raw and shining from shoulders to waist, and now it was said that the man truly wore the red coat of a soldier. Most men bit their lips or their tongues after their first cry, but this determination to keep a defiant silence did not last long, and they found there could be some small relief in a groan or a shriek. In time there was a great and throbbing pain upon which the lash fell with the agonising lightness of a feather. When a man had received a hundred lashes he was often in a state of convulsion, arching his back and jerking his head against the restraining pull of a belt held by a drummer to his front. Two hundred and fifty strokes were the most he was believed capable of enduring at one time, and if his sentence called for more he was brought to the halberds again the next day, and the next until the number was completed. Some officers and surgeons were more interested in the reactions of those who witnessed a flogging than of the man who received it, and they said that the hands and feet of the watchers often turned cold, whatever the temperature of the day. There was also a peculiar manifestation of emotion which the men commonly called "sniffing". With each stroke of the cat the assembled soldiers drew in their breath sharply, through their nostrils and open mouths. If they wept, as many did, they also sucked in the tears that ran from their cheeks to their lips. Once heard, this hoarse, bronchial sound from five hundred or a thousand throats was more vividly recalled than the memory of the victim's red and quivering body.

As Oughton and Lord Frederick had hoped, the sight of their comrades' pain and humiliation broke the spirit of the Argyll men and reduced them to traumatic obedience. When the last man was cut down, the triangle dismantled and the halberds wiped clean of glutinous blood, the drums beat a flam and a long roll for the breaking of square into line. It had been Oughton's intention to return three of the five companies to the Castle and to send the others to quarters in the country. Sergeant Mac-Dougal had long since left for Edinburgh with an emptied wagon, to collect the knapsacks of these two companies whom Lord Frederick said had been the most mutinous and disaffected. But while the fourth man was being flogged alarming news had come from the city, and Montgomerie now told Oughton that however docile the Highlanders might be at this moment he could not answer for their behaviour when they heard what was happening in the Castle. Good sense demanded that they should be immediately dispersed about the countryside, that as little communication as possible should be allowed between one company and another. Oughton wearily accepted the advice. The day had gone badly after all, what had been done for the good of all had resulted in further evil. He sent Major Campbell of Melfort into the city, to see what might be achieved by fair

words alone, but having no faith now in any Highlander, officer
or soldier, he asked Mordaunt to follow with three troops of his
command. Escorted by the remaining dragoons, each rider with
his carbine loaded and loose on the ring, the Argyll men were then
marched away to quarters about Musselburgh, Haddington and
Dalkeith. Lord Frederick told them that they were being sent
into the country "by way of disgrace", and before each humbled
company left the links it took its belts and pouches from where
the wagons had unloaded them.

The flogged men were placed on one of the carts and covered
with their blood-soaked plaids. They were carried into Leith, to
a warship in the harbour, that the Navy might make what use it
wished of them.

"Jealous, mutinous, and obstinate to a degree of ferocity"

THE NEWS WAS brought to the Castle by the men of Sergeant MacDougal's baggage-party. "Whereupon," said the officer of the guard, "John Brown sallied forth from his barrack, with his sword in his hand." MacDougal had no orders to keep silent about what was happening on the links, and he could not in any case have prevented his soldiers from talking. When he had taken the wagon to Palace Yard in the citadel, and entered the North Barracks with Private John MacNeil, the other men of his party ran out of Foog's Gate to Hawk Hill, shouting that they had been betrayed, that four of their comrades were being flogged on the links. John Brown was a private soldier in one of the companies Lord Frederick had declared to be the most mutinous of the regiment. Recovering from the fever, he was lying clothed on his bed when MacDougal came into the barrack-room, and the evidence of what happened then is conflicting. MacNeil later said he was ordered to gather Brown's knapsack and arms and take them to the wagon, which he did. Corporal Donald MacKechnie, another convalescent in the room, said that Brown was told to pack his own baggage, that he replied he would do so bye and bye. Neither witness said that Brown refused to obey, but it would appear from MacDougal's evidence that when the soldier heard the angry shouting outside he rose from the bed and went to the door of the building. Either there, or in the Yard beyond, MacDougal stopped him, ordering him to load the wagon. "Hold your tongue," shouted Brown, now enraged, "or it'll be the worst for you! You'll not get the baggage this easy!"

At that moment Lieutenant John Gilfillan, a young Breadalbane gentleman of Clan Macnab, came from the officers' quarters on the west side of the Yard, languidly aroused by the noise. MacDougal went to him for support, but Brown pushed between them and foully abused the lieutenant in Gaelic. The echoing richness of his language filled the windows of the North Barracks with white faces, their voices calling for an explanation. MacDougal abruptly left the Yard, running out of the gate to Hawk Hill where he was immediately surrounded by convalescents and walking-sick, shocked and angry men. Gilfillan did nothing, or nothing that seemed to him more sensible than a discreet return to his quarters. When the lieutenant was gone, Brown went back into the barracks for his broadsword. Holding it by the sheathed blade, he ran to the head of the Lang Stairs and down their steep fall to the inner barrier, shouting for the drawbridge to be raised.

MacDougal did not stay long on Hawk Hill where his calls for order were ignored. He walked round the western escarpment of the citadel, intending to get out of the Castle if he could and away to Leith with the news that the garrison was in revolt. He saw Brown at the drawbridge, which was now raised, and there were a dozen Highlanders with him, all angry. He put his hand on the chain to lower the bridge but was roughly dragged away and told not to interfere. More shouting men were now coming through the arch of the Portcullis, some with muskets and some with swords. The Sergeant stepped back, or was forced back to the wall of the Three Gun Battery, and as he looked up to the Half Moon high above him he saw other soldiers leaning over the embrasures, calling incoherently and waving their weapons. No one man seemed to be the leader, but Brown's voice was the loudest, demanding that no one should be allowed to enter the Castle. "Keep out all but our friends!" he shouted over his shoulder as he ran back up the hill.

Pressed against the wall of the battery, seeing little in the narrow stone lane but waving swords and angry faces, MacDougal did not know where Brown went, but Private Neil Maclean met the angry man at the foot of the Lang Stairs and asked him what

was happening and where he was going. "I've got six cartridges,"
said Brown, "and I'm going for more!" Maclean was alarmed,
and his only wish was to leave the Castle, but when he asked the
men at the bridge to let him through, that he might attend to
some private business in the city, one soldier struck him heavily
on the chest with the hilt of a sword. Another said that he was a
dog to think of deserting his comrades, that he deserved a thrust
with the point.

The officer of the guard that day was Lieutenant Dugald
Campbell from Lorne, and when the revolt began he was
pleasantly taking his ease in the guard-room, his waistcoat buttons
undone and his stock loosened. As he looked from his window
he was astonished to see Brown running across the court, sword
in hand. He went out immediately to Hawk Hill, shouting
impotently against a red and green sea of protest. His duty at this
moment, and indeed Gilfillan's earlier, was clearly defined in
Roger Stevenson's *Military Instructions for Officers*, a pocket-book
which most Fencible commanders strongly recommended to the
gentleman of their companies. Mutiny, said Mr. Stevenson, never
took hold of a whole party at once, it began with the seditious
behaviour of two or three men, before whom an officer should
not lose courage. Since matters had plainly gone beyond this nice
point, Campbell did not follow Stevenson's advice on what
next to do: "Instantly command them to be silent, and if they
continue, lay hold of the first firelock and break the heads of the
chief mutineers without mercy, threatening to hang all who fail
in subordination." The Lieutenant wisely turned away instead,
going back into the citadel and across the court behind the North
Barracks to the Lang Stairs. When he reached the drawbridge
below, and uneasily faced the mob, he ordered the Castle to be
opened at once but was told to stand off. "It'll not be raised!"
shouted a bold voice above him, and he turned to it. Brown had
returned, and was now sitting on the wall of the Three Gun
Battery some yards from the bridge, his legs hanging down and
his sword across his knees. "No man gets in," he cried, "not till
our friends come from Leith!"

Later than Mr. Stevenson would have thought advisable, Campbell put a hand in the hilt of his sword, but an angry surge of the mob thrust him against the wall, making it impossible for the weapon to be drawn. He saw three or four non-commissioned officers, convalescents from the hospital, bravely fighting with fists and elbows to reach the chain-work of the bridge. Sergeant Charles MacArthur was there first, limping painfully on an injured foot, and when he ordered the soldiers to let him out he too was told to stand back. "Not even our Chief would get out now!" said a man of his company, and Brown began to shout for powder and ball, for proper sentries to be placed on the bridge. At this John MacLeod, whose bayonet was already locked to his musket, pulled back the dog-head and screwed in a new flint. Dugald Campbell was now convinced there was to be a desperate battle on this cramped ground and in the lane leading to the citadel. He pushed away the men who surrounded him, drew his sword at last and used its hilt to hammer a path to the chain-work. His intention, perhaps, was to cut down the nearest man when the first shot was fired and to die in an attempt to lower the bridge, but a dozen Highlanders immediately drew their broadswords and faced him resolutely. Near to tears in anger and shame, he sheathed the blade and turned away.

For what seemed to him to be an hour, but was probably less, he listened helplessly to the noise from Hawk Hill above, to the useless, angry appeals of his sergeants. Then there was a call from Castle Hill beyond, and a soldier on the Half Moon Battery shouted that the Major was come. Melfort was a popular man, and some of the Highlanders said he should be admitted. Dugald MacArthur, a convalescent of the Major's company, put his hand on the chain and emotionally begged his friends to lower the bridge. As a noisy argument began on Melfort's personal merits and faults, Lieutenant Campbell struggled through the crowd until he stood before MacLeod. "I'm in your power," he said, "but let the Major in and tell him what you want. I give you my word. No one else need come in, and if I deceive you, you may put your bayonet in my breast!" This theatrical declaration cunningly or instinctively appealed to the Highlanders' admiration of flamboyant courage, and they cheered the Lieutenant, calling him a brave fellow who could be trusted.

When Melfort rode in he went no further than the Three Gun Battery some yards from the bridge. It was clear from what he saw and from Dugald Campbell's breathless report that the time for fair words was long past. Brown was shouting hysterically for the bridge to be raised again, but before this could be done Melfort swung his horse about and rode out of the Castle. He went down Castle Hill at a sliding gallop, passing Sergeant-major Duncan Livingstone to whom he shouted an order to get into the Castle if possible, and then rode on to meet the dragoons on the Leith Road. Livingstone did his best with the professional power of his lungs, alone on the edge of the dry ditch, an unarmed David before a Goliath of stone. He was answered by John Brown, now standing in an embrasure of the Battery. "No man shall enter until the companies return from Leith!" The Sergeant-major remembered the undrawn sword in John Brown's hand, and remembered too that the soldier's right fist was wrapped in a bloody bandage.

Livingstone's shout for admission was heard by MacDougal and he made one last effort to get the bridge lowered. He ordered a man of his baggage party, Donald McConnell, to haul on the chain, but the soldier was immediately pulled away and both he and the Sergeant were told that they would be killed if they touched the bridge again. MacDougal was ready to risk that, but there was another voice calling from Castle Hill. Ninian Imrie had come with Oughton's ultimatum. Dragoons were on the way, he said, "If you do not instantly surrender you will all be put to the sword without mercy!" When he received no answer, if indeed his English had been understood, he turned his back with deliberate contempt and rode slowly toward the Royal Mile.

The mutiny had been an explosion of passion, without direction or control, an angry protest against betrayal. No one had seen beyond the raising of the bridge and none knew what should or could be done now. After two hours of exhausting noise and emotion some of the men began to drift away from the inner barrier, to the citadel or Hawk Hill, and Brown's voice was no longer heard on the Half Moon Battery. Upon Corporal Mac-Kechnie's civil demand, John MacLeod meekly surrendered his musket and bayonet and went up the hill to the Back-Barracks, but the swordsmen still remained by the chain and the barrier, uneasy yet steadfast in their refusal to lower the bridge.

There was a trumpet call and the sound of hooves on the stones of the Lawnmarket. Three troops of the 10th Dragoons halted at the Bowhead, two of them dismounting and moving toward the fortress. They could be seen from the Half Moon Battery as they came up the shadowed throat of Hill Street and deployed in the sunlight of the open mound, carbine in hand and thrusting their gauntlets into their belts. Once in line and extended order, three ranks deep like a company of infantry, they waited until a cornet advanced with their colour, until Thomas Mordaunt took his place in the van with a drawn sword. Upon his command, the elegant lift and sweep of his hat, they moved forward in lines of red, yellow and black, bodies bent against the slope of the hill. The assault was of course absurd, an advance by dismounted horsemen upon one of the most powerful strongholds in Britain, a castle that had taken Cromwell three months to subdue, across ground that could be cleared by one discharge of grape from the Half Moon Battery. But the confidence of this unhesitating march, their own lack of resolve and purpose, broke the dispirited resistance of the Highlanders, most of them fever-weak from the beginning. They moved from the bridge and the barrier, hurrying to Hawk Hill and the barrack blocks. Lieutenant Campbell and the sergeants lowered the bridge, and it had not touched the ground before the first files of heavy-booted dragoons leapt upon it, running to take the Portcullis Gate before it could be closed. The twelfth, the last, and the shortest siege in the Castle's recorded history was over.

The dragoons pursued the Highlanders like cattle, driving them into the hospital and the Back-Barracks. Brown was found

alone in the Palace Yard, and MacLeod upon his bed in a listless
state of shock. With three others, also marked down as ringleaders
by Lieutenant Campbell and Sergeant MacDougal, they were
heavily ironed and sent to the guard-house. At sunset both men
were thrown into the Black Hole below the casemate, and later
that night a sentry moved closer to hear their soft and secretive
whispering. Brown asked MacLeod what had been done with
"what was in the handkerchief", and was told that it had been
thrown from a barrack window. This curious conversation was
considered important enough to be repeated at the court-martial
later, and although no explanation was given, the prosecution's
implication was that the handkerchief had contained the six
cartridges mentioned in Neil Maclean's evidence.

When James Oughton received Mordaunt's report that the
Castle was once more in the King's hands, he came into the city
by coach, and at four o'clock that afternoon he sat down in the
Governor's House to finish the dispatch he had begun at noon in
Leith. He asked Amherst for English regiments. He begged to be
freed from troublesome Highlanders who were "extremely
capricious, jealous, mutinous, and obstinate to a degree of
ferocity". With only the dragoons to maintain order, he could
not wait for Amherst's reply however, and he wrote next to
Lord Adam Gordon, commanding the Northern District at
Newcastle. "I must beg your Lordship will send me two or three
hundred good men with as much dispatch as possible." This
letter was sent by express that evening and reached Newcastle
early the next morning, putting Gordon in an ill-humour. He
was an uncle of the Duke of Gordon, a conscientious, middle-
aged soldier with a paternal sympathy for the Highlanders,
thinking of himself as one and believing them to be more often
misunderstood than wilfully mutinous. When Oughton's mud-
spattered galloper reached him, he responded immediately,
ordering three hundred Scottish Borderers of the 25th to march
that day for Edinburgh. They were the best soldiers he had and
he was reluctant to part with them. He told Amherst that he now
had only a regiment of Huntingdon militia and some green

recruits of the 10th to deal with mobbing miners in Durham and Lancashire. He implied that these dangerous men were a greater threat to the security of the nation than Lord Frederick's Highlanders or General Oughton's anti-Papist mob, and within a week, when five hundred pitmen rioted in Chester-le-Street, he wrote again and again for the return of his men from Scotland.

Oughton spent the night of the mutiny and the whole of the following day at his writing-desk, sending dispatches to Amherst, to the Secretary of State and the Secretary at War. He was now aware that he was more than very tired, and he perhaps feared another stroke. He desperately longed for rest, for the curative waters and tranquil society of Bath, but would not yet ask for leave of absence. He was also plagued by Lord Frederick who was writing to London in another room, complaining that the candle-light strained his eyes and obsessed with the notion that his Highlanders had been seduced by the citizens of Edinburgh. "The good people of this town," he told Amherst, "have taken great pains to make my regiment as mutinous and as useless as they have made every new regiment which has been quartered here." He stubbornly believed this, despite a report that the two companies on detachment in Dundee had now thrown away their pouches and sporrans. "I have no excuse to make for my regiment," he said abjectly, "from whom I had far different expectations." He asked Oughton to send Melfort at once to Dundee, with a troop of dragoons to bring the rogues to their proper obedience.

His belief in the guilt of the people of Edinburgh was shared by Oughton, who was now convinced that no Scots regiment, and particularly no Highlanders, should be used for the defence of the northern kingdom. He wanted English foot-soldiers about him, honest, loyal men who did not give a fig for the disaffected talk of seditious civilians. He told Lord Weymouth that even the Fencibles, enlisted for service in Scotland only, should none the less be sent into England where they would be safe from infection.

I discover too many seeds of discontent, especially among the lower people. Great number of the dissenting ministers, and several of the established clergy, are avowedly republicans and Americans, and the Popery Bill gave these people a handle to inflame the minds of the populace.

That troublesome fellow Lord George Gordon, a nephew of Lord Adam, was travelling about Scotland, brazenly exciting men's minds with his maniacal zeal and his call for the extirpation of all signs of idolatrous Popery. He had been received with great honour in the south-west where some ministers had offered to raise a regiment of a thousand men, for whatever use Lord George desired. Oughton may have wished that their power to call up so many men had been more properly employed when their parishes were asked for levies. The mad champion of Protestant liberty was accompanied on his travels by one Ralph Bowie, by his name a Highlander and a Clan Donald man, although Oughton did not say this. It was damnable enough that the rascal was a trouble-maker. "He is an able, crafty fellow, and was Secretary to the Committee of Correspondence in the Popery Bill riot." Oughton's past enthusiasm for the Highland people, as unrealistic as the Ossianic mythology that had inspired it, was now a sour memory only. The Argyll men, like the mutineers on Leith Shore, on Arthur's Seat or the hill above Burntisland, might have been brave enough in the face of a foreign enemy, but at home the Government would be wise to disperse them among English or Lowland regiments. He was no longer pleased by the sentimental nonsense of New Town drawing-rooms. The Highland gentry resident in Edinburgh, spending their mountain rents on the comforts of the city, had been rudely shaken by the mutinies. They were also tormented by unpleasant doubts and emotions, by a fear that their Lowland neighbours now despised them, by the suspicions that the Highland soldiers might have been betrayed. A writer to the *Mercury* said that he was almost ashamed to call himself a Highlander, and asked what had happened to the ancient attachments between

chief and clan. Had the chiefs, by acts of oppression, lost the right
to expect loyalty? Had the clansmen thrown off every virtue that
had made their ancestors remarkable? More pertinently, he asked,

> Can the officers of any regiment impose upon their men what
> articles they please, and at any price they think proper; and in
> case these are refused by the men, on account of overcharge or
> otherwise, and the men are compelled to take them or suffer
> punishment, can they have any redress at common law in a
> civil court?

Such questions, in Oughton's mind, were undoubtedly evidence of the republican and American ideas all too common in
Edinburgh society. He was relieved when Major James Flint
brought the light infantrymen of the 25th into the city, small
vigorous men in the new short coats designed for colonial campaigns, their red caps trimmed with black fur and badged with a
metal thistle, the arrogant Latin boast that no one could touch
them with impunity. Although they were Scots, they were a
regular battalion, Border men who were proudly if paradoxically
known as The Edinburgh Regiment and might be relied upon to
protect the city's good name. He stubbornly resisted Lord Adam's
repeated requests for their return, determined that they should not
leave until he had the English soldiers he earnestly desired. His
health was now so poor that he could attend to important matters
only. Even these essential burdens were almost too great to bear
but he applied himself to them without mercy, determined that
his mind and body should obey his will. He ordered a Court of
Inquiry into the mutiny, preparatory to a general court-martial,
believing that this would persuade the Argyll men that their complaints would be justly considered. But now Lord Frederick's
officers were angered by a rumour that the regiment was to be
sent into England, declaring that this would be a mark of disgrace
upon them, that they would obey the marching-orders but would
then resign their commissions. "I think it highly probable they
would do so," Oughton told Amherst, "and still more that the

men would not obey, knowing well that by the terms of their engagements they are not obliged to march out of Scotland."

Of the five men arrested only Brown and MacLeod were brought to trial. The court sat in the Great Hall of the Castle on Monday, November 8, Lieutenant-colonel Mordaunt presiding and Sir James Dunbar as the Deputy-Judge-Advocate. Once again, Mr. MacGregor of the Gaelic chapel came to give his countrymen comfort and to act as their interpreter. After three days both men were found guilty of mutiny and incitement to mutiny. Despite the weight of evidence against them, they denied the charges. Brown said that he was drunk on the morning of the mutiny and had remained so throughout the day, that he had not injured his hand when raising the drawbridge, but while lowering it "to let out one MacDonald of the Invalids down to the city". He denied that he had any cartridges, or knew where to find more, "and if he did say so, he said what was not truth". MacLeod said that another man had locked the bayonet to his musket, that he had been compelled to stand sentry on the bridge. "In answer to Maclean's evidence, the Prisoner says that the handkerchief belonged to Brown and was put out at the window to dry, and when Brown asked what was become of it, he said he had taken it in, and no other conversation happened about it." Brown was sentenced to death by shooting, and MacLeod "to receive one thousand lashes on his bare back with a cat and nine tails by the Drummers of the regiment".

When Sir Charles Gould received a report of the court-martial he was as displeased by it as he had been with the trial of the Leith mutineers, and he told Sir James Dunbar that there should have been a stricter regard for the Articles of War. He was also irritated by Dunbar's nagging demands for extra expenses. Those incurred at the earlier trial had been greater than what was usually allowed but now, said Sir James, "I had more trouble in attending and running about than on any others." Gould would not authorise the payment until the demand was signed and approved by Oughton, who appeared to be too ill, too irresolute in mind to attend to this. The Judge-Advocate-General was troubled by the improper conduct of a trial that should have been as blameless as custom and honour required. The charges had been inexact and the Articles quoted were in excess of what were required. "You will not take offence at my recommending to you, that every sentence and the Articles of War upon which it is founded, should exactly apply to the charge upon which the prisoner is arraigned." Gould had no sympathy with mutineers and was as firm an advocate of the lash and the firing-squad as any general officer, but the meticulous application of the Law transcended all else. Although the sentences were richly deserved, he wished that they had been based upon precise reference to the relevant Articles. If a man was to be shot or flogged, he implied, the fellow should have the reassurance that he had received the full protection allowed him under God, Crown and Parliament. The report of the court-martial had come to London with a letter from Oughton, a plea for clemency and expedient mercy, and it was almost his last act as Commander-in-Chief of North Britain. The anger and bitterness he felt at the time of the mutiny had quickly cooled into sadness, a feeling that there had been humiliation, pain and bloodshed enough. He remained at his desk and his duty until the court-martial was over, and then retired to his bed for a week, seen by no one but his wife and his stepson. It was said that he had suffered another stroke, and both his physicians and his staff urged him to take the cure at Bath. He was close to the end of his career and his life. The brief months of his command had been a *via dolorosa*, the country of his adoption a Calvary of failure, but he was reluctant to abandon either.

Charles Gould was in no haste to put Oughton's plea or his own doubts before the King, whose mind at this moment was occupied with the opening of Parliament. When an audience was possible, George III asked for time to consider the Judge-Advocate-General's advice, and two days later his decision was sent to Edinburgh. In the first week of December Brown and MacLeod were brought from the Black Hole to the frost-rimed parade of Hawk Hill, to the centre of a square formed by the impassive Borderers of the 25th, two troops of dismounted dragoons and a grieving company of their own regiment. They were told that the sentence of death upon John Brown would be set aside if he agreed "to serve a term of fourteen years in such of His Majesty's dominions beyond the seas or foreign parts, and in such a corps as His Majesty shall from time to time be pleased to appoint". John MacLeod was offered a similar choice, the thousand lashes awarded him or an exile of five years. The King hoped that his clemency, if accepted, would have a proper effect on the minds of all men in the Argyll regiment, but they should know that any future offence would be punished to the full extent of the Articles of War. When Mr. MacGregor had translated this, the two men fell upon their knees and wept, thanking God and the King for such mercy. Two days before Christmas a warship took them south to the Thames, to the dank cells of the Savoy Prison from whence they were eventually sent to the fever-heat and certain death of a far West Indian garrison.

Oughton stayed at Caroline Park until the New Year, in nominal command but his duties sadly neglected. When he went south he still had not put his approving signature upon Sir James Dunbar's expenses. Gould did not press the sick man, saying that when Oughton came to London again this tiresome formality could be concluded. He did not come again. He died in Bath that spring, when the trees were already in leaf. His will asked that he be buried as a soldier, with no more display and expense than decency required. His most treasured possession, the plate-mounted pistols the Great Duke had given his father, were left to his stepson Hew Dalrymple, now first-major of the Duke of Atholl's Highlanders.

"All traitors go to hell, who thought the 77th to sell"

DAVID STEWART OF GARTH was thirteen when it was decided that he should now carry a colour in the Duke of Atholl's regiment. "The boy is of low stature," said his father's application, "but well made and strong; others agree that he is very promising, so that want of years is a fault that is always mending." Although he was gazetted ensign he never joined the battalion, but his regard for it was second only to his admiration of the Black Watch with which he later served. Remembering the brave recruiters of the Atholl companies, green drummers in Strathtay and the firelit scarlet of his uncle's coat, he said that the officers and men were all remarkable. "The former were young and spirited, the latter of the best description in respect of morals, bodily strength and personal appearance." With one exception the regiment was at all times loyal and obedient, an example to the rest of the Army. That exception, however, was as dramatic and as significant as the eruption which transforms a placid mountain into a volcano. In January, 1783, the private men of the 77th Highlanders turned upon their officers, beat those who did not run, closed the citadel of Portsmouth and held it in defiance for a week.

The offer to raise a thousand men from the Duke's broad lands in Perthshire was first made at the beginning of the American Revolution by his uncle, James Murray of Strowan. It was not accepted, but two years later the Duke himself went to the King in London and secured a letter of service and a colonel's commission for his kinsman. Strowan was at that moment commanding the Scots Guards in New Jersey, a scarred veteran who had begun his career at fifteen in a whitecoat regiment of Saxony,

transferring to the 42nd and taking his first wound beneath the
bloody breastworks of Ticonderoga. He was an emotional man
of impetuous courage and impulsive anger, and once responded
to a cry of "*Stand and deliver!*" by leaning from his coach and
grasping the ears of the highwayman's horse. Pain was his in-
separable companion, the understandable reason for his shortness
of temper. Leading a company of the Watch in the capture of
Martinique he was struck by a musket-ball that entered his body
below the lower rib, passed upward through the left lung and
lodged itself permanently under his right scapula. For the rest of
his life he rode with difficulty, was never able to lie down, and
slept upright against a wall of pillows. In Whitehall he was
known as The Forester of Atholl because of his protective pride
in his regiment and his boast that he could call up as many men
as he desired from his clan grounds. Garth said that the soldiers
of the 77th thought of him as their father, but an anonymous
ballad written by one of them suggests that their feelings were
substantially less than filial.

> If writing keeps his memory
> His deeds shall not forgotten be,
> It makes my blood run chill in me
>   To think of Murray's roguery!
>
> Upon earth short shall he dwell,
> But like all traitors go to hell
> Who thought the 77th to sell,
>   But God detects his roguery!

The song was composed in a Portsmouth ale-house during the
mutiny, and was secretly in print before the men of the 77th
marched northward to the Border, stripped of the arms they
were believed to have dishonoured, despised and feared by their
officers. Its venomous hatred was perhaps directed at the Atholl
family in general rather than Strowan in particular, for he did
not deserve the accusation that he had sold his soldiers to the
East Indies, that he had sworn to see them dead if they would not

go aboard the transports. The name of Murray, said one verse, should stink in every Scotsman's nose, and behind this contempt lay two generations of lingering hostility. The ballad was sung to the music of that derisive rant *Hey, Johnnie Cope!*, but the choice of a Jacobite air was ironic. At the time of the last Rebellion the Murray dukedom had two heads, one Hanoverian and one Jacobite, and the harsh effect of such conflicting loyalties was felt in every cottage on the Braes of Atholl. The young men who were called out to fight for the Stuarts were subject to more pressure, more threats of roof-burning and eviction than most clan regiments in the Pretender's Army, and they had also the highest rate of desertion. Despite this lack of enthusiasm they responded to a last call upon their ancient valour, fighting with spectacular and suicidal courage at Culloden, winnowed by the enfilade fire of Campbell militia and the volleys of Wolfe's regulars. The methods by which they had been recruited and the manner in which they were wastefully sacrificed were bitterly remembered by their sons and grandsons, and the echoing voice of their resentment would still be heard fifty years later,[*] before it was choked by the romanticism of the 19th century. When the men of the 77th mutinied it was inevitable that Strowan should be the object of some detestation for he was the second son of Lord George Murray, commander of the Jacobite Army and a relentless recruiter of the Atholl Brigade in the service of Charles Edward Stuart.

> Your father commanded in Forty-five,
> The Young Pretender could not thrive,
> As witness many men alive
>   How treacherously he sold them!

The Duke was the grandson of Lord George but the balladeer ignored him by name. A red-haired and heavy-eyed young man he was one of the most powerful proprietors in the Highlands, a high Tory whose consuming ambition was to be the equal of the greatest and grandest of English landowners. He called upon

[*] The Perthshire militia riots of 1797. See Part 4, p. 395.

architect and arboriculturalist to create a mountain framework
of parks and dells for the realisation of that desire, and would in
time build roads, bridges and villages with a creative energy
worthy of the Book of Genesis. In his wish to be taken for an
English lord he was at this moment the subject of one of the
earliest of Scottish conversational paintings, in which David
Allan pictured him against a landscape of remodelled nature, in
little kilt and feathered bonnet, surrounded by his young family
and a representative selection of game brought down by his
double-barrelled gun. At the beginning of the century his great-
grandfather, who lived in unequalled pomp and state according
to Daniel Defoe, could summon six thousand men to the fiery
cross within a week, Murrays, Robertsons, Farquharsons,
Menzies, MacGregors, Campbells, Stewarts, and all others over
whom he had superiority. More modestly, the fourth duke
believed that he could call upon half that number with ease, but
he soon discovered that without his tireless personal appeal and
the pressure of his gentry, without the distribution of engraved
watches and bounties of ten or twenty guineas, he could not
hope to compete with the wide-ranging recruiters of other
regiments. In the end, that he might muster a thousand men by
the time promised, he was forced to take more than three hundred
from the Lowlands as well as the usual handful of hungry Irish
and English. "Our fathers you sold on Culloden field," recalled
the ballad, and this may have been the reason why so many
Atholl cottages were deaf or defiant when *Am Moreach Mór* rode
into their glens and asked for their young men.

The battalion was embodied at Perth. Upon Robert Skene's
instructions, hardened senior non-commissioned officers from
the Guards taught the new soldiers "to *march*, to understand rank
and file, *to break and rally again* in their own places, and *above all*
to keep their *arms clean* and in good order". They wore high
black bonnets gaily slashed with a red hackle, belted plaids of
Government tartan, scarlet coatees faced with green, white
waistcoats and diced hose of crimson and white. Their drummers
were dressed in forest-green and a tartan which Hew Dalrymple

had found at Blair Castle, "of the sett of a philabeg of the Duke's, which was thought very pretty, it has no black in it, but is composed of red, green and dark blue". For reasons that were never clearly explained, the War Office did not acknowledge the existence of pipers in Highland regiments, and they were always equipped and paid at the Colonel's expense. In all the Duke's lands there was no piper young enough, skilled or handsome enough to play his Highlanders into battle, and Mr. James MacLaggan the minister of Blair was sent to the Isle of Skye in the belief that he would there find a MacCrimmon. He reported miserably that the members of this legendary race of pipers were now all gone, but for one old man who existed on a pension from MacLeod of MacLeod. There were indeed younger men on the island, of other piping families but renowned for their art and virtuosity. They were so saucy in manner, however, that there was no talking to them about enlistment. Garth's uncle Charles, a lieutenant of the 77th, eventually found an old piper in Appin of Dull who was willing to bring two or three young men up to the required standard. They were schooled in a shed behind Garth House, or more fittingly in the open where pipes are meant to be played, on the high hills northward to Rannoch, below the gentle curve of Schiehallion's breast.

Strowan did not return from America until September, 1778, his departure delayed by a fall from his horse in Philadelphia, by the breaking of a collar-bone already plagued by that resident bullet. He was kept informed of his regiment's progress by John Mackay, his pay-sergeant in the Guards and now quartermaster of the 77th. In execrable English, but with painstaking care Mackay told his Colonel of each new order and decision. Pipers, drummers and grenadiers only were to carry broadswords, and by a sad departure from tradition no new Highland regiment was to be armed with pistols. The rent of Strowan's London house was being regularly paid, as were the wages of his dear housekeeper Mistress Anne. Murray's splendid sword, a basket-hilted weapon he had not been able to wear in the Guards, was being cleaned, and Mr. Dickey the regimental clothier was making his uniform, "ten buttons on each lappall, 4 on each sleeve, and 4 on each pocket, all in tows". Cartridge-pouches, to be worn on black leather belts, would hold sixty rounds and more, and the officers were to have silver lace on their coats. Mackay was an old soldier and a good soldier, and by his persistent attendance at the Tower of London he made sure that the 77th was issued with the best muskets available, "as good as ever com".

Upon Oughton's earnest representation no doubt, the Duke originally agreed to recommend Hew Dalrymple for the lieutenant-colonelcy of the battalion, but the King thought he was too young and inexperienced, a handicap which did not prevent the granting of a lieutenant's commission to the Duke's feckless brother William, aged fifteen. His pride hurt by the snub, Dalrymple transferred to another regiment as soon as he could. The man whom Strowan earnestly wished to have as his second-in-command was John Reid of Straloch, his friend and Captain in the 42nd, and had this appointment been approved there might have been no mutiny at Portsmouth. He was the son of a Strathardle family whose name was Robertson, but claiming the title of Baron Reid it had taken that as a surname. He was a gentle-eyed, middle-aged widower, suffering from increasing deafness but still alert in mind and body, and could have been created by Providence to demonstrate that it was possible for one Highland gentleman at least to possess those qualities which Garth and others attributed to all. He was a man of scrupulous honour and warm compassion, dedicated in his concern for the soldiers of his race. "Born a Highlander and understanding their language," he said in pride, "I repeatedly led them on to victory and have bled with them. Knowing the temper and disposition of the Highlanders, I value them more than the influence of either birth or fortune."

He had been educated at Edinburgh University for the practice of Law, but like many other young clan gentlemen so committed by their anxious parents he had turned from its sedentary miseries to the Army, raising enough men from his father's land in 1745 to get himself a commission in Loudon's regiment. He was taken

prisoner at Prestonpans, was back with his company before the
following spring, and by skill and courage captured a Jacobite
treasure chest which the French had landed on the northern
coast of Sutherland. His family was poor, their estate wasted by
the Rebels, and he could advance by wounds and long service
only, eventually securing the temporary command of the Black
Watch. Fortune came to him at last and by way of the marriage
bed, from an American wife who brought him an estate of
35,000 acres, but these had been lost upon the outbreak of the
Revolution and he was once again poor. He was not only a
soldier of skill but also a man of artistic tastes and talents, an
accomplished flautist, the composer of marching-tunes paradoxically scored for stringed instruments. He published them with
pride and one – written for two violins, a violincello and two
horns – is still the slow march of the Black Watch. When the
American Revolution came he was retired on half-pay, grieving
for his wife, devoting himself to his memories and music, but
repeatedly offering himself as the commander of a battalion of
his countrymen. He petitioned Amherst, to whose wife he had
dedicated some of his music, asking for the lieutenant-colonelcy
of the 77th. Supported by Strowan's preferment, he went to
London, lodging in Frith Street, calling upon Amherst with the
recommendation and with another from Francis Farquharson of
Monaltrie. This aging Jacobite, forbidden to return to Scotland
but living as close to it as he could in Durham, said that Reid's
capture of the French treasure in 1746 had forced Charles Stuart
to take "that desperate resolution to engage the King's Army at
Culloden".

When the Duke of Atholl abandoned his earlier and lukewarm
support of Reid's candidature the old soldier accepted the blow
with dignity and returned to Strathardle and his music. At the
end of the war his finances improved and he was able to sell some
of his estates in Nova Scotia for £52,000. He left little of this
to his only child, who had dismayed him by marrying a vile
apothecary. Almost all of it went to the University of Edinburgh
for a chair of music, upon the simple condition that every year

on or about the February day of his birth a concert should be given, that among the pieces played should be a march and a minuet of his own composition, to show the tastes of his century. The performance is still held, and in the sweetest possible way it perpetuates the memory of an amiable man to whom, according to a brother officer, the private soldiers of his race were "much attached for his poetry, his music, and his bravery".

Reid had warned Amherst that the conduct of a Highland regiment principally depended upon the proper choice of officers, and he cannot have been thinking of Charles Gordon of Sheelagreen, to whom Atholl eventually gave the lieutenant-colonelcy. This proud and arrogant man was not yet forty, the son of an undistinguished family in Aberdeenshire, a brave and spirited officer during his service with the 89th Gordon Highlanders in India, and a major in Oughton's regiment when influence and preferment appointed him to the 77th. He spoke no Gaelic and had little understanding of or regard for the Highlanders. He was the only officer of whom Garth wrote with disapproval. His portrait in the *Sketches* is seen through a Venetian blind, the slatted darkness of which emphasises the illuminated faults. He was too much of the German school, said Garth, unwilling to trust his men, "too apt to enforce his orders with a strictness which did not always yield to circumstances". He looked upon his soldiers as pieces of machinery who must obey his orders without thought or reflection. If he did not often impose the corporal punishment he believed essential for the maintenance of discipline, no credit was due to him but to the honourable behaviour of his men. They hated him. They called him Charley in contempt not affection. Long before the mutiny some of them had sworn to comb his hair, and when they did so they boasted of an oath fulfilled, "as witness bears his bloody head!"

The men of the 77th spent the whole of their service in Ireland, dispersed by companies, and impressing all other regiments by their ability to march thirty miles a day for several days without any sign of exhaustion. They harried Irish rebels and suppressed

Irish riots with bayonet and musket-butt, and with an enthusiastic zeal that justified the Government's policy of using Celt against Celt, of employing one subject people in the suppression of another. When Strowan came home from America he spent as much time with the battalion as the affairs of Parliament and his estates allowed. He kept his junior subalterns on constant recruiting, slowly replacing many of the Lowlanders with drafts from the mountains, and if he did not always get the Atholl men he desired his recruiters brought him Stewarts and Camerons, surrendered at a price by the gentlemen of Appin and Lochaber. Some of his officers, pursuing their ambitions into other regiments angered Murray by selling their commissions to Irishmen. He wrote in protest to London, saying that a Highland regiment should be commanded by Highlanders, angrily objecting to the fact that the War Office had approved these transfers without reference to him. His soldiers, he said, had been raised by their chief . . .

> . . . under a kind of confidence of being commanded by him, his family or friends, and a belief that they are ever under his patronage; their provincial attachments are stronger, and require to be managed with greater delicacy, and even gratified as far as is consistent with the good and general rules of the Service, and I hope they will never discover that their Colonel is not of importance enough to be consulted in the appointment of officers. The idea of meeting their countrymen as companions and officers is a very strong motive to engage Highlanders to enter the service, and this prejudice is still more inveterate amongst Highlanders raised at once, as my regiment, by the influence of a Chief, and if it is once known that Irish officers are to command them I am sure I shall not find another recruit in that country.

His protest was successful, and when the regiment left Ireland toward the end of 1782 most of its officers were once more Highland gentlemen from Atholl and Breadalbane. The first-major was now Sir Robert Stuart of Tilliecoultry who was admired as much as Sheelagreen was hated. "A soldier bold," said the ballad, "of birth and fame, and long may he maintain the same." The battalion landed at Bideford in August, and in October it marched into Hampshire to be quartered about Basingstoke, Alton, Andover and Whitchurch. Strowan had recently become a major-general and was thus removed from direct command, but his distant pride and concern, Atholl's purse and Sheelagreen's harsh discipline, kept the regiment to the standards he had always demanded. Until the quartering became a burden, the Hampshire villagers were excited by these strange men, tartan figures at their firesides, black bonnets and red coats plunging through the autumn woods, the sound of sad music at sunset. When that novelty passed, as it quickly did, the principal inhabitants of every village, the innkeepers and victuallers, petitioned the Secretary at War for the speedy removal of their now unwelcome guests.

No one could see any further reason for so many soldiers. The American War was virtually over. It was true that men were still killing each other in distant parts of the earth, maintaining a right to ground or water until the leisurely formalities of peace were concluded, but a treaty with the Americans was signed in November that year, and another with France and Spain was expected any week. Like most regiments raised during the Revolution, the men of the 77th had been enlisted for three years or the duration of the war. Beyond their joy at reaching the end of this commitment, there was much to pull their hearts and minds toward the Highlands. There was near-famine throughout Scotland, particularly in the mountains, and the price of meal was higher than it had ever been. The harvest had been almost destroyed by early and continued frosts. Starvation was common in many glens and there were brutal food riots in the Lowlands. The Lord Justice Clerk, Thomas Miller, said that public unrest was so serious that the King's servants in North Britain were of opinion that all Fencible regiments should not be disbanded until troops of the peace establishment could be garrisoned in Scotland. "The fatal success of the mobs against Papists and Popish chapels," he said, "awakened religious enthusiasm, the most dangerous ingredient in the temper of the people of this country. But the present and immediate cause of the disorders and mobbings, which now prevail in Scotland, is the great scarcity and high prices of corn."

It was natural that soldiers who had not seen their homes and their families for three, four and often five years, should now think of nothing but a return to them, and they justly believed that the Government had no power to prolong their service. But although a great war was ending, a man-consuming fire still burnt in India. There Hyder Ali, the Sultan of Mysore, and his son Tipoo persisted in their struggle against British supremacy, whatever terms their late allies the French might be making. The need to refuel this war with fresh battalions and healthy men was threatened by the nature of the private soldier's enlistment. From the beginning the thought of losing him after three years had been unpopular with most general officers who believed that for the good of the service a man should wear the red coat until his usefulness was destroyed by death, fever, or wounds. Amherst had no doubt of this and had opposed any change, any adoption of foreign practices which could only confuse the minds of honest soldiers.

> Why turn their thoughts to a term of enlistment when it is not at present in their thoughts? Can anyone acquainted with the Army say that the man who enlists with his thoughts turned to the term of his enlistment, enters into the service with equal spirit, and is so likely to make the good soldier as the man who enlists for life? We conquered in the last war with soldiers enlisted for life. It may be a dangerous experiment for this country to attempt an innovation.

The Government's problem at the end of 1782 was distressing. By the imminent signing of a treaty with France and Spain it would be compelled to disband almost all the regiments the Crown had raised for the war. At the same time it was obliged to maintain the conflict against Hyder Ali, to assist the East India

Company, and to defend a capital investment of £18,000,000 in the Indian sub-continent. It could of course have claimed that the war referred to in a soldier's enlistment paper included that against the Mahrattas, but this specious argument was not attempted. Instead, the Government decided to put as many regiments as possible aboard the transports, to hold its breath in the hope that the vessels would be hull down in the Channel before peace became an inconvenient reality.

There was not a time-serving soldier in Britain who did not believe that he would soon be entitled to his discharge. The men of the 77th had also been told by Atholl's recruiters that they would be sent home with honour when the terms of their enlistment allowed. Elsewhere in Hampshire was another Highland regiment of the same mind, the 81st which had been raised by William Gordon, brother of the third Earl of Aberdeen. It was a quarrelsome, sullen battalion, the loyalty of its companies strained by the fact that the Gordon gentry who had enlisted them had passed them back and forth between the 81st and a regiment of fencibles raised by the Duke of Gordon. So strong had been this competition for men that rival bands of recruiters had marched through Huntly lands at night, led by torches and pipers, buying and selling recruits like drovers at a tryst.

On December 14 the commanders of the 77th and the 81st were told to hold their regiments in readiness for foreign service. This order was kept from the men, but the companies were moved about the Hampshire villages at frequent intervals. Most of the men of the 77th were already much closer to Portsmouth than they had been when they came from Bideford, the explanation given by the Deputy-Adjutant-General being that the moves were "to prevent the regiment having so long a march at this time of the year". In the New Year the treaty with France and Spain was still unsigned, and on Tuesday, January 21, the Secretary at War sent Sheelagreen a brief list of the regulations necessary for his battalion while at sea. On the same day another rider delivered the Secretary's instructions to Major-general Francis Smith, deputy-commander at Portsmouth.

I have the honour to acquaint you that orders are this day forwarded by Special Messenger for the 77th Regiment of Foot to march as soon as possible after the receipt of their respective orders, without the normal halting days, to Portsmouth and Portsmouth Common, from whence they are to embark on board the East India ships destined for their reception.

The news that they were to sail for India was made known to the Highlanders the following day. They marched on Friday, the companies converging from their village quarters and proceeding by divisions, the last three companies entering Portsmouth on Saturday morning. They do not appear to have been alarmed or resentful of the orders to embark, nor by the first sight of the Indiamen, bare yards and masts on the winter water. The young and spirited adjutant of the regiment, Lieutenant Patrick Mackenzie, left Andover with his company at dawn on Friday, and he later sent an account of that day and the others following to his friend Charles Stewart, on sick-leave at Garth House.

I think I never saw men march from quarters with more cheerfulness and sobriety in my life than they did, and it was the general concern on the march how they would treat Hyder Ali Can when they should take him prisoner. Nay, even within a few miles of Portsmouth, they expressed their wishes that they might be immediately embarked to escape being quartered in that damned place Portsmouth, as they called it.

When Stewart's nephew David repeated the substance of this in his *Sketches* he tailored it to fit his own belief of what would have been the Highlanders' proper behaviour. "They showed no reluctance to embark," he wrote, "nor any desire to claim their discharge, to which their letters of service entitled them. On the contrary, when they came in sight of the fleet at Spithead, as they marched across Portsmouth Hill, they pulled off their bonnets and gave three cheers for a brush with Hyder Ali." But the two

accounts make it clear that since the treaty of peace had not yet
been finally signed the Highlanders honourably and willingly
accepted a continued call upon their services. At his lodgings in
the High Street, where he had been for thirty-six hours before the
last division marched through the Land Port Gate, Sheelagreen
wrote to Strowan, telling him that forty-one officers and a
thousand men were now quartered in the narrow streets or upon
the Common, and he hoped to have them all aboard the transports
by dusk on Monday. He had spent some time with representatives
of the East India Company and had been assured that everything
needed by the Highlanders would be found aboard the vessels,
including checked shirts and trousers. As he wrote this letter he
already knew what every man of the 77th was to know before
the beating of taptoo that night. Peace was a fact. The Lord
Mayor had received, and made known to the press that afternoon,
a dispatch from the Foreign Secretary informing him that the
preliminary treaty with France and Spain had been signed six
days before. The same express from London brought no cancella-
tion of the embarkation orders. If Gordon was alarmed by the
thought of what this news might do to the temper of his battalion
he did not immediately say so, but he wished that Murray were
there. "If you could, without any great inconvenience to yourself,
in my humble opinion you should come down and see the
regiment, were it but for a day, before our departure, but in that
you are the best judge."

And then, in a postscript, he betrayed his deep unease. He said
that this was a moment of particular crisis. "Though you may
rest assured that I shall do everything in my power to prevent
grumbling, which I apprehend is impossible." He may have
believed, he may have hoped that the trouble coming would be
grumbling only.

"*We are not to be sold by you, nor by General James Murray*"

AT DUSK ON Sunday, when the bells of Saint Thomas were calling above the walled town, two letters were written to Lord George Gordon and left at the Crown Inn for the night coach to London. Both were unsigned, except in the name of the Highlanders of the 77th Regiment, but it was later said that one was composed by a grenadier named Cummings and the other by John Charles, a Lowlander of Strowan's company. That which Gordon made public told him that because the Atholl men were deeply impressed by his exertions on behalf of the religion and liberties of Scotland, they felt bold enough to ask for his help, that justice might be done.

> We are to imbark to-morrow; but there is every appearance at present of a desperate resistance being made by the men. How it will end, time alone must determine. We assure your Lordship, that we were never so much as informed of any such intention till last Wednesday, that we got the route from Andover to this place; and notwithstanding peace being signed, we have received fresh orders for imbarkation to-morrow morning at ten o'clock. We beg leave to assure your Lordship, that we entirely depend upon your interposition and support at this time.

The impression which George Gordon has left upon history, with the unsympathetic assistance of Charles Dickens, is that of an obsessed zealot, an anti-Catholic bigot whose rabble-rousing was principally responsible for a week of bloody riot in June 1780, the storming of Newgate Prison, an assault on the House of

Commons, and the killing of several thousand Londoners. This
monstrous chimera, which eventually frightened him more than
it did others, obscures a young man whom William Hickey
described as gay, volatile and elegant, with the most affable and
engaging manners. The sincerity of his religious convictions was
always reinforced by political ambition, and he was ruined by the
ferocity of both, but his extraordinary charm, his power to
express a nation's ignorant fear in explosive if sometimes confused
language, made him the accepted champion of such diverse
peoples as the London mob, Gaelic Highlanders, and austere kirk
folk of the Galloway hills. The ironies in his character and life
were many, not the least being that so violent a Protestant should
come from a ducal family of past Catholic or Episcopalian
persuasion, that it should be his sister's husband, an officer of the
Guards, who was the first to order volley-firing upon the rioters
who cried his name and wore the blue cockade of his cause. His
affection for the people of the Highlands was sentimental and
romantic, and only a little less sincere than their emotional
response to it. As a midshipman in the Navy he had spent some
time in the Hebrides where he learnt to speak Gaelic and to play
the pipes, to dance a reel lightly and to sing a love-song with
affecting grace. He wore tartan trews wherever possible, even in
the Palace of Westminster, and when he campaigned for Inverness
against General Simon Fraser he spent most of his time among the
common people, none of whom had the power of a single vote.
He emptied his purse to hold a great ball, sending his yacht to
Skye for fifteen of Clan MacLeod's most beautiful girls, and his
popularity eventually alarmed his opponent. The great houses of
Gordon and Fraser wisely conferred, and the General agreed that
if he were allowed to have the Inverness seat he would buy Lord
George a pocket-borough in Wiltshire.

The young man came to Parliament as the leader of Protestant
liberty, condemning the war against the Americans, opposing the
Catholic emancipation bill, declaring that the people of Scotland
were naked before the agents of Popery, one of whom, he said,
was believed to be the King himself. His house in Welbeck Street

was open to any Scot, and regardless of rank or station each was
gravely and politely welcomed at the door by John MacQueen, a
Skye man who was Gordon's loyal servant and friend. What
arguable future this strange demagogue might have had was
washed away in the tidal blood of the riots, and his guilt was not
removed by his acquittal on a charge of high treason. He was now
a long-haired, wild-eyed ghost, walking in mourning-clothes
along the edge of sanity. Although he had been terrified by the
angry brute he had aroused in ignorant minds, and had thrown
away his blue riband before the riots were over, he knew that he
was still trusted by many men in both kingdoms, and perhaps
hoped for political advancement therefrom. The letters he
received from Portsmouth, however, were more than evidence of
Highlanders' continuing attachment: they offered him an opportunity for personal revenge against the Colonel of the 77th.
When the mob came to the door of the Commons James Murray
of Strowan had rested the point of his sword on Gordon's breast,
declaring that if one of the rogues got into the building he would
take pleasure in passing the blade through his lordship's body.
Forced to apologise on his knees before the Speaker, Murray had
underlined the threat with a contemptuous insult. As he arose,
delicately dusting his breeches with a handkerchief, he looked at
Gordon and said, "Damned dirty House this. The sooner it's
cleaned the better."

Lord George's response to their appeal was not what the Atholl
men may have hoped. He sent a copy of one of the letters to the
King's first minister, Lord Shelburne, but he did not protest
against the injustice that was being done, he did not demand that
the soldiers should be discharged as the terms of their enlistment
required. He clearly saw an opportunity to place the administration in his debt, to confound Murray's arrogance by removing
or encouraging disorder in the Colonel's regiment. He told
Shelburne that since the men of the 77th had such a good opinion
of him he was ready to put himself at the disposal of the Cabinet,
to leave at once for Portsmouth, to send a letter, a verbal message
by his man, "or do anything that is just, and fair, and honourable".

He was curtly thanked and told that His Majesty's ministers were
taking every measure that was necessary. This cold rebuff was
perhaps expected, for John MacQueen had already left on the
Portsmouth coach from the General Post Office. When he
alighted at the Crown, seventy-three miles later, the mutiny was
three days old.

> The twenty-seventh of January,
> The year seventeen hundred and eighty-three
> The Highland boys would not agree
>   To ship for Colonel Gordon!
>
> Charley are you waking yet?
> Or are you sleeping? I would wait.
> The Highland drums to arms do beat,
> Will you go on board this morning?

The first indication of the grumbling expected by Sheelagreen
had come on Sunday morning, when some of his officers reported
their servants' gossip. "The men are talking that they ought to
be discharged now that peace is signed." He believed that he
would be able to bring them to order at the morning parade, to
subdue or satisfy their doubts, to persuade them to embark
without protest on Monday. The wooden drums called a sonorous
assembly fifteen minutes before noon, three green-coat men
standing before the Market House in the High Street. The
Highlanders came dutifully from their quarters and as the orders
of the night required, each man neatly dressed and armed. To
their front on the wide parade was the Main Guard and the sea-
wall, the heavy cannon on the saluting-platform. As they took
their dressing, looking to their right through fitful bursts of rain,
they could see the top-masts of the Indiamen in the northern
harbour, lying between Gosport and the Gun Wharfe. When
his company commanders had reported, Sheelagreen walked
along the line from the grenadiers on the right to his own men
on the left, repeating the same, short unemotional words to each
of the ten companies. They would parade again at nine o'clock
the next morning, ready to go aboard the ships' boats at the

Victualling Key, every man with musket, bayonet, pouch and knapsack. From their former good behaviour he had no doubt that they would maintain the high standards that had always distinguished the Duke of Atholl's Highlanders and he hoped that no man would be absent, that none would be the worse for drink. They should not be afraid of going to India, he had soldiered there himself and knew it to be a good service in a good climate. He said nothing of the terms of their enlistment or the recent treaty of peace. The companies listened to him silently and without movement, but Patrick Mackenzie saw the discontent in many faces, particularly among the grenadiers.

The Highlanders were left to themselves until the next day, except those marked down for the main guard and the inlying picquet. Although rain was now falling steadily, few of the men returned to their quarters. "They were frequently seen in small numbers," Mackenzie told Charles Stewart, "at the corners of streets and lanes consulting, but I cannot learn that one of them on that day spoke a word to any of their own officers." As always, civilians were blamed for this black and hostile mood. Mackenzie said that the inhabitants of Portsmouth told the Highlanders that they should not embark, that they had been betrayed, that their officers would not go to India with them. "Nay, before my face the people had the assurance to tell them these circumstances, which they being willing to believe had more effect than my rhetoric." He and other subalterns bravely remained in the streets throughout the day, hopefully believing that by their calm presence they would quieten the soldiers' discontent. At dusk it was bitterly cold, a rising gale blew salt spume and cutting sleet over the sea-wall and into the town, but still the Highlanders did not return to their quarters. They pulled their plaids about their shoulders and stood in dark clumps at tavern-doors and lane-heads. Atholl historians, anxious to protect the myths they were perpetuating, said that the Lowlanders in the regiment were responsible for the mutiny, and some of the officers supported this claim at the time, naming men of Fife, Lanark, Ayr and Stirling as the principal ringleaders. They were reluctant to believe that their clansmen could turn against them, for this would be to admit a lack of the love, the trust and the loyalty that supported their own pretensions. It is true that Lowlanders in the grenadier company gave the mutiny an English voice and some were more violent when the physical struggle came, but the revolt was almost unanimous, and by definition a Highland-man could not give blind obedience to or accept the unquestioned leadership of common men from beyond the hills.

In this desire to find a reason for the mutiny that did not admit the Highlanders' justified sense of betrayal, many of the officers also said that the soldiers were pot-valiant only. There was indeed much drinking that long and idle Sunday, and was perhaps necessary to give desperate men the courage to risk the lash and the firing-squad, but only the protective prejudice of rank and class could think it more reprehensible than the cynical dishonesty the men were challenging. Once that day was past, that challenge irrevocably made, there would be little or no drinking. When Strowan wrote his report however, upon information given by his officers, he said that by Sunday evening many of the soldiers were drunk and riotous, prowling the dark streets

. . . looking for their officers to obtain money; some under pretext of sending their wives home, others to purchase necessaries for the voyage, but it has since too plainly appeared all with a view to get liquor, altho' they cloaked all their pretentions under the specious demands of the several balances due to them, which were paid to the greater number.

Murray did not think much of the soldiers' claim that they should now be discharged, saying that it was the result of "advice given them by the lower class of inhabitants". The words of his report are not those of Garth's hero, loved and loving as a father, but they do show the sad confusion in the Highlanders' minds, a determination to resist embarkation if they could, a need to care for families whose existence was officially ignored and who must be left behind should the regiment be forced aboard. Young officers like Mackenzie who were still abroad at nightfall gave the men what money they could from their own purses, believing that they were perhaps being duped but hoping that the payments would be enough to lower the temperature of revolt. When there was no more money the subalterns promised the soldiers "that every farthing due would be paid the moment they set foot on board of ship". It was an old promise, and it was not believed.

Sheelagreen was not in the city, having ridden through the Land Port Gate at three o'clock to dine at the General's house two miles along the London road. He and Smith were pleasantly at ease when they were told that six Highlanders were at the door, humbly asking for the General. Smith went to them in an ill-temper, angered by this insolent breach of regulations. The English-speaker who led the deputation was a man called Mitchell of Captain William Morrison's company. Another, who had been enlisted by Lieutenant James Graham of Fintry, gave the General a worn and creased leaflet which he had kept in his sporran for four years. It declared that all men whom Fintry recruited would have their discharge in three years or at the end of the war. A third man produced an advertisement from a Dundee journal, announcing the same promises in Atholl's name. As Smith stared with distaste at these thumb-greased papers Mitchell asked him whether he agreed with the soldiers of the 77th that such assurances entitled them to their discharge, that they should not now be embarked for India. Smith's reply was explosively short. The war was *not* over, he said, and in his opinion they could be and would be sent wherever the King desired. He then returned to his interrupted dinner, and the deputation walked back through the rain to Portsmouth. Smith's lie had been foolish and calamitous. At another time, at an hour less affected by good port and civil company, he might have been more cautious. He was only the deputy-commander of the Portsmouth area, acting in the absence of Lord George Lennox then in London, and like many men in such a temporary position his conceit exceeded his good sense. He also failed to understand

the peculiar temperament of these men who had stood politely
at his door in their wet plaids, asking for his protection.

> Were it to fight 'gainst France and Spain,
> We would with pleasure cross the main,
> But like bullocks to be sold for gain,
>   Our Highland blood abhors it!

When Sheelagreen returned to his lodgings in Portsmouth he
reluctantly approved the advances which his subalterns had made
to the men, but he told the paymaster John Farquharson to make
out a correct list of arrears, that it might be known which
scoundrel had or had not made a just demand. That done, he
retired to bed and did no more. The Highlanders had a long
night to decide what they must do. The letters to Lord George
Gordon had already been left at the Crown and now, in tavern-
smoke or a tallow-lit room, a third letter was written. It was
found at Sheelagreen's door and taken to him before he rose for
breakfast.

To Colonel Gordon, Lying at Portsmouth
Atholl Highlanders

Colonel Gordon,—This comes to let you know that if you
come in front of the Regiment to-morrow that you will
certainly be killed, as we sent to the Commander in Chieff of
His Majesty's forces in England and that he told us if we was
so great fools as to go aboard we might, but you cannot
compel us to it. As we only listed for three years or during
the American War, as our Bargain, we will assure you that
we will stand to it as long as we can. You need not doubt but
we will do for you if we go, and before we go. We are not
to be sold by you, nor by General James Murray, nor by any
treachrous vilans such as you are, for none but such treachrous
vilans as you would do so.

Sheelagreen dismissed the letter with brave contempt. The
Commander-in-Chief to whom it referred was Henry Seymour

Conway, a versifying veteran who had represented almost as many pocket-boroughs in Parliament as he had served in battles since he first wore a cornet's sash at Dettingen. He was hot-tempered and theatrically emotional. During the Gordon Riots he had seized Lord George by the collar and shouted, "I am a military man and I shall protect the freedom of debate with my sword! Do not imagine that we will be intimidated by a rabble!" That such a man would correspond with private soldiers in the manner suggested was impossible, and the pathetic absurdity of the boast encouraged Sheelagreen to ignore the anonymous threat, to believe it to be the work of one infamous man only, or even a civilian.

Sunrise on Monday was hidden by low-bellied clouds. Heavy rain darkened the cream-stone houses about the Main Parade and moved in shuddering curtains across the cobbles. A high tide was running, a gale-force wind lifting the waves to the embrasures of the saluting-platform, and since no boats could reach the Indiamen, Sheelagreen postponed the hour of assembly until noon. His grateful officers sat down to a late breakfast at ten but were almost immediately aroused by the news that some of the Highlanders had broken into the guard-house, releasing three soldiers held in the Black Hole. The junior officers ran into the High Street, looping their sword-belts over their shoulders and standing in line to face more than two hundred men who were marching up the street with the prisoners on their shoulders. When the subalterns were joined by Sheelagreen and Robert Stuart they advanced boldly on the mob and seized the prisoners. Patrick Mackenzie, who joined in the struggle with spirited enthusiasm, said that as well as insults several half-bricks were thrown at Sheelagreen, although whether by civilians or soldiers he could not say. The prisoners were returned to the guard-house and what might have become a bloody mobbing curiously subsided into a shouting, swearing argument. "The Colonel, Sir Robert and the officers endeavoured then to explain to them their mistake, and to pacify them, but they were too drunk, too clamourous and self-sufficient to hear or be convinced."

The soldiers dispersed noisily, but now Sheelagreen was alarmed and decided not to insist upon embarkation that day. "If it could not be accomplished by fair means," he later explained to Strowan, "and to await the determination of the Government on the business." He should therefore have cancelled the parade he had ordered but he did not, unsure of his power to do so. Instead he sent Stuart to General Smith, to report what had happened and to ask for further orders. The rain stopped and the wind fell as noon approached, but Stuart did not return. Fifteen minutes before mid-day three companies assembled on the open square before the saluting-platform, the grenadiers, Charles Murray's, and a third captained by John Balneavis of Cairnbeddie. The seven others gathered outside their quarters in the town or on the Common beyond the Land Port, as was the custom before all marched to the grand parade. Patrick Mackenzie watched from the wind-break of the Main Guard with his brother Alexander, the regimental chaplain, waiting for the drum-tap that would call the first three companies to their markers and oblige him to dress their ranks as adjutant. He thought that many of the soldiers were still drunk, particularly the grenadiers and some of the men commanded by his friend Balneavis, and those few who dutifully brought their knapsacks had the slings cut immediately by their angry comrades. Officers and men faced each other uneasily across the wet stones, the drummer looked to Sheelagreen for the order to beat, and he stared toward the head of the High Street, hoping for Robert Stuart's reassuring appearance. When he was at last asked what should be done he said that he would speak to the battalion, company by company when it was fully assembled, that he would say there was to be no embarkation, that any soldier who had a just grievance should place it before his captain in a soldier-like manner. There could be no further delay. The drums of the other companies were beating in the town, from Colewort Barracks to the Old Armoury, and soon they would be marching to the main parade. Sheelagreen asked his officers to move to their places. It may have occurred to some of them, as they raised their bonnets in salute and walked away, that nothing Gordon could now say would be believed by their men.

> The Highland boys did him deny,
> Said "We will fight until we die,
> But you and Murray we defy,
>   We'll comb your hair this morning!"

"Parading by hundreds in the streets, beating to arms"

THE YOUNG DRUMMER raised his sticks in line, buttons to his lips.
He held time in suspension for five seconds and then brought the
woods down upon the skin in the brisk *tow-row-dow* of the
Troop. The three companies fell in upon their markers without
hesitation, although there was some muttering as they came
forward. Sheelagreen ignored this hostile growl, and now that
his officers had gone to their company positions he stood alone
before the parade. In the shelter of the Main Guard, Chaplain
Mackenzie watched with pride as his young brother Patrick
dressed the ranks, first the grenadiers and then Balneavis's
company. In the Adjutant's opinion he had never before done
this so well, nor had his orders been more willingly obeyed; and
for a brief moment his spirits rose with the thought that there was
to be no trouble after all. But as he moved on to the third company
this euphoria was abruptly ended. "I went to the left of the
grenadiers," he told Stewart, "and was standing with Robert
Ferguson the right of Balneavis's (where, by the by, it is likely
you would have been had you been with us) when I observed a
flash of pan near the right of the grenadiers."

Once dressed and steady in line the grenadiers had not moved,
but angry voices cried from the second and the third ranks. They
would not go aboard the transports. They had been sold like
bullocks to the Indies. Sheelagreen could not let any further
insolence go unchecked and to his martinet's mind the irregularity
of the noise was more insufferable than the meaning of the words.
"For shame, grenadiers!" he called, "Be quiet in the ranks!"
This mild reprimand, or its apparent indifference to the cause of

the discontent, destroyed the discipline he hoped to maintain. A young soldier, John Robertson, stepped from the right of the front rank, raised his piece and shouted "By God, I'll shoot you!" The pan flashed and the musket misfired, but there was a responsive yell from the rest of the company. It wheeled upon its left-flank marker, for a moment in perfect order and then closing about Gordon like a fist. Balneavis' men broke almost immediately, running past Patrick Mackenzie to join the grenadiers, and within seconds the third company turned upon its officers. "I saw Captain Murray in the rear of his company after being knocked down," said Mackenzie. "I run to his assistance and by the time I got to him he was forced off by some of his well-wishers from the parade." Charles Murray's officers made a short and ineffectual attempt to calm their men and then ran, to the narrow entrance of Governor's Green or down Great Penny Street, pursued by shouting Highlanders and hurrahed by delighted civilians.

Sheelagreen had bravely stood his ground, without drawing his sword or raising a defensive arm. He saw the approach of impassioned faces and flowing plaids, heard the threats to comb his hair, felt spittle on his face, and was then overwhelmed. Robertson swung his musket by the barrel but another grenadier, Alexander Milroy, pushed him aside and knocked Gordon to the ground with a forward butt-stroke. As he fell he was hit again on the head and shoulders by George Carlow and Robertson. "How shocking the next thing that catch'd my eye," said Mackenzie, "the Colonel in the midst of the Grenadiers, upon both his knees with his hands over his head and his face covered with blood." Gordon would undoubtedly have been clubbed to death in a few seconds had not one of Balneavis' men, an old soldier, John Grant, bent over him to take some of the blows on his own back. The Chaplain also thrust his way to Sheelagreen, taking a glancing musket-blow from the enraged Robertson. Coming to his brother's help with a shout of anger, Patrick Mackenzie was immediately knocked down. He took Gordon in his arms protectively and was then struck four or five times on the head and shoulders. He fell on his face, almost insensible, seeing nothing but the cobbles enamelled with his blood. Paymaster Farquharson now came into the fight, roaring a protest. He was a huge man affectionately known as Big John, and it was his popularity as much as his flailing arms that enabled him to clear a space about Sheelagreen. In the moment's pause, John Grant and another soldier dragged Gordon out of the mob and across the ground toward the security of the Main Guard. When some of the Highlanders fixed their bayonets and turned to follow, Farquharson stepped before them, shouting to them in Gaelic and calling them rogues and cowards. The small regard they had for him was soon exhausted and they reversed their muskets, striking him on the head and shoulders, but although his face was masked by blood he did not fall. On the ground below the Paymasters' straddled legs, Patrick Mackenzie struggled to rise. He saw nothing but was suddenly aware that he was being pulled away. At the head of the High Street he wiped the blood and mud from his face and looked up. His rescuers were the drum-major, Sergeant Dewar, and a private soldier of the grenadiers who "though he assisted me, is a great mutineer".

Farquharson now ran, half-blinded and stumbling in pain but reaching the High Street some strides ahead of his pursuers. There he blundered into men of his own company whose names and faces he could not remember but who carried him to a shuttered building on the corner, beating on its door until it was opened and then thrusting him inside. The terrified shopkeeper locked the door again and took Lieutenant Farquharson to a back room, begging him to leave before the mutineers broke in and murdered them both. The Paymaster took off his bonnet, wiped his bloody face, and covered his uniform with a coachman's great-coat. He climbed the garden wall to Saint Thomas's Street and walked boldly to the Town Key where a boatman rowed him across the harbour to Gosport.

Sergeant Dewar had left Patrick Mackenzie at the door of another shop in the High Street, swearing to throttle the owner if he did not give the adjutant shelter. From the window of a garret to which he was reluctantly taken Mackenzie looked down upon the bonnets of cheering mutineers, the flash and smoke of their joyous musketry, and Sheelagreen's feathered cap held high in triumph. He stayed in the attic until they were gone, until he was joined by Sergeant Murdoch of his own company, and together they left the house. They were seen at the head of Fighting Cock Lane, were called upon to stand and die but ran down Lombard Street to the Key, falling into a boat some yards ahead of the first skirling Highlanders. Mackenzie was unconscious when the boat reached the jetty at Gosport, and it was five days before he felt able to stand upon his feet.

John Grant had not thrown the last bolt of the Main Guard door before the mutineers were hammering on it with fists and muskets, firing into the thick wood or stabbing it with their bayonets. They swore at Sheelagreen for a coward, telling him to come out and face the men he would have sold to the Indies. He pulled himself to his feet, bitter with humiliation and pain. From the distant shots and angry cries he knew that the other companies had also mutinied. "I was determined," he later told Strowan, "to sell my life as dear as I could, but finding they were firing in the town, and the very small probability of our being able to prevent them from breaking in, I thought of an expedient." There was more desperation than cunning in this device. Someone must go outside, someone who would tell the mutineers that he was dying and no longer worth their attention. The Garrison Guard that day was supplied by the 41st Regiment of Invalids, and its commander was an old officer with one leg. Upon his own suggestion, or upon Gordon's orders, he limped through the quickly opened door and had time enough to shout the message before he was thrown aside on a heap of builder's lime. He would have been smothered had not some of the Highlanders pulled him free, regretting this rough treatment of a disabled veteran with whom they had no quarrel. What he had said was momentarily believed and the grenadiers turned away toward Great Penny Street, calling upon all officers to come out of hiding, to surrender their lives like brave men. In the silence Gordon hurriedly pulled off his red coatee and trews, dressing himself in the blue and scarlet uniform of an Invalid. He was then taken from the Main Guard and across the parade, half carried in John Grant's arms and unable to see for the blood that still ran from his head. In the High Street he was recognised by Sergeant Dewar who took him into a coffee-house where he once more collapsed.

Dewar told Grant to find Sheelagreen some other clothes, to bring him to the Point where the sergeant hoped to have a boat waiting. Left alone with his commander, Grant gently washed Gordon's face and dressed him in a sailor's jacket and trousers supplied by the owner of the house. With some of his strength if not all of his wits restored, Sheelagreen said he would go alone to the Point. He pulled a knitted cap over his bloody head and walked out to the parade-ground. There was no one between the High Street and Saint James's Gate two hundred yards away, but to his left a dozen shouting grenadiers were returning to the Main Guard with bayonets fixed. He ignored them until they called to him and then he boldly halted, lifting a hand in greeting. They wanted to brag. They said that if their damned rogue of a colonel were not done with dying they would finish the work for him. He waved again, went through the Gate and over the bridge to the Point, quickening his pace but taking the narrow lane past the Round Tower until he could turn right to the Victualling Key. There he found the loyal drum-major, a bright-eyed midshipman, and a man-of-war's boat, its white oars lifted above the tarpaulin hats of its crew. Once in the boat, his head supported by Dewar, he lost consciousness. He was rowed past the black and white walls of the Indiamen to Gosport where the midshipman took him to Haslar Hospital, to the lodgings of its physician Doctor Lind.

The four companies that had paraded on the Common beyond the Land Port made no attempt to join the mutiny, and when dismissed they returned quietly to their tented quarters. On open ground they were exposed to any attack by mounted troops from Hilsea Barracks, three miles to the north on the neck of Portsea Island, but their sympathies were with the Highlanders in the town. "Had they been there," said Mackenzie with contempt, "they might have probably been as busy as the others." Within the walls no officer was to be seen. Some had left by boat from the Point or the Town Key, others were hiding where they could in back rooms or attics. "The soldiers now grew perfectly outrageous," said Strowan's report, "searching every public house for their officers, to put them to death, and parading by hundreds in the streets, beating to arms, and carrying the Colonel's bonnet upon a bayonet as a trophy of their victory." They broke into the regimental store by the Main Guard, taking broadswords and ball cartridges, firing volleys into the air. When Sir Robert Stuart rode to the bridge of the North Bastion shortly before three o'clock he heard these distant shots and the wild rant of Garth's young pipers, the throb of drums sounding every call from the Point of War to the Chamade. General Smith's indecision had delayed the Major's return and no one recorded the orders he had finally given in response to Sheelagreen's appeal, nor might they have made any difference. There was a young officer of the light company outside the Bastion, angry tears in his eyes, and when he had told Stuart all he could the Major returned at once to Smith.

The General was even more incapable now of resolute thought, and the best his addled mind could suggest was that Stuart should ride into the town in the hope or restoring order. This the Major bravely did, coming through the Land Port Gate at four o'clock and halting his horse by the Market House in the High Street. He was at once surrounded by mutineers, bayonets swaying above their black bonnets, but they greeted him civilly and listened politely when he told them that they would not be sent aboard, that the naval commander of Portsmouth, Sir Thomas Pye, had said he would embark no man who was not willing to sail. Stuart had no authority to make this promise, although he may have sincerely believed it would be honoured. Admiral Pye was a man of meagre abilities who had been advanced by political interest rather than by blue-water service, and the future of his satisfying career was now threatened by the crews of three line-of-battle

ships under orders to escort the Indiamen. The sailors were ready
to mutiny if they were not given their discharge, and the Admiral
undoubtedly felt that he had trouble enough in the fleet without
shipping redcoats of a like mind. The Atholl men thanked Stuart
for his assurance but refused to lay down their arms until they had
a similar promise from the Commander-in-Chief. He rode back
to Smith in a rising temper, and he might have been more angry
had he known that the Highlanders now thought of him as an
ally.

> Our Major, like a soldier bold,
> He said, "My lads, you shan't be sold,
> For of your hand I'll take a hold
> And bring you off this morning!"

The Lord Mayor of Portsmouth, Sir John Carter, was stouter
in heart than Smith, and since the King's officers seemed unable
to protect his citizens or cleanse his streets of riot and mobbing
he decided to do so himself. Before Stuart was gone the commander of the 41st Invalids was asked to assemble his aging
veterans and march them against the Highlanders. They came to
the parade-ground in good spirits, advancing upon the Main
Guard with bayonets fixed until they were stopped by sudden
shots, by the ragged flash of musketry in the falling dusk. The
firing was perhaps intended as a warning, but it wounded two
men and killed a third, and the Invalids wisely withdrew. The
loss of a life that had survived more desperate actions against
the King's enemies deeply distressed the Highlanders, and their
response to it was impulsive and emotional. Earlier that day
they had struggled among themselves to crush the skull of
Sheelagreen. Now they wept for an old soldier, and that night
they opened a fund for his widow to which every man of the
regiment eventually subscribed what he could.

Early on Tuesday morning some of the junior officers came
into the town, cautiously and in hope of bringing the men to
order. They were not molested and they were told that the
companies would willingly parade for inspection and drill, but

no man would go aboard and none would leave Portsmouth until
he had been assured of his discharge. Some of the grenadiers were
still drunk, the subalterns told Stuart, but the rest were sober and
civil, their uniforms clean and their arms bright. All of them were
full of hatred for Murray and Sheelagreen, and vastly disappointed
to hear that Gordon was not dead. Mackenzie thought this sobriety was due to lack of opportunity. "When the inhabitants
found that the men's money was done, they had no more liquor."
But the people of Portsmouth had also realised that the Highlanders' quarrel was with their officers only, and providing they
were not provoked the town was in no danger. Like an audience
encouraged by a spirited first act, the citizens now awaited the
rest of the melodrama with confident expectation. In the absence
of orders from London all responsibility rested upon General
Francis Smith, and he was still in suspended animation, leaving
matters to Providence or Robert Stuart.

Half an hour before noon the Major rode into Portsmouth
with two captains, Charles Murray and James Menzies of Inver-
gowrie, the former with courage since the mutineers had been
intent on killing him twenty-four hours before. The companies
were all assembled on the parade, falling in upon their markers
and accepting their dressing with willing enthusiasm. They
listened politely when Stuart repeated the promise he had given
on Monday. This time he called upon some of the men by name
and they answered him honestly, but with a bluntness he foolishly
thought was insolence. They said they were sorry for their
behaviour, but it had been forced upon them and if they were
ordered to embark they must again resist. They demanded their
subsistence, the sevenpence to which each man was daily entitled
for bread, meat and small beer. He gave it to them. He said later
that he had no doubt the money would again be spent on
spirituous waters, but he did not explain how, in the absence
of any looting, they were thus supplying themselves with
food. Strowan's report confirmed this prevailing suspicion.
"Toward evening a number of them were very much in liquor
. . . which made it absolutely necessary for every officer and non-

commissioned officer not concerned to keep out of the way for fear of being insulted." On Wednesday morning the companies once more paraded before Stuart and the captains. Many men came as before with muskets loaded and primed, but none was drunk and all obeyed their orders without insolence. This day Stuart walked among the ranks as the pay-sergeants distributed the subsistence. He spoke in comradely friendship, placing a hand upon one man's shoulder, another's arm. He said that James Murray had now come from London and all would be for the best, that their General would permit none of his brave lads to be forced aboard. He was shocked to discover that they did not wish to see Strowan. "Their answer was that they were glad he did not make his appearance, as they could by no means say what they would do in such an event." When the parade was dismissed, and before he left the town, his sergeants told him that the men were exulting in their triumph, boasting that they would be happy to kill Murray if he came among them.

The newspapers said that Atholl had also arrived from London, but if so he remained discreetly outside the town, making no attempt to end the mutiny and risking nothing that might bring him the distinction of being the first Highland chief to be killed by his own people. James Murray had left London by coach on Tuesday, upon the prompting of the Government and his own outraged pride. The weather was rain-whipped and stormy, the roads rutted and water-logged from Putney Heath to Petersfield where he was forced to spend the night upright in a tavern bed and kept awake by pain and anger. He was on the road again long before dawn on Wednesday, travelling by Horndean and Cosham and with as much haste as the foul weather and roads permitted. He reached Smith's house at seven o'clock, pausing only for a hot drink and for any fresh news before going on to the Land Port Gate. There, at eight o'clock, he found Stuart and some of the company commanders, miserably sheltering from the morning rain. They strongly advised him against entering the town where "the mutineers would certainly tear you to pieces". This information was a great shock to his self-conceit and momentarily robbed him of decision. He made no protest when Stuart took him north about the town to the Gun Wharfe, to a boat for Gosport. Once across the harbour he talked to Sheelagreen and to other officers. "The poor General," said Mackenzie, "is indeed vastly distressed on account of the villains' behaviour, and I think it has added half a score years to his looks." That night Strowan wrote his report to London and confessed himself at a loss to explain the reasons for this wanton mutiny, the ferocity of a hatred that desired his death and Sheelagreen's. The Government must be the best judge of the proper steps to be taken, but as the mutinous spirit was general throughout his regiment some good might be done if the Highlanders' fear of embarkation were removed, if they could be withdrawn from Portsmouth and dispersed about the country. He did not say how this might be done, nor did he suggest that the men's demand for their discharge was justified. Like Lord Frederick Campbell three years before, he wanted to draw them from their position of strength, to isolate and punish the most guilty.

> The Ringleaders are many, and are well known by their officers, and so soon as the Regiment can be disarmed there is little doubt that, very severe examples being made will have the good effect of bringing back the rest to that discipline and sense of their duty which as soldiers they have ever been taught to observe, altho' upon this unfortunate occasion they have in so conspicuous a manner laid aside.

While Murray sat at Sheelagreen's sickbed, debating how the Highland cat might be belled, and Gordon swore that he would never again go before such rebellious rogues as their Lieutenant-colonel, General Smith emerged from cataleptic inanimation and made two attempts to end the mutiny by force. His first proposal was that the Artillerymen in the town should be ordered to turn the rampart guns upon the Main Guard when the Highlanders came to parade. This bloody suggestion was wisely abandoned, for even had the cannon been capable of such an unintended bearing the effect of their fire would have been disastrous upon citizens as well as mutineers. Smith then called up an English marching-regiment from Hampshire and sent it against the Land Port Gate with drums beating and colours advanced, but the men of the 77th drew up the bridge, mounted the wall and held it in calm defiance until Smith was persuaded that an assault would be no less murderous than his first brave proposal.

The Highlanders were now left to themselves, in virtual occupation of the town but willing and ready to parade, to mount guards and picquets, to accept all orders given nightly at Retreat except those which obliged them to go aboard the Indiamen. The paradox of their civil and courteous behaviour defused their officers' angry frustration. They held Portsmouth like a garrison under siege, ready to resist force if it were sent against them, but placing their weapons and ammunition in the Armoury and mounting a guard upon them. There was now no drunkenness, and they treated the citizens with respect. "The whole regiment have conducted themselves with a regularity that is surprising," wrote a correspondent to the Scots Magazine, "for what might not have been expected from upward a thousand let loose from all restraint?" They came in honour to the burial of the Invalid they had killed, and many of them again wept as the coffin was lowered into its grave. Every morning they assembled before the Main Guard, their uniforms clean and their cheeks freshly shaven, admitting the Deputy-Adjutant and any captain who wished to put them through their drill and exercises. The officers hated this docility, believing it to be excessively insolent, but accepting it because it at least gave them a tenuous hold on the mutiny. Even captains who had been pursued with murderous intent on Monday were now saluted with respect when they came to evening Roll Call, standing with empty authority before their companies.

News of the triumphant mutiny had been carried to all the regiments quartered in the county, Scots and English, and they became increasingly hostile to their officers. As the same insolent spirit spread to the men-of-war at Spithead, Sir Thomas Pye was more alarmed by the thought of a naval mutiny than he ever was by the revolt of the 77th. Once taken by its crew, a line-of-battle ship was a floating mine, and he could see his whole career disintegrated by a subsequent chain-explosion throughout the fleet, but his reaction to the situation seems to have been a compound of masterly indecision and pious hope. Some men of the 81st Highlanders had been embarked upon an Indiamen before the 77th arrived in Portsmouth, and when the bumboat-women brought news of the mutiny they noisily demanded to be set ashore. The captain of the transport was naturally reluctant to have his white holystoned decks turned into a battleground, and against the protests of the Gordon officers he quickly sent the Highlanders where they wished. They marched behind a piper to the Hampshire villages in which the rest of the companies were quartered, and by nightfall the whole regiment resolutely declared that it would not embark for India, that it would have its discharge as the law and common justice required. Men of the 68th, an English regiment already embarked for the West Indies and lying out to sea, loaded their muskets and forced the crews to get the ships under way for the harbour. A frigate captain fired across the bows of the transports and stopped all but one which ran in to South Beach. There the cheering soldiers were ferried ashore, but their landing coincided with the arrival from London of Lord George Lennox. He took power and decision from Smith's irresolute hands and ordered a squadron of dragoons to mount and ride. Before dusk every man of the 68th was a prisoner at Hilsea.

Lennox would perhaps have wished to act against the 77th with the same speed and success, but the Commander-in-Chief had ordered him to treat with the mutineers, to read them a letter in which Conway assured them "that no force whatever will be used to make you embark contrary to your engagements". Before Lennox could do this, before he could be assured that a general officer could go before the Highlanders without provoking another outburst of violence, he had to restrain Strowan's renewed desire to bring the regiment to order by the force of his own personality. Murray proposed to do this at the

morning parade on Friday but was stopped by a tart letter from
Lennox who had no doubt that Strowan's life would still be at
risk if he went into the town. At last the Forester of Atholl
swallowed the bitter fact that he could no longer inspire the
loyalty of the men he had raised, and he stiffly accepted Lennox's
advice. Like Sheelagreen, he turned his back with contempt. If
he could do no good in Portsmouth

> ... neither do I think that I could with any propriety be seen
> as their Colonel until the soldiers become sensible of their
> late improper behaviour and of the falsity representing my
> having sold them to the East India Company. So soon as they
> come to this wished for disposition, I should hope my presence
> on the Parade, instead of being attended with any circum-
> stances of disrespect, ought to be at their special desire. I make
> no doubt your Lordship will agree with me in opinion that
> it would be letting down the service for the Colonel ever to
> appear there on any other terms.

Captain Menzies read Conway's letter at Retreat on Friday,
or at morning parade on Saturday. The mutineers thanked him
for it and said that they believed the Commander-in-Chief
wished them well, but the promise that they would not be
embarked against their will was only a part of what they
demanded. They had as yet received no assurance that their
enlistment was over, that they could now march homeward to
their glens. Encouraged by John MacQueen, who attended their
parades and sat with them in their quarters, they believed that
Lord George Gordon was pleading their cause in London and
would soon send word that he had won all they desired. The
Skye man sent daily letters to his master, and occasionally rode
out of town to posting-houses as far as Guildford to make sure
that they were not being taken from the mail-coaches by agents
of the Government. The mutiny was now a public spectacle, a
bold humiliation of an increasingly unpopular administration,
more effective than the best of political squibs. "The inns of
Portsmouth are full of company from London," said the *Morning*

Chronicle, "and the country people from Sussex and twenty miles round flock in to see the Highlanders." On Sunday these visitors lined the streets to cheer the companies as they marched to church. It was said that the soldiers prayed with great humility and devotion, but their armed sentinels stood at the door of the church or walked among the leaning headstones of the little graveyard.

"Their perseverance originates in moral obligation"

ON WEDNESDAY, AS James Murray was rowed across the harbour
to the humiliating security of Gosport, the aged member for
Lincoln, Robert Vyner, rose in the Commons to say that while
he did not know all the circumstances the information he had
received from Portsmouth persuaded him that the protest of the
Highlanders was in some measure justified. If they had indeed
been enlisted upon the terms they claimed, then Government
should keep faith with them. They should not have been ordered
to embark for the Indies, and they should not now be punished
as men guilty of mutiny without provocation. He called upon
the King's ministers to declare what they knew of the matter.

The Home Secretary, Thomas Townshend, admitted that he
had heard of the affair, which was scarcely remarkable since there
was no man in the House who had not. He was more eager,
however, to protect the administration than to acknowledge its
duplicity and he blamed the officers of the 77th for using un-
authorised methods of enlistment in order to gain rank, for
making promises they were not entitled to give. They deserved
the severest reprehension for this, he said, but the context of his
words suggested that he believed they had offended more by
embarrassing the Government than by deluding their men. In
his opinion the methods used to raise such regiments as the 77th
were both dangerous and impolitic, but since the attestation
papers of many of the Highlanders did show that they had been
enlisted for three years or the duration of the war these conditions
must be observed. It should be remembered, however, that the
Atholl Highlanders were a marching-regiment, raised to serve in
the King's dominions, and as such could be required to embark
for the East Indies or anywhere else His Majesty desired. Edmund

Burke could not let this fence-straddling pass without tipping Mr. Townshend to one side or the other. While he had no good words to say of the methods of enlistment, he said, peace was here and the men "were perfectly right in not going to the East Indies".

General Joseph Smith interrupted Mr. Burke at this point, aroused less by the matter of the debate than by the word Indies and its evocation of a campaigning youth under a benign oriental sun. He hoped the House would not give the world the impression that soldiers had an aversion to service in India. He remembered that when the 83rd Regiment had been ordered thence from Guernsey (or Jersey, he could not recall which) the soldiers had gone to church and given thanks for the opportunity to serve in that theatre of war. With an irony that was perhaps lost upon the nostalgic veteran, Mr. Burke said that he had not meant to convey the idea that India was a bad place to send a soldier. On the contrary, he believed it to be the best.

Lord Maitland, the young son of the Earl of Lauderdale, remembered the raising of the Atholl companies, and that they had indeed been enlisted upon the terms claimed. Many of the soldiers could not speak English, but the promise that they would serve for three years or the duration of the war had been explained to them in their own language. Therefore he was not surprised by their reluctance to go to the Indies from whence, in all probability, they would never return. That the House and the country might know the truth he asked that the letter of service for raising the 77th be laid on the table. Suddenly aware that the debate was moving in the wrong direction, Townshend suggested that it should be postponed until inquiries could be made in Portsmouth, and he was supported in this by George Dempster, the member for Forfar and Fife burghs, who also suggested that Murray of Strowan should be present. Sir Richard Hotham, a London hatter with business interests in the East and thus a proper regard for priorities, informed the House that some speedy action should be taken, "for keeping the Indiamen at Portsmouth is a great expense to the proprietors".

The snub which Joseph Smith had received from Burke acted as a spur on others of his rank, and the first to rise was General Sir George Howard, well over seventy years in age and a veteran of most campaigns since Fontenoy and Culloden. He had no doubt the men had been enlisted as they claimed, and he knew the conditions were written upon the back of their attestations. General Conway, the Commander-in-Chief, coming late to the debate, admitted that he had ordered the 77th abroad. He had chosen the Highlanders because they were up to strength and other regiments were weak in numbers. Peace, he said, had come suddenly, and nobody reminded him that sudden or not the nation had been awaiting the treaty for two months. He ended his indignant self-defence with the claim that he knew nothing of any assurance that the soldiers would serve for three years or the duration of the war. Either this bold disavowal provoked a noisy uproar or the next speaker, General Charles Ross, had difficulty in voice projection. "He spoke a considerable time," said a reporter, "but we were not able to hear him."

When the debate ended at lamp-light the letter of service was ordered to lie upon the table until Strowan came to the House, and Townshend promised that the men of the 77th would not be sent abroad until there had been a full inquiry. The Government perhaps hoped that this would be the last of the matter in the Commons, and that the War Office would be left to settle it in its own way. But on Friday Maitland rose again and said that he had been making himself a perfect master of the affair and he trusted that his labours had not been wasted. He held a paper above his head dramatically, and with youthful passion declared that it proved that there was not a man in the regiment who was not entitled to his discharge. It was, he said, an advertisement signed by the past Secretary at War, Lord Barrington, and printed in the *London Gazette* of December 16, 1775.

It is His Majesty's pleasure that from the date hereof, and during the continuance of the rebellion now subsisting in North America, every person who shall enlist as a soldier in any of His Majesty's marching-regiments of Foot, shall be entitled to his discharge after serving three years or at the end of the said rebellion, at the option of His Majesty.

Faced with this triumphant reminder that they had inherited the promises made by a previous administration, the King's ministers were silent, leaving General Conway to make what defence he could. He was concerned, he said, that so delicate a question should be publicly discussed. If the King's enemies – he did not say who they might now be – discovered that two-thirds of the British Army were about to be discharged what dangerous consequences might not follow? There never had been any intention to force the Highlanders to do anything contrary to their engagement, but their orders were to serve wherever war was raging, and when peace came suddenly on . . . Charles James Fox interrupted the rambling rhetoric, blandly surprised that peace had come so suddenly upon the Commander-in-Chief. He could safely say that it had not come upon him suddenly, nor upon the public. It had been expected since the beginning of December. It was now here and the war was ended, but if Parliament wished to break the treaty "then it must be called a new war, so that, if the whole army has been enlisted to serve during the former war, the present treaty, once ratified, puts a complete and legal period to their service".

While Conway was considering this stunning logic, General Smith rose again to the defence of a professional if not a political colleague, but soon lost his way in the undergrowth of his thoughts and memories. He emerged into the light at last, blinking at the brilliant irrelevance of his argument. Had not Sir Eyre Coote, commander of the King's forces in India, asked that no more Highlanders be sent to him, since they were unable to endure the heat of the country? Conway now found his voice and agreed that no Highland regiment should be ordered to the Indies. Compassionately perhaps, no one reminded him that such an order, issued by him, had provoked both the mutiny and this debate.

Archibald Fraser was the only Highland voice to speak on the matter. He was the son of the old fox of Tower Hill, and upon the recent death of his step-brother, Simon, had inherited the General's Inverness seat and title of *MacShimidh*, chief of Clan Fraser. With extravagant but splendid emotion he praised the common men of his Gaelic race, their civil character and martial spirit. He reminded the House that no people in the world were more tenacious in honour, in promises made or given.

> There is no service, however disagreeable or dangerous, provided they have consented to or engaged in it, which they will not perform. Their perseverance originates in moral obligation, and it is unavailing to endeavour to force them to continue beyond the specified time without a fresh agreement. The sense of moral obligation which, with religious principles, is instilled into their minds in the early part of their lives, inspires them with that willing activity, sobriety and perseverance for which they are so eminently distinguished. I flatter myself, therefore, with the hope that every gentle, every humane, every consistent measure will be adopted on this occasion, that the recruiting service might not hereafter suffer in those parts of the kingdom by anything now done here.

This impassioned sincerity deflated the spirit of the partisan debate, and it now limped to an indecisive end. It was moved and agreed that Maitland's paper should lie on the table with other relevant documents. The Government had accepted its moral defeat. The weight of public and Parliamentary opinion supported the mutineers, and since they could not be dislodged from the citadel of Portsmouth without bloodshed their demands must be met. On the evening of Tuesday, February 4, the *London Gazette* published a declaration signed by George Yonge the Secretary at War.

> WHEREAS doubts have arisen with respect to the extent, and meaning of His Majesty's orders, dated War Office, Dec. 16, 1775, relative to the terms of inlistment of soldiers

since that time in the marching regiments of infantry; His Majesty doth hereby declare, That all men now serving in any marching regiment, or corps of infantry, who have been inlisted since the date of the said order, shall on the ratification of the definitive treaty of peace be discharged, provided they shall have served three years from the dates of their attestation; and all men inlisted, and serving as above, who have not so completed their full term of service, shall be discharged at the expiration of three years from the dates of their respective attestations; and that, in the mean time, no person inlisted under the conditions above mentioned, shall be sent on any foreign service, unless he shall be re-enlisted into His Majesty's service.

From reports in the London newspapers, read aloud in Portsmouth taverns, the Atholl men knew of their victory before the six companies left the citadel and marched to the Common, to hear of the Government's decision from Lord George Lennox and to parade at last before James Murray of Strowan. They came behind their greencoat pipers and arrogant drums, swaggering in the thin February sun, their arms bright, their uniforms clean, and their cheeks as always freshly shaven. The Secretary's order was read to them and translated into Gaelic, and they listened in dignified silence. His florid complexion made even ruddier by the brisk morning gallop from his brother's house at Goodwood, Lennox briefly exhorted them to do their duty now as loyal soldiers, obedient in the love and trust of His Majesty. They cheered him warmly, for they bore him no ill-will.

> Lord George Lennox, a soldier brave,
> How generously he did behave,
> His word of honour to us gave
> That we should not be sent away!

Although he had sworn never to appear before his regiment except at its request, Strowan had been persuaded to ignore its obstinate refusal to ask for him. He stood before it now in earnest sincerity, imploring it to believe that he had meant it no injury and had always wished it well. Standing at his Colonel's side and still weak from his injuries, Patrick Mackenzie was convinced that no man on parade believed this honest assurance. Strowan also sensed the distrust, and before dusk he would angrily leave by coach for London, nursing his humiliation and an aching shoulder. Sheelagreen had kept his bitter word and did not come to the Common. He had long since dismissed the ingrate battalion from his mind and was now buying the lieutenant-colonelcy of the 61st Foot. One last effort was made by Lennox to save the Government's self-respect, encouraged by the Highlanders' emotional declaration that they would march wherever it pleased the King's Majesty to send them within his kingdom, and there take their discharge. He told them that any man who re-enlisted and embarked for India would receive a new bounty. Some of the younger soldiers were ready to go, but quickly lost their enthusiasm when they were told that the money would not be paid until they were aboard, and not at all if less than five hundred men of the regiment volunteered. "Our friends," said Patrick Mackenzie with hurt and contempt, "are too great scoundrels themselves to trust anyone else."

Two days later the companies marched from Portsmouth to quarters in Hampshire and Surrey, there to await orders for Scotland and their discharge. After the parade on the Common, according to Stuart's report, they had been dutiful and well-spirited, but now they were sullen and suspicious, alarmed by the fact that their muskets, which they had themselves placed in the magazine, had not been re-issued. Along the march and in their new quarters they were openly hostile to their officers, most of whom feared another and more violent mutiny. At Guildford, where the grenadiers and Balneavis' company were quartered, Surgeon George Renny wrote to Strowan in distress, saying that the situation was as grave as it had been on the first day of revolt. The ringleaders, who should have been arrested and punished, were boldly encouraging a new spirit of mutiny, abusing Strowan at every opportunity. Like many gentlemen of the regiment,

Renny believed that the Government had betrayed its officers, but that even now an example could be safely made of the worst offenders. "Their threats and insolent behaviour, instead of showing courage, are to me very convincing proofs that the greater part are cowards at heart, and would tamely submit to anything that had the appearance of resolution in the order of Government."

But the administration had no intention of provoking the Atholl men to further violence, and the officers were compelled to endure the contempt of their men. Most galling to their pride was the continuing presence of John MacQueen. He moved freely among the companies, one day here at Farnham, another there at Guildford, Alton or Petersfield. His tall black figure was seen on a village green at morning parade, an unsmiling face beyond a Highlander's shoulder, and his soft island Gaelic was heard from a tavern window as the officer of the night passed by on Rounds. It was known that he had sent his master a letter in which the Atholl men thanked Lord George for his support, innocently believing that the wild young man had been responsible for the Government's surrender. John Charles and the grenadier Cummings were now publicly boasting that they had appealed for Gordon's support, and their officers hotly insisted that both should be taken up and punished. Strowan agreed, and he sent a spy among the soldiers, an unknown and unnamed man who, if he were not a soldier of the regiment, seemed able to pass as one. His purpose was to trap MacQueen into an admission of Gordon's complicity, but he failed. "Understanding yesterday where he set up, I went to his quarters, and found means to introduce myself to his company, with a view to discover the intention of his journey, but finding who I was, he returned mystical answers to my questions."

Murray was obsessed with a desire to bring the ringleaders to punishment, even though the Government clearly wished the regiment to be disbanded without further trouble. He urged his officers to gather what evidence they could, to secure from other men a promise that they would "sign a paper disavowing their having any concern in the mutiny". Captain William Robertson, younger of Lude, flattered himself that he had prevailed upon his non-commissioned officers to disown any sympathy with the mutiny and to declare their faith in Strowan's good intentions, but Charles Murray said that his sergeants were now so afraid that they would lay no evidence against any man. Old John Grant, who had saved Sheelagreen's life, had been threatened and would certainly be murdered if he were not quickly given a pass to London and safety. Murray also said that he had done his best to pacify his soldiers, giving them every farthing they claimed was owing, but they had shown no gratitude. Although they were without muskets, he knew that many still had powder and shot and he could think of no way these might be taken from them without violence. The spirit of defiance was still strongest among the grenadiers, and Renny appealed to Strowan for resolute action.

> Something decisive ought to be done with this mutinous company to strike terror into the rest, and if the resolutions of the Government, be what they may, are not speedily put into execution, the very worst consequences are to be dreaded . . . Were force of any consequence employed, the business of securing the ringleaders might be effected without any opposition. Scoundrels divested of principle, and engaged in so bad a cause, tho' ever so desperate when danger is at a distance, would tremble the nearer it approached.

The officers could not believe that the Government intended to take no action to restore their damaged reputations, but when Strowan's demands were repeatedly ignored he and his captains were at last compelled to accept their final humiliation. James Murray suffered it with resignation, but he was in London and unlike his embittered officers he did not hear the tavern song of the triumphant soldiers.

> We Atholl men go home to rest,
> For sure we are we've done our best,

> But her nainsel'* has been opprest
> By Murray who fairly sold us!

They went home to rest at the beginning of April, northward through an early spring, not as a regiment nor yet by divisions, but piecemeal, company by company and ignobly disarmed, each a week's march behind another. They had been told that they would be disbanded at Perth, in the county where they had been raised, that the Government would honour the assurance given in Strowan's letter of service. They were marched no further than Berwick, England's bitter gateway to Scotland, the last company coming wearily over the bridge at the beginning of May. The town was crowded with Dragoons and Foot and quarters were bad, increasing the Highlanders' anger. In a greatness of spirit he had not shown during the past vengeful weeks, James Murray came to Berwick to be with them, prematurely aged and bitter at heart. Upon his earnest appeals to the War Office, each man received his due pay and enough subsistence to buy meat and meal on his long walk home, but the Secretary had insisted that proper deductions should be made for any new clothing recently issued. The men blamed Strowan for this last act of spite, and they did not know that he had angrily protested against its petty parsimony.

Before June the last Atholl Highlander had gone northward over the Lammermuir Hills, and with him went the echo of his enduring hatred.

> There have been traitors, you may see,
> In Forty-five and Eighty-three,
> But let Murray still branded be,
>   And all good men abhor him!

* One's own self, a common reference to a Highlander.

3
THE YOUNG MEN WITH THEIR TARTANS

The 6th Northern (Gordon) Fencibles
Edinburgh, March 1794

The 1st Strathspey (Grant) Fencibles
Linlithgow, March 1794

The 4th Earl of Breadalbane's Fencibles
Glasgow, December 1794

The 1st Strathspey (Grant) Fencibles
Dumfries, June 1795

"And money coming down like a shower of gold"

A PROPHECY WAS fulfilled. In the years following the American Revolution an old seer had travelled from township to township in the glens of Ross, crying *"Mo thruaighe ort a third, tha'n caoraich mhor a' reachd!"* Woe to thee, oh land, the great sheep is coming! Now it was come: the white-faced Cheviot, the hornless, docile animal which the homeward soldiers of the 77th may have passed unthinking on the high ground of the Lammermuirs. A man-made beast, cunningly evolved from native ewes, from Ryeland, Spanish, and Lincolnshire rams, capable of flourishing on the alpine mosses of the mountains and surviving the worst of their winters. It was the Four-footed Clansman, the devourer of men. It was replacing a black-cattle economy, it would soon clothe and feed the greatest army Britain had ever assembled. It offered a rich alternative to the wasteful anachronism of run-rig husbandry, and if it did not alone destroy the vestigial inter-dependence of the *ceann-cinnidh* and his children it was the principal and most powerful instrument of that destruction. Once cleared of men, a laird's land could be leased to Lowland graziers and his fortune assured, his debts paid and his southern fancies indulged. Although relieved of familiar responsibility, the fabric of his ancient dignity as a *duine-uasal* could still be maintained, his plain house rebuilt in castellated splendour, his body clothed in an expensive and theatrical imitation of his people's ancient dress. There was as yet only the beginning of great change, of the clearances that would continue with increasing intensity for the next sixty years, but that change was already ennobled by the word Improvement, and the removal of men and women from their homes was already justified by the belief that they were thus rescued from a life of sloth, ignorance and superstition. *Mo thruaighe ort a third . . .*

By 1790 the white wave had washed northward from the Pentlands to the Great Glen and the Cromarty Firth. Sir John Sinclair of Ulbster, the hawk-nosed agriculturist who then introduced the Cheviot to Caithness, protested against the inhumanity of removing men to free grazing lands. He pleaded for slow and considerate change, but greed was more powerful than compassion, and cautious advice less effective than his claim that where lean Highland cattle had once brought £200,000 in a good year "the same ground under the Cheviot or True Mountain Breed will produce at least £900,000 of fine wool". After half a century of shabby gentility and purse-poor ambition a land-rich chief was delighted to discover that a meagre yield of twopence an acre could now become two shillings or more under sheep. A glen that had once supported five townships of his children, giving him little more than their affection and loyalty, could make him richer than many Englishmen if he replaced them with four shepherds, six dogs, and three thousand lowing clansmen of the True Mountain Breed.

Sinclair was perhaps the only proprietor to advise or practise caution. "We have heard," said Sir George Mackenzie of Coul, himself a great Improver, "but a few voices against the necessity of removing the former possessors to make way for shepherds." Among those voices he would not have included the bitter lament of Clan Chisholm's bard: "Our chief is losing his children! He prefers sheep in his glen and his young men away in the camp of the Army!" Such protests came from common men and could be ignored by members of the British Wool Society, but when they were translated into action they were immediately met by the military strength of outraged authority. In the July heat of 1792, long remembered as *Bliadhna nan Caorach*, the Year of the Sheep, the men of Ross gathered on the green banks of the Oykel and began to drive the Great Cheviot from their county.

This peaceful rising, believed by some proprietors to be the work of Jacobin republicans, was suppressed and dispersed by armed gentry and by soldiers of the 42nd Royal Highland Regiment, many of whom were kinsmen of the drovers they pursued through the dark glens below Ben Wyvis. Stewart of Garth was there as a young lieutenant of the Black Watch and he admitted that never again were his emotions so powerfully disturbed. He did his duty, placing that obligation above all others, and he was proud that his soldiers accepted "the necessity of turning their arms against their friends and relations". But he was also distressed by the grief and rage of Highlandmen who would not be driven from their homes and who would not be replaced by sheep.

Lord Adam Gordon, now the aged Commander-in-Chief of North Britain, was equally resolute in his duty and determined to tolerate no riotous assemblies, but he told the Home Secretary that there had been no spirit of rebellion among the men of Ross, no disloyalty or dislike of the King's person, only a deep fear of eviction and dispersal. He believed this fear to be justified, and the reason for it a matter of national concern. Once the mountains lost their native people, he said, "I am convinced that no temptation under the sun will be able to bring inhabitants to such Highland property from any part of the world." His warm feeling for the Highlanders was sincere, but as a general officer he was perhaps more alarmed by the effect this Diaspora might have upon future recruiting, upon what had until now appeared to be an almost inexhaustible supply of superb soldiers, nurtured in a warlike tradition and isolated from the corrupting influence of democratic principles.

There was indeed an ironic paradox in the changes brought by the Great Cheviot, and one that was half-seen by the bard of Clan Chisholm on the braes of Strathglass. Over-population in the Highlands, with concomitant famine and deprivation, had become an increasing problem which a sheep economy now promised to solve by removing its victims. But a new war, a global struggle that was to last almost unbroken for a quarter of a century, needed the peculiar qualities of that unique race

under threat of dispersal. At a time when the proprietors were
anxious to be quit of most of their dependants they would be
asked to supply more companies, more battalions of Highland
soldiers than ever before. At a moment when wealth could be
secured by the emptying of their glens they were more eager for
the rank and reward, the profit and renown to be got from
delivering the best of their children to the Army. Thus the right
arm of the paradox clasped hands with the left. The fear of
eviction, which had always persuaded tenants-at-will to give a
son or a brother to support the commissions of their chief's
kinsmen, was stronger now that he had more pressing reasons
for removing them. The war with France only delayed the
ambitious plans of many proprietors. "Gentlemen who still
had the means of influencing their tenantry," wrote Lord Selkirk
in 1805, "suspended for a time the extension of sheep-farming,
and the progress of the advance of rents." Estates which were
ripe for change, he said, would have been let to graziers seven or
eight years since, if peace had not been interrupted. But the threat
was there and known to the people, and they may have innocently
hoped that the surrender of their sons would save them from its
execution. Lairds who had once opposed emigration because it
robbed them of their tenants, and who might now have welcomed
it when it freed their valleys for sheep, opposed it still because it
would reduce the number of recruits they were obliged or were
anxious to find for the King's Highland battalions. In this confusion of greed and compulsion, the present and eventual losers
were the common people of the clans. Some of the young men
who went eagerly or reluctantly into the new regiments must
have known that if they survived battle and disease they might
come home to roofless cottages, to scattered families, to the sound
of sheep in empty glens. The brassy music of the martial life to
which they were committed drowned all but the voices of their
recruiters, yet there was a sadness in their thoughts, and their
valour was salted by the bitterness of betrayal. "If I were as I
used to be," sang Archibald Stewart, who had been a hunter in
Glen Avon before he was sent for a soldier,

> If I were as I used to be,
> amongst the hills,
> I would not mount guard
> as long as I lived,
> nor would I stand on parade,
> nor for the rest of my life
> would I ever put on a red coat.

The strength of the British Army in February, 1793, when the allied powers decided to destroy Revolutionary France, was less than a hundred thousand, including the forces at home, in Ireland, and in the colonies. It was also in the worst state of preparedness, ill-trained, ill-disciplined, ill-equipped and in-efficiently commanded. From colonel to ensign its officers were frequently ignorant or neglectful of their duties, corrupted or constrained by a system of commission-by-purchase that made lieutenant-colonels of green boys and placed them above veteran captains with empty purses. While this method of advancement occasionally gave early opportunity to such brilliant men as John Moore or Arthur Wellesley it more often placed military power in the hands of incompetents and brutes. John Fortescue says that there was an open and scandalous traffic in the sale of commissions conducted by unscrupulous brokers who, according to an officer of the Guards, "would dance any beardless youth who would come up to their price from one newly raised corps to another, and for the greater douceur, by an exchange into an old regiment, would procure him a permanent situation in the standing army." The private soldiers such men commanded were bought like cattle and were almost as highly valued. Recruits were found and sold by speculators and crimps who were as much military contractors as the venal clothiers and provisioners, selling men at twenty, thirty and sometimes fifty guineas a head to the rich fathers of ambitious sons. In the desperate demand for men, the need to treble the strength of the Army within two years, the administration did little to check the abuses of enlist-ment, although William Windham, the scholarly Secretary at

War, reminded regimental commanders that the King disapproved of methods that were "equally injurious to his service
and offensive to the Law". The cynical indifference of other
great men, however, was justified by the ordinary Englishman's
reluctance to go for a soldier unless he were caught up while
drink-sodden at the door of a tavern, desperate on the edge of
starvation, or terrified at the foot of the gallows.

A few months spent on battalion recruitment offered handsome profits to those junior officers who were anxious to avoid
foreign service, or were eager for the money that would buy
them promotion. Pryse Lockhart Gordon was the son of a poor
Nairnshire manse, an ambitious snob who became a recruiter
before he was twenty, beating the valleys of Aberdeenshire with
a crimson sash across his chest, coloured ribbons in his hat, and
a sergeant and drummer for his escort. He was told by his captain
that at a guinea a man he should make twelve in a week, and
more if he milked the bounties due to the men he enlisted. "Never
could I have hoped for such good fortune," he wrote, in his
entertaining and neglected *Memoirs*. "Kind friends, good society,
and money coming down like a shower of gold!" He enlisted
nearly three hundred men by coercion, blandishment and the
ale-pot, but it was only by effort and perseverance that he
received his due pay from the Government. He then squandered
it "in taverns, dress, horses, at the billiard-tables and fives-
court". However, he was as adroit a social climber as he was a
recruiter and he advanced as high as he desired in the Army
without ever seeing an advancing tricolour through the smoke
of a rolling volley.

Gordon's small corruption, his cheerful amorality, were
commonplace, lost in the dark shadow cast by greater men like
Colonel Oliver Delancey, the first Barrackmaster-general of the
King's Forces. The decision to house soldiers in barracks rather
than the cottages and taverns in which they had been previously
quartered was as much a political necessity as a progressive
reform. As the strength of the Army increased so did civilian
objection to obligatory quartering, and the growth of radical and

republican thought made it essential that soldiers, the only adequate police force, should be insulated from disaffection and garrisoned where they could be quickly assembled and deployed against mobbing and riot. Any plan involving the large expenditure of public funds invites adventurous peculation, and when William Pitt the younger gave Delancey the responsibility of supervising the building of the new barracks the Colonel met the challenge with enthusiasm and imagination. In the eight years he was Barrackmaster-general he was consistently inefficient, incompetent or corrupt. He had the uncontrolled right to purchase land, to issue contracts and dispose of offices, and the number of grateful barrackmasters he appointed seemed to be in indirect proportion to the number of barracks he built. He was granted vast sums for personal expenses without being required to explain how they were spent, and when his high-riding career was finally brought to an end it was discovered that more than £9,000,000 had been issued to his department and that no detailed account of its expenditure had been kept. Since the responsibility for this breath-taking piracy rested upon the two men who had appointed him, Pitt and Windham, he could not be brought down without the risk of burying them in the ruins of his collapse. He was advised to resign and was helped to this public-spirited decision by a pension of six pounds a day, almost two hundred times the pay of a fighting foot-soldier.

The Highlanders' contribution to the augmentation of an army so inefficiently commanded and corruptly managed was as disproportionate as always. Four new marching-regiments had already been raised in the mountains and eight more would be recruited before the end of the decade. With second or third battalions, recurrent replacements, this meant the enlistment of between fifteen and twenty thousand young men, more than five per cent of the probable population of the Highlands. But they were not all that could be taken and would be taken, the astonishing heart still beat and the artery still bled. Once raised, all line regiments were soon sent abroad, to Flanders, to the Mediterranean, to India, Canada and the Cape of Good Hope, and there was a consequent need for a permanent force to protect the United Kingdom from invasion or insurrection. In 1793 it was once more decided to reform the corps of Fencibles,* drawn from the shires of England, Scotland and Wales. The proposal was made in a memorandum composed by the Home Secretary, Henry Dundas, and circulated among those land-owners with persuasive or coercive influence over their tenantry. Dundas was a brilliant and ambitious politician, a younger son of a modest Scots legal family which had climbed to national power since the Act of Union. His capacity for survival in the hazardous alleyways of political intrigue depended upon an elasticity of principle that enabled him to support or abandon his colleagues without once appearing to depart from the highest of disinterested motives, and his skill at exploiting the Scots electoral system made him a zealous opponent of its reform. He was admired or detested with an intensity of emotion that occasionally approached the fringe of paranoia, so partisan or hostile that his friends and enemies could not understand the logic of each other's judgement. His loud Scots voice offended sensitive English ears, and his raw good looks were too bucolic for elegant taste, but the governing class enjoyed his hospitality, envied his easy sexual charm, and admired his ability to remain in his chair when his dinner-companions had slipped to the floor in a stupor. These virtues were un-appreciated by the common people of Scotland whom he directed with contempt and efficiency, and who occasionally celebrated the King's birthday by burning his tall figure in effigy. He and his bright-eyed little nephew, the malleable Lord Advocate Robert Dundas, were said to rule North Britain as Sultan and Grand Vizier, as if it were "a lodge at a great man's gate". He believed himself eminently qualified to hold the power he was given or assumed, and would perhaps think it proper that his public statue in Edinburgh, surmounting a pillar one hundred and

* A shortened form of *defensible* which was first used in the 16th century to describe those men fit and able for defensive military service. In the 18th century it was also intended that Fencible battalions should provide trained men who could be re-mustered or re-enlisted in marching-regiments.

thirty-five feet in height, is more than two and a half times his natural size.

Dundas's inspired energy in military administration – the suggestion of an improved barracks system was originally his – would shortly transfer him from the Home Office to the Secretaryship of War, and it might be thought that he had earned this position by the generous manner in which he had drummed up his countrymen for martial disposal by the Crown. The population of Scotland was one-fifth that of England and Wales, and only three per cent of the King's subjects lived in the Highlands. During the next seven years sixty regiments of Fencible Foot and forty-six of Horse would be raised in Britain, and of these Scotland would supply thirty-seven of infantry and fourteen of cavalry. A people who numbered fifteen per cent of the nation's whole were thus to find sixty per cent of its Fencible foot-soldiers and thirty per cent of its horsemen. It is true that, unlike England and Wales, Scotland was not yet required to raise regiments of militia, but this demand too would shortly be made. The disproportion is even more remarkable. Of the thirty-seven battalions found by Scotland twenty-three were Highland, and so three per cent of Britain's population provided the King with thirty-eight per cent of his Fencible infantry. Such prodigal use of the nation's minorities was not uncommon. In many nominally English regiments of the line the rank and file were predominantly Scots and Irish, and this imbalance, to a greater or lesser degree, would continue throughout the next hundred years. Not until the citizens' wars of the 20th century would the Army of the United Kingdom correctly reflect the proportions of its diverse peoples.

Beyond their real or imagined enthusiasm for military service, the decaying social structure that still made it easy to muster them in large numbers, there was another reason for the prodigious calls made upon the Highlanders. It was believed with some justice that they were politically innocent or naïve, uncorrupted by democratic thought. Lowlanders might be recruited to serve in marching-regiments abroad, but the administration was unwilling to trust too many of them with the internal defence of the country. Less than Ireland, but more so than England, the growing industrial area of Scotland between the Border counties and the Highland Line was a centre of violent political dissent. The passionate voice of its alarming anger was heard in its anonymous pamphlets and proclamations. The more politically conscious of the worker class, weavers and miners, had no doubt that the new Fencible regiments were primarily intended to suppress their societies, to stifle their complaints and to silence their opposition to the war. Robert Dundas told his uncle that common people in Paisley rejoiced in the early reverses of the Army, and the Duke of Hamilton, as Lord Lieutenant of Lanarkshire, sent the Home Secretary a revolutionary manifesto that was passing from town to town in the county.

> IN THE NAME OF GOD we do cast of the Authority of that Tyrant and Usurper known by the Name of George III Rex for his treachery and perjury in violating the whole laws of both God and man usurping the Hedship of the Church, introducing Popery and Slavery, imposing enormous taxes, squandering the Public revenues, overawing the Parliments, by filling it up with his Creatures, oppressing the People of Britain and Irland with packed Courts, vagabond lawyers, Gadgers, half pay Officers, Liqwise carring on an unjust & unlawful war, contrary to the minds of the people. . . .

The lairds and lords of the Highlands responded enthusiastically when they received Dundas' invitation to muster their tenants, and in June, 1793, six of them met in Holyroodhouse to discuss their progress with Lord Adam Gordon. There was no argument about their willingness or their professed ability to raise the regiments required of them, their main concern would appear to have been with precedence. This was sensibly settled by the drawing of lots, and the honour of commanding the First or Strathspey Regiment of Fencible Men went to Sir James Grant of Grant, Laird of his name, the Good Sir James who had parleyed with the Seaforth mutineers on Arthur's Seat fourteen years

Samuel M.ᶜPherson Corporal in his Highland Ridgmentals; the most
Active in the Desertion: The Posture in presenting his Firelock at Cap.ᵗ Ball in Lady Wood
And was Shot at the Tower, July 18ᵗʰ 1743. Bickham jun. delin. fe. London 1.ᵗ Aug.ᵗ

SAMUEL MACPHERSON OF THE 43RD

"Seeing we must suffer, we chuse loose our lives in making our way if our
ardon will not be granted.''

2. A CONTEMPORARY ENGLISH VIEW OF HIGHLAND SOLDIERS

"Away false northern kern, well you deserve the greatest punishment – at home to starve."

3. DONALD MACDONNELL, A VARIATION OF A POPULAR PRINT

"His pipes were a weapon of war . . ."

4. AN OFFICER OF A LATE 18TH CENTURY REGIMENT, INCORRECTLY DESCRIBED AS THE 76TH

"A mockery of Highland dress."

5. A PRINT OF SAMUEL MACPHERSON, SOLD AFTER HIS EXECUTION

"My blood, I hope, will contribute to your liberty."

. SIR JAMES GRANT OF GRANT

"Few men could with more confidence tep forward with an offer to his King."

7. FARQUHAR SHAW

"A generous disposition of mind, seldom found among men in more elevated stations."

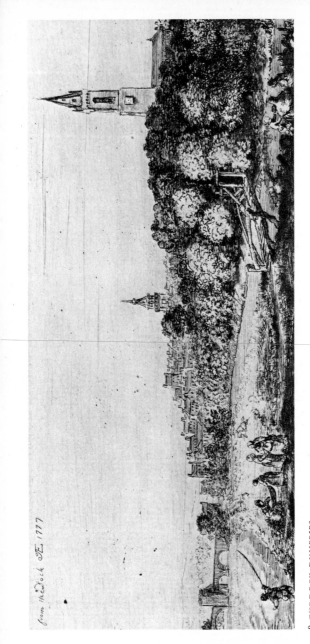

from the Dock Æ 1777

8. THE DOCK, DUMFRIES

"The Strathspey men gathered beneath the trees, not in ranks but in dark scarlet groups."

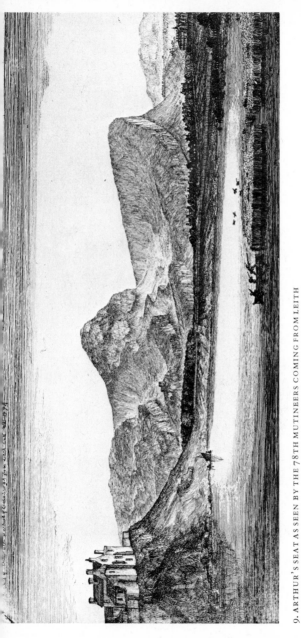

9. ARTHUR'S SEAT AS SEEN BY THE 78TH MUTINEERS COMING FROM LEITH

"Before dusk they had posted sentinels along the escarpment."

10. EDINBURGH CASTLE

"However necessary, it was not advisable to employ force while the Highlanders remained in possession."

11. TAYMOUTH CASTLE

"If the people came to Lord Breadalbane's grounds they got no weapons, or none that was seen in their hands."

12. KENMORE

"On Sunday, Angus Cameron and James Menzies went to hear the Gaelic sermon at the kirk, upon a green headland above Loch Tay."

13. LINLITHGOW PALACE

"When the first mutineer was seen between its roofless gables, musket raised, there was a sigh from the soldiers on the field."

14. LT.-GEN. SIR JAMES ADOLPHUS OUGHTON

"And now, my Lord, I must entreat you, send me down an English regiment."

15. DAVID STEWART OF GARTH

"He could feel the chill egalitarianism of the Industrial Age, coming with the wind from Loch Tay."

16. LORD MACDONALD

"If you cannot complete a regiment, you will lose nothing as Government will buy your men from you."

17. LORD ADAM GORDON

"I *expect* the Prisoners individually to state their acceptance, or refusal, to His Majesty's gracious condescension."

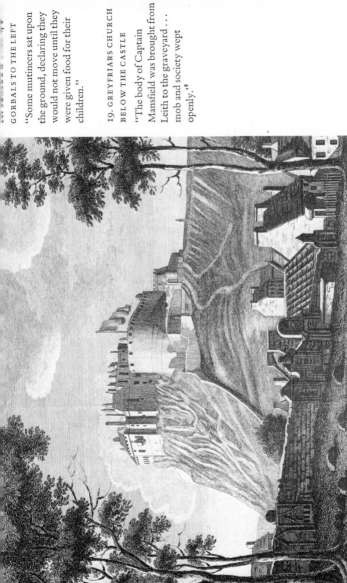

GORBALS TO THE LEFT

"Some mutineers sat upon the ground, declaring they would not move until they were given food for their children."

19. GREYFRIARS CHURCH BELOW THE CASTLE

"The body of Captain Mansfield was brought from Leith to the graveyard . . . . mob and society wept openly."

20. MEN OF THE 6TH (GORDON) FENCIBLES

"The Duke had expended a great deal upon a regiment intended to reflect the fading power of his family."

21. A HIGHLAND OFFICER AND SERGEANT

"Meeting their countrymen as companions and officers is a strong motive to engage Highlanders."

22. HIGHLAND SOLDIERS

". . . it is unavailing to endeavour to force them."

3. CAPTAIN ALASDAIR RANALDSON MACDONELL OF GLENGARRY

A young chieftain composed of vanity and folly . . .''

4. MALCOLM MACPHERSON OF THE 43RD

He sensed the coming change and had no taste for it.''

5. LEITH FROM THE EAST

When the first files appeared about the Tower they were faced by MacIver
and MacWilliam.''

26. LADY YESTER'S CHURCH

"Wrapped in their bloody plaids the dead men lay in the shadows of Lady Yester's Church. Young Walter Scott was attracted to this macabre mortuary."

27. LEITH AND THE FIRTH FROM THE SOUTH

"What the Mackenzie sentinel saw was soon known by all the companies."

THE SHORE, LEITH HARBOUR

"Captain Innes found the mutineers with their backs to the houses between
Bernard Street and the Signal Tower."

PORTSMOUTH HARBOUR. THE ATHOLL MEN MUTINIED ON THE
PARADE BEYOND THE SEA-WALL

"A high tide was running, lifting the waves to the saluting platform."

30. THE BLACK WATCH MUTINEERS ARE BROUGHT TO THE TOWER BY BALL'S DRAGOONS AND THE FIRST GUARDS

"Early in the afternoon they crossed the moat and entered their prison."

before. Second was William Wemyss of that Ilk, descendant of the Earls of Sutherland and of the Earls of Wemyss. As a Coldstream subaltern of nineteen he had raised and commanded the first regiment of Sutherland Fencibles in 1779 and now, as Member of Parliament for that shire and the cousin of its Countess, he offered to call again upon the young men of Strath Fleet, Strath Naver and Strath Helmsdale.* The other Highland gentlemen were the Duke of Gordon, the Earl of Breadalbane and the Marquis of Lorne, heir to the dukedom of Argyll. Two Lowland regiments only were lotted at this meeting, one to be raised by the Earl of Hopetoun and the other by Hugh Montgomerie of Coilsfield, first-major of the Argyll Fencibles during the American Revolution. At Montgomerie's request, the lieutenant-colonelcy of his battalion was given to old Alexander Donaldson, who had risen from his sick-bed to reason with Lord Macdonald's mutineers on the hill above Burntisland. Royal warrants and letters of service had already been issued, and the conditions of service were made clear upon all attestation papers. There was to be no drafting, volunteers only would be taken, and none would be required to serve beyond Scotland except in the event of a landing by the enemy upon the coast of England. The administration would soon regret the precise wording of this last clause.

The twenty-three regiments of Highland Fencibles raised during the next six years were the most extravagantly and expensively dressed of all battalions, and the caricature of their national dress which Lord Frederick Campbell's men had found so humiliating reached an apogee of absurdity. A tasselled sporran would soon hang below the soldier's knees, and twenty-four inches would be added to his height by a monstrous feathered bonnet. The belted plaid of his ancestors became a tight, pleated swathe, the loose jacket was replaced by a high-collared, throat-choking tunic. The men of the Caithness Fencibles were subjected to the particular sartorial fancies of their Colonel, Sir John

---

* Six years later many of these recruits were re-mustered in a marching-regiment, the 93rd Sutherland Highlanders. Before the end of the war, the glens they had left were already being cleared and placed under sheep.

Sinclair, who believed that trews and not the kilt were the ancient clothing of a Highlandman, as indeed they probably were in Caithness. He was proud of the uniform he designed. In his splendid portrait by Raeburn his ruddy falcon's head is lifted above a yellow and scarlet coat, his breast swells against the folds of a silken plaid, and his tight trews end high enough on his calves to expose his elegant hose of crimson and white. He also composed a marching-song for his soldiers, in clumsy rhyme and with unintentional ambiguity.

> Let others boast of philibeg,
>   Of kilt and belted plaid,
> Whilst we the ancient trews will wear
>   In which our fathers bled.

Despite the confident assurances of those first proprietors in Holyroodhouse, and others later, they were again forced to use threat and bribe to find the men they had promised. The marching regiments had taken the best or the most eager of young Highlanders, and Fencible recruiters were soon beating in glens far from their Colonels' lands. Sir James Grant and the Duke of Gordon were great proprietors with a large tenantry but both were compelled to write to The Chisholm in Strathglass, to Cameron and MacDonell gentry in Lochaber, offering a captain's or a lieutenant's commission in return for a hundred, for fifty stout lads between the ages of eighteen and twenty-four. Colin Campbell of Stonefield, who had promised the Crown a regiment of Dumbarton Fencibles, asked Henry Dundas if he could have three hundred Prussian deserters then imprisoned in England. The suggestion was not without appeal to the administration, for Stonefield said that in return for their liberty the Prussians would surely serve wherever the Crown wished. But Dundas thought it might have a damaging effect on recruiting for other Highland regiments, and Campbell was told that he must find what men he could in Scotland.

Once more the people were the victims of bribery and coercion, their fears increased by the northward drift of the Great Cheviot.

Their clan loyalties were still strong, and the disposal of their young men without concern for these feelings caused bitter pain and humiliation. William Munro was a man of Ross living on Lochtayside, and when he was summarily ordered into the Breadalbane regiment by the Earl's law-agent he wrote sorrowfully to his noble Colonel. The other men of his company, he said, derided him and insulted his clan, declaring "My kindred is all thieves, and they never knew or heard of Munroes but as rogues." He asked to be transferred to another company, another regiment where his pride and his clan would be treated with respect. There is no record that his request was granted, nor any indication that it was not dismissed as a trivial impertinence, but his voice is a melancholy note above the great noise of recruiting drums, and must be set against the boasting of greater men. The old attachments between the gentry and the commons of a clan were almost broken, and this would be realised too late by many Highland soldiers. Alasdair Grant, a bard of Glenmoriston, spent his brief manhood in the King's red coat, and when he returned he died at the mouth of his valley, within a morning's walk of his home. His Soldier's Song, composed when he was still under arms, acknowledged the bitter difference between a dream and the reality. *'S fhad o'n chuala tu 'chainnt . . .*

> You have long heard the saying,
> as the verse has it,
> "A tardy repentance does little good."
>
> I knew at the time
> I was put in the ranks,
> that the commander had no thought for us.
>
> When in France, he does not
> recognise Highlander or Lowlander,
> when he takes out his pen to do his clerking.
>
> When he is in command,
> my loss is no matter to him.
> Oh, I have been in a knot since that first day!

"Four regiments are in a state of what I cannot name"

"HIGHLANDERS HAVE A natural aversion to the sea," said Pryse Lockhart Gordon, "and are extremely jealous of any infringement on what they consider their rights." A round, fleshy man with alert eyes, he was now a Highland officer, his sedulous attention to his own advancement having secured him a lieutenancy and a quartermastership in the Gordon Fencibles, the gifts of his *friend* the Duke. Within a few months he was commanding a company, and by the same noble preferment he had obtained an ensign's commission for his son William, aged seven, who was also given the vacated post of Quartermaster. Gordon was thus in Edinburgh when that natural aversion and extreme jealousy were subjected to what he called "an electric shock", and his regiment came close to mutiny if not to the act itself. "The example of the 77th Regiment," he said, "had not been forgotten in the Highlands, and no sooner were orders given for the embarkation of the Scots fencibles than discontent and murmurs broke out."

It was inevitable that Westminster should regret its assurance that the eight battalions of Fencibles already raised in Scotland would not be required to march from thence until the enemy had landed in England. The war had of course begun badly, and the re-appointment of Lord Amherst as Commander-in-Chief, nearing eighty and weak in body and spirit, had been more an act of desperation than confidence. A derisory expeditionary force of three battalions sent to Europe had shared the Allies' incompetent failure to defeat a no less disorganised French Army, and in the West Indies a terrible drain of youth and blood had already begun. There would be eighty thousand casualties in those pleasant isles

276

within three years, half of them dead from disease, despair, and gunshot. By February, 1794, there was a real fear of a French invasion, and the Government naturally believed that the proper place for Scots Fencibles was in Kent or Sussex, to dissuade such a landing or to meet it while the enemy's feet were still wet. Amherst acknowledged this need but honourably insisted that the Crown should not break the promises it had given. Upon Dundas' assurance that the terms of the soldiers' enlistment would not be altered without their consent, the old soldier wrote to Lord Adam Gordon in the King's name, asking for two thousand volunteers, two hundred and fifty of the best men from each of the Fencible battalions.

The Scottish Commander-in-Chief was not enthusiastic, but he told Dundas that he would send the drafts as soon as he could. The Fencibles were dispersed throughout Scotland and since time would be wasted by marching them into England he asked for ships, a transport or an old naval forty-four to be sent to Leith, and two more of the same to Inverness, "which vessels would completely carry up to 1,000 from each place". He was told that no men-of-war were available, even obsolescent forty-fours, but transports would be sent. Since wind and weather were unreliable at this season, Dundas urged Lord Adam not to abandon the original proposal to send the Fencibles by land. A week later Gordon suggested that five hundred men should be taken from each of four battalions only. "It would answer us here *much better* in every point, and if you would take the *one half* the number at Newcastle over land, and the other half from Fort George by sea to the Nore, it would be fully as soon executed, and for less expense." He would thus retain five hundred men in Glasgow and the same in Edinburgh, with a thousand elsewhere to deal with the omnipresent threat of civil unrest. He believed that it would be easier to get five hundred men from a battalion than two hundred and fifty. "I think it will be more readily gone into than if a separation took place, for Highlanders do not like to part company, or so well to go by water as by land." He had correctly understood their attachment to the company of their own fellows, but even he believed they had a childish fear of the sea. Not now and not ever would authority understand that past breaches of faith had given the Highlander an unshakeable belief that once below decks he would be sent to the Indies, to wherever the Crown wished.

No word had yet passed between Dundas and Gordon to explain how the Fencibles were to be persuaded to go into England. In a letter of March 3, peppered as usual with italics and written to Evan Nepean, the Under-Secretary of War, Lord Adam said that he knew Dundas had promised Amherst that no man would be called upon without his free consent, but "I should be very happy indeed if this business goes on *without hesitation* on the part of the men, but that I *can* not, nor *will* not, answer for." None of the battalion commanders had yet been asked whether his men would volunteer in the numbers required, whether they would go cheerfully south to English counties that had not yet seen a French soldier or a French landing-craft. Nepean told Gordon that Lord Amherst thought, and Mr. Secretary Dundas agreed, that a bounty of a guinea to each volunteer, an adequate supply of blankets aboard ship, should inspire enough men to their proper duty. As for the proposal to take five hundred men from four battalions only, Lord Adam must do what good sense and the needs of his command required. He was still unhappy, and he told Amherst that he would use what influence he had with the Highlanders, but he could not promise that they would respond. Amherst passed this letter to Dundas who, suffering as much from ill-health as impatience, sent a curt reply to Edinburgh.

> I thought this point had been clearly ascertained, but in case I should be mistaken and my apprehension on this subject be well founded, your Lordship will exert your influence in such a manner as may be necessary for removing any difficulties on that head, but there must be no exercise whatever of compulsion.

Left thus to himself, to take all credit or blame, Lord Adam decided to call upon five Fencible battalions. Three of them were

Highland. the Grants, the Gordons and the Breadalbane men, and two were Lowland, Lord Hopetoun's and Hugh Montgomerie's. Letters to their Colonels were dispatched in the first week of March. "I have directed all concerned to use *every persuasion* in their power," he told Amherst, "to induce obedience to His Majesty's wishes." But even if he got the volunteers he did not know how they could be embarked, for the transports had not yet arrived. "I beg to have His Majesty's *pointed orders,* how I am to proceed? *What is to be done?*" He did not tell London that he had already received a clear warning from his nephew, the Duke of Gordon, that there would be no zealous response to an appeal for volunteers. The Duke did not like the proposal at all, and he told his uncle that he hoped his Fencibles would not be of the same mind. He thought that if they were invited to march into England they might go readily enough, "but whether they will *Boat* is more than I can answer for". There was perhaps another reason for his disapproval. He had been given a letter of service to raise a marching-regiment which his middle-aged but still handsome Duchess would shortly recruit, riding behind six pipers and offering a guinea and a kiss to every volunteer. If it were thought that promises made to the Fencibles were being broken, however cunningly, neither kiss nor coin would be enough to attract men into the 92nd Gordon Highlanders. His pessimism was justified, for the first hostile reaction to Lord Adam's call – or the first that the Commander-in-Chief was aware of, since it happened within a mile of his headquarters at Holyroodhouse – came from the Duke of Gordon's Northern Fencibles in Edinburgh Castle.

The Duke had expended a great deal of money upon a regiment that was intended to reflect the fading power of his family. Its great and splendid King's colour carried the painted figure of Saint Andrew, a Union wreath of thistles and roses, and the words *Clue le Cruadal,* an approximate rendering of the Gaelic for *Renown with Hardiness.* He chose its plaiding from three patterns supplied by a manufacturer of Huntly, selecting a variation of the Government's black sett with a yellow stripe, thus giving future men of his name something they could believe was the ancient tartan of their clan. He chose a lieutenant-colonel with less care, granting the commission to his brother-in-law John Woodford, the stiff-necked drill-book Englishman whose Grenadier Guards had been the first to fire upon the Gordon Rioters in 1780. Pryse Gordon despised the Lieutenant-colonel, sneering at his farcical claim to be a Highlander and deriding his naïve belief in the love of his soldiers, but the minister's son was envious of Woodford's marital connection with the House of Gordon, and piqued that such good fortune should be lightly regarded. Woodford was at this moment enjoying an affair with his paymaster's wife, and would eventually be bludgeoned through the streets of Ayr by the outraged cuckold.

The Duke had confidently hoped that he would be able to raise the battalion from his own estates in the north-east. There were encouraging precedents. In 1760, when he was sixteen, his mother had recruited the 89th Highland Regiment from the *Gordonach*, and he would have gone to India with it had not George II said that since there were only nine dukes in the kingdom of Scotland the absence of one, however patriotic, was unthinkable. In 1778 he raised a Fencible regiment in Aberdeen, Moray and Banff, so healthy and efficient a body of men, said Garth, that only twenty-four died in the five years of its existence. But now the response from the Duke's tenantry was so meagre that he was forced to call upon those chiefs over whom his family held an ancient feudal superiority, or with whom he had personal influence – Camerons and MacDonalds in Lochaber, Robertsons in Perthshire and Macphersons in Inverness.* They were all men of touchy pride, insistent upon the particular precedence and peculiar rights they believed were due to their clans. Their jealousy of each other, and their dislike of their martinet Lieutenant-colonel, was naturally reflected in the bewildered discontent of their companies.

---

* Despite the liberal affections of the Duchess, the same lack of enthusiasm in the north-east affected recruiting for the 92nd. Officers and men of this marching-regiment largely came from MacDonald, Macpherson, Maclean and Cameron clans. Only five of its officers were Gordons, including its Lieutenant-colonel, the Duke's son.

The most arrogant of the Highland officers was Captain Donald Cameron, ninth or twenty-second chief of his name according to partisan numbering, lately come of age and the grandson of the all-but-canonised Gentle Lochiel of Jacobite hagiolatry. Long forfeited, and then managed by trustees of whom the principal was Henry Dundas, the Lochiel estates had been only recently restored to this tall and graceful boy. Bred in France and England, he had come to Lochaber for the first time in 1790, and by some overnight miracle had slipped at once into the traditional skin of a Highland chief. "Many old Jacobites were still living," said Pryse Gordon, "and they puffed up the stripling with ideas of power which no longer existed." Gordon detested the young man, of course, with all the envious contempt of a parvenu. He said that Cameron was unpopular with other officers, and those who were not Highland probably did resent Lochiel's unregimental familiarity with the soldiers of his company, his insistence that as his clansmen they should be treated as *gentlemen*. Such concern for them was perhaps the least return he could make in gratitude, since their fathers and grandfathers had paid their rents twice over to support his in exile. He brought eighty of his young tenants to the regiment, promising them that they would be commanded by him alone, and when he was told that he must part with some, to complete the flank companies, he was preposterously defiant. On the night he publicly refused to obey the order he had invited some civilian gentlemen of his clan to the mess on Palace Yard. "His *tail*," said Gordon, "half a dozen yahoos in great jackets and tartan trews." For their benefit, perhaps, Cameron said that if Woodford dared to take one man from his company he would order his piper to sound Lochiel's Gathering and march the rest home to Lochaber. To emphasise this threat he boasted that this was the first time the banner of *Mac Dhomnuill Duibh* had flown under the Gordon standard, that never before had a chief of Lochiel been required to serve with men whose customary dress was small-clothes and breeches. Remembering this years later, and trimming the memory to fit his self-conceit, Pryse Gordon said he felt compelled to defend the honour of his family, being the only member of it present. "You forget, Captain," he said, "what might have been a good doctrine fifty years ago avails but little at the present moment. These fine fellows are now soldiers, and you will find your chieftainship no longer exists, and, should you continue to keep company with your *soi-disant* gentlemen, that the breeches-men will not associate with *you*!" In a flurry of further insults, and until they were restrained, these two absurd men almost came to blows, Captain Gordon with his hand in the basket-hilt of what he naturally called his "good Andrea di Ferrara".

When Woodford did transfer two-thirds of the Cameron men into the flank companies he was indifferent to the effect it might have upon the morale of his battalion. The mixed clans who had been brought into the Gordon Fencibles by their ambitious gentry were already unhappy, and a lack of concern for the ties of ancient loyalties, the breaking of a promise made by a chief, however insufferable he might be in pride, now strengthened their fear of intended betrayal. This fear was dramatically demonstrated on Monday, March 8, when they were paraded on Hawk Hill and Lord Adam's appeal for volunteers was read to each company by its Captain. There was no protest, no demonstration, but no man stepped forward. Later that day, said Gordon, "they were seen in knots, talking in Gaelic with an air of mystery". William Scot, a political informer smelling out disaffection wherever it might be suspected, told Amherst that members of the Society of Friends of the People, middle-class radicals from the elegant crescents and squares of the New Town, had urged the Fencibles not to volunteer, assuring them that they would certainly be deceived. He did not explain how the Friends had learnt of Lord Adam's appeal so soon, or how they had been able to talk so freely with a regiment which, according to Pryse Gordon, "was locked up in the Castle". The Highlanders' refusal was more probably the result of simple reasoning. They had been enlisted upon a promise that they would not be required to serve beyond the Borders until England was invaded. Since there was no invasion, no need to go aboard ship when good roads were there to march, the Government must therefore mean to betray them, as the men of the 78th and the 77th would have been betrayed had they not refused to sail.

That evening after dusk, delegates from every company called upon their captains in Palace Yard, politely asking for reassurance but swearing that no man would volunteer, that none would embark. Scot the spy was in the Castle, looking for Woodford and for information, but the Lieutenant-colonel had not been seen since the morning parade and was perhaps in the comforting arms of Katherine Gordon, the paymaster's wife. He came to the citadel on Tuesday, however, confident that he could bring the Highlanders to their duty. "He marched them by detachments into the garrison chapel," said Pryse Gordon, "and mounting the pulpit, lectured away for a couple of hours, but, as might have been expected, without effect, and it was evident to every one but himself that he was throwing away his time." William Scot waited in the Yard until the last of the companies had listened to Woodford's wasted rhetoric. When he spoke to the spy, the Lieutenant-colonel angrily accused the townspeople, particularly the Friends, of seducing his soldiers, and swore that he would soon produce evidence of this. And then, perversely, he said that he had brought all the companies round, that they had cheered him and declared their willingness to march or embark for England whenever he wished.

Three days later, however, the regiment was still hostile and semi-mutinous. Some of the companies, their captains told Woodford, might agree to go to England, but only if they were *marched*. Others, particularly the Lochaber men, were stubborn in suspicious defiance. On Saturday morning Woodford sent a subaltern down the Royal Mile with a report for Lord Adam, a contradictory expression of hope and despair.

> Although the men of the regiment under my command have generally assented to go by sea to England, and that the majority would cheerfully follow me, yet I am clear that there is so strong an aversion and suspicion in many attending it,

that I should fear an embarkation would be attended with unpleasant circumstances, and should anything unfortunate happen on the voyage all future confidence might be lost.

Since it was clear from this confused letter that Woodford had failed to influence his men, it was decided to bring the regiment's Colonel south to Edinburgh. Lord Adam probably wrote to his nephew, although Pryse Gordon claimed that he had himself prevailed upon Woodford to make the appeal. "I advised him to summon the Duke, as the only chance of checking a mutiny that was ready to break out at every moment, but he continued lecturing for three days, when he found that his eloquence produced no good effect; and at length he despatched an express to Gordon Castle."

While he awaited his nephew's arrival, Lord Adam was increasingly distressed by the reports he received from other Fencible commanders. He had now written to all of them, but his hopes were destroyed by the suspicious hostility of their men. William Morrison, commanding the first battalion of the Breadalbane regiment in Aberdeen, said that he had used every means in his power to persuade his soldiers to volunteer, but although they had listened to him civilly they had refused to come forward. Andrew MacDouall, Lieutenant-colonel of the second battalion at Musselburgh, angrily declared that he was dishonoured and discredited by the insolent manner in which his companies had rejected the appeal. The Argyll Fencibles, said Alexander Campbell of Lochnell, were influenced by a stubborn minority who noisily refused to volunteer. In Glasgow, where his regiment had replaced the Strathspey men, William Wemyss called the Sutherland companies to the Green, believing that they would all go south to England. "But I am very sorry to say, when ordered to turn out, they did not come forward so as to enable me to say they would either march or embark." Despite this, they then went through the drill and exercises he ordered, with a good-natured obedience that only increased his chagrin. Both regiments of Lowland Fencibles were also obstinately unresponsive, and like the Highlanders they resented the fact that the call for volunteers was put to them in the form of an order rather than a request. Unlike the Highlanders, however, they reacted with violence. On March 12 old Alexander Donaldson, who must have thought that one mutiny had been plague enough upon an honest officer, wrote from Inverness to say that the men of Hugh Montgomerie's battalion had at first seemed willing to go,

> . . . but about 8 o'clock I was surprised by a number of men getting together, with their arms and bayonets fixed, huzzaing, and in liquor, saying they would never embark, that they would march to any part of England, but embark they would not, as that was no part of their engagement, that they were sold, and that they understood some troops of Horse were at Elgin to force them aboard. They forced the Guard, obliged a fifer and drummer to beat to arms, broke open the stores, took the made-up cartridges and served them out among themselves. I find they have now mounted a Guard, have placed Sentries on the stores, and thus the matter now rests at 12 o'clock at night.

Lord Hopetoun's regiment was at Banff, and when it heard of the resistance made by Montgomerie's men seventy miles to the west, it violently declared that not a man would go aboard the transports. The officers of the battalion lost their heads in alarm, and at dusk that evening they took the ammunition from the battalion stores and threw it into the sea. "Which, however," said Hopetoun with disgust, "being done in haste proved partly ineffectual, and some was picked out again."

Lord Adam wrote daily to Dundas, miserable dispatches, each with fresh news of the Fencibles' hostility. He asked for help, for guidance, and received none. What if the regiments agreed to embark and then refused? What should he do? The question was academic, for the promised transports had not arrived, at Leith or at Fort George. He had urged the Fencible officers to temporise with their men, but he was not confident. "It is my duty to state that the situation is *critical*, and that Mutiny is very contagious, more easily prevented than quelled." His letters, sometimes three or four a day, blew across the Border like wasted leaves, and there was no encouraging reply. Hugh Montgomerie rode express to Inverness where, by the force of his personality, he brought his mutinous regiment back to its duty. He told Lord Adam that the men were now cheerful and willing to embark if *ordered*, but he said nothing of volunteers. William Wemyss did not go again to Glasgow. He told Lord Adam that the affairs of his constituency required his presence in Sutherland, meanwhile he hoped that his officers, those who were not themselves absent, would persuade his soldiers to honour the call made upon them. When they did, he would go to England with them. "I am much hurt that their ignorance, assisted by the evil inhabitants of Glasgow, should have created suspicions in their minds which I hope they will be ashamed of."

Lord Adam's military problems were also bedevilled by a noisy clamour from those citizens of Edinburgh and Glasgow who feared a weavers' revolt more than a French invasion, and who were angered by a proposal that abandoned them to the *sans-culottes* of Lanarkshire. One who signed himself *A Justice of the Peace of Edinburgh* wrote to Dundas in protest, declaring that it was the most unpopular and impolitic measure that could have been devised, creating disorder among the only soldiers available for the defence of respectable society.

> Two thousand men to the assistance of England can be of but little consequence, but to Men that do not look upon themselves as treated according to bargain and faith, as they say, the order has affected the whole of the kingdom, and at this instant the four regiments ordered are in a state of what I cannot name, and the consequences *dreadful to look to*. You Sir, are Scotland's friend, and *as such* for the love of *God*, of *peace*, of *Internal Quiet and good order*, take some *immediate* steps to put a stop to our present licentious appearance in consequence of this order.

Dundas was at last moved to ask Lord Adam when this tiresome business would be settled. Past two o'clock in the afternoon of Friday, March 19, the Commander-in-Chief wrote a brief and weary reply. Though matters were still in a fermented state, he said, he hoped that he would soon send four Fencible battalions to England by one route or another. He had some reason for confidence. Hugh Montgomerie had reported that his men were now willing to march or embark. Lord Hopetoun was also certain that his regiment would go wherever he desired, and there was a hopeful if less positive assurance from Lochnell of the Argyll Fencibles. As he sat alone, by a window overlooking the quadrangle of Holyroodhouse, writing in a bold hand that curiously resembled the slanting muskets of an infantry line, Lord Adam was perhaps happy that there was now no doubt about the reliability of the fourth regiment. His nephew had come at last to Edinburgh and was at this moment in the Castle, talking to his soldiers.

His Grace had arrived in his own time, spending forty-eight hours on the journey from Castle Gordon. His battalion was paraded before him on Hawk Hill, facing its colours, and he spoke to it winningly, mixing compliments with parental admonition. They had been called, he said, to the defence of their country. "If any man is such a disloyal dastard as to refuse, he can step out of the ranks and he shall have his discharge, for though you were raised for the defence of Scotland, England is now in danger, and none but cowards would refuse such a call!" That, at least, was how Pryse Gordon remembered the occasion years later, and in an age when it was comfortably assumed that upon the news of England's adversity Highland soldiers would spring eagerly to her aid. "This short harangue," he said, "was received with the greatest applause, every bonnet was elevated, and every voice cheered, that they were ready to follow his Grace to the world's end." A correspondent to *The Times* wrote less effusively, but in the same inspiring mood.

> The Duke of Gordon asked them on parade, if they were willing? All of them answered by three cheers, His Grace

then asked if they would embark? They again answered by three cheers, and God save the King! This manly conduct, we hope, will be followed by all the other Fencible Regiments.

It was Lord Adam's hope, too. How his nephew had succeeded in bringing a semi-mutinous battalion to willing obedience was less important than the influence its change of heart might have upon others. But, as a new week began, it became clear that only the Gordons and Montgomerie's West Lowland Regiment were willing to go to England. The Highlanders of the Sutherland, Breadalbane, and Argyll battalions were perversely intractable, unmoved by the offer of a guinea to every volunteer. Lord Adam generously hoped that this would not dissuade the War Office from paying it to the men of the Duke's regiment or to the Lowlanders. "As it has been promised," he told Dundas, "I trust you will have the goodness to see that it is complied with, by being made good by the public."

The volunteers could be embarked within a few days, now that "two shabby transports" had arrived at Leith, and the Duke had promised his battalion that he would be the first man to leap aboard. Any joy Lord Adam may have felt at this small, small success was embittered by the knowledge that in Linlithgow the soldiers of Sir James Grant's Regiment were still in a state of armed, defiant, and desperate mutiny.

"Come forward then . . . step forth and vie with each other!"

THE MARCH SUN was bright on the field of exercise, upon young grass and the black water of the loch. The laird of Grant stood alone before the wrack of his regiment, comical and unmilitary, the hook of his nose jutting beyond the ostrich feathers of his bonnet, his pot-belly swelling against his white cashmere waist-coat. Every officer, and every soldier remaining in the ranks was staring westward to where Captain MacDonell's men – with others of the grenadier company, the Colonel's, the Lieutenant-colonel's and Glenmoriston's – were running about the lake to the grey-harled town of Linlithgow. The shouting figures were lost for a few moments in a copse of bare oak and then were seen again on the other side of the water. Some turned eastward into the town-street by the West Port, others followed the shore of the loch, leaping garden walls like the red deer running, all moving toward the great keep of the old palace. When the first man was seen on its north-western tower, between the roofless gables, plaid flowing and musket raised in skirling triumph, there was a responsive sigh from the soldiers on the field and the Laird's numbed astonishment changed to fatiguing despair. His second call for volunteers had failed. Twelve thousand rounds of cartridge and ball, stored in the palace five days before, were now in the hands of the men who had violently rejected his appeal.

Sir James Grant, Laird of Grant, third baronet and eighteenth chief, Lord Lieutenant of Inverness and Member of Parliament for the shires of Moray and Banff, was in his fifty-sixth year, a devout Presbyterian, uxorious father of fourteen children, and one of the richest proprietors in the Highlands. In justice to such merit and might, Stewart of Garth abandoned his own talent for eulogy and paraphrased Clarendon's encomium on Charles I: "He was the worthiest master, the best husband, the best father, and the best Christian of the district to which he was an honour and a blessing." That district was the wide and fertile valley of the Spey, much of which he owned or controlled through the gentry of his clan. His Highland home was a placid island in a green ocean of natural pine, a discreet distance from Grantown which he had built in Georgian splendour on a desolate moor, inspired by the improving fever of the age. When in residence he enjoyed the dignity of a *ceann-cinnidh*, although he disliked the indecent play-acting of chiefs like Lochiel, having too much good sense to believe that history could be reversed by the belting of a plaid. During the shooting season he entertained no less than fifty guests, seating them according to rank in his great dining-hall. Those below the invisible cellar of salt were served with whisky-punch instead of wine, but all were waited upon by country boys dressed in his livery of scarlet and green. His generous hospitality at Castle Grant was stiffened by the con- descension of a great chief, a man whose Norman ancestor had placed a foot upon this land more than five centuries before, but he was also the anglicised product of Westminster School and Cambridge, happiest on George Square in Edinburgh or at his town house in London, dedicated to the politics and loyalties of a southern ascendancy. His good nature had restored much of the damage done to his family name by his father Ludovick, a weather-cock who had confirmed his belated allegiance to the Hanoverian cause by surrendering a hundred of his Jacobite clansmen to imprisonment and transportation. The debts which the Good Sir James had also inherited from this equivocal parent had been paid by the sale of clan lands and the people upon them, a profitable conveyance that brought him £100,000, to which was added another £12,000 which the Crown granted him in compensation for his father's services during the Rebellion of 1745. The administration's long delay in acknowledging those services reflected Sir Ludovick's own hesitation in offering them, for he had waited upon the result of the battle of Culloden before declaring his unqualified support for the victor.

The clan gentry over whom Sir James exercised a firm and paternal influence were thickly settled in Strathspey from Rothiemurchus to Craigellachie, but there were others westward across the sleeping giant of the Monadhliath, the Grants of Glen Urquhart and Glenmoriston whose unfortunate people Sir Ludovick had abandoned to Cumberland's justice. Military ambition came late to the Good Sir James, and for no clear reason other than gratitude or a desire for personal advancement, but he followed its prompting with energetic zeal and in the belief that he was able to call up more young soldiers than most chiefs. "Few men," said Garth, "could with more confidence step forward with an offer to his King." He had stepped forward before Mr. Dundas' proposals were sent to Scotland, and it was thus fitting that the lotting in Holyroodhouse gave him the right to raise and command the First Regiment of Highland Fencibles. He sent his fiery cross by coach from the General Post Office in London, carefully phrased letters to the cadet houses of his family, cousins close and distant, appealing to their affection and asking for their loyalty. "I trust," he said, "that the spirit of the clan will enable us soon to embody the regiment." The response was gratifying. Twenty-one of the gentlemen to whom he gave commissions, upon their assurance that they could fulfil their quotas, were men of his own name, as were the Chaplain and Surgeon. Although the Government was giving a bounty of three guineas to each man enlisted, the Good and Thrifty Sir James modified this, that there might be some margin of profit to encourage the recruiters.

> You are requested to beat up for no more than two guineas and a crown for each man, of which you are to deduct the price of a knapsack, and also furnish each recruit with two good shirts and a pair of shoes out of the said bounty. But notwithstanding, you are to understand that a good man is not to be parted with if he accepts of three guineas.

Delayed in London by the business of the Commons, "tied to the House" he said, the Laird did not come to Scotland until the summer of 1793, stopping in Edinburgh to enjoy its society, to attend the lotting, before travelling on to Castle Grant. The raising of his regiment, even at a distance, was agreeable to his family pride and he began to think of a second and a third battalion, envious of the Earl of Breadalbane who had been granted permission for such augmentation, but he was wisely dissuaded by his regimental agents in London. It would be more profitable, they said, if he recruited a marching-regiment instead. There would be more men to find, more commissions to sell, and the certainty of half-pay for himself upon its disbanding. "You will also have the emoluments arising from clothing of a regiment abroad which is considerable." He accepted this persuasive argument and offered the Crown a Strathspey Regiment of the line, asking only the right to grant a captain's or a major's commission to his favoured son Frank, aged fifteen. The less valuable majorities in his Fencible battalion fortunately went to veterans of the Indian and American campaigns, both called John Grant, one of Glenmoriston and the other of Auchindown. If not a Grant by name, the Lieutenant-colonel was at least a member of the Laird's family, for like the Duke of Gordon Sir James gave the commission to a brother-in-law, Alexander Cumming of Altyre in Elgin, whose surname would shortly and as a result of compulsive inheritances pass through confusing permutations, from Cumming to Penrose-Cumming, thence to Cumming-Gordon and finally for evermore to Gordon-Cumming. His marriage to the Laird's sister Helen was said by one aged aunt "to weigh like heavy gold with hopes of success", but neither Lord Amherst nor Lord Adam Gordon were as optimistic about his appointment to the Strathspey Fencibles. He was known to be an ill-tempered and thoughtless man, with enough reckless bravery to make those faults dangerous, and he was thus as foolish a choice for the acting command of a Highland regiment as Sheelagreen and Woodford had been.

The response from gentlemen of his clan was deeply gratifying to the Laird, but since most of them were unable to inspire the same enthusiasm among their reluctant people he was soon writing begging letters to chiefs beyond the Monadhliath and the Great Glen. Thus he acquired forty men brought to him by Simon Fraser of Foyers, the brother-in-law of Glenmoriston. He also wrote to William Chisholm, the sickly, money-hungry chief so bitterly accused by Clan Chisholm's bard. *An Siosalach* had recently inherited the title from his half-brother and was about to marry a spirited Glengarry MacDonell whose mother had taught her the value of eviction and clearance, and who was now urging her prospective groom to apply those lessons upon his estates. He had already leased some ground to the Lowland sheep-farmer Thomas Gillespie, the Great Cheviot grazed within sight of his windows at Comar and the people it had replaced were gone to the emigrant ships at Inverness or the slums of Glasgow. The invitation to sell some of his superfluous young men to the Laird of Grant was naturally attractive, but there were tiresome problems. "The raising of a hundred men in the present general confusion of recruiting," he replied, "is no easy task, and what would throw an additional embarrassment upon me with regard to that circumstance is that the tenants upon my property obtained from my late brother leases of a disreputable description, and are besides naturally averse to the military life." He meant that his compassionate half-brother, Alexander the Fair-haired, had given some of the clansmen a protective security of tenure and since they believed themselves safe from threats of eviction they would not part with their sons. With the encouragement of his wife and the example of his mother-in-law, William Chisholm would soon break many of those leases, but even now, as he told Sir James, he would drum up a hundred recruits with great cheerfulness were the price worth his time and trouble. That price was too high for the Laird, however, and the Chisholm's greedy mind was turned to more satisfying opportunities for profit. When Elizabeth MacDonell became the lady of Comar House, Thomas Gillespie was invited to pasture more sheep on the braes of Strathglass.

Elizabeth's brother, Alasdair Ranaldson MacDonell of Glengarry, was the Laird of Grant's ward and when his "only father" appealed to him for a hundred recruits he produced them without hesitation. This gave the Good Sir James great satisfaction, although he would later regret the gift. The ease with which the MacDonells were brought to the Strathspey Fencibles may have been due to the improving energy of Alasdair's relentless mother, a Grant of Dalvey known as Light-head Marjorie. In 1785 she had evicted five hundred people from Glenquoich, sending them to Canada and replacing them with Thomas Gillespie's sheep. She evicted still more in 1787, and more again the following year, using some of Mr. Gillespie's welcome money to erect a tasteless mausoleum over the grave of her ineffectual husband. The unspoken threat of similar misfortune thus had more effect upon the Glengarry sub-tenants than all the recruiting rodomontade of her son. This arrogant young man was cast from the same ridiculous mould as his neighbour Lochiel, incarnating all the real or imagined characteristics of a clan chief. He was tall and handsome, with a heart-shaped face and a thin nose like the blade of an axe. He wore nothing but Highland dress, including the bonnet of his own design that perpetuates his memory. He strapped himself with barbaric arms and rarely stepped abroad without a chief's ancient tail of henchman, bard, piper and gillies. In time he would become the friend of Walter Scott, to whom he gave a great wolf-hound, and by whom he was immortalised as Fergus MacIver of *Waverley*, forever alive in death like a bright-coloured fly in amber. He lived out of his life on a wave-curl of passion, passionate in friendship and passionate in enmity, killing Flora MacDonald's grandson in a duel, alternately treating his clansmen as beloved children or brutish serfs. Opposing any change that threatened to wake him from his dreams, he conducted his own war against the building of the Caledonian Canal, and would eventually and ironically stumble to his death from a wrecked steamer on that waterway. Awed by the man's monstrous absurdity, Pryse Lockhart Gordon thought he was as ludicrous as Lochiel, but none the less admired his grand and eccentric manners. They met once in Italy when Alasdair Ranaldson came to dine with a Florentine noble, wearing tartan, dirk, pistols, and broadsword, and while demonstrating how his ancestors had once captured and dismembered wild cattle he almost pulled the marchese's arms from their sockets.

There was one difficulty in enlisting the MacDonells for like their chief most of them were Catholics. The English Relief Act of 1791 had removed the restrictions that prevented the recruiting of Papists, but a similar Bill for Scotland was yet to pass through Parliament. The attestation forms signed by the Laird of Grant's Fencibles should thus have included a declaration that as well as being free from rupture, lameness, and fits, they were also Protestants. The exclusion of Catholics was an irritating obstacle to the recruitment of Highlanders, for many of the most warlike in tradition were also Roman, and since the beginning of the war there had been attempts to persuade the Crown to raise Highland regiments that were avowedly and exclusively Catholic. Those evicted people of Glengarry now living in Glasgow squalor were presumed to be burning with martial ardour, anxious to give their lives for a family that had no further use for their labour. They were tended in body and spirit by Alexander MacDonell from Inshlaggan, a selfless priest who was also a distant kinsman of Alasdair Ranaldson. Upon his chief's instruction he wrote to the Earl of Fife, proposing a battalion of Glasgow MacDonells and a colonel's commission for young *Mac-'ic'-Alasdair*. Fife was shocked by the suggestion, and by the fact that it was put to him by a man who, he said, had been a baker before he became a priest. He informed Henry Dundas that the recruiting of such a battalion would be a dangerous precedent, and if Catholics were to be enlisted they should be widely dispersed among Protestant regiments. It was not long since, he said, that a Jesuit priest had gone through the Highlands, telling simple men of his own faith that they would soon be masters of their own lands again.

The substance of Fife's objection was supported by Colonel James Fraser of Belladrum who was raising a Fencible regiment from his clan, despite the continuing pain of wounds received at Quebec forty years before. The enlistment of a Catholic battalion, he said, might encourage good members of the Kirk in their suspicion that "the present war was undertaken to restore the Catholic religion in France". He did not believe this himself, he reported the opinion in order to demonstrate its absurdity, saying that he could enlist one hundred and thirty good Romans from Morar and Kintail who were as loyal subjects of the Crown as any in the country. When Dundas rejected Father MacDonell's offer it was not from religious prejudice or respect for the Law, but in the sensible realisation that the wild boy chief of Glengarry could not be trusted with a colonel's commission. In anticipation of the Scottish Relief Act, and providing the matter did not provoke mobbing or riot, the colonels of the new Fencible regiments were allowed to omit the excepting clause from the attestation papers. The Good Sir James was particularly pleased. In March, 1793, he had been forced to reject a Papist recruit offered him at a reasonable price by the Laird of Mayen. "I cannot desire you to do an illegal act, though I am convinced many Roman Catholics are good subjects and I am sorry to lose a fine young fellow, and above all a Grant." Now, when Alasdair Ranaldson brought him a hundred young Catholics, half of them surnamed MacDonell, he accepted them with joy and gave Glengarry the right to select his junior officers. The senior lieutenancy naturally went to Alasdair's young brother James, later to hold the château of Hougomont throughout the long June day of Waterloo. The second subaltern was their cousin Ranald, whose notion of military service was that it should be spent on leave in Lochaber, protected by a steady supply of medical certificates from the physicians among his kinsmen.

The men of Clan Donald, from Glengarry, Scotus, Clanranald and others, were the largest contingent in what was intended to be a Grant regiment. A great number of the soldiers did come from Strathspey, but there were only eighty men of the Laird's name, no more than twice the strength of the Frasers brought in by the Laird of Foyers. Other clans well represented were Mackintoshes, Mackenzies, Macphersons, MacGregors and MacLeods, indicating that although the Grant gentry had willingly answered their chief's appeal they had been forced to beat in glens far from their own lands. Their desire to fulfil the quotas promised was sustained by the knowledge that they were obliged to pay Sir James three guineas for every man short of the number agreed. The recruiting was directed by Lieutenant-colonel Cumming from his fine house at Altyre. He was to spend much of his regimental career at home, which was perhaps fortunate, for when he and the battalion came to closer contact, particularly at Dumfries, the result was disastrous. The Laird's purse-pinching hope that he would raise his men for less than the Government's bounty was soon shattered. Captain Allan Grant, ignoring orders that no one under sixteen was to be enlisted, reported that he had acquired "a fine boy, fourteen years of age, and five feet four inches", but had been obliged to pay twelve guineas to the greedy young warrior. John Rose of Holme, approaching fifty and unwilling to tire himself with too much travel, recruited his company within a week by offering fifteen guineas to every sturdy man who stepped behind his drummer. The difference between such lavish bounties and the three guineas advanced by the Government came from the Laird's own pocket, and his understandable irritation was made worse by Lord Adam Gordon who did not approve of a colonel who stayed in Edinburgh when his battalion was being raised in the mountains. "I must think," he told Sir James, "the *longer* you keep near each other, and the *more* you keep together, the better for the Regiment and the Service."

The Laird accepted the rebuke and went north, arriving at Castle Grant a month after his soldiers had been inspected and embodied. The companies were paraded before him on a moor above Forres and his thin blood was excited by their brave drums. Like the country boys in his dining-hall during the shooting season, they wore his livery of geranium-red faced with green. Their tartan, the old black sett with a glowing stripe of red, had been chosen by himself and supplied by John Gloag, clothier of Edinburgh. Much of their clothing was made in London, including their tall bonnets of bearskin, their cockades, scarlet garters, tailored hose of caddis cloth, diced in crimson, green and white. The officers' shoulders glistened with gold bullion, and minute bells, each costing twenty-three shillings, rang softly on the tassels of their badger-skin sporrans. Sir James did not know what kind of fighting-men he had dressed in this peacock fashion. Three months before they had been drovers, farmers and shepherds, masons, wrights and weavers, one a printer, another a hairdresser, a third a dancing-master escaping from his debts perhaps. Now each man or boy was like his fellow, a red feather in his bonnet, head erect above a choking stock, hair clubbed by a leather rosette, chest embraced in black cross-belts and shoulders squared against a green canvas knapsack. Alexander Cumming assured Sir James that with drill and discipline, yet more discipline and drill, he would soon have soldiers of whom he could be truly proud. It was easy for the Laird to believe this as the companies marched away from the review, the sun warm on the cherry-brown of their muskets, a piper playing the bold march of the clan.

When the battalion was sent to garrison duty in the Lowlands the Laird returned to Edinburgh, to the candle-lit elegance of his house on George Square and the matronly company of his wife Jane. The Strathspey men wintered on straw beds in Glasgow, along the Clyde, in Paisley and Largs, and their officers would later claim that their mutinous behaviour was the result of too long an exposure to the democratic influence of pike-forging weavers and pamphlet-writing lawyers. Oliver Delancey had yet to build adequate barracks in Glasgow, and the soldiers were quartered upon citizens of that city and neighbouring towns. The Friends of the People would naturally have attempted to seduce them from their duty, since that might well include the bloody suppression of all reforming and revolutionary societies. There is no evidence, however, that the two mutinies in the First Fencibles were the result of anything but the Highlanders' resentment of promises broken, of offences to their self-respect, and they were probably more outraged by the degradation of their Gaelic countrymen in the ghettoes of Glasgow than they were provoked by the egalitarian arguments of its middle-class republicans.

On Monday, March 10, 1794, two days after Lord Adam issued his appeal for volunteers, the Strathspey Fencibles were ordered to march from Glasgow to Linlithgow in two divisions. The first and largest left on Thursday, when the Edinburgh *Courant* reported that the regiment would proceed from Linlithgow to Leith, there to embark for England. The appeal for volunteers had not been put to them and still had not been made on the following Monday when the second division came through the dust of the Stirling road to the West Port. The companies were quartered along the narrow street between the eastern and western gates, their ammunition and stores placed under a grenadier guard below the great Lion's Chamber of the old palace.

The failure to call for volunteers in Glasgow had been due to the absence of the Colonel and Lieutenant-colonel. Cumming was still at Altyre, kept there by a daughter's sickness. Sir James was coming post-haste from London, a rocking week of discomfort made the more unpleasant by the obligation to go straight to Linlithgow without calling upon Lady Grant in George Square. He came with his son Frank, who was boyishly proud to be given the honour of bringing the Fencibles' new colours, but more eager to take up a commission in his father's marching-regiment, now embodied as the 97th Strathspey Highlanders. They arrived in the little town a day before the coming of the second division, and the Laird's weary spirits were lifted by a waiting letter from his wife, full of town gossip and gentle love. She said the latest news from London was that the French invasion army was now rumoured to be in great distress, and unlikely to cross the Channel. "May it be so, My Dearest Life, and God grant you all comfort and happiness."

But there was little comfort or happiness. First, a brief letter from Lord Adam Gordon, superscribed *Private*, told Sir James of the disorder in other Fencible regiments, of a report that the soldiers of one were buying powder and ball from disaffected civilians. "When your people are assured that no force was meant, or intended to be used, and that they certainly never will be compelled to embark, I should think they would rest satisfied." From what the Laird was told by Glenmoriston and Auchindown there was no reason to expect such satisfaction. Blindly he believed that the only cause of the discontent reported by his majors was the influence of republican societies in Glasgow, and he was unhappy that his regiment should now be quartered in Linlithgow, a pestilential source of sedition. "I am informed from the first authority," he told Lord Adam, "that there is no place in Scotland worse for conveying *hidden poison*." He cannot have believed that his men were ignorant of the proposal to send the Fencibles to England. He could not yet know that some of them had received letters from their kinsmen in the Gordon battalion, urging them to resist the Government's intention to ship them against their will. The foolish failure to put Lord Adam's appeal to the Strathspey men before they marched from Glasgow, before the *Courant* announced that ships were awaiting them at Leith, before they heard of the Gordons' defiance, had confirmed their fear of betrayal, their belief that they were to be embarked without choice and under compulsion. Inevitably perhaps, the men of Alasdair Ranaldson's company were loudest in tavern protest. The MacDonells had been troublesome since the day they had marched to Forres behind their chief's aquiline brother. They were fiercely proud, contemptuous of other clans, jealous of their Catholicism, and quick to resent any real or imagined slight upon it. They steadfastly thought of themselves as a clan levy and not a regimental company, and their independent conceit was encouraged by young Glengarry, now come of age and acknowledging no man's authority. Like Lochiel, he preferred the companionship of his clansmen to that of his brother-officers. He jested with them in Gaelic when they should have been mute and immobile in the ranks behind him. After Retreat in the evenings he walked with them to their quarters, his arms about their shoulders, offering them whisky from his own flask, and he refused to discipline them when other officers complained of their insolence and insubordination.

On the evening of Monday, March 17, some hours after the second division arrived, Sir James Grant wrote a long and affectionate address which he had decided to read to the battalion the following morning, believing its personal appeal most proper and persuasive. He came to the field of exercise before noon on Tuesday, to the gentle meadow slope upon which his silent regiment stood in line, staring eyelessly across the loch to the great fortress palace where Mary Stuart had begun her troubled life. It was a fine, mild day, the light strong on young brown faces, on painted drums, bayonets bright and the polished brass of shoe-buckles. The Laird was in a good humour, proud of the brave appearance of his soldiers and confident of their loyalty, pleased to have heard this morning that his wife and his daughter Margaret would shortly join him at the Golden Lion in Linlithgow. The first words he read from his address, the paper held close to his eyes, were an admission that its appeal would not be a surprise to the men paraded before him. "My friends and fellow-soldiers," he said, "you know that we are come here in consequence of a call from His Majesty to go to the south of England . . ." He read as quickly as he could, but lifting his voice that it might carry to the furthest rank, and only occasionally did he wait for his words to be translated into Gaelic. He asked for five hundred volunteers, good-looking men with vigour, youth and strength. It was the King's wish that they should go by sea, for His Majesty believed this would be the least fatiguing, the least expensive method of transportation. If they wished, their Colonel would go with them, by sea or by land, and they could trust in his continuing love and concern.

Come forward then, my friends! Let every brave man and lover of his country step forth and vie with each other who shall be first in so noble a cause! Be assured you have not your own welfare and happiness more at heart than I have. You will find England excellent quarters. The soldier lives much better there than he can do here, and however you look at present, I expect every one of you will look ten times better before you have been a month in England . . .

But no man stepped forward, and before he had finished he heard a sullen murmur, an angry shout of defiance. When he lowered the paper and stared myopically at the red ranks before him, the shouting increased. The MacDonell men cried out that they would not go to England for this had not been in their papers, they would rather stand their ground and die like their comrades in the Gordon regiment. Stunned by their anger, Sir James turned away and left them, returning to the Golden Lion where he miserably awaited the reports of his officers. When they came to him they told him that although the regiment had marched from the parade in good order not one man had come forward in answer to their earnest appeals. He was shocked, he had not thought such obstinacy possible. "Till this day," he wrote to Lord Adam that night, "I had every reason to believe they would embark for England without hesitation, provided their officers went with them." He asked Gordon for time, for the news of his regiment's behaviour to be kept from London until he could bring it to its duty. He sent the letter to Edinburgh on the Linlithgow Fly at eight o'clock the next morning, by the hand of a grenadier lieutenant, John Grant of Delcroy. Long past sunset the weary subaltern returned with a welcome letter from Lady Grant to her "very dear Sir James". It chattered with gossip. Young Frank's recruiters had enlisted some remarkably fine men for his commission in the 97th. Alexander Cumming was in Edinburgh and would soon leave for Linlithgow. Lord Adam had described Glengarry as "a young chieftain composed of vanity and folly". The small domestic warmth of the letter was chilled by a dispatch which Delcroy also brought from Gordon. No time could be given, said the Commander-in-Chief, nor could the matter be properly kept from London, and copies of the Laird's unhappy report had thus gone to Lord Amherst and Mr. Secretary Dundas. He demanded Sir James' presence at Holyrood-house as soon as possible, with an assurance that his battalion was now willing to supply the volunteers required.

The Laird of Grant was reluctant to leave Linlithgow and unwilling to call again upon his soldiers until they had been given an opportunity to regret their insolent behaviour. At supper he was encouraged by Captain Simon Fraser's assurance that the men of his Light Company were now eager to volunteer. To occupy the minds and bodies of all the companies, to isolate them from the corrupting influence of the town's evil-minded citizens, Grant ordered extra drills on the lochside field. From early morning until dusk on Wednesday and Thursday the drums beat across the idle water, and at Retreat the officers reported that the Highlanders had gone through their exercises in good spirits. Now more hopeful, Grant decided to make a second appeal on Friday. By this time Alexander Cumming should have arrived, although his alarmingly cheerful letters from Altyre could not have inspired confidence in his influence. He said that all the Fencible regiments in the north had been playing hell, seizing ammunition and setting order at defiance. "I hope our lads will escape the contagion, but I rather wish than expect it."

Before he left his officers to their wine and retired to bed on Thursday, Sir James decided that the morning parade would also be a felicitous occasion for displaying the new colours his son had brought from London. They would replace the temporary painted flags, now much cracked and weathered, and must surely please the vanity and prime the loyalty of his soldiers. For five days the two standards had remained in young Frank's travelling-chest, wrapped in lacquered leather, and the Laird's delay in lodging them before the battalion was a sad mistake. Many of the Highlanders, particularly the grenadiers and the Glengarry men, had become increasingly suspicious and by the fifth day a wild tavern-rumour was accepted as bitter truth. It was said that one of the colours was the flag of the Duke of York, His Majesty's second son and the Commander-in-Chief of the British Army before Tourcoing. The Strathspey Fencibles were thus already sold to Flanders, and the call to march to England's defence was a trick to lure them from their home country.

"The situation in which we stand, without a single cartridge"

TWO ENSIGNS OF Clan Grant carried the new colours to the lochside on Friday morning, escorted by a grenadier guard with bayonets fixed. They marched with Alexander Cumming, John of Glenmoriston and Sir James. When they reached the meadow-slope they turned away from the field-officers and took the positions ordered, their backs to the water and their feet apart in straddling pride. As each young man extended his right arm in ritual custom the embroidered silk broke from varnished poles, forest-green of the Regimental colour and the Union of the King's, roses and thistles delicately entwined upon the saltire of Scotland and the red cross of England. The companies came at ten o'clock, separately from their quarters, a single drummer beating. They were followed along the cobbles to the West Port by a large crowd of leather-workers and weavers, and these democratical town rascals, as the Highland officers called them, cheered the Fencibles and shouted "There go the brave fellows who won't be blinded!" But there was a sad blindness of distrust and suspicion. The new King's colour was only a silken copy of the familiar painted flag, but the soldiers saw what they feared to see and believed it to be the standard of His Majesty's son, the Duke of York in Flanders.

The battalion assembled in line for review, in close order by seniority of companies, two paces apart. Sir James had decided against a second reading of his lovingly composed address. He ordered Adjutant Watson to dress the line, and when this was done to his satisfaction the captains and lieutenants walked along the ranks of their companies, repeating his appeal in their own words, asking for volunteers to step forward and form again behind the new colours. "We represented fully that there was to be no force," said John Grant of Delcroy, "it was to be only choice, but all to no purpose." No one clearly remembered how the revolt began. As if the shock had robbed his memory of detail, Sir James told Lord Adam that to his regret and astonishment many of the soldiers broke away without orders. Writing to the factor at Castle Grant, Delcroy said that the grenadiers to whom he and Captain Robert Cumming were speaking suddenly began to huzza in a dastardly manner and then left the ranks. A political informer called Wishart, who may have been in Linlithgow to spy upon the workers' societies, reported to Henry Dundas that "Considerably more than the one half joined the standard, but the rest of them refused and McDonald of Glengarrie's Company (who are all Catholicks) not only refused to go but in a tumultuous manner runn off the field." He was the only witness who said that some of the Highlanders came forward to the waiting colours. Certainly, in one second it seemed, the First Regiment of Strathspey Fencibles changed from an orderly battalion into a riotous mob. At first there was that barking shout from the grenadiers on the right flank, twenty or thirty muskets raised in defiance, and then running men in scarlet and green. Upon this the Colonel's men and Glenmoriston's broke their ranks, turning their backs in protest, and some of them followed the grenadiers. All of Alasdair Ranaldson's company, *"that black sett of MacDonells"* said Delcroy in hate, wheeled from the centre of the line, for a moment steady and then crumbling. They ran westward, outpacing the grenadiers, and Glengarry did nothing to stop them. The last company to break was the Lieutenant-colonel's on the left flank. Ignoring Cumming's angry call of *"Stand fast!"*, a dozen or more men lifted their muskets above their heads and stepped forward with a shout, pausing briefly before they too ran from the green.

As they splashed through a burn that drained the loch the mutineers passed Lady Grant's carriage, at this moment turning from the Bo'ness road to the field. She and her daughter were

not alarmed but two riders who accompanied them, both gentlemen of the Laird's clan and his law-agents in Edinburgh, pulled
their horses closer to the carriage in protection. Grant of Delcroy
thought that the arrival of his chief's lady at this point was the
worst event of the morning, making her a shameful witness to
her husband's humiliation.

The MacDonells took the shorter route through the lochside
gardens of Linlithgow, over dry-stone walls and the tannery
yard to the school-house, climbing the terraced graveyard of
Saint Michael's church. They were the first to reach the ruined
palace. They ran through the outward gate, and the Highlander
who guarded it wisely stepped aside or was knocked to his knees.
The grenadiers went about the great keep, through a skirt of
skeleton trees to the eastern door, and entered below the sculp-
tured arms of Scotland's kings. Inside the palace they joined the
Glengarry men on the central courtyard, their voices echoing
against its stair-towers, the stone flowers and heraldic beasts still
green-black from the smoke of Cumberland's arsonists. They
climbed upon the ruined fountain that had once flowed with
wine for royal birth and marriage, for a Jacobite prince fifty
years before, and their defiant slogans filled the sky with wheeling
birds. Other men broke into the ammunition store, carrying
kegs and cartridges to the great Lion Chamber, a roofless hall of
wet stone and dead memories. The first MacDonell to climb to
the high roof stood alone for a moment, calling across the loch
to the remaining soldiers on the field. Then he was joined by
others, and all fired their muskets in anger or joy, the white
smoke blown back into their faces and the noise bouncing from
roof to roof in the town.

Staring in disbelief at the wild and distant figures, Sir James
was immobilised by shock. If he felt anything at this moment it
was perhaps relief that his law-agents had the good sense to turn
Lady Grant's carriage about and lead it from the field. Grant of
Delcroy said that nothing was done for ten minutes, and then
"We got those that remained with us put into some order, and
after taking a list of the present and the absent marched back to

town." Cumming had taken command from the Laird's listless hands. With drums beating bravely, he led the companies eastward about the shore of the loch and into the town by way of the churchyard to the Cross. Leaning from the yellow walls and narrow windows of the palace, the mutineers shouted insults to the officers as they passed, and some of the younger subalterns, wretched with impotent shame, snapped their useless pistols at the faces above them. "Laying our account," said Delcroy, "for being fired upon by the dastardly rascals, but they thought proper to decline that."

Three platoons of Fraser's reliable Light Company were kept under arms at the Cross as a Reserve Guard, and the remaining men were dismissed to their quarters. Two hundred of them, however, shouldered their muskets with an astonishing shout of defiance and marched northward up the Kirkgate to the south door of the palace where the MacDonells and the grenadiers welcomed them with cheers. Between three and four hundred men, more than a third of the battalion, were now in a state of mutiny, holding a strong defensive post and in possession of all the regiment's powder, shot and flints.

The Strathspey officers stood glumly about their Colonel, reloading their pistols or grasping their sword-hilts, protected from the gathering mob by a glistening hedge of bayonets. The high tower and roof of Saint Michael's church masked their view of the palace and muted an occasional shot, a ragged *feu de joie* from the derisive mutineers. The Laird's irresolution and Cumming's near-apopleptic anger were mocked by the jeers of the leather-workers who pressed upon the Light Company men, filling the air with a tannery stink and the more offensive cries of political reform. Upon Cumming's order, or perhaps his own arrogant suggestion, Alasdair Ranaldson was at last sent up the cobbles in the hope that his persuasive influence would bring his clansmen out. He was told to take his junior subaltern with him, the Adjutant James Watson who had long since replaced the malingerer Ranald MacDonell, transferred *in absentia* to Fraser's company. Watson's assistance at this moment cannot have pleased Glengarry, for the sturdy middle-aged Lieutenant was not Highland and no gentleman at all by Clan Donald's exclusive standards. He was a Lowlander, lately a sergeant of the Royal Artillery whose experience and diligence had persuaded the Laird to give him a commission. But he was a brave man and showed no alarm when the mutineers, having admitted both officers, told them that they were now prisoners and hostages. Watson despised the MacDonells, believing them to be a curse upon his good-hearted benefactor, but he kept this contempt behind an impassive face. For ten minutes, while Glengarry laughed and talked with his emotional children, the Adjutant coolly watched and remembered the efforts that were being made to prepare the palace for attack. "They had sentries posted at every hole and corner," he later told Delcroy, "and on one pass they had no less than twelve men posted, and they began to make new posts of defence as they expected at every moment to be attacked by dragoons." He made no attempt to recall the mutineers to their duty, believing that to be Glengarry's responsibility, but when he saw that some of them were now breaking into the powder-kegs with heavy stones he decided that calm unconcern would not save him and them, if not the town of Linlithgow as well, from a sudden heavenward ascent. He called to them sharply. Since most of them were idle, he said, they must fall to their exercises and he would instruct them. Amused by the impudence of the proposal, they willingly paraded on the grass-grown courtyard and for two hours he took them through the standing drill with the musket – Rest, Order and Club, Secure, Shoulder and Present. He called the orders in a loud voice, boldly facing the levelled muskets, although "Every man's piece," he said, "was properly flinted and for the most part loaded."

It was now past one o'clock. Lady Grant and her daughter had long since returned to Edinburgh. The officers were gone to their quarters, the Reserve Guard had been discreetly withdrawn from the Cross and the noisy provocation of the mob. In the Laird's room at the Golden Lion he and Cumming discussed what could and what should be done next, since it was clear that Glengarry and Watson were prisoners if not already foully murdered. A decision was made for them by Surgeon Peter Grant, son of the factor at Grantown and a young man well liked by the Mac-Donells. He said that he would gladly go into the palace and ask the defenders what terms they required for their submission. He was briefly gone, returning when Sir James was still writing his first unhappy dispatch to Lord Adam Gordon. Captain MacDonell and the Adjutant were both unharmed, said the Surgeon, and the mutineers were willing to return to their duty upon a written assurance that they would not be sent into England, that the appeal would not be put to them again until the French had landed. The demand was improper and out-rageous, and Sir James told Peter Grant to return and make that plain, in whatever language the young man thought appropriate. The Laird then picked up his pen and continued his letter. The MacDonells, he wrote, had ever been the bane of good order and discipline, and until the regiment was moved to country quarters, away from poisonous towns like Glasgow and Linlithgow, it could not be brought to obedience, discipline, and duty. He had not the strength of spirit, perhaps, nor the calmness of mind to give Lord Adam a full account of the day, and the immediate future was too depressing to contemplate. Nor could he order his loyal companies to attack the palace.

> In the situation in which we stand at present, without a single cartridge, it is not in the power of the well affected to enforce obedience. For particulars I beg leave to refer your lordship to Captain Grant who is sent in express. You can easily believe that our situation is very distressing and unpleasant.

Captain John Grant of Rippachie, who rode immediately to Edinburgh with this dispatch, was not long gone before the Surgeon returned. The Glengarry men, he reported, now said they would go wherever the King required, provided their chief was allowed to march before them. This conditional offer irritated the Laird's sense of propriety, the rogues could not be allowed to put their attachment to Captain MacDonell above their duty to the Crown. He may have suspected that the insolent proposal had originated in Alasdair Ranaldson's ambitious mind. In his travelling-desk at this moment was a petition from the troublesome young man, asking leave of absence to London where his brother-officers believed he intended to offer the King a whole regiment of MacDonell men in return for a colonel's commission. Surgeon Grant assured his commander that the demand was not exclusive and should not be taken seriously, for all the mutineers were now agreed that they would not insist upon a written assurance. If Sir James and Major John of Glenmoriston came to the palace alone and gave their word of honour that no man would be sent to England, that no volunteers would be required until the enemy landed, then they were willing to march out and obey all orders given to them.

He went as they asked, at four o'clock and with Glenmoriston. Cane in hand, he waited like a beggar at the outward gate, below the high walls, the darkening carvings of the King's orders of knighthood, Garter, Thistle, Fleece and Holy Ghost. He gave his word of honour to a deputation of men from the grenadiers and from his own company, and when this was done the mutineers cheered him and some of them came from the palace behind Watson and Glengarry. The Adjutant was undoubtedly pleased to be quit of the place, for when they grew tired of his musket-drill the Highlanders had returned to their violent and enthusiastic assault on the powder-kegs. Although all of the MacDonells accepted the Laird's word, most of them remained in the palace, declaring it more satisfactory than their quarters in the town. He wisely decided to treat this as childish conceit and not continued defiance, even though they thus remained in possession of the cartridges and flints. He returned to his lodgings and wrote at once to Lord Adam, more happily and calling upon classical imagery. "By a temperance, which perhaps could not be justified by anything but the necessity of the case, we have induced them to quit the Aventine Mountain." He did not say that the antique

Romans of Clan Donald still held that hill, but the thought of
their insolent independence lay behind his acknowledgement that
there could be no thought of sending the regiment to England.

> I have now only to request of your lordship, as soon as it suits
> your conveniency, to move us to some place where the
> discipline of the Regiment may be in some degree restored,
> and where the men may have a constant and unremitted duty
> which may keep their minds employed and prevent their being
> prey to every officious intermeddler.

He sent the letter by the hand of Alexander Grant, one of the
lawyers who had ridden with Lady Grant to the field of exercise,
and when the officer of the night reported that all was tranquil in
the town he retired early to bed, if not serene in spirit at least more
confident than he had felt at any time this week. He rose and
broke his fast early on Saturday morning, listening to his officers
as he ate in his room. James Watson boldly offered to go again
into the palace and persuade the MacDonells to surrender the
ammunition, although he suspected that many of the others had
filled their pouches with cartridges before leaving. Glenmoriston
and Robert Cumming of the grenadiers assured the Colonel that
their men now regretted their behaviour. Grant of Rippachie had
returned from Edinburgh in the night, waiting without sleep for
the Laird's awakening that he might deliver Lord Adam's letter as
soon as possible. The Commander-in-Chief said that he had been
hurt beyond description by what had happened in Linlithgow,
no understatement since the news had come while he was still
wondering what was to be done with the Gordons in the Castle.
He did not censure Sir James for what had happened, but advised
him "to be cool and temperate, to tell those who are well affected
that no man will be desired to march out of Scotland without his
consent". The morning was cold, the rain heavy, but such was the
sunny state of the Laird's euphoria that he wrote at once to Lord
Adam, declaring that he would not be surprised if all his regiment
now offered to march into England. He saw no contradiction
between this startling optimism and Watson's troubling report

that sometime before midnight the mutineers had sent two or three emissaries to Edinburgh. "Probably," wrote Sir James with no great concern, "to satisfy themselves as to the conduct of the Gordons."

Lord Adam had assured Sir James that the regiment must remain in Linlithgow until further orders, until all the misguided men had returned to their duty, but it was hard for the Laird to decide whether he had a loyal battalion ready to obey him or a quiescent mob that might again break into mutiny. The Mac-Donells came from the palace that week-end, although many of them returned to it at the first rough word from an officer or sergeant. They had surrendered what cartridges remained below the Lion Chamber, but Watson was unable to recover a single flint. The Laird now began to think of his reputation, the respect of the public, and with an influence that later men of his rank and power might envy he succeeded in stifling the suspicious curiosity of the Edinburgh newspapers. On Friday the *Advertiser* had reported that although two companies of the Strathspey Regiment had volunteered for England there was doubt about the enthusiasm of the others. Alexander Grant discovered that the source of this report was Sheriff Clark of Edinburgh, an intriguing busybody who had informants in Linlithgow and in all the towns where the Fencibles were quartered. The lawyer therefore called upon the sheriff and showed him a letter in which Margaret Grant declared, with more loyalty than truth, that all was well in her father's battalion. Mr. Clark was happy to accept this information, not because he believed it, perhaps, but because he was also ordered to call at Holyroodhouse and explain his improper conduct to Lord Adam Gordon. There remained the newspapers, but Alexander Grant quickly dealt with them. "I have requested all the Printers," he told Sir James, "rather to insert nothing than to insert anything contradictory of the *Advertiser*, except what they may receive from you or the Commander-in-Chief."

The Laird of Grant remained in Linlithgow for five more days, despite Lord Adam's repeated requests for his presence in Edinburgh. He sent Alexander Cumming with a verbal report of all that had happened, with an assurance that his soldiers continued in good humour and dutiful obedience. Cumming returned with Gordon's tart insistence that if all were indeed well in Linlithgow there was nothing to detain Sir James. So he went at last, and Cumming rode with him for six miles as far as Winchburgh. He arrived in George Square after lamp-light on Friday, March 28, and wrote at once to Holyroodhouse, sending the letter by Delcroy's hand and imploring Lord Adam to believe that the mutineers "in general repent deeply of their mis.onduct which their sudden paroxysm of groundless folly occasioned". What passed between the two men when they met the next morning was unrecorded, but Sir James was certain that if Lord Adam again appealed to the Strathspey men they would all volunteer. Gordon did not make the appeal. Henry Dundas' scheme was in miserable ruins, broken upon the ignorance, the obstinacy, the pride and fear of the Highlanders. Only Montgomerie's Low-landers and the Gordons, now brought to a proper understanding of their groundless folly, were to go to England. Young Delcroy walked down Leith Walk to watch the sunlit embarkation of the Northern Fencibles. His martial ardour was stirred by the boats full of red coats and tartan plaids, by the grand example of the Duke of Gordon, but he also felt degraded by the shameful behaviour of his own regiment, and he wept publicly on the Shore.

The Strathspey Fencibles were now being disciplined by Alexander Cumming. He had begun the moment he parted from the Laird at Winchburgh. Turning about he saw the arrival of the Edinburgh coach from Linlithgow and there, sitting boldly atop it, was a villainous Light Company man called Mackay, whom Cumming knew to have been refused a pass that morning. The unfortunate fellow was dragged down, accused of desertion, and returned to Linlithgow in the charge of a party of Argyll Fencibles marching that way for Falkirk. "Could we punish him," Cumming advised Sir James, "he is a proper subject." From early morning until dusk, the Lieutenant-colonel kept the companies at exercise, on the simple and effective principle that an exhausted body produces an inactive mind. He ordered firing-drill on alternate days, and since there was no ammunition to be issued the soldiers were forced to use the powder and ball they had carried from the palace. This not only improved their skill but soon exhausted the cartridges they had secreted in their pouches. When their flints were also gone, Sir James was forced to pay for replacements from his own purse. He came one afternoon with Lady Grant to watch the firing, offering a pair of eight-shilling shoes to the best shots, and he told Lord Adam that no finer marksmen were to be found in the King's army. The Lieutenant-colonel's harsh discipline, his firm belief in the Black Hole and the threat of the lash, brought the battalion to dutiful if sullen subordination, and some of the officers soon felt secure enough to ask for leave of absence. To Cumming's rough amusement, John Grant of Glenmoriston went "upon a whoring expedition to his piece in Glasgow", and most of the subalterns were eager for the society of Edinburgh. The mutiny, it seemed, was over, and in the first week of April the Laird confidently assured Henry Dundas that four hundred of his men were now willing to march into England. If the Secretary was encouraged by this to think again of calling upon the Strathspey Regiment his mind was quickly changed by the Laird's qualifying paragraph. "At the same time, such is the effect the MacDonell company's example may have, I cannot pledge myself for a certainty of no change of sentiment, but I trust in God there will be none."

Alexander Cumming did not see why the matter should be left to Providence, and he was anxious to be rid of all MacDonells, chief and clansmen. In his diligent efforts to discover those men who might be properly hanged or flogged as ringleaders, he now knew that an emissary from the Gordon Fencibles had come to Linlithgow two days before the mutiny, the brother of a Glengarry soldier called MacLachlan. The Gordon man had been seen by several sergeants in the Red Lion or the Crown, clearly identifiable in his distinctive tartan and yellow-faced jacket. It was as a result of his visit, his appeal for support, that three emissaries from the MacDonell company had gone to Edinburgh. Cumming had the names of these rascals and he hoped that they would be court-martialled in Edinburgh, for it would be hazardous to try them in Linlithgow. The Laird refused to proceed against them, believing that no good could come of it. Cumming accepted this under protest and he urged Sir James to get rid of Alasdair Ranaldson and all his insufferable clansmen. The impudent young man had publicly insulted Surgeon Grant and far from apologising was demanding satisfaction for the injuries he claimed to have received.

> Notwithstanding the humiliating situation to which he was lately reduced, he is again returned to his playing and joking with the men in the ranks, and yesterday there was hardly one of them that he did not entertain with whisky. This behaviour, you may easily conceive, frets and disgusts all the officers who are certain neither the company nor the regiment will ever do good while he is with us.

Glengarry solved the problem himself. He once more applied for leave of absence, explaining that he wished to lead a deputation of loyal Catholic Highlanders to the King in London. More than this, since he was now come of age, the pressure of family affairs preceded his regimental obligations. Providence had intervened after all, and Alexander Cumming was grateful. The chief of Glengarry left one morning on the Fly, enjoying the valedictory tears of his clansmen who may have wondered why he was now deserting them, since they had come from the palace upon his assurance that he would lead them wherever they went. His departure made little difference to their insubordinate mood, and although their hostility was generally suppressed it exploded in one last gesture of defiance. As Catholics they were exempted from the Sabbath parade, and like all non-conforming soldiers at all times they resented this being used as an excuse for extra duties. When one of them refused to mount guard on Sunday he was thrown into the Black Hole from which five of his comrades rescued him, and carried him shoulder-high from the Cross to the West Port. The disgraceful incident was reported to Lord

Adam Gordon who wisely decided to refuse Cumming's demand for a court-martial. He wrote a letter of censure, naming the guilty men and ordering it to be read before the whole battalion. He told Cumming that this was to be the end of the matter.

Gordon had done his best to deal with the Fencible mutinies with circumspection, and like Oughton he thought that the cat and the firing-squad could do more harm than good to the special qualities of the Highland soldier. But like other mistaken men he also believed that the real cause of the recent disorder had been the pernicious wickedness of the reforming societies. In June, when the Strathspey Regiment was at last sent to the comparatively innocent glens of Galloway, he issued a circular letter to all commanding officers in Scotland.

> I think it necessary to apprize you that in these particular times it will be proper you should be very cautious what men you enlist, such as may have belonged to any of the different Levelling Societies, or who have been concerned in any late riots should be avoided. Precaution is likewise necessary to be used in the case of any person who may be proposed to be brought in as an officer.

Not since the shooting of Farquhar Shaw, of Malcolm and Samuel Macpherson against the chapel wall of the Tower, had any Highland soldier been executed for mutiny, and the lash had only been used against the wretched Argyll Fencibles on the links of Leith. The administration's leniency had not been based upon Christian compassion, but upon concern for the peculiar qualities and circumstances that brought a Highlander to the colours. It acknowledged, however reluctantly, that too harsh a punishment for his transgressions might dry up the wondrous well of man-power from which he was drawn. This special consideration would no longer be respected in the face of a more bloody threat to Crown, Church and Government. The King was not only at war with the Republic of France but also with some of his subjects, particularly in Scotland where his servants were said to be among the most corrupt in Europe. The merchants of Leith in public meeting might declare that the British constitution was the happiest ever devised by man, but the cries of "God save the people!" and "A sow's tail for Geordie!" mocked such complacency as they drove to the play-house. Book and ballad diverted society with Jacobite romanticism, but three printers were sent to gaol for drinking a toast to "*George the Third and last, and damnation to all crowned heads!*" An eighth of the population of Edinburgh lived on bitter charity, falling harvests had doubled the price of bread within a year, and six baker's boys were transported without trial for raising their voices in a High Street riot. The *Rights of Man* was a banned book but was read more hopefully than the Bible, and *Ca Ira* was sung with more sincerity than the National Anthem. Shelley dedicated a poem to the Friends of the People, and Robert Burns' *Tree of Liberty* was declaimed in the candle-lit hush of poor Lanarkshire cottages. Strikes immobilised seaports, and the weavers of Paisley were known to be buying arms. Forged at night and distributed secretly, the pike threatened to become the political weapon of distressed and unfranchised workers, and if their passion had not been filtered through the cautious reformism of the middle-class radicals who led their societies they might have overturned that happy constitution of which the Leith merchants were so proud. Transportation, the hangman's noose and knife, judges who saw the face of Jehovah in their shaving-glasses, were able to suppress but could not totally silence the angry call for liberty, and the gallows confession of that mysterious conspirator Robert Watt told a frightened establishment that five thousand Lowland workers, armed with pikes, guns and grenades, had been ready to transfer power to the patriot societies.

The King's regiments garrisoned in Britain were the only defence against this real or chimerical menace. Mercy toward the Highland mutineer, the suborned or disaffected soldier, was thus no longer expedient, reasonable, or compassionate.

"We shall see the officers' guts about their heels"

WHEN DUNCAN BAN MACINTYRE retired from the Edinburgh City Guard he left the little howff in the Lawnmarket where his wife distilled and sold whisky and he became a soldier in the Earl of Breadalbane's Regiment. The sweet-tongued singer was now beyond seventy, too old even for the aged Guard, and his enlistment by the Fencibles can have been a gentle favour only, an honourable recognition of his skill and of his loyalty to the leaders of Clan Campbell whose qualities he happily immortalised in song. He cannot have been required to fulfil any duties, to march or stand guard, and he may have earned his soldier's pay as an officer's servant, the pet of Glenfalloch's grenadier company, silencing a tap-room or bivouac with the imagery of his verse. The old world he had loved was long gone, but his heart was once more quickened by the sight of the Campbell boar on a banner of silk, and he sang of his new comrades as if they were the young men of the Watch with whom he had marched fifty years before.

> Comely to behold
> on a clear level field,
> were the young men with their tartans
> pleated into a kilt.

He composed a song to the noble Colonel who had called them forth. "Thou wilt not be daunted," he said, "with thy virile fighters, and thou directing them." The young Earl directed his regiment as little as possible, his ambitions being more political than martial, and only the strenuous efforts of Henry Dundas and Lord Amherst would later persuade him to return to Scotland and his mutinous soldiers. Duncan Ban wrote nothing of that. He could think no ill of *Mac-Chailein 'ic Dhonnachaidh*, the brave chief who welcomed him into the Breadalbane Regiment, who replaced his fox-skin cap and faded kilt with a soldier's brave dress, who gave him a fine sword with an Islay hilt and a blade so keen that it could neatly cleave a floating apple. He composed no song about the mutiny on Candleriggs Street, although he must have been in Glasgow when it occurred. He did not sing of the nine-tailed cat on the red back of John MacMartin, or the polished muskets that ended the life of Alexander Sutherland on Musselburgh sands.

Duncan Ban had been born in Glenorchy, the twisting valley whence the bandit lords of Breadalbane had come. In two and a half centuries, by guile, terror and blackmail, they extended their lands eastward to the borders of Atholl's grounds. When the greatest of them secured an earldom, serpent-wise and full of caution, he made certain that it could be inherited not only by his children's children but by those of his collateral predecessors should his own line become extinct. It was by such cunning foresight that John Campbell, a descendant of that first Earl's uncle, had now become the fourth holder of the title. The great swathe of his mountain lands stretched for ninety miles from east to west, from Perthshire into Argyll, and no man could ride across it in less than three days. In the last decade of the 18th century its adult population was more than fifteen thousand, so attached to Lord Breadalbane by the nature of their tenancy if not the decaying ties of clanship that he raised the greatest part of three Fencible battalions and one marching-regiment from their sons, completing the numbers with quotas from his cousins in Argyll. He was vain and proud, selfish and self-seeking. He was a gracious hero, said Duncan Ban, expert in ruling, but this was how the old singer saw all the great men of Clan Diarmid. More restrained in admiration, Garth said that his lordship managed his vast property with such patriarchal kindness that upon his call to arms his young men came forward readily in great numbers. For many of them, like the aggrieved William Munro, that ancient call was in truth a peremptory order from Breadalbane's agents, its threat of eviction spoken or implied.

The Earl was as eager as Sir James Grant to raise a Fencible corps, aware of its political value at Westminster and Windsor, and although his offer perhaps anticipated the Laird's, the subsequent lotting at Holyroodhouse placed his regiment fourth in precedence. When his recruiters began their beating for the first battalion they gathered five hundred men in less than a week, drawn from the sod and stone townships between Taymouth and the brown slope of Cruachan, and within a month more recruits from the sea-lochs of Argyll completed the required strength of two flank and six battalion companies. Ten commissions only were taken up by Clan Campbell, and of these two alone were captaincies. The lairds of Breadalbane willingly supplied their sub-tenants but they sold the commissions thus acquired to outland gentlemen, pursing the money or loyally surrendering it to their chief. The Major of the regiment was Alexander Maclean of Coll, a veteran Hebridean who brought in enough islanders of his clan and others to support his own commission, a captaincy and two lieutenancies for his kinsmen. The Lieutenant-colonel was William Maxwell Morrison, whose interchanging names suggest his doubt as to whether he should be Highland or Lowland, for as William Morrison Maxwell he had commanded the Light Company of the 77th at Portsmouth ten years before, and since then had been living but indifferently on half-pay and hope.

The first battalion of Breadalbane men was originally known as the Perthshire Regiment of Fencibles, but its Colonel soon persuaded the Crown to change the title to his own. He was with the companies when they were mustered on a river-field by Taymouth Castle, and Duncan Ban's heart throbbed with pride.

> Thou art wise and generous;
> the men who march with thee
> are a goodly company;
> 'tis thou did raise hundreds

of Fiann descendants,
and, in time of action,
swift in strife were they.

Among these descendants of the legendary Fingalians less than
forty were named Campbell, and there were almost as many
MacDonalds. But the common people of the Highlands were
only now adopting the surnames required by southern clerks, by
parish-registers and muster-rolls, and whatever their patronymics
or descriptive names most of the men of the battalion were the
children of Clan Campbell or the lesser tribes upon Breadalbane
ground. They were now all one, the King's soldiers in tight red
jackets faced with yellow, green plaids, leather stocks and flat
bonnets. The Earl's vanity required them to complement his
own magnificence. On that April day at Taymouth he rode
before them like a demi-god, his shoulders dripping with gold,
his bonnet dressed with eagle feather and tumbling fur, his trews
and plaid of gentle silk, a sword-belt of soft reindeer leather, fine
bearskin on his pistol holsters. This spurious evocation of Gaelic
splendour was the work of his lordship's London tailor. His horse
furniture had been made by a saddler in the Haymarket, his
bullion and foaming linen supplied by the brothers Hewetson of
Covent Garden, lace-makers to His Majesty's Great Wardrobe.

Soon back in London, at number fifteen Wigmore Street, the
Earl secured letters of service for the raising of a second battalion
and was given hope to think his offer of a third would be accepted.
He was so enthusiastic that Lord Amherst cautioned him against
taking drafts from the first to make up the strength of the others,
an unnecessary warning since Breadalbane land was fruitful with
young men. The Earl was pleased that his battalions did not
disgrace themselves in the disorders of March, 1794, or at least did
not carry their sullen refusal to volunteer into open mutiny.
When that trouble passed he believed that all discontent was
over. The first battalion was sent to Aberdeen where, said
Duncan Ban, "We drank of strong drink, as much as we could
enjoy, lest we should be taunted for coming home sober." But

the high spirits of the first spring muster were gone, and a grumbling suspicion, a fear of betrayal, darkened the minds of many men. In May that year four companies of the second battalion at Dundee objected to stoppages from their pay and again came close to mutiny. Lieutenant-colonel Andrew Mac-Douall told Breadalbane that the soldiers resented a deduction of 1s 3d for turnscrew pickers and brushes, both essential for the cleaning of their muskets. "They found that they could have furnished themselves with the same articles of equal workmanship at one half the price." They also claimed that the tartan caddis for their hose was less than needed, and that they were over-charged for the belts that supported their white fur sporrans. MacDouall's good sense settled the business by a compromise, and when the battalion was inspected a month later the men behaved so well that he ordered hogsheads of porter to be distributed among them.

The discontent in the first battalion was more bitter and began to sour the enthusiasm of the companies before they marched south to the Lowlands. They too were meanly robbed by excessive deductions. They too believed that the Crown and their officers had attempted to betray them, that the call for volunteers had been a trick, but something worse had outraged their self-respect. Early in July, 1794, they were paraded in hollow square to watch the bloody flogging of Malcolm MacFarlane of the Light Company and the effect of this experience would be disastrous. That night in a tavern Private John Malloch told three soldiers of Captain Nairne's company that before another Breadalbane man was so foully treated *"We shall see the officers' guts about their heels!"* The punishment had been ordered by Maclean of Coll. Morrison was rarely with the battalion, absent through sickness, family affairs or indifference, and all command and responsibility rested upon the Major. He should have been aware of the Highlanders' particular abhorrence of corporal punishment. He may have known that the Perthshire men in the battalion resented him, believing rightly or wrongly that he favoured his islanders above them. But he had been an officer of

the Crown for a quarter of a century and he placed his duty
before the paternal concern that was once the instinctive reaction
of a Highland gentleman.

He brought the battalion to Glasgow toward the end of that
July and quartered it in the centre of the city, in the narrow lanes
between the Trongate and the stinking Shambles on the Clyde.
The companies were exercised daily on the Low Green above the
river, marching there behind pipes and drums, watched by idle
schoolboys and suffering the obscene derision of laundrywomen
at the Washing House. At Retreat the soldiers dispersed to their
mean lodgings and, in the opinion of their officers, to the seditious
influence of the levelling societies. It was perhaps a fear of such
political contagion that intensified the discipline imposed by
Maclean and his company commanders, as if they believed that
hard sweat and relentless abuse would exorcise the demon of
disaffection.

The battalion guard-house, the explosive centre of the coming
mutiny, was in Candleriggs Street, on the west side and a few
yards north of the Trongate corner. It was a solid building of
grey stone, two storeys high, recently removed from its original
position in the Trongate and reassembled here on the site of the
old weigh-house, between the meal-market and the herb-
market. It had bizarre, classical pretensions, a microcosm of
Mediterranean grandeur. It was fronted by a covered piazza a
foot above the street, the roof supported by four Ionic columns
with entablature. Here at night a single lantern drew marching
shadows from two sentries, pacing in time and turning together.
The echoing ground floor was one stone-flagged chamber where
the soldiers of the guard sat and slept, held for twenty-four hours
in the inexorable embrace of cross-belts and knapsack. An inside
stair led to two rooms above, a store-cupboard and a bed-
chamber for the officers on duty. The street outside was straight
and narrow, five hundred yards northward from the Trongate to
the facing windows of Ramshorn Church on Back Cow Lane.
The buildings leant toward each other in decaying sadness, stone,
wood and thatch, crow-step gables and flaking plaster, a sugar-

house and a soap-works, a cooperage, builder's yard and charity school, a mansion that once flattered the conceit of a glass-maker but was now a wretched tenement, its outside stairs hung with children from dawn until dusk. Almost opposite the guard-house was Bell's Wynd, leading to the scarlet horror of a fleshmarket and the roof-top offices of the Glasgow *Herald*. Halfway up the street and on the east side was a large bowling-green, unfashionable but still in use, and between its crumbling wall and the cobbles was a shallow ditch, a septic wound, moving with maggots and foul with the smell of rotting kail-stalks and butcher's refuse.

On the night of Thursday, November 27, the men of the guard were drawn from Captain Francis Gray's Light Company, the companions of Malcolm MacFarlane. There was one prisoner only, a Highland deserter from the 68th Foot, John Stewart, whose wife had been allowed into the guard-house to comfort and sustain his courage. There was no privy in or near the building, and at seven o'clock on Friday morning, while it was still dark, Stewart asked leave to make water. Sergeant Henderson sent him into the street, with his wife and escorted by Private Hugh Robertson. When nature had been eased into the ditch the Stewarts asked Robertson if they might go into a tavern for a little food, and he good-naturedly agreed. He became uneasy, however, when they delayed over the meal, and he suddenly grasped Stewart's coat and pulled him toward the door. There he was attacked by the prisoner's wife who threw her arms about him, shouting for her husband to run. Stewart did so, through the door and into the darkness of Candleriggs Street.

When he was released by the screaming woman, Robertson went back to the guard-house and told Sergeant Henderson what had happened. Together they went into the street, walking its length in the foolish hope of finding the lurking deserter. Robertson was now aware of the enormity of his error, the punishment he must suffer, and again and again he told the Sergeant of his remorse. The Lieutenant of the guard was John Cameron, a young Lochaber gentleman recently come to the regiment, and when he was called down to the lower chamber he angrily ordered Robertson to be relieved of his musket and bayonet and placed under restraint until the Major's will was known. Aroused from his bed at the Star Inn on the Trongate, Maclean did no less than was required of him by the Articles of War. He told Cameron to keep Robertson in close arrest, and shortly after breakfast he instructed the Adjutant, his kinsman Hector Maclean, to arrange a regimental court-martial for the first convenient day after the Sabbath. The punishment inevitably awaiting Robertson was thus not less than three hundred lashes and not more than a thousand, to be publicly administered on the Low Green and on one or more days according to the length of the sentence and the advice of a surgeon. Alexander Maclean may have already known, as he certainly knew later, that the flogging of Malcolm MacFarlane had deeply angered the battalion. As a lieutenant of the Argyll Fencibles he had seen what Highlanders would do in protest against such brutal punishment, but he could not ignore Robertson's offence, and in the absence of Breadalbane and Morrison there was no one to whom he might transfer the awful responsibility of decision.

Early in the morning of Monday, December 1, when the members of the court-martial were assembling in the upper chamber of the guard-house, all the men of the Light Company came to Candleriggs Street. Many carried muskets, or had bayonets at their belts. They stood before the piazza, calling for Robertson's release, declaring that they would not permit another of their comrades to be flogged. The noise attracted a great crowd, women and children from the tenement, workmen in iron shoes from the soap-works, coopers with hammers in their hands, butchers in bloody aprons. Some of them were Highland and they shouted encouragement in Gaelic, urging the soldiers to attack the building. The guard that day was formed by Glenfalloch's grenadiers, and although they were unhappy with their duty the two sentries kept the Light Company men from the floor of the piazza. Their captain was here now to sit as president of the court. He leant from the upper window, ordering the rioting soldiers to return to their quarters, but the only response was a great shout of anger, and the Light Company men rushed upon the piazza. The sentries fell back to the door, barring it with crossed muskets, and behind them stood Sergeant Nicolson with his halberd advanced, shouting violent oaths.

Two junior lieutenants, Maitland and MacLaurin, had come late to sit on the court, and had been delayed further by the mob between the bowling-green and Back Cow Lane. They used their fists, the weight of their bodies, to reach the piazza. There they were joined by Hector Maclean, a powerful man who had once been a sergeant of the Scots Guards, and together the three officers cleared a space, room enough for Campbell of Glenfalloch to come from the guard-house with dignity. He was a just and kind man, well-liked by the Highland soldiers, some of whom had known him since childhood and had gralloched the red deer he killed on the braes of Ben More. He held his arms above his head, appealing again for them to disperse, but they shouted him down. Boldly he turned his back upon them and called out the rest of the Guard. The grenadier sentinels formed a line upon the piazza, an arm's length apart, and upon Glenfalloch's next order they stepped down to the cobbles, driving the mutineers before them with bayonets fixed and charged. They marched forward three paces before they halted, the flank-men making a half-turn to the left and the right. The mutineers fell back against the houses opposite, toward the Trongate and Back Cow Lane, but they would not leave the street. As if his thin screen of grenadiers were a battalion in line, Glenfalloch calmly waited for the arrival of Maclean of Coll, standing on the piazza in the position of rest, one knee bent, left fist on his hip above his sword-hilt.

The Major came within the hour, pushing through the crowd with Captain Alexander Nairne and ignoring the jeers and abuse. When he entered the guard-house he at once ordered the Adjutant to carry the news of the disturbance to the civil authorities, and young Maclean went quickly out of a rear door, over the walls to Brunswick Street and thence to the Town House on the Trongate. The Major then walked on to the piazza and told the mutineers to return to their quarters, warning them of the extreme penalty they faced if they refused. Some did go, but calling over their shoulders that they would shortly return, with their arms and those who had already brought their muskets now fixed their bayonets. They moved toward the Guard, a shuffling, cautious advance, upon which Maclean withdrew the sentinels to the floor of the piazza, standing before them and enduring the spittle-laden abuse, the weapons pointed at his chest. His air of indifferent courage concealed his increasing unease. Men of Lord Breadalbane's company and some of Glenfalloch's grenadiers had now joined the mutineers. Workmen from the soap-works and cooperage, boys from the tenements, were pulling stones from the wall of the bowling-green and passing them to the nearest Highlanders. Maclean's reaction to this threat was improper and doubtful in law, for the presence of so many citizens in the mob before him made this a civil riot as much as a mutiny, and there was no magistrate to read the Act. He called upon the sentinels to prime and load. That there might be time for the gravity of his intention to be understood he gave the commands slowly and clearly, from *Open your pans* to *Handle your cartridge*, from *Load with cartridge* to *Ram* and *Shoulder*, but before the twenty-one complicated motions were completed, before the last order to present, the mutineers cried out against his voice, telling him that they were not afraid, that they knew how to fire as well as any grenadier of the Guard.

Glenfalloch and Nairne pleaded with Maclean, urging him to compromise, to avoid the shedding of blood, and perhaps he was relieved to have their support for his own unhappy doubts. He did not complete the firing-orders but he kept the Guard at the shoulder. There had been no movement forward since he first called *Prime and load . . . one!* If he were not to open fire he could do no more until he heard from the Town House, although he did not know how the Lord Provost could help him, there being no adequate police force in the city, no reliable force at all to maintain the law except the Breadalbane Fencibles who now stood in defiance of it. Like all professional officers, Maclean had no faith in the citizen warriors of the Glasgow Volunteer Companies, shop-keepers and counting-house clerks in comic uniforms of their own fantastic design. He had told Hector Maclean that the Lord Provost must send word at once to Hamilton where there was a regiment of dragoons, but he knew that long before the horsemen arrived, if indeed they could come today, he must make a decision that would end this unhappy affair. It was almost noon, and some of the mutineers had already stepped upon the piazza, when the Major at last capitulated. Later that day, by a dispatch to Edinburgh, he explained his surrender in a single wordy sentence that almost concealed his anger and shame.

> After trying every argument, without effect to induce them to go home, and seeing every appearance of matters coming to an extremity, I was induced by the persuasion of several officers to give up the prisoner, upon condition of his being again returned to the guard-house and a Court-martial proceeded in to-morrow.

Thus was Hugh Robertson delivered to his triumphant comrades of the Light Company, carried on their shoulders across the Trongate and into the labyrinth of lanes beyond. Despite the assurances willingly given to Maclean, or demanded by him, he cannot have believed that the prisoner would be returned the next day, and it may be that Robertson was not pleased by his rescue. If he were indeed surrendered to the court he would still be flogged, and if he were not he might well be shot for his innocent but influential part in the mutiny.

Alexander Maclean of Coll stood erect on the piazza until the last of the mutineers and the mob were gone from Candleriggs Street. His humiliation had been total, but his emotions had not blinded him to his duty, and he had marked down those men he would later name as ring-leaders. There was John Malloch, of course, the young man from Loch Tay who had already threatened to disembowel his officers. There was Ludovick MacNaughton, also from Breadalbane and a soldier in his lordship's company. When the trouble began he had been wearing civilian clothes, or at least a coloured coat instead of his uniform tunic. He had been among the first to go for his musket, returning from his quarters within the half hour and now dressed in tartan and scarlet, as if they would ennoble his mutinous conduct. No man had been more active, thought Maclean, than the youngest soldier in Lord Breadalbane's company, Duncan Stewart. "Though without arms," the Major would write that evening, "he never ceased instigating the rest and fomenting mutiny as much as possible."

When the breathless Adjutant arrived at the Town House, mired to the thighs by his ignominious journey over garden walls, Lord Provost John Dunlop did not know what was expected of him, and not knowing he accordingly did nothing. In addition to his civic responsibilities of which he was excessively proud, haughty to those below him and obsequious to those above, he was a writer of sentimental songs. He had composed the lyrics of that popular air *Here's to the year that's awa'*, although he might not have wished to be reminded of it as this twelve-month ended. Like other Scots in his position he was obsessed by the fear of civil insurrection, and what had been a recurring nightmare for three years seemed now to have become a terrifying reality. If a Highland regiment, which was intended to stand between the Crown's authority and republican revolt, was itself in a state of rebellion what was there to prevent a dreadful catastrophe? Maclean of Coll came to the Town House that afternoon, with a copy of the report he had written to Lord Adam Gordon. Neither soldier nor Provost drew much reassurance from their meeting, aware that the true power in the streets of Glasgow at this moment was the Breadalbane Regiment. Their conversation was stiff with suspicion, and Dunlop was angered by Maclean's complaint that the townspeople were supplying his mutinous men with powder and ball. When they parted, the Lord Provost wrote at once to Robert Dundas in Edinburgh, ordering his clerk to make a reciprocal copy for the Major. He told the Lord Advocate that he and his brother magistrates would do all that was required of them to preserve the peace of the city "which I cannot help thinking endangered in some degree by an example so outrageous and so contrary to law and discipline". He had written to the Lord Lieutenant, the Duke of Hamilton, and to the Colonel of the dragoon regiment, but instead of reassuring squadrons of horse only Colonel Clavering had come. The cavalry commander told the Lord Provost that he could not bring his riders into the city without an order from Lord Adam. "If that is necessary," Dunlop told Robert Dundas, "I request your Lordship that the order may be made a standing order, as I presume it is principally with a view to the peace of this great city that dragoons are quartered at Hamilton."

That Monday evening the city magistrates met at the Town House, expecting it to be stormed at any moment by wild Highlanders and a seditious mob. With more hope than faith in the decision, they agreed that the Glasgow Volunteers should be ordered to hold themselves in readiness. This regiment was a continuing source of amusement to battalions of the line, and a sad caricature of the valiant Enthusiasts who had fought at Falkirk. It consisted of three hundred young merchants and superior artisans of the middle class who served without pay. They were mustered in small companies under titles of their own invention, The Sharp-Shooters, The Grocer's Corps, the Canal Volunteer Corps. There was also a Light Horse Company, made even lighter by the fact that it was yet to be mounted, and it was commanded by the Town Clerk, John Orr, whose rake-helly, fox-hunting youth had long since surrendered to the puritanical self-denial of middle age. The Saturday soldiering of these companies on the Low Green had equipped none of them with the skill or courage to face a desperate enemy in the night-dark of Glasgow streets, but until a proper force arrived they were all that John Dunlop might call upon.

The Breadalbane officers wisely kept to their lodgings, believing that their appearance abroad would only provoke the mutineers. Hugh Robertson was not surrendered at the guard-house on Tuesday, and the members of the court discreetly returned to their quarters by the back lanes. At nightfall too, John Dunlop was alarmed to hear that some Highlanders had attempted to buy powder and ball, and although the ironmonger who reported this had turned them away they might well have been successful elsewhere. He sent this information to Robert Dundas by the morning coach, adding that although the night had been tranquil, with no mob or mutineers in the streets, he was uneasy about the future. There was a general alarm throughout the city, and all good people felt themselves at the mercy of the Breadalbane men, "a military force devoid of proper subordination and therefore dangerous to the extreme". If Wednesday night again passed without incident he proposed to call upon the Lord Advocate and the Commander-in-Chief in Edinburgh. The quiet in the city, after the fear of bloody insurrection, now persuaded him that the mutineers should not be provoked, and he begged Dundas to believe that good men should act with prudence and caution. "A rash step might be in the present situation of the country, and of this town in particular, be irrevocable."

Dunlop's letter reached Hugh Cameron's Tavern by the Cross in Edinburgh at five that evening, and within the hour Robert Dundas was with Lord Adam Gordon at Holyroodhouse. The Commander-in-Chief was not greatly alarmed by the Glasgow mob, but he was angered by the mutiny and he believed that duty and good sense required him to crush it immediately beneath a dragoon's boot. Upon the receipt of Maclean's first dispatch he had sent a rider to the west, a young aide galloping hard to Major-general Sir James Steuart commanding that district, with orders to gather all the forces that might be necessary "and to take such steps as may appear proper for securing the ring-leaders and preserving the peace of the city". Steuart was a realist, that is he took cautious advice from his doubts, and he was perhaps glad that Lord Adam's orders left him room for independent decision. The only forces immediately available to him were four troops of Clavering's dragoons, and no man would thank him if he sacrificed them in a bloody street battle with His Majesty's soldiers and subjects, however disaffected these might be. He ordered the horsemen closer to Glasgow, that the threat of their blue coats and steel scabbards might be seen in the winter daylight, their trumpets heard at night. He then left by coach for Edinburgh, riding in cold and aching discomfort with John Dunlop and John Orr.

They arrived at the Cross too late on Thursday for Lord Adam to see them, but they met him at the breakfast hour next morning. So unanimous was their gloom, their belief that the dragoons were too weak to subdue the Highlanders, that Gordon withdrew the proposal for the moment. He did so under protest. Mutiny, he said, grew stronger with every minute it was unopposed, and it was insufferable that a thousand men should be allowed to hold a kingdom at defiance and in breach of their soldier's oath. The little Lord Advocate, who also came that morning, was as bright-eyed and amiable as always, stepping neatly from one bland equivocation to another. If he were original and positive in any belief it was in his firm conviction, as Lord Cockburn said, that his main public duty was resistance to revolution. This duty, however, was weakened by the present frailty of those who should be its resolute instrument. The principal purpose of garrison troops in Scotland was to suppress civil discontent, yet the necessary presence of those regiments in urban areas exposed them to that disaffection. In the Lord Advocate's opinion, frequently if irrelevantly expressed, the Breadalbane Fencibles should never have been sent to Glasgow. The security of the nation would be at less risk if they and Sir James Grant's insubordinate companies were immediately disbanded. But before this could be done, if it should be done, the Breadalbane men must be returned to their duty, and the King's servants who gathered above the quiet quadrangle of Holyroodhouse were obliged to find the means and method of that compulsion. It was another day, another breakfast, supported now by his deputy Alexander Leslie, before Lord Adam was able to persuade Mr. Dunlop that troops *must* be sent into his city. This small victory was immediately lost in Sir James Steuart's continuing caution. The extra forces he would need, he said, could not be brought to a state of readiness within forty-eight hours. He was told to dispose them as the daily situation demanded, ready or not. His lack of enthusiasm, however, forced Lord Adam to agree that the Glasgow Volunteers should be issued with ball cartridges, but he insisted that none should be fired without express orders from the general officer commanding.

That night the old man wrote urgently to Lord Amherst, upon a matter that had angered him since the first news of the mutiny. The proper place for Lord Breadalbane, he said, was in Glasgow not Wigmore Street, and upon his insistence Robert Dundas repeated this advice to the Home Secretary, the Duke of Portland. "It is hoped that his lordship's presence and influence will at least have the effect of detaching the well affected and orderly of the corps from those who have been principals in the mutiny."

The nation's press had still published no account of the affair, but the printer of the *Herald*, whose offices were within sight and sound of the riot on Candleriggs Street, should not be charged with lack of enterprise. The report of a political spy in Edinburgh, sent to Henry Dundas on Friday, suggests that if the Secretary of War were no longer the Sultan of Scotland the Lord Advocate was still its Grand Vizier, loyal to his uncle's belief that tolerance of a free press was incompatible with responsible government.

(The mutiny) is very properly hushed here as much as possible, and none of the papers have as yet taken any notice of it, so I should hope it will not soon reach London thro' that medium at least. There is however no doubt of the fact several private letters from Glasgow to the most respectable people here mentioning it. The particulars I have thus given you were related to me by one who was present, and may be depended on. It is a very bad business in whatever way it ends.

Although their city was apparently in the hands of rebellious Highlandmen, and might at any moment be sacked by a republican mob, the Lord Provost and the Town Clerk were not eager to return to it. They remained in Edinburgh at Cameron's Tavern until Sunday, December 7. That Sabbath morning, with Steuart and Dundas, they again called upon Lord Adam who must by now have been weary of so many guests, so often and so early. The meeting was decisive, however. Dunlop and Orr were persuaded to return to Glasgow on the evening Fly, and Steuart agreed to march into the city on Tuesday, if his regiments were at last ready. Before this irrevocable step was taken, John Dunlop insisted that Major Maclean should arrest the ringleaders of the mutiny. He did not explain how this was to be done. Lord Adam no doubt thought the proposal an insult to Maclean's intelligence and a probable risk to his life, but as an alternative to the use of force it should be at least tried. Throughout the summer Gordon had feared that another mutiny in another Fencible regiment would be followed by the sympathetic revolt of others, and he had expected this daily since the first news from Glasgow. He was therefore reassured that Sunday when Campbell of Lochnell told him that the Argyll regiment in the Castle was quiet and obedient. William Wemyss, coming to Holyroodhouse upon express orders, also said that his Sutherland men had never been in better spirits. But there were three companies of the Strathspey Regiment at Paisley, close enough for them to be seduced by the mutineers, and Lord Adam sent orders at once for them to march south, to join the rest of the battalion in Dumfries.

He dined early on Sunday, alone for the first time that week. He believed that Breadalbane would arrive in Scotland at any hour now, and would bring his mutinous people to order, but at four o'clock, when candles were being lit against an early dusk, a subaltern of his lordship's regiment came to Holyroodhouse with a most discouraging letter from Major Maclean.

"*The mutineers have not shown any contrition*"

"I WILL FREELY confess to you," wrote Alexander Maclean, "that I am afraid even Lord Breadalbane's presence would not be sufficient to induce the companies that are mutinously disposed to give up voluntarily the principal delinquents." The most to be expected from the arrival of *Mac-Chailein 'ic Dhonnachaidh* might be that the soldiers from his own estates would refrain from further outrageous behaviour. In the Major's opinion, bluntly expressed to Lord Adam, the mutinous spirit of the battalion arose entirely from the arrogance of the Breadalbane men, their belief that they were superior to other Highlanders in the regiment, and their resolve that no man from their country would be punished at the halberds. Maclean clearly resented this impertinence, both as an officer of the Crown and a gentleman of Coll whose islanders, the children of Gillean of the Battle-axe, were the equal of any mainland Campbell. He was also angered by the fact that all responsibility for ending the mutiny by peaceful means had been placed upon him, that Lieutenant-colonel Morrison, who should be in Glasgow, was still absent upon his own affairs, petitioning the Government for permission to raise a regiment under his own name.

Maclean would receive little credit for the fact that after the angry protest in Candleriggs Street he prevented any further violence and even imposed a bizarre discipline on the mutinous battalion. Ignoring the near-panic of the city's inhabitants, the lathered galloping of Steuart's aides from suburban villages to the Volunteers' headquarters at the Tontine Inn, he persuaded the companies to assemble for the guards and parades he ordered, to gather each day for their subsistence money and to disperse quietly when dismissed. He repeatedly asked the known ringleaders to come forward for punishment and thus save their comrades from an inevitable assault by Steuart's Horse and Foot. If it were true, as John Dunlop claimed, that some of the soldiers wished to march homeward to their glens, it was Maclean and company commanders like Glenfalloch who dissuaded them and thus stopped a suicidal encounter with the waiting dragoons. The Major knew that the Highlanders' self-respect and traditional concern for their honour would compel them to behave well once their protest had been made, that if they were treated with fairness and courtesy they would respond in a like mood. He exploited this simple nobility in the hope of strengthening his tenuous hold over them. Although they had resisted military brutality they had a perverse pride in themselves as soldiers and were easily shamed by any suggestion that they were less than this conceit maintained. For three days Maclean refused to post any orders for the men of the Light Company, letting them know that this was because they had disgraced themselves before the guard-house, and when he returned them to their duty he made it plain that it was not because they had been forgiven but because he would no longer impose an extra burden upon the other companies. The Light Company accepted the rebuke with remarkable docility.

Despite this, the soldiers were still in a state of mutiny. They would not deliver Hugh Robertson to the guardhouse, and they told their officers that they would resist any attempt to take ringleaders from among them. But the curious calm created by their orderly behaviour and by the lack of any movement against them began to unnerve their courage. A correspondent to *The Times* said that they believed the quiet to be the forerunner of a storm.

The Lord Provost was not impressed by the civil manner of the Highlanders. Once returned to Glasgow, and having failed to persuade Maclean to imprison the ringleaders so adamantly demanded by outraged authority, he told Lord Adam that although the city was peaceful "The mutineers have not shown any contrition for the atrocious offence committed." He wrote to London in the same indignant tone, warning Henry Dundas and Portland that the sixty thousand inhabitants of Glasgow, so inadequately protected by three hundred Volunteers, were at the mercy of a thousand Highlanders. He, too, had no faith in the battalion's tardy Colonel. "My belief is that Lord Breadalbane's presence, in the sentiments the regiment are under, will be ineffectual, and that they will not permit of their comrades to be touched."

Sir James Steuart finally left Edinburgh for his command on Tuesday, December 9, accompanied by Lord Adam's deputy, General Alexander Leslie. The three men were agreed that if Breadalbane did not shortly arrive then Steuart must enter the city with all the Foot he could muster. It was eight days since the riot in Candleriggs Street, and in that time not one positive step had been taken to bring the mutiny to an end. Lord Adam Gordon's faith in the merciful use of immediate and irrestible force – a sophisticated version of Mr. Stevenson's belief that the first mutinous dog to open his mouth should be knocked down with his own firelock – had foundered upon Steuart's dilatory incompetence and upon the Lord Advocate's chimerical fear of civil insurrection. "An unsuccessful attempt to seize the mutineers," Robert Dundas had told Portland "would be followed with consequences of the most serious and alarming nature to the tranquility of this country." Indecision and irresolution thus compelled continued reliance upon the one man whom nobody now believed would truly bring the Highlanders to submission.

In his first request for Breadalbane's attendance, written two days after the riot in Candleriggs Street, Lord Adam told Amherst that "if his lordship's parliamentary presence can be dispensed with" the Earl would be welcomed in Scotland. This tart sarcasm was forwarded to Wigmore Street with a brief covering letter, and was agreeably acknowledged the same evening by Breadalbane's assurance that he would leave for Scotland without loss of

time. The next morning Amherst wrote again, as if overnight
his tired and aged mind had at last seen the cunning game the
Campbell might be playing. He said that he was exceedingly
glad that the Earl had decided to go to Glasgow, and he would
now write immediately to the War Office "that the Letter of
Service for your third battalion may be prepared as soon as
possible". If Breadalbane had indeed been idling in London until
this coveted favour was granted he made no haste to pay for it.
He was still in London two days later on Monday, December 8,
when he received Lord Adam's peremptory order to rejoin his
regiment at once. He acknowledged the letter with lofty politeness and asked what commands he might expect when he arrived
in Glasgow. Gordon received this on Thursday, the eleventh day
of the mutiny, and he answered with controlled anger.

> I lose no time to state, what I hope, and expect from your
> Lordship, as Colonel of the 4th Regiment of Fencibles, and
> as indispensably necessary for the existence of Military
> Discipline and Order. Your Lordship's 1st Battalion being at
> present and ever since their outrageous behaviour on the
> 1st inst. in a state of absolute Mutiny and Disobedience to
> their officers, examples must be made, and I expect from your
> Lordship that you will use what means you chuse to cause
> delivered up in order for trial by a General Court Martial,
> the ringleaders and principal actors in the said mutiny, as
> without this previous step is taken no measure or moving of
> your 1st Battalion can be admitted, and if it is not complied
> with by consent, all the force under my command here, of
> Infantry and Cavalry, must be recurred to, to procure Justice
> and to restore Order and Discipline.

Gordon sent these orders to the Star Inn at Glasgow, but when
the dispatch arrived on Thursday evening there was nobody to
open it. The Earl of Breadalbane was still on the Great North
Road, coming leisurely northward to his duty. For three more
days Lord Adam fretted at the enforced inaction, unconsoled by
the Home Secretary's approval of all he had done. The Duke of

Portland was now less concerned with the resolution of the mutiny than with what steps might be taken to prevent a repetition of it in other regiments. He agreed with Robert Dundas that all Highland Fencibles should be removed at once to some part of England where they would be isolated from their disaffected countrymen, and he seemed to have forgotten that this would be a breach of their engagement, that such a proposal had been the cause of their discontent in the spring. He also had no confidence in the Earl of Breadalbane, and he again echoed the advice given to him by the Lord Advocate. If the man were able to separate the good from the bad among his troublesome soldiers it would at least enable Sir James Steuart to chastise the latter.

The Earl arrived at the Star toward dusk on Sunday, coming to the Gorbals bridge through the blue-coat pickets of the Queen's Dragoons whom Steuart had now advanced within carbine-shot of the river. He was relieved to discover that the company at the inn would not be entirely tedious, that the Duke of Hamilton was lodging there, with Campbell of Lochnell and his lady. William Morrison had also arrived in Glasgow on Saturday with a handsome offer of assistance to Maclean of Coll, which the Major may have thought more obligatory than handsome and as worthless now as it was belated. Breadalbane did not appear at the morning parade of the companies on Monday, to upbraid his men or demand the surrender of Hugh Robertson and the ringleaders named by Maclean. He was perhaps fatigued by an arduous and unwelcome journey of four hundred miles in three days, content to let the knowledge of his awesome if unseen presence work what influence it could upon his clansmen and his soldiers. At supper on Sunday, Alexander Maclean had told him that three grenadiers had declared themselves willing to suffer trial, if that would save the battalion from further punishment, and he had thus arrived at a most felicitous moment for his bruised reputation, when the resistance of the mutineers had reached the point of collapse.

For ten days Maclean and the company commanders had

talked earnestly and emotionally with the soldiers, warning them that continued obstinacy must result in the use of force, in the death of many and the punishment of more than were already under its threat. They appealed to regimental and clan loyalties, and again and again they asked John Malloch and others to submit and prevent a useless slaughter. Their appeals and arguments were reinforced by the sight of black-horse'd dragoons across the Clyde, white cord braiding on dark shell-jackets, the bright challenge of bridle and chain. By Monday, December 15, when the drummers of Steuart's infantry were clearly heard on the high ground beyond Barrowfield, the Breadalbane men at last believed that the storm they had feared could now break upon them in terrible vengeance.

At two o'clock that afternoon four soldiers came to Colin Campbell of Glenfalloch at the Tontine and offered to stand trial on behalf of all the mutineers. They were Lochtayside men from the Earl's lands. Two belonged to the Light Company, John Malloch and Duncan Stewart. A third, Ludovick Mac-Naughton, was from Lord Breadalbane's company, and the fourth was a grenadier, John MacMartin. None of them was older than twenty-four. Despite his claim to be eighteen, Stewart was in fact three years younger and had enlisted at the age of fourteen. It would be easy to believe that their frightened comrades had forced them to surrender, but John Dunlop said that a fifth volunteer, eager to share their self-sacrifice, was forcibly restrained by his fellow-grenadiers. The submission of the four men was noble and naïve, and would be regretted only when they lay in darkness below the casemate of Edinburgh Castle, when fear of death or mutilation compelled them to give the names of ten other Highlanders who, they said, were as guilty as they. When they came to Glenfalloch they believed that by their surrender the rest of the battalion would suffer no reprisals, and they may also have agreed with the officers and sergeants who told them that they had shamed their families and their chief. Later that afternoon Hugh Robertson came to the guard-house and was placed in manacles and leg-irons with the others. At the evening parade, as each company assembled before its quarters, the soldiers told their officers that they would now obey all orders given to them.

John Dunlop was exultant. At three o'clock on Tuesday afternoon he wrote to the Duke of Portland, telling the Home Secretary that the four prisoners were already on their way to Edinburgh Castle, guarded by men of their own regiment and commanded by Captain Campbell of Glenfalloch. Now that the affair was seemingly over, the rhyming Provost breathed vainglorious fire. The Glasgow Volunteers, he said, were in excellent order, ready to do all that was required of them. "I can also depend upon the assistance of a very respectable body of Gentlemen of this City who have enrolled themselves as special constables, to act in the district over which I have the honour of acting as Depute Lieutenant." At this point in the writing of his dispatch his loyal euphoria was unpleasantly interrupted by the news that the mob was again abroad, menacing life and property and determined to rescue the Highlanders.

Alexander Maclean had feared this, and had urged the wisdom of sending the prisoners from the city as soon as possible. He had opposed Lord Adam's earlier intention to hold the necessary court-martial in Glasgow, and he was supported by John Dunlop who wanted no more provocation and riot. The four men were taken away at noon, still manacled and marching by the Gallowgate to the Edinburgh road. By one o'clock there were two mobs on the streets. The first, which included a number of unhappy Breadalbane men and corporals, was orderly enough if noisy. It gathered before the door of the Star on the Trongate, shouting for the release of the departed prisoners, and the correspondent to *The Times* soon left it in search of something more exciting. He joined the second mob, now moving down West Gallowgate under the leadership of a number of Friends of the People, one of whom, said the correspondent, was a democratical rascal called Russel who had been involved in the trial of Thomas Muir the previous year. This crowd was more violent in intent, and was armed with stones and clubs, but it was too late in leaving the city to come up with Glenfalloch's party. At the outskirts it met two officers who had marched some way with Colin Campbell, the Adjutant Hector Maclean and General Leslie's kinsman and aide, Major John Leslie. The mob fell upon both officers, hurling stones which knocked Leslie to the ground where he would then have been beaten to death had not Maclean dragged him into a house. They were besieged for nearly an hour, while the mob beat on the doors and broke the windows. The most eager in this assault was a Breadalbane soldier of Captain Gavin Drummond's company, Alexander Sutherland from Caithness, driven by anger and grief to this violence and thus to his eventual execution. In a bizarre paradox it was not the Glasgow Volunteer Regiment or the Gentleman Constables who restored order, but a company of the Breadalbane Fencibles sent by Maclean of Coll. They drove the mob away at the point of bayonet and they brought Alexander Sutherland to the guard-house on Candleriggs Street. There he was joined that night or on Wednesday morning by two other mutineers who may have come voluntarily in surrender or under compulsion. Both were men of Francis Gray's Light Company and one was an old soldier of thirty, John Scrimgeour. The second was Donald MacCallum whom Major Maclean had already marked down among the most mutinous. In the attempt to release Hugh Robertson he had leapt upon the piazza, waving his musket and shouting "Let us get the bugger out!"

On Tuesday night a troop of the Queen's Dragoons came over the Gorbals bridge and patrolled the city with the Volunteers. Before dawn they had apprehended the democrat Russel and two members of the Society. The Lord Provost publicly thanked the Breadalbane Fencibles for their part in the rescue of the two officers to whose help he and the city magistrates had come so belatedly. He offered a reward of £50 for information against any other guilty members of the Society of Friends and he placed an advertisement in the *Courier* urging "Masters and Mistresses of Families to keep their Children, Servants and Apprentices in their respective houses during the evenings and night times."

Glenfalloch's melancholy march to Edinburgh with his four

prisoners took two days. At nightfall on Tuesday, when he quartered his command beyond Airdrie, he received an astonishing request from the grenadier John MacMartin. He made no report of this to Lord Adam, or of his action in response, but many years later he told the story to Garth who included it in his *Sketches* as an example of "the honour and fidelity to his word and to his officer in a common Highland soldier". MacMartin said that he knew he must be shot for his offence but he had promised a favour to a friend in Glasgow and was distressed that he had not yet kept his word.

> He could not die in peace unless the business was settled, and that, if the officer would suffer him to return to Glasgow, a few hours there would be sufficient, and he would join him before he reached Edinburgh, and march as a prisoner with the party. "You have known me since I was a child; you know my country and kindred, and you may believe I shall never bring you to any blame by a breach of the promise I now make, to be with you in full time to be delivered up in the Castle."

Glenfalloch did not ask what this business was, or if he did he did not tell Garth. He released MacMartin that night and was not alarmed by the grenadier's failure to return before Thursday morning, when the party entered the western suburbs of Edinburgh. Campbell led his command slowly to the West Port and the Grassmarket, and when he could delay no longer, since his approach had been seen from the walls of the Castle, he marched up to the fortress. "As he was delivering over the prisoners," said Garth, "but before any report was given in, MacMartin rushed in among his fellow prisoners, all pale with anxiety and fatigue, and breathless with apprehension of the consequences in which his delay might have involved his benefactor." He had come from Glasgow by night, travelling across country to the south of the Whiteburn road, and had lost his way in unfamiliar woods and hills.

Hugh Robertson was tried by a regimental court-martial in the

Candleriggs guard-house on Friday, December 19, Captain Gavin Drummond presiding over four subalterns of the battalion. The hearing was brief and he was quickly found guilty of a breach of the second article of the twenty-third section of the Articles of War. He was sentenced to receive three hundred lashes on the bare back, to be delivered in the usual manner by the drummers of the regiment, but Drummond's report strongly urged mercy, arguing Robertson's previous good character and the fact that his offence had been accidental. In his first recorded official act since arriving in Glasgow, Breadalbane was graciously pleased to accept the recommendation, and Hugh Robertson was accordingly returned to his duties without the wet red coat that military justice had demanded.

Before the week ended Alexander Sutherland, John Scrimgeour and Donald MacCallum joined the other prisoners in Edinburgh Castle, and no one in authority believed that they deserved mercy. "We have at last got the better of the mutinous Fencibles," Robert Dundas informed London, "and I hope our military gentlemen will persevere in carrying through steadily the system of vigour which has been adopted regarding them." Lord Adam Gordon compassionately advised Breadalbane to settle any reasonable complaints his battalion might have, but the Lord Advocate believed its distemper would be improved by what he called *The Windsor Remedy*, immediate dispatch across the Border. "But my countrymen have taken it into their wise heads to object to going into England, and they cannot by the terms of their enlistment be compelled." John Dunlop was glad that his city would be quit of the Breadalbane men before Christmas. They were to be sent to the Falkirk district, and he hoped that Lochnell's Argyll Fencibles, who were to replace them, were the steady fellows everybody claimed them to be. He was keeping his Volunteers under arms, their banners hung from the windows of the Tontine and they paraded daily before it in their splendid uniforms. Glasgow was now to become an armed city. In addition to the Argyll soldiers, two six-pounders and a regiment of dragoons were shortly to arrive, and Dunlop hoped that this would encourage the Crown's servants to complete Delancey's long-overdue barracks on the Gallowgate. His preening pride, his belief that he had saved the city from insurrection and anarchy would be warmly confirmed in the New Year by a letter from the Duke of Portland. "I most sincerely congratulate you, and desire you to accept my best acknowledgements for the very conspicuous and meritorious part you have taken, and to be assured that it will give me peculiar pleasure to represent to His Majesty the distinguished service you have rendered."

The first division of Lord Breadalbane's Regiment left for the Falkirk district on December 20, its sick and baggage carried by track boat on the new Forth–Clyde Canal. The last companies reached their quarters on Christmas Day, frost on their bonnets and their bare hands blue with cold, but they were told that his lordship would pay for all they could eat and drink in celebration of their Saviour's birth. Lieutenant Alexander Campbell of the Light Company, who had passionately recommended Hugh Robertson's good character to the mercy of the court, was responsible for distributing the Earl's generosity among the companies quartered at Bathgate. With great difficulty he found an inn-keeper who would supply food at sixpence a head, porter and whisky at the usual prices. It was a cold season, the worst for several years, and although the landlord could serve a meal he had no fuel. The conscientious Lieutenant found the coals and a cart to carry them, begging both from a magistrate who charged the cost to the lord of the manor.

Few men in the battalion, at Falkirk, Linlithgow or Bathgate, can have enjoyed their Colonel's seasonable liberality. It was now known that if the prisoners were sentenced to death their own regiment would provide the firing-party, and would be paraded in hollow square to watch their ritual execution.

"We would wish they would spend their lives in your service"

WHILE HE WAITED for his trial, lying in a stone cell beneath the Castle, the boy Stewart made his will. He left the balance of his pay and what little else he possessed to his brother, a soldier in the Major's company, but the brother died of a winter fever before Duncan Stewart was brought to the court, before he knew whether he was himself to live or die.

No action was taken against the ten men whom the prisoners were persuaded to accuse, it being thought that seven were enough to carry the burden of guilt and become an example in punishment. They were tried with more scrupulous attention to Military Law than other Highland mutineers had been, and this was due to the fairness of Colonel Hugh Montgomerie who presided over the Court, and to Alexander Fraser Tytler, the Judge Advocate of North Britain.* Tytler was the second of three generations of scholarly historians, the Professor of Universal History at Edinburgh, and later a steady light in the radiant awakening of Scottish historical studies. Cockburn thought he was no lawyer, and said it would do his memory no kindness to believe that he was a man of genius or influence. But his amiable nature and honest mind, his respect for the Law throughout the trial, prevented what could have been a more spiteful act of vengeance against the Breadalbane men, the revenge of a society determined that someone should pay for its recurring nightmare of republican revolt.

Since the surrender of the first prisoners on December 16,

* He took the title of Lord Woodhouselee when he became a judge of the Court of Session in 1802.

347

Hector Maclean had been responsible for the gathering of evidence against them all, the preparation of exculpatory witnesses, the assembly of testimony as to what John Malloch had said, what MacCallum had shouted, what young Stewart had been seen to do. The duty was difficult and exhausting, and in order to bring some witnesses to Edinburgh from their quarters about Falkirk he was forced to pay their fare from his own pocket, believing they would not arrive in time if they marched by road. The hire of a post-chaise was twenty-four shillings, with half a crown to the driver and another for turnpike dues, and he had little money beyond his subaltern's pay. It was many weeks before the Deputy-Adjutant-General acknowledged his desperate requests for re-imbursement.

There was no sympathy for the accused among the officers of other Highland regiments. Major George Sutherland of Rearquhar, who had been ordered south with the Sutherland Fencibles as a precautionary measure in mid-December, expressed a general opinion when he said the Breadalbane men were rascally fellows. "The cause of giving us so much unseasonable and distressing a march, even tho' we were more fortunate in weather than could be expected in this season of the year." When the court-martial first assembled on Tuesday, January 6, in the great chamber of the officers' quarters on Palace Yard, those mild days were gone, replaced by cold sleet and snow, fierce winds and flying slates in the air above the Lawnmarket. The fire that burned in the chamber may have warmed the sixteen members of the court who sat closest to it, but it can have been little comfort to the prisoners, already weakened in body and spirit by depressing fears and the near-zero temperature of the Black Hole. The trial lasted until January 23, with frequent adjournments and interruptions. The first of these was when the court postponed its business on four consecutive mornings, during which a soldier of the second battalion of the Breadalbane Fencibles received a thousand lashes on Hawk Hill. Drunk while on guard at Leith, he had discharged his musket through an innocent window. Later the court set aside the principal trial and quickly dealt with Dugald

Cameron, once a private soldier of the Strathspey Fencibles and now a recruit in the regiment being raised by Alasdair Ranaldson MacDonell. He was given five hundred lashes for wantonly striking an officer. Returned to their cells below the casemate, the Breadalbane prisoners did not hear the cries of these suffering Highlanders, but they would have heard the beat of drums before each stroke of the lash.

The verdict of the court upon them was inevitable. All were found guilty of a breach of the third article of the second section of the Articles of War, that which defined mutiny and incitement to mutiny. Glenfalloch had given evidence of the previous good character of Malloch, MacMartin and MacNaughton, and the court acknowledged that there were degrees in culpability and in the enormity of the crime. The behaviour of Sutherland, Mac-Callum, Malloch and the boy Stewart was held to be most heinous, and all were sentenced to death. MacNaughton was awarded fifteen hundred lashes, Scrimgeour and MacMartin a thousand each. Informed now that Stewart was not yet sixteen, despite the age given at his enlistment, the court recommended him to mercy. Mercy was also asked for John MacMartin, on the grounds of "certain alleviating circumstances" which may have been brought to the court's attention by Colin Campbell of Glenfalloch. The Reverend Mr. Robertson MacGregor, growing old in the service of the Gaelic Chapel-at-Ease, had once again accepted the melancholy duty of interpreter and comforter, and he accompanied the prisoners when they returned to their cells, staying with them as long as they wished.

The sentences were confirmed by Lord Adam Gordon, and that duty and compassion might be served without cruel delay he ordered the executions to be carried out on the following Tuesday, January 27, publicly and upon the sands of Musselburgh. This news was taken to the prisoners by Captain William Cunningham of their regiment, and he was said to be greatly moved by the duty.

Tuesday was colder yet. Old Rearquhar could not remember such a day in this part of Scotland for fifty years. The white snow and the white light muted all colour, turning scarlet, blue and gold to black. A strong and relentless wind blew across the sands, and men and horses leant against it. Drawn up in a three-sided square, their backs to the north, east and west, were six companies of the Sutherland Fencibles and five of the Scotch Brigade, three troops of the Queen's Dragoons, a detachment of artillery, and selected companies from the first battalion of the Breadalbane Regiment in full dress. A great crowd had come from Leith and Edinburgh, well-wrapped against the weather and held at a respectable distance from the square by plodding patrols of dragoons.

The four prisoners left the Castle at ten o'clock in two mourning-coaches, their white and expressionless faces sometimes seen at the curtained windows. They were accompanied by a captain's escort of the Third Dragoons and a half-company of the Scotch Brigade. Mr. MacGregor rode in the first coach, changing to the second before the journey was over, that he might pray with all the condemned men, and take note of any last words they wished to send to their friends and kindred. They reached the sands at noon. Their hands were now tied behind them and they walked toward the centre of the square. Before each man marched a sergeant with halberd reversed, its point directed at the prisoner's breast, reminding him that he must be in no indecent haste to surrender his life. A firing-party of twelve Breadalbane men waited in three ranks, with muskets at the rest. They too wore the dress uniform of the regiment, belted plaids and yellow-faced scarlet, diced and gartered hose, eleven brown tassels on white sporrans, the snow-light bright on metal buttons, each engraved with the boast that no one might touch a Scot with impunity. Ten yards before the firing-party were four plain coffins and there the prisoners halted, facing their eyeless executioners and the bitter wind from the sea. Sir James Steuart then came to the centre of the square, standing before the prisoners and lifting his voice to read the verdict of the court and the consequent decision of the Commander-in-Chief in North Britain. Mr. MacGregor whispered a translation to two of the men who spoke little English, and his voice may have quickened with joy as Steuart came to the surprising end of Lord Adam's order.

> As it appears to me of the utmost consequence, that crimes of so dangerous a tendency as disobedience and mutiny, should be punished with rigour, Alexander Sutherland, the most notorious offender, has been offered to suffer death; but knowing how much it has always been His Majesty's wish that justice should be tempered with mercy, the punishments so justly awarded to all the other prisoners are suspended until His Majesty's pleasure shall be known.

Three sergeants turned about, taking Malloch, MacCallum and Stewart by the arm and leading them away. All but one of the coffins were removed by drummers, and Alexander Sutherland stood alone with the minister and the fourth sergeant. "That poor, unfortunate Caithness man!" said Rearquhar, remembering the scene later. He was now greatly distressed that he must watch the death of a man of his own name. He looked to his rear, to the ranks of the Sutherland Fencibles, and he saw that the cheeks of many were wet with tears. Across the square, the Breadalbane men were also weeping. Sutherland was quickly shot. The day was too cold to prolong the ceremony. "He met his fate," said the Edinburgh *Advertiser*, "with becoming patience and fortitude." The words were customary. They helped an age of naked emotions to accept the obscenity of any public execution, for if a man were said to die in penitence there was no unpleasant censure on the morality that had condemned him. Sutherland prayed for a few minutes, kneeling beside his coffin with Mr. MacGregor, and then he rose smartly, staring boldly at the firing-party until the sergeant tied a handkerchief about his eyes. When they had gently guided him to his knees again, the sergeant and the minister walked away, and the firing-party moved forward to within seven paces of their waiting victim. He was killed instantly by a volley from the first and second ranks, and there was no call for a compassionate musket from the reserve.

Lord Adam had suspended the other sentences upon his own

responsibility, confident of subsequent confirmation by the King. There had been four days only between the close of the court-martial and the execution, and in this time there could be no hope of an approving word from London. The Commander-in-Chief now began to work for some commutation that would be both merciful and salutary, unnecessarily plagued by Lord Breadalbane who wanted the same, for more selfish reasons. George III had been closely informed of every stage of the mutiny, and had been greatly disturbed by it. He had insisted that it should be ended without bloodshed if possible, but once it was over he told Amherst that discipline must be restored by the suitable punishment of the most guilty. On Christmas Eve he said that if Lord Adam were satisfied with the decision of the coming court-martial he should order its instant execution, "and only send to the Advocate General if he has a doubt about the propriety of the sentence". The convenient ambiguity of this encouraged Gordon to believe that if one man only were shot he could suggest a conditional mercy for the others, and he now argued this so cogently that the King gave his approval. On February 9 the prisoners in the Castle were told that the three men under a suspended sentence of death would be pardoned if they enlisted in those companies of the 60th Royal American Regiment at present serving in the West Indies. The flogging of the others would be set aside if they joined units of the same battalion in British North America. Lord Adam ordered the terms of this clemency, and its harsh alternative, to be read at the head of every regiment, corps, troop, company and detachment in Scotland, assuring the soldiers of his command that "Their own and their country's approbation will be the sure consequence of good behaviour to every individual, whereas a contrary line of conduct cannot fail of exposing to disgrace and punishment all such as shall quit the paths of Duty and Honour".

Seen across two centuries the choice before the wretched men in the Castle is deceptively generous, but there was not a man in the British Army at that time who did not fear and hate the thought of service as a green-coated rifleman of the Royal

Americans. The regiment had been raised in 1755, from Pennsylvania frontiersmen who were sent to fight the French and Indians along the Mohawk and Monongahela rivers. Now it served in the graveyard garrisons of the Caribbean and the rotting forts beyond the Ottawa, its fever-thinned companies inadequately filled by German mercenaries and condemned men from British courts-martial. In all but name it was thus an expendable penal battalion from which few men were discharged except by death. Even so, it offered a longer lease on life than would be given by a firing-party on Musselburgh sands, and the choice was accepted by Malloch, MacCallum and Stewart. But the other three said they would go to the halberds. They were Highland and the lash destroyed their self-respect. They were Highland and they had mutinied to prevent the use of the cat upon a comrade. But they would be flogged rather than go to exile and death with the Royal Americans. Their decision dismayed Lord Adam, for he believed that the best interests of the Service as well as their own would be served by their transportation. To give time and persuasion an opportunity to change their minds he delayed the order for their flogging.

The sentence of the court, the shooting of Sutherland and the suspension of punishment upon the others, had a remarkable effect upon the mind of Lord Breadalbane, filling its languid chambers with unusual alarm and indignation. He was at this moment completing the third battalion of his Fencibles, and his recruiters were beating up the last drafts for his marching-regiment, the 116th Perthshire Highlanders. But recruits were now difficult to find in his country, the mutiny in Glasgow had soured the hearts of his people. Before the execution of Sutherland he had the first of many interviews with Lord Adam, and wrote the first of many letters pleading for special consideration, for the mercy which (although he did not say this) would restore his good name among his clan.

There is something in the character of these men which requires a very different mode of treatment from others, and it is from this consideration that I have deliberately formed my judgement, and I again repeat to your Lordship that if a capital punishment is inflicted it may leave a wound which will not be easily healed, and put an end to any future exertions in the district of the Highlands with which I am most connected, that may be thought necessary for me to make in the service of Government to which both my life and fortune is devoted.

This failed to save the life of Sutherland, but when the Earl heard of the choice that was to be given to the others he asked for them to be drafted into the 116th or the third battalion of his Fencibles. His regimental agent in London wrote to the Duke of York in his name, declaring that he was sensible of the atrocity of the crimes committed but an awesome example had been made of one of "these fine young men" and no good purpose could be served by the punishment of the others. At the beginning of February, before Lord Adam's alternative to the sentences had been confirmed by the Crown and communicated to the prisoners, two Highlanders arrived in Edinburgh from Lochtayside. Peter MacMartin and Patrick Malloch came to petition their chief and plead for their sons. MacMartin's grief was further troubled by a sense of personal responsibility. Two years before, he had approved of his son's desire to enlist, in pride perhaps or because the Earl's agents demanded it, but his wife went in tears to Glenfalloch's recruiter at Milton on Loch Tay, begging so affectingly that the young man was turned away from the colours. Angered by her interference, MacMartin sent his son to the Earl at Taymouth Castle, with a letter asking for the boy's enlistment and apologising for his wife's behaviour. "When the lad heard of it he was exceedingly sorry, and wants to enlist whether his mother is pleased or not. I hope your Lordship will be pleased to recruit him as he is a good recruit." Breadalbane was so pleased and the lad was taken up, his enlistment dated from the day he had walked about the loch to Milton. Now the father came with his friend Patrick Malloch to ask mercy for their erring sons. There is no record that they saw the Earl, and the petition they signed with labouring hands had been dictated to another.

> We came on purpose from Breadalbane to thank your Lordship for your humanity to these poor Lads who were so unfortunate as to incur the Displeasure of their officers and you the Chief. We are very sensible that it is owing to your Lordship's interest at Court and your application to His Majesty that their Lives were spared. All we can say that not only us (who are so nearly connected with these deluded boys) thank your Lordship but the whole Country. Lady Breadalbane we hear and we believe has interfered if possible farther than your Lordship we pray for her prosperity here and her happiness hereafter. Your getting these men their pardon has endeared you to your numerous Tenants in our Country more than we can express and as you have saved their lives we would wish that they would spend their lives in your service we don't presume to dictate but if it could be done to get them to serve under your Lordship it would greatly add to the general happiness that the news of their respite diffused over the whole country.

On the day he received this, February 6, Breadalbane also heard from Lord Adam that it was the King's wish that no prisoner should be allowed to enlist in the Earl's regiments, that they must go to the Royal Americans or suffer the sentences given by their court-martial. If he saw the petition from the fathers, Gordon was perhaps less moved by its simple sincerity than irritated by its clear indication that Breadalbane's people believed their chief to be responsible for the mercy already shown. When the Campbell again asked for the men to be sent to his battalions, and added that he would petition the King upon the subject, Lord Adam told him to accept the situation as it was. The old man's anger was evident in the violent underscoring of the letter.

I *expect* the Prisoners individually, to state their acceptance, or refusal, to His Majesty's gracious condescension and when that is received, *then* will be your Lordship's proper time for making further application to His Majesty, *if you shall so think fit.*

The Lord Advocate was not impressed by Breadalbane's emotional pleading on behalf of the mutineers, and he suspected that outraged pride if not political ambition was leading the Earl into darker intrigue. One of the informers employed by Robert Dundas told him that two days before the execution of Sutherland his lordship had presided over a large dinner party at Fortune's Tavern, a fashionable house in Stamp Office Close renowned for claret, conversation and conspiracy. That Breadalbane, with Maclean of Coll, should dine with thirty gentlemen, advocates, scholars and surgeons, might have been of no consequence had it not been for the political nature of some of them. One was the ambitious young Whig Adam Gillies who had been counsel for Robert Watt and David Downie, tried five months before for their part in the Pike Plot. There were others more reprehensible.

Some of them are looked upon as the most decided Republicans in this country, the others must certainly have a fellow feeling when they thus associate with persons of that description. I could not get a list of their toasts: for this reason, that immediately after dinner one of the party called Fortune aside and told him they did not wish to be attended by him or anybody else but one particular waiter.

The Lord Advocate was not able to discover what had been said or discussed at the dinner, and that one particular waiter was nobly silent, even under determined interrogation by Thomas Elder, the Lord Provost who had boldly dispersed the first Convention of the Friends of the People, without assistance according to loyal mythology. Whatever Breadalbane may have hoped from the meeting, or it from him, nothing came of it, and he now devoted his time to the protection of his reputation in

Perthshire. Since the Crown would not give him the prisoners, and both the Duke of York and Henry Dundas had bluntly informed him that the King's decision would not be changed, he must prevent the flogging if he could. Like the parents of Malloch and MacMartin, many of his tenants believed that he and his emotional young wife had secured the first stay of execution, and this innocent faith in the omnipotence of their *ceann-cinnidh* was encouraged by John Kennedy, his lordship's factor at Taymouth. But if MacMartin, Scrimgeour and MacNaughton went obstinately to the halberds it would appear that the Earl had betrayed them. Kennedy was told that the friends and relatives of the prisoners must urge the young men to accept enlistment with the Royal Americans. Every family in Breadalbane should know that the Earl was making powerful applications on their behalf. And then a cynical deception or a cruel lie. "It may be just as well for themselves that they are away from their own regiment, and if they behave well after a few years there will be no difficulty in getting them transferred."

But the three men steadfastly refused to change their decision. Ten weeks after the choice was put to them, seventeen since they were first locked in the half-light below the Castle, Lord Adam finally ended the squalid delay. They were given what they wished. They were taken to the halberds on the clear, mild morning of Saint George's Day, and each received the first two hundred and fifty lashes of his sentence. MacNaughton and Scrimgeour endured the agony with firmness, but MacMartin behaved insolently, or so it was reported to Kennedy. They were sent to the barrack hospital, to the care of a surgeon engaged by Breadalbane's law-agent, and in the morning their crusted backs were again broken open by another two hundred and fifty strokes of the lash. That night none of them could endure the thought that such agony must continue for at least two days more. They asked for mercy and said they were now willing to join the 60th.

In May, when the whipped flesh was not yet healed, all six prisoners were taken by ship to the Savoy Prison in London.

A month later they marched to Portsmouth where they joined a hundred convicted soldiers, all awaiting transport to the Royal Americans. The fact that Scrimgeour, MacMartin and MacNaughton were to go to Canada was lost in bureaucratic indifference, and they were marked down for the West Indies with the rest. But an officer to whom they appealed, or another who conscientiously observed his duty, informed the War Office of the mistake and they were transferred to a draft of Royal Fusiliers, then embarking for the Saint Lawrence river. Malloch, MacCallum and Stewart went to the fevers of the Indies.

The spirit of the Breadalbane Regiment remained darkened by the mutiny, and so few Highlanders came forward as replacements that the Earl was forced to recruit more often in the Lowlands. In April, 1799, when most Fencible regiments were disbanded, the men of all three battalions were asked to re-enlist for service in Ireland, but only the third agreed. The men of the first battalion were marched to Fort George on the Moray Firth. The hills of the Black Isle threw back the echo of the last Retreat beaten by their drums, and in the morning they were dismissed to their homes. Duncan Ban Macintyre had already composed a sorrowing valediction. '*S muladach ma theid ar sgaoileadh* . . .

> 'Tis woeful if we are disbanded
> when 'tis our wish to be as we are.
>
> If we go to farm labour
> our shoulders will be bent with delving.
>
> Much better to be gentlemen,
> lining up in the battalion.

"You'll not have him out! With my life I'll guard this door!"

SEVEN WEEKS AFTER his emotional farewell at Linlithgow Alasdair Ranaldson MacDonell resigned his commission in the Strathspey Fencibles. Now that he had come of age, he said, the affairs of his estates demanded all his time and attention. His departure was not regretted, and Alexander Cumming prayed that the other two gentlemen from Glengarry would shortly follow their cub of a chief. James MacDonell did indeed leave within a month of his brother, seeking fire and glory in a regiment of the line, but their little kinsman Ranald was as reluctant to surrender his lieutenancy in the Light Company as he was to abandon his convenient sick-bed in the Highlands. The Grant officers asked for his dismissal, declaring that his insolent absence was injurious to discipline, but before he could be removed he had first to be recalled to a proper understanding of his duty. In December, 1794 Lord Amherst said that the young man should be told that unless he sent in his resignation, or joined his regiment without delay, he would be tried by a general court-martial. Cumming was ordered to prise the absentee from his distant glen, but the only response to a further blunt recall was yet another medical certificate which, said the Lieutenant-colonel, was easily got for a guinea from "some Doctor Roy". This obliging man was Alexander MacDonald of Kilmalew, *An Dotair Ruadh* the red-haired physician who had studied medicine at Aberdeen and practised it so profitably on the island of Lewis that he was said to have returned to the mainland with two thousand pounds, securely tied in a stocking. His loyal diagnoses continued to protect young Ranald until Cumming decided that the lieutenant should be summarily discharged from the regiment without benefit of court-martial. "As you are free of the rest of the pack," he advised Sir James in January, "you should insist on Lord Amherst clearing you of him too, as he was a shameful imposition on you from the beginning and ought to be sent after the Cub." The Laird accepted the proposal, and the Commander-in-Chief persuaded the King to withdraw Lieutenant Ranald's commission.

The rest of the pack, the troublesome MacDonell company, had been discharged from the regiment before Christmas. No one had been surprised to discover that Alasdair Ranaldson's concern for the problems of his estates was an excuse only, that his real desire was to advance by one leap from a captain of the Strathspeys to a colonel of his own Glengarry Fencibles. With the removal of the restrictions on the enlistment of Catholics he had been granted letters of service and was now beating the shores of Loch Quoich and Loch Garry. Some young men took to the high braes to escape his urgent drums and others came in unwillingly, forced into service by threats of eviction against their kindred. They were lacklustre recruits, and to stiffen their spirits, to give them an inspiring example to follow, Alasdair Ranaldson asked for the Strathspey company to be transferred to his new regiment. The Laird was willing enough to be quit of the ingrates who had caused him so much shame and heartache, but he saw no reason why he should part with them without replacement or repayment. This purse-conscious hesitation angered the young chief and he wrote an indignant letter of protest to Henry Dundas.

> I brought a hundred men into the Grant Fencibles, *all* my own tenants' sons who followed me from mere attachment. You cannot therefore be surprised if I should have every inclination to have as many of them or any others out of that regiment as would chose to follow me to the number permitted by the Government, which would be the *means* not only of *completing*, but also of *disciplining* my regiment in a very short time.

He was advised to call upon Sir James and argue his plea in person, and he arrived at Castle Grant with an arrogant tail of gillies and a petition signed by seventy-two members of the MacDonell company, privates, corporals and sergeants. They told their most honoured and renowned Colonel – they meant Alasdair Ranaldson, not the Laird – that it was their earnest and ardent wish to follow him to any part of the earth His Majesty might direct, seeking no bounty or recompense, only the satisfaction of serving under his banner and sharing the dangers that might face him. They had been kindly treated by the Strathspey officers in whose care he had left them, but now they desired to be under his protection once more. They had asked nothing of him when they were enlisted, because he was not then of age . . .

> Yet we hope now that you are your own master and have it in your power that our aged parents our wives and children and such of our friends as depend upon us should have something for our sake during our absence and if we chance to return home ourselves that we may know where to betake ourselves, indeed we expect to enjoy those possessions which our ancestors so long enjoyed under your ancestors, though now in the hands of Strangers, as we do not wish that you should lose by us we shall give as high rent as any of your Lowland shepherds ever give and we shall all become bound for any one whose circumstances may afford you room to mistrust. As our paper runs short we shall conclude by assuring your honour that all and every one of us unite in the same sentiments of attachment to you and shall continue in that attachment while the breath of life remains in us.

More than half of the signators had the same surname as their chief, and all the others were the familiar names of his lands. Their moving petition was an appeal to the obsolescent loyalties of a quickly dying world, the love and interdependence between the *ceann-cinnidh* and his children. They recognised with sorrow the fact that rents must now be more important to their chief than men, and they innocently offered to compete in kind with the wealth to be got from the Great Cheviot Sheep. They made no reference to the warrior history of their clan but declared them-

selves ready to become hostages for the security of their dependants, and asked no more of Glengarry than the protection his
forefathers had given theirs. He did not acknowledge this obligation when he sent a copy of the petition to Henry Dundas, he
said that the letter clearly indicated the soldiers' loyalty to his
person and "their willingness to enter upon a more extensive
service". His meeting with Sir James Grant that November was
bitter and indecisive and he complained to Dundas that malicious
people had grossly misrepresented him to his former guardian.
"Envy has occasioned me many enemies but I shall ever trust that
your goodness will put it in my power to confute any mis-
representations . . . Gratitude is a ruling passion in my breast, and
as long as blood circulates in my veins, it shall be my study
continually to merit that confidence which you have so early
placed in me."

To stimulate that confidence, he told Dundas that he had the
power to call the Gaelic youth of Glasgow into the King's service.
There were more than eighty Highland societies in that city,
including one of his own name and another formed by gentlemen
of Clan MacInnes who, he boldly declared, should more properly
be spoken of as MacDonells. In the event of invasion or public
tumult they would all be eager to follow his leadership. When
Lord Provost Dunlop was told of this he warned the Duke of
Portland not to believe the claims of "that hot-headed, weak
young man", for there were not more than five people in Glasgow
who came from Glengarry's country and "they are infernal
Democrats and very likely to have put this nonsense into his
head". It would be a sorry day, he said, if any Highlander in the
city placed attachment to a chief before obedience to the magistrates, and none should be entrusted with a musket. The warning
was accepted, but although Alasdair Ranaldson was not allowed
to lead a *levée en masse* from the urban clans he was at last given
his soldiers from the Strathspey regiment. They joined him at
Invergarry in December, by the burnt husk of his castle, below
the winter birch on the Raven's Rock. The simple assurance they
had asked of him was not kept, if ever given. When the Glengarry

Fencibles were disbanded in 1802 his self-indulgence was increasing his debts to £80,000, almost sixteen times the annual rent he could expect from his tenants, and much of the land the returning soldiers had hoped to enjoy was already leased to Lowland shepherds. "*A cross has been placed upon us!*" sang the blind bard of the clan, "*Poor men are naked beneath it!*" The regimental chaplain, Father Alexander MacDonell who had once urged the King's ministers to make soldiers of his Catholic clansmen, now saved them from the harsh consequences of that service. He secured grants of forest land in Canada, between the Ottawa river and the Saint Lawrence, and when a thousand men, women and children sailed from Fort William he went with them as their priest. They called their new home Glengarry. Alasdair Ranaldson was bitterly hurt by what he thought to be their desertion, but the grazing Cheviot which replaced them now paid some of his debts and enabled him to found The True Society of Highlanders, for the preservation of "the Dress, Language, Music and Characteristics of our Illustrious and Ancient Race".

Those Strathspey officers who had hoped that the removal of the MacDonell company would restore the morale of the regiment were soon disappointed. After the battalion's departure from Linlithgow it spent much of its service in the south-west where Lord Adam Gordon believed the Highlanders would be uncontaminated by the pernicious influence of the levelling societies. Continued inaction, however, sustained their lingering sense of betrayal, and their corporate spirit was weakened by the Laird's insistence that they should supply drafts for his marching-regiment, for the company which his boy Frank now needed to secure a majority in Fraser's Fencibles. Although Sir James ordered Glenmoriston and Auchindown to part with none but the old and the ill-disciplined the effect on those who remained was demoralising. Alexander Cumming still spent much of his time in the north, ostensibly beating up replacements and inefficiently assisted by the battalion Sergeant-major who, he said, "sacrifices so deeply to Bacchus that no dependence can be put in him". Cumming had not forgotten or forgiven the unpunished insolence at Linlithgow, and even from a distance he insisted upon harsh discipline, the use or threat of the lash. A bitter epidemic of influenza throughout Scotland further lowered the morale of the companies, although its effect on the soldiers in Dumfries would have been worse without the professional dedication of Surgeon John Grant, who had come from the 97th to replace his kinsman Peter.

The black lochs and forests of Galloway, the Gaelic still spoken by some of its hill people, must have reminded the Highlanders of their homeland but did not soften their longing to be in their own glens. The news they received from their families was bitter, news of famine, disease and death. The failed harvest of 1794 had been followed by a hard winter, a cold spring lingering into summer, late frosts and rotting days of rain. Cumming told Sir James that sheep were dying on the hills, and in many areas the wretched people were not only eating straw but also precious seed-corn needed for planting. Although he did not say so, deprivation and despair made it easy to find replacements for the Laird's regiments. There was no shrewd bargaining now by reluctant parents, and their sons willingly accepted the docked bounty of fifty-five shillings, twenty upon a declared intention to enlist and the remainder upon approval by Doctor John. They brought with them a sullen resentment that increased the growing hostility of the Fencibles, and when Cumming came to Dumfries towards the end of May he was immediately aware of what he later called their "tumultuous manner". He believed it to contain a threat to his life.

His response to this real or imagined menace was to intensify discipline and to increase the hours of exercise. Every morning at seven the companies were paraded before their quarters in Dumfries and marched to the open country beyond the Lochmaben road, returning to the town at four in the afternoon. On Thursdays they were brought back at one o'clock, that they might buy meal at the weekly market ordered by the magistrates, but on one such day, June 4, Cumming was dissatisfied with their drill and kept them on the field until past four. They were thus unable to buy their meal, or were forced to pay higher prices to profiteering merchants. They did not hide their anger, and boldly declared that they would not endure such treatment again.

On the evening of Tuesday, June 9, before the next meal-market, detachments of the Grenadier and Light Companies were issued with powder and ball and joined a party of constables in a march against the King's enemies. The threat to His Majesty's peace came from a family of Irish tinkers, John O'Neill and his two sons, who lived with their women and children in one cottage outside the town. Their wandering trade made them proper victims of the Comprehending Act, the statute which empowered magistrates to impress all vagrants and idlers into the Army or Navy. The Catholic O'Neills were resolute, independent men and had already had one violent brush with authority. In October 1793 a party of Breadalbane Fencibles, looking for deserters, had been fired upon by John O'Neill. He wounded two soldiers, but since he received six months only for the offence it may be presumed that the Fencibles were held to be more at fault than he. The Catholic families of Dumfries, the radical, liberty-toasting middle class, not unnaturally regarded the tinkers as heroic victims of tyranny and this, as much as the demands of the Act, made the magistrates determined to remove them. The constables and the Strathspey men arrived at the isolated cottage an hour before sunset, and when there was no answer to a demand for surrender Sergeant Beaton and two soldiers broke down the barred door with the butts of their muskets. The O'Neills screamed in wild defiance and fired seven times, not ball or bird-shot but rugged slugs. Beaton was hit in the head and groin, and the legs of Grenadier John Grant were brutally mangled. A fowling-piece was thrust against the breast of Alexander Fraser of the Light Company, and had his arms not been raised, holding his musket at the port, his heart would have been blown from his body. The fallen soldiers blocked the narrow doorway, and in the moment's pause O'Neill's sons escaped by a back window. When more Fencibles pushed into the smoke and darkness, the tinker called for mercy and by some miracle of forbearance he was not bayoneted where he knelt.

Two other men crouched beside him, but when they were dragged outside they were seen to be women in their husbands' clothes. The Strathspey men came back to Dumfries in an angry humour, their bloody wounded on a cart, the tinker walking behind with a halter about his neck.

The mood of the regiment was still black when the companies paraded for exercise on Thursday. The surgeons at the Infirmary had not as yet been able to extract the slugs from the groin of Sergeant Beaton or the arms of Private Fraser. One of John Grant's legs had been successfully amputated below the knee, but it was known that he would die before the other could be removed. The Catholics and radicals of Dumfries were already raising a fund for the defence of the O'Neills, and the young and beautiful poet of Woodley Park, Mrs. Maria Riddell, interrupted a passionate quarrel with her dying friend Burns to announce that she would go to Edinburgh on the tinkers' behalf, and there secure the services of the great advocate Henry Erskine. There was no public commendation of the Fencibles, and no talk yet of a fund for the wounded men in the Infirmary.

When the companies came from their quarters to battalion parade in the High Street, on the wide cobbles southward from Fish Cross, ill-temper was plain in their manner and their faces. This was the day of the meal-market, and a fear that they would again be kept on the field until past four o'clock aggravated the grief and resentment caused by the affray with the O'Neills. Big John Grant of Glenmoriston understood their ·mood and sympathised with it. He told the Adjutant, James Watson, that the men must be brought back before the market closed, for the magistrates had taken great pains to bring in the meal from the country. The soldiers were already marching down the Loch-maben road when Alexander Cumming clattered from the stable-yard of the George Inn, deciding upon impulse to conduct the field exercises himself. He wore tartan trews and a red tail-coat, ostrich feathers dripping from his bonnet. Since he was mounted he carried no broadsword, but two pistols were thrust into his belt, primed and loaded. He did not tell his officers why he believed the weapons necessary, and none of them thought it wise to ask.

At one o'clock Watson came to Cumming's stirrup and reminded him that the battalion should now return to Dumfries for the meal, and the Lieutenant-colonel agreeably told him to inform the men that the exercises were over. Watson did so, explaining in unnecessary detail why there would be no more drill that day. He was interrupted by an impatient young grenadier, John Anderson, who shouted "There's no reason for an excuse, we've been here long enough!" Watson would have been wise to let the small insolence pass, but with Cumming's eyes upon him he stepped toward the man. "Your conduct under arms is very improper!" he said. "I shall take you before the Colonel." Cumming placed the grenadier in arrest, and so that the remainder of the regiment might understand that he would tolerate no petty insubordination he continued the exercises for another ten minutes. It was almost two o'clock when he led the battalion into Dumfries, erect in the saddle, the pistols crossed in his belt. The companies were dismissed on the Dock, the long green promenade on a river-curve of the Nith, and when the last man was gone, running towards the meal-market, Cumming rode south to the parkland of Castledykes. A brisk canter, he evidently thought, would give him an appetite for dinner.

Watson returned to the George where the long mess-room on the first floor was full of Strathspey officers, all relieved that the morning had passed with no trouble more serious than Anderson's hasty impertinence. The Adjutant talked with them for fifteen minutes and then went to rest in his own room. Almost immediately he was aroused by the officer of the Guard, Ensign James Grant the son of Auchindown. A body of Highlanders, said the agitated boy, had come to him at the guard-house and boldly demanded the release of Anderson. Watson was too shocked to speak, but he slipped his sword-belt over his right shoulder, picked up his bonnet and cane and ran from the inn. The guard-house was three hundred yards away on English Street, a small stone building that had once been the town's

House of Correction, and twenty or thirty angry soldiers were now standing before it. Watson could not understand their Gaelic and none answered in English when he asked what they wanted, but upon the fourth time of asking Private James Forsyth roughly declared that they would take Anderson from the prison. Watson seized the young soldier's coat in a fury. In that case, he said, Forsyth would go to prison too. He pulled the man through the crowd to the gaol, but its door was blocked by Sergeant Peter Mackay and two soldiers of the Guard. The mutineers now closed upon Watson and a voice twice shouted "*Damn it, have him!*", which the Adjutant understood to mean that Forsyth should be rescued. He pushed the prisoner behind Mackay and turned. "You'll *not* have him out!" he called, "With my life I'll guard this door!" When the Highlanders still pressed forward he beat at their shoulders with his cane, paradoxically regretting the blows for he had never before struck a soldier of the regiment. "Don't blame me! I'm determined you shan't have him!" The slender wand was a feather-touch on the thick plaids and he drew his broadsword instead, clearing a space with a stamping guard in carte. "The first man that comes nigh this door I shall run through the body!"

As the soldiers fell back from the blade Mackay called out the Guard, forming them in line with bayonets charged. Watson was astonished to see that Forsyth had now rejoined his friends and was shouting abuse over their shoulders. The little Adjutant was as bold as he had been in the palace yard of Linlithgow, and with his sword advanced he strode forward and twisted his left hand in the jeering soldier's coat. "Sir!" he said, "I'm determined to secure you!" So unexpected was this courageous action that no one prevented him from dragging Forsyth into the guard-house, where he pushed the man face down on a bench and ordered Anderson to remove his belt and bayonet. When he returned to the street, resolved to die if necessary, the Highlanders were gone, running toward the High Street. They passed the Captain of the Day, William Grant, who walked on to the guard-house in astonishment and asked what was the matter of the disturbance.

"Matter enough, Captain William," said Watson in angry despair, "the men are in a state of mutiny, and I'm glad to see you."

Grant told him to break open the ammunition-box and issue cartridge and ball to Mackay's men. There was a great noise of shouting beyond the distant roofs, and the doors and windows of English Street were now full of curious civilians. More officers came running to the guard-house, some without bonnets and some with sheathed swords. When Major Grant of Auchindown arrived he told Watson to reinforce his son's Guard with a subaltern and thirty loyal men, if any such could be mustered. The officers then walked back to the George to await their absent commander. They sat glumly in the dusk of the low-ceilinged mess-room, or stood at the windows of their chambers, listening to the shouts and cries of their soldiers. Cumming returned two hours later at four o'clock, refreshed by his ride and in a rough good humour. He had noticed nothing unusual in the streets, or pretended that he had not, although the pistols were still in his belt. He saw Watson sitting alone, a bent scarlet figure at the foot of the table and he called out jovially. "You're a good deal confused, what's the matter with you? Out with it!" The Adjutant had been despondently reflecting that because the discipline of the battalion was his immediate responsibility, this serious breach of it would be charged against him. "Colonel," he said, "there is a good deal the matter with me. I am sorry to have to inform you . . ."

Cumming's astonishment was emotional enough to make nonsense of the precautionary pistols at his belt. The scoundrels had no justification for mutiny, he shouted, no reason to take up the trade of the MacDonells. Never had soldiers been more kindly treated by their officers. Forsyth and Anderson must be punished by a garrison court-martial that evening. He took Glenmoriston and two captains into his room to discuss the procedure of the trial and was joined there by Colonel Blackwood of the Ulster Light Dragoons, who also lodged at the George. Cumming's anger, the fear that had obsessed him since his arrival in Dumfries, now took his reason to the angry edge of insanity. He told Blackwood that the Highlanders had been behaving in a tumultuous manner for some days, and that they had sworn to shoot the Adjutant if the prisoners were flogged. He asked for the assistance of the dragoons whenever and wherever they might be needed, and he told Glenmoriston that while the court was sitting all Strathspey officers must be armed with loaded pistols. But no one in that small bed-chamber knew how the trial should be conducted or what charges should be properly laid against the accused, and Cumming was still turning the pages of the Articles of War when Corporal Michael Meredith brought the prisoners to the inn. There had been no attempt to rescue them in the streets.

The trial was briefly held in the mess-room, Cumming presiding over Blackwood and two dragoon officers. Before six o'clock both unhappy soldiers were found guilty and were remanded to the guard-house in the charge of Sergeant-major Hugh MacBean. Cumming then went into Blackwood's room with the cavalry commander, that they might find and agree upon which Article of War and for what crime the prisoners could be justly flogged. Glenmoriston and the remaining officers stood at the window of the mess-room, miserably watching the gathering crowd of Highlanders below. As MacBean and the prisoners appeared from the arch of the stable-yard there was a great shout of rage, a movement like a red wave turning. The noise was heard by Cumming, and he came quickly from Blackwood's chamber to the mess-room, one hand holding the Articles of War, the other pushing a pistol into a tail-pocket. He called cheerfully to the officers, as if he were a hunter sighting a quarry. "Our fellows are playing the fool! Follow me!" And he ran down the stairs.

After his distressing duty as prosecutor at the court-martial, James Watson had gone to his room. He too heard the cries of anger. Sword in hand, he went first to the mess-room, which was now empty, and then to the stable-yard stairs. At the bottom his arms were seized by two citizens. "For God's sake!" said one, "Don't go into the street if you value your life!"

"You are all cowards! None of you dare meet me man to man!"

HUGH MACBEAN WAS a Clan Chattan man from Moy. He had received his warrant as sergeant-major a week before the affair with the O'Neills, when his predecessor made a last sacrifice to Bacchus. He was an old soldier, a Chelsea out-pensioner who had had enough of wounds and excitement with Lord MacLeod's regiment, and some of his courage had been expended with his blood on the dust of India. When he came from the arch of the yard with his prisoners, with Corporal Meredith and six men of the escort, he first thought that the Highlanders in the street were assembling for the evening parade, but then he saw the bayonets fixed to their muskets and he was afraid. They shouted *"Give us the men!"* A pace or two from the arch, toward the door of the inn, Sergeant Robert Grant called to them to have patience, they would get the men, and he was never asked to explain this curious promise. MacBean was thrust back against the wall by the sudden rush of the mob. Two men of the escort charged their bayonets, but he shouted to them in alarm, telling them that resistance was useless, and thus Anderson and Forsyth were carried away in triumph. MacBean could not clearly remember the rest of the day, and he said later that he had been "a little blinded" by what had happened at the entrance to the stable-yard.

Alexander Cumming leapt from the door of the inn with a shout and plunged into the crowd like a man welcoming the violent embrace of the sea. Auchindown came out behind him, but went no further than the bottom of the steps, for the men who closed behind Cumming now turned against him. He took a pace to his right, put his back against the wall and drew his

371

broadsword. By his side Sergeant John Grant of the grenadiers, a hated disciplinarian, swore at the mutineers and warned them against harming their officers, whereupon Duncan MacDougal presented his bayonet at Grant's chest and said "You're worse than any officer!" Auchindown pressed down the musket with his sword and softly appealed to the soldiers to return to their quarters. They told him they would have the prisoners first. "Aye, so you may," he said, "but that won't save them, even though they go to the utmost corners of the earth!" He stared anxiously across their heads to the tall figure of Cumming, wading through a red flood. Outside the George the High Street narrowed in its fall to Nith Place, and at its widest was no more than twelve yards, but the crush of angry men was so great that it took Cumming some time to pass through. He had seen Anderson and Forsyth in the evening sunlight on the far side and he called their names as he breasted a way toward them. They turned into a close to escape, but he followed. The alleyway was narrow and low-roofed, its red-black sandstones dank with condensation, and at its end was a small courtyard, a deep well of light. There the two men turned to face Cumming. "You damned fools," he said, "are you not ashamed?" They were awed by his bullying lack of fear, and they meekly told him that they had been rescued against their will, that they were sorry and would follow him wherever he wished. "Take hold of my coat," he said, as if they were penitent children, "and I'll lead you to the guard-house." They did so, and went with him through a building to another close, and by that to the High Street again, northward of the George.

James Watson at last freed himself from the hands of the anxious citizens, but they once more begged him not to go into the street. One of them, who spoke Gaelic, said that he had heard the mutineers calling the Adjutant's name and threatening to kill him. "I don't care," said Watson, "no good man will injure me!" He ran from the yard to the street, joining a red and green line of Strathspey officers who now had their backs to the windows of the inn, facing the mutineers with drawn swords. The Highlanders called for the release of Anderson and Forsyth, swearing that no man should be flogged, that none should endure Cumming's ill-treatment. "Good God!" said Watson to Grant of Delcroy, "is there no way of getting them to unfix their bayonets?" At that moment three men charged their muskets at him, but their voices were more sorrowful than angry. They told him that they had always respected him until this day, until he had beaten them with his cane. "Get out of here, Watson!" said Delcroy, but the Adjutant pushed the weapons aside in contempt. "Unfix your bayonets," he said, "it's shameful for you to behave in this way." He pulled back the green facings of his coat. "Here! If I'm the only obnoxious creature amongst you, now's the time!" Delcroy stepped to his side, sword lifted, and the muskets were brought to the recover. The three mutineers shook their heads, but behind them Private Charles Mackintosh shouted angrily. "Damn the officer who strikes me, for he'll not strike me twice!"

Glenmoriston was the first officer to leave the defensive position against the wall of the inn. He was out of patience with this day, for it had not gone as idly as he had hoped. He had not been required upon the field of exercise, and the disturbance outside the guard-house had unpleasantly called him from a *matinée* held by his sister, Captain Fraser's wife. Now this insufferable humiliation. When he saw Cumming enter the close he forced his way across the street to its black mouth, turning there with broadsword advanced. He allowed no man to enter the alley, but none of the mutineers obeyed him when he ordered them to disperse. They swore at him cheerfully, for they admired his dark womanising charm, but more malevolently they cursed the Lieutenant-colonel for a rogue who liked to see good men flogged. Other officers followed the first-major's example, moving into the mob, punching a passage with their fists and the brass hilts of their swords, shouting threats or appeals into the sweating faces, angry with their men, with the failure of their own authority, with the jeers of the civilians at the windows above and with the stupidity of those who now blocked the street at either end. The sultry warmth of the June evening was increased by the press of bodies, the thickness of scarlet and plaid, the salt stench of sweating flesh and damp cloth. For all their anger, however, no officer or man had yet struck a blow with intent to harm. Captain John Rose, the fat and amiable Laird of Holme, argued with the soldiers in Gaelic, telling them that their behaviour was foolish, and when they said that Forsyth and Anderson should not be flogged for so trivial an offence he damned their infernal impudence, they were not the best judges of such matters. He saw a tall grenadier from a parish next to his own, Lachlan Mackintosh, and he put a hand on the man's shoulder, begging him to set an example, to go to his quarters. "Time enough for that!" said Mackintosh, pushing the hand away. And then there was a great shout, a cry that the Lieutenant-colonel had come into the street again.

Cumming stepped from a close on the east side, twenty yards from the inn, Anderson and Forsyth walking meekly behind him and holding the tail of his coat. The mob moved about all three, a wave about a rock, and when it subsided Cumming was alone. He shouted in fury, calling for the prisoners to come back, damning the others for dogs and cowards. The wave returned, white surf of the bayonets lowered. He stood his ground, his chin lifted in contempt. The officers fought to reach him, swords above their heads, but only Delcroy and Glenmoriston could get to his side, and at that moment Duncan MacDougal and Alexander Fraser* pressed their bayonets against Cumming's body. He understood none of the Gaelic shouted into his face, but Delcroy later told him that Fraser or MacDougal cried *"Devil damn you!"* and others behind called *"Stick him! Stick him!"* The weapons rested upon his waistcoat briefly before he brushed them aside. He pulled the pistol from the tail of his coat, forced back the lock with the ball of his left hand and pushed the weapon toward Fraser's head. The soldier fell back, either in astonishment or because he had been struck by the barrel, and all the mutineers pressed away from Cumming, taking Delcroy and Glenmoriston

---

* There were nine Alexander Frasers in the battalion, including the man wounded by the O'Neills, all recruited by and serving in the Light Company commanded by Captain Simon Fraser of Foyers.

with them. With his arm rigidly extended, pistol levelled, Cumming turned slowly about, widening the circle still further, and halting when the gun was again levelled at Fraser. There was a sudden silence, and some yards away at the door of the inn Auchindown cried out in alarm. "For God's sake, Colonel, don't fire it!"

Cumming glanced briefly at Auchindown, in reassurance the second-major believed. He pulled the Articles of War from inside his waistcoat and stepped toward the nearest mutineer, the braggart Light Company man Charles Mackintosh. If this confrontation was fortuitous it was also bizarrely symbolic, for Cumming was taller than any man in the battalion and Mackinosh was the smallest. With a backward movement of his left hand, the officer hit the soldier across the face with the book. "You blockhead!" he said with cheerful contempt, "what are you doing here?" Mackintosh put a hand to his cheek and there were tears in his eyes. "Damn you for a bugger!" he shouted, "why do you strike me?" Cumming did not answer, he returned the book to his waistcoat and looked calmly across the street to the steps of the inn. He called to Watson, ordering the Adjutant to beat the evening parade. The silent mob opened before him as he then walked slowly to the George, the pistol loose in one hand and the other fastidiously tidying his disordered stock.

It was some minutes before Watson was able to find the Drum-major, and almost eight o'clock when the sticks at last began to sound throughout the town, across crow-step gables in Castle Street and the old Fleshmarket, by Nith Place and Irish Street. The mob of soldiers outside the inn at first hesitated and then instinctively obeyed the drubbing persuasion of the company beat. Above their heads, from the windows and stairs, disappointed citizens jeered at them and called them cowards. At the arch of the stable-yard, Sergeant-major Hugh MacBean listened uneasily to a gossiping woman who told him that a merchant had told her that some of the Highlanders had powder and ball in their pockets.

Once assembled before its quarters, once inspected by its

platoon officers, it was the custom for each company to march to the Dock behind its Captain. This evening, however, most of the company commanders went alone to the river-bank, and the soldiers came as they wished, with bayonets fixed, some in orderly files behind a subaltern and a drummer, others singly or in shouting groups, and excited civilians followed them. Cumming left the rear of the George with Watson, walking down Irish Street, and at the corner of Nith Place they saw Lachlan Mackintosh leaning against a wall with his arms folded and his coat open. The Adjutant had already told Cumming that the grenadier had been most active in exciting a spirit of revolt throughout the day, "going backward and forward holding committees with the men", and the Lieutenant-colonel now stopped, pointing an angry finger. "I've marked you!" he called, "I've marked your conduct. Fall in with your company, sir!" The soldier did not move, but answered defiantly. "I don't care whether you've marked me or not. And I'll not fall in!" The order was repeated, and when it was again ignored Cumming and Watson walked on to the Dock.

The long summer twilight was moving to dusk, blue shadows from the chestnut colonnade along the promenade. There were boys fishing in the Nith, children calling from the garden walls. The soldiers gathered in company order beneath the trees, not in ranks but in dark scarlet groups, their unhappy officers and sergeants standing before them. When Cumming arrived he did not cry *"Markers!"* or command the companies to parade in battalion line. He told the senior ensigns to stand behind him, their faces to the river and their colours unfurled. He then called for silence, and called for it again and again until there was some response, white faces turning toward him in the shadow of the leaves. In a strong voice he shouted "First Fencible Regiment . . . *march to the Colours!*" It was the same invitation to re-affirm their willingness to serve that the Laird had given on the lochside at Linlithgow, and as before it was rejected. Some of the officers put their hands in the hilts of their swords and looked at Cumming uneasily, but he smiled and beckoned to the soldiers, encouraging them to gather about him in a semi-circle. They came forward reluctantly and stood at rest, leaning on their muskets and looking at him through the tilting hedge of their bayonets. He raised an arm, keeping it in the air until there was silence and then he took the Articles of War from his pocket. In a clear voice he read those paragraphs relevant to mutiny and the punishments for mutiny, and then he lowered the book, staring at the soldiers. "You are all cowards!" he said at last. "You are cowards to attack one man. None of you here dare meet me, or any of your officers, man to man! However, I'll swear some of you are honest men who blush for the conduct of the rest and who will stand by your officers and your colours to the last." He turned his back upon them and ordered the ensigns to open march, halting them when they were fifteen paces apart. He faced the soldiers again. "Now then! All of you who wish to be true to your King and Country.... *march to the Colours!*"

There was at first a sullen hesitation, and then a movement forward, the sound of feet shuffling as each rank took its dressing, the metallic chatter of bayonets unlocked, the whispering thud of musket-butts on the earth of the Dock. Soldiers who still lurked in the wynds that led to Nith Place and Saint Michael's Street now ran to join their companies. One of them was Lachlan Mackintosh, but Cumming saw him and again pointed a stabbing finger. "Not you, sir! I see you. Stand your ground there!" But the soldier came on and took his place in the rear rank of the grenadiers. When the companies were still, their files straightened by sergeants' halberds, Cumming marched to their front. He ordered them to break ranks, to gather about him again. "Now you are come to a new engagement," he said, "I promise you that you will see justice done between your officers and those who have been mutinous." He ordered his drummer to beat and the soldiers fell back into line.

Cumming walked along the battalion front from company to company, slowly and deliberately with Watson and Glenmoriston. Six times he stopped and pointed at a soldier whom he believed to have been forward in the mutiny or whose name had been

given to him by the officers. He ordered each man to step from
the ranks, to march to the rear and fall in behind Sergeant-major
MacBean. In this manner were selected Charles Mackintosh and
Lachlan Mackintosh, Duncan MacDougal, Alexander Fraser and
two others. They obeyed without protest, and there was no noise
but the crunching tread of boots as MacBean's escort marched
them away. When they were gone Cumming returned to the
front of the battalion. He said there was another matter of which
he must speak, although it gave him pain. Two respectable
citizens of the town had informed him that soldiers of the First
Fencibles had bought powder and swan-shot, with the declared
intention of killing their officers. He asked those men to throw it
now upon the ground before him. At first there was no response,
and then two or three twists of powder and ball curved through
the dusk and fell before him. He was not satisfied. He ordered
every captain of every company to go along the ranks of his
command with its sergeants and subalterns, to search the pockets
of every soldier. This the officers did, perhaps glad that the
increasing darkness hid the casual speed with which they carried
out the shameful duty. One man only, a grenadier, was found to
have a cartridge. He said it had been issued for the march against
the O'Neills and since forgotten. His captain, the Lieutenant-
colonel's kinsman Robert Cumming, swore to his honesty and
the excuse was accepted.

The humiliating parade was over. The drums beat a dismissal,
the companies marched to their quarters and the ensigns returned
to the George, each with a colour sloped on his shoulder, its green
or blue silk gathered in his right hand. The mutiny which had
begun with such terrible menace had ended in anti-climax, cowed
by a blow with a book, by Cumming's courage, by his extraordinary indifference to the fear that had obsessed him for days.
At Taptoo the town was again quiet, no soldiers abroad but the
sentries outside the guard-house and the inn, the marching patrol
of the flying picquet. After supper with his officers Cumming
went to English Street upon the earnest request of Ensign James
Grant, whose tour of duty at the guard-house had been the most

exciting day of his life. The boy said that he believed the last two men selected on the Dock were innocent of any part in the mutiny, and his sincerity or the proof he offered persuaded Cumming to order the men's release. Before midnight, however, the remaining four were joined by a fifth, James MacDonald of the Light Company whom Captain Simon Fraser now accused of leading the riot outside the George.

On Friday morning, after the first parade passed without incident and the battalion marched to the field of exercise, Cumming wrote a brief report which Glenmoriston carried to Sir James in Edinburgh. He began the letter by congratulating the Colonel on the marriage that week of his favoured daughter Margaret, and then said that Major Grant would give more details of the bad behaviour of the regiment, the sad news that many of the Laird's own people had "taken up the trade of the MacDonells". All the officers were heart-broken by such in-gratitude, for never had soldiers been more kindly treated. He wrote again on Saturday morning, reporting that sorrow had now properly replaced the mutinous spirit of the battalion. The captain who rode with this dispatch met Sir James on the coaching-road to Dumfries, for the Laird had left Edinburgh immediately upon receipt of Cumming's first letter. He arrived before the George at one o'clock on Sunday morning, anxious and weary but glad to hear from Cumming, who arose from bed to greet his brother-in-law, that there had been no further insubordination. He slept little, and at the morning church-parade he came before the battalion on the Dock, pot-belly tight against his breeches and scarlet coat. He was pleased by their good order, by their captains' assurance that they felt nothing but regret and shame. He told them that he had welcome orders from Lord Adam Gordon, that they were to leave this week for the Peebles district, and he promised them that he would march with them every step of the way. The rest of the day he spent in the mess-room at the inn, presiding over a Court of Inquiry, but in the evening he went to see the prisoners in the guard-house. He chided them gravely, warning them of the terrible penalty they faced,

and advising them that their only hope of salvation in this world
or the next was an appeal for mercy and an honest display of
contrition.

Isolated now from their friends, held by leg-irons and manacles,
the prisoners' apologetic sorrow was convincing, although the
Laird could not assure Lord Adam that they repented *all* their
folly. Two days later each man put his boldly drawn signature or
a trembling cross below a petition for mercy.

> Colonel Sir James Grant
> Sir, Our destination seems to us awfull, but we as Candidates
> for mercy, sensible of the Crimes we have been guilty of;
> Implore forgiveness and promises in the strength of divine
> providence; still to morass any systim that may prove injurious
> to Character or Country And if it is in your Honours power
> to act as a Mediator betwixt Lord Adam Gordon & us we
> trust it is to acquitt us, We totally Rely upon your Goodness
> hitherto experiencedd. Had we been sensible of the danger to
> accrue, we should have been mute; but Rely and depend upon
> your mercy, willing to Return to our duty as Tyrants against
> such practices as we have been accustomed to, and devotees
> for Establishment, Crown & Dignity.
>
> > Lachlan M'Intosh
> > Charles M'Intosh
> > Alexr. Fraser
> > Duncan M'Dougald
> Dumfries June 16th 1795   James M'Donald

Two of the prisoners were Strathspey men from the Laird's
own lands. Fraser was the son of a Foyers man who had settled in
Abernethy south-west of Grantown, and Little Charles Mackintosh was a labourer from Inverallan below the hills of Cromdale.
Big Lachlan, who was not yet twenty-two, had been a tailor,
one of several of his clan who came to the regiment from their
country about Loch Moy. MacDougal had been recruited by
Grant of Glenmoriston in Urquhart, and MacDonald was
another young man from the same valley, but he had been a

waiter at Balmain's tavern in Linlithgow when he abandoned his napkin for a musket in Alexander Cumming's company.

The Laird sent their petition to Lord Adam. He said that his officers believed it to be unworthy of attention, for all the prisoners were manifestly guilty.

"These poor, unfortunate young men, in the bloom of life . . ."

THE FIRST DIVISION of the regiment, one advance company, marched from Dumfries on the morning the prisoners' sad petition was handed to the Laird. By the week's end all the battalion was gone and was now quartered along the curling valley of the upper Tweed. Sir James rode with three companies to Peebles where he established his headquarters at the Tontine Inn, and where he at last decided to be rid of the prisoners. The charges against Anderson and Forsyth, the inconclusive result of their court-martial, had been discreetly forgotten for the moment, but fear of another outbreak had prevented the Laird from posting any orders for the disposal of the others. Now, at a late hour during their first night in the guard-house at Peebles, the five men were told that they must be sent to Edinburgh and there tried for mutiny and incitement to mutiny. They left before noon on Monday, June 22, handcuffed in a carter's wagon and escorted by James Watson, two sergeants, two corporals, a drummer and twenty private men. The morning sun was strong above the northward road by Eddleston Water, but despite the heat on their backs and the dust in their throats the party travelled at a steady pace, reaching the village of Howgate by three o'clock. There Watson halted at the inn for rest and refreshment, gloomily watching the rainclouds gathering above the Pentlands. He wrote a brief report to Sir James in thin ink and on poor paper supplied by the landlord, entrusting it to a young soldier who had fallen sick with a foul stomach and who was told to return to Peebles in his own time. Everything had so far gone as the Laird would wish, said the Adjutant, the escort good and obedient and the prisoners full of repentance and sorrow.

The storm broke before the march was resumed and continued with varying force until seven o'clock when the party reached the Castle, stained with mud and black with rain, the muskets of the escort secured under their plaids. Watson's pride was humiliated by the reception of his command. The first battalion of the Scotch Brigade was in garrison and the officer of the guard kept the Strathspey men waiting on Hawk Hill until he could find his adjutant or Colonel Thomas Scott, both of whom seemed reluctant to interrupt their supper for so trivial a matter. The prisoners had been brave enough on the march but now they were frightened by the great fortress, the grey-black stones glistening with rain, the sound of disembodied voices on Palace Yard, the silent shell of the new barracks rising above the south-western escarpment. "Entering the Barrier Gate," said Watson in his report to the Laird that night, "and *walking* up to the Main Guard, *threw* a *damp* upon all their spirits, but more particularly (Charles) Mackintosh, indeed the whole of them were stagger'd at the *unwelcome* reception they met with at the Guard-house." Colonel Scott would give no receipt for the prisoners until he was satisfied that his imprest funds would not thereby become responsible for any subsistence money due to them. They said that none was owing, they had no claims against their officers. They spoke well of their regiment, and although Watson thought this cunning and dissembling he parted from them with sympathy. He told Sir James that at the next guard-mounting they were to be placed in separate cells and allowed no contact with each other. "This will mortify them beyond anything that could possibly happen to them, for they depended much upon enjoying one another's society."

The five men remained in dark isolation below the casemate until July 4, and their only friendly visitors were Mr. MacGregor from the Gaelic Chapel-at-Ease and James Grant, chaplain to the First Fencibles. Grant was admired and respected by most men in the battalion, particularly the soldiers of Glenmoriston's company, and he accepted his spiritual and military responsibilities more conscientiously than many regimental chaplains who took a lieutenant's pay and rarely left the manse. He came from a ministerial family of Strathspey which had given devoted service to the common people of Clan Grant, and his predecessor in the parish of Urquhart and Glenmoriston had been his uncle, John Grant, one of those whom the Laird's father betrayed to the Duke of Cumberland and the hulks at Tilbury. James Grant did what he could for the prisoners, and although he could promise them little mercy in this world he diligently prepared their souls for the next by prayer, psalm and precept.

The Strathspey Regiment came to Musselburgh camp at the beginning of July, that some of the officers and men might give evidence before the court-martial and supply the firing-party required by its probable verdict. The long dunes above the firth were already white with tents, the orderly lines of four troops of dragoons, a company of artillery, and the first battalions of the Sutherland and Breadalbane Fencibles. Major Sutherland of Rearquhar had been told that he would be a member of the court over which his Colonel, William Wemyss, would preside. The links were more pleasing to the old man's eye than six months before, that snow-cold day when the Breadalbane muti-neer had been shot, but the officers' tenting of his regiment had not yet arrived and rather than lie upon a truss of straw in a soldiers' tent, like other gentlemen of his corps, he had taken expensive lodgings in Musselburgh. He suffered painfully from his rheumatic complaints, a severe cough and sores on his mouth, and his infirmities cannot have cleared a mind that must shortly decide upon another's life or death. It was regrettable that the preliminary duties of the trial did not allow him to visit Edin-burgh, to purchase bed and bedding, but he was delighted by the brave appearance of the camp, the inspiring admiration of the citizens who came daily to watch the parade of scarlet and blue, bright sabres and brown muskets in the long hours of sunlight.

The prisoners were brought from the Castle two days before the trial. They were strongly guarded and heavily ironed but they were together again, and the clean sea-winds blowing through their tent, the sight of their comrades and the familiar beat of their company drums restored some of their spirits. The court first assembled at ten o'clock on Monday, July 6, in a great tent with the walls brailed up to cool the air. Ten field officers and four captains, one of whom was Colin Campbell of Glenfalloch, sat at a long board table, their bonnets and hats before them, gold lace and geranium-red coats glowing in the yellow light. There were many witnesses, the evidence given was long and detailed. Nineteen officers and men appeared for the Crown, and the seven who came forward for the accused spoke mainly of their previous good behaviour, their respect for their officers and their obedient attention to their duty. Watson's opening evidence for the Crown took almost a day and he appeared again before the court to swear, in the strongest words he said he knew, that during the nineteen years he had spent in the King's service he had never known a better behaved soldier than the young James MacDonald. The Laird found the whole business too painful to attend, nor was his presence required. He remained at his town-house on George Square and it was there on the third day of the trial, that he had a visitor from the north, Angus Mackintosh the brother of Big Lachlan. The troubled man brought with him a letter from his master, Alexander Grant the minister of Calder, who begged the Laird's forgiveness for such presumption and said that he would not, in ordinary circumstances, have made any application in favour of such a rascal as Lachlan. However, Angus Mackintosh was a well-disposed, good-natured fellow and had accepted the condition the minister imposed before writing to Sir James. This was that he should declare himself ready to enlist in the Strathspey Fencibles, and that although he had resisted previous attempts to recruit him he was now willing to join the colours if this could in any way save Lachlan from terrible punishment. The miserable man was deeply sensible of the enormity of his brother's crime, said Mr. Grant, and mourned over it night and day. "I hope you will forgive this interposition, as I never meant to say a word in favour of the culprit."

The Laird could not accept the despairing offer, having no authority to do so and perhaps no desire, but the probable fate of the prisoners had been troubling him, and he knew that since the execution of the Breadalbane man the Crown was determined upon such exemplary punishment in future. On the day the trial ended, but before its verdict was known, he wrote an earnest appeal to Lord Adam Gordon. He said that he shuddered at the thought of what the sentence might be. He recalled the good behaviour of his Fencibles before and since the mutiny, the suffering of the brave fellows wounded by the Irish tinkers, and he reminded the Commander-in-Chief that the five prisoners, all simple men without malevolent intent, were the sons of good and loyal subjects.

> May I supplicate that their youth and inexperience may plead in their favour. The manner in which His Majestys mercy (if such shall be his pleasure) may be exerted, I will not pretend to suggest. But I trust in God, it would not be misplaced. These poor, unfortunate young men, in the bloom of life, may yet serve their King and Country with merit, either in the Army or Navy, and in the full confidence that sufficient warning of the consequences of such crimes has now been impressed, I once more Humbly supplicate His Majestys mercy in their favour.

That afternoon the court decided that the charges against the five men were proven. As a result of James Watson's passionate plea in his favour, MacDonald was mercifully sentenced to a thousand lashes. The others were to be shot.

Early in the morning of Friday, July 17, the assembling beat of the General was drummed through the Musselburgh camp, a carrier-wave for the brittle call of cavalry trumpets. With the exception of the camp guard and inlying picquet every man was ordered to parade and march in full dress, the Strathspey, Breadalbane and Sutherland battalions, three troops of the Fourth Dragoons, a company of Hopetoun's Fencibles and the blue-coat gunners of the artillery. The prisoners were placed in two mourning-coaches with the ministers, and when the column had formed about them it marched to the north-east, ten miles to the

links on Gullane Bay, a desolate waste, a land-sea of moving sand
that had twice drowned the villages bravely built upon it. Here
on tussocked grass bent by grieving winds were more soldiers,
two battalions of the Scotch Brigade from Edinburgh, six troops
of cavalry from Haddington and Dunbar. Lord Adam's deputy,
Major-general James Hamilton in cocked hat and gold-drenched
scarlet, waited in the saddle at the roadside, surrounded by his
young staff and his genteel friends from the New Town. The
long column from Musselburgh arrived at noon, and the prisoners
remained in the hot and curtained darkness of the coaches until
the regiments and battalions had formed a great three-sided
square, facing the broken sunlight on the waters of the firth.
The horsemen, in three ranks to the rear of each side, carried
drawn sabres, and in the centre of the Fourth Dragoons were two
six-pounders, their mouths closed against the driving sand by
brass tompions.

When the prisoners at last stepped from the coaches, blinking
at the strong light, a sergeant's escort took them to the middle of
the square where they saw the triangle of halberds, four lidless
coffins and a firing-party of twelve men from their own regiment.
The verdict of the court was then read to them and they knelt
with Mr. MacGregor and Chaplain Grant. They sang psalms
above the wind until a dragoon captain from Hamilton's staff
softly interrupted them and told them that they must rise, that he
must now read Lord Adam's Orders of the Day. The sentences
were all confirmed, but the King had extended his mercy and
had instructed Lord Adam to suspend MacDonald's punishment
and the shooting of two others until his further pleasure was
known. For Alexander Fraser there was no mercy, but his three
companions could let chance decide who was to live and who
was to die with him. The lotting was soon done, trembling hands
grasping a scrap of paper from a sergeant's bonnet, and that taken
by Little Mackintosh had the cross of death upon it. MacDonald,
MacDougal and Lachlan Mackintosh were quickly marched to
the rear of their battalion, the triangle was dismantled and two
coffins removed. The correspondents to the *Courant* and the

Advertiser, standing far away on the wings of the square, would not agree later upon which man faced death with fortitude and which struggled against it. At that distance, with eyes narrowed against sun and sand, there was nothing to distinguish the bare-headed, kneeling men. Both were short and dark-haired, both wore green-faced scarlet, a belted plaid now loosened about their waists. The writer to the *Courant* said that Fraser resisted turbulently until he was bound hand and foot, that Charles Macintosh was nobly calm and submissive. The *Advertiser* reversed the names, but the end was the same for both young men, darkness as the caps were pulled over their eyes, the sound of muskets cocked, of butt-plates sliding over buttons to the shoulder, and then death before they could hear the rolling echo of the volley. Their bodies lay face down beside the coffins, untouched until all the battalions, the companies and troops, had marched past them in slow time.

Within a week the pardoned men were informed of the King's pleasure. They were to go to the 60th in the Caribbean where yellow fever, by death or debility, had already robbed His Majesty of forty thousand useful soldiers. They were taken by ship to London, to the Savoy Prison from which they then marched to Portsmouth. Before they left Scotland they had asked their company commanders to save them from certain death in the Indies, and Simon Fraser of Foyers had promised them that the Laird would do all in his power to secure their transfer to his marching-regiment, the 97th, where they would be among men of their own race and country. They heard no more of this proposal, which the Crown undoubtedly rejected without hesitation, and when they reached Hilsea Barracks in September they were told that they would be drafted into a brigade of infantry now being raised to serve in the penal settlements of New South Wales. This melancholy exile seemed to them to be no better and perhaps far worse than the Caribbean. The 97th was quartered in villages three miles from Portsmouth, weakened and demoralised by service as a marine corps aboard Lord Howe's fleet, and the simple reasoning of the prisoners encouraged them to believe that with the regiment so close there should be no difficulty in their transfer. MacDougal and Mackintosh wrote to the Laird, reminding him of the assurance given by Fraser at Musselburgh. They lived, they said, in daily hope of delivery.

> If you will for this one time Endevour to Get us in to the 97th you shall always find that We shall behave ourselves like Soldiers and in a Soldire like manner for the futer and as We Got no ansure of the Lines Was Delivered to you in Musselburgh So therefor we hope your honour Will let us know and your petitioners Will for every pray.

They asked for a reply addressed to the Main Guard at Portsmouth, but none came. Instead they were visited by Lieutenant John Grant, the Paymaster of the 97th, who told them that his regiment was now to be disbanded but Sir James had not forgotten them. He had secured the King's permission for them to enlist in any of the companies which several Strathspey lairds had recently raised and which were now to be embodied in regiments ordered to the West Indies. One of these gentlemen, James Grant of Kinchurdy, was willing to take them and would promise them more gentle treatment than they could expect from the officers of the South Wales Brigade. The pendulum had again swung to the Caribbean, but life there among their own kind seemed preferable to the brutal miseries of an Australian stockade, and they willingly volunteered. Paymaster Grant sent this news to Sir James, adding that Kinchurdy was that day writing to his own colonel, asking leave to enlist the prisoners. "Of which I assume there can be no doubt, and that the poor fellows shall soon be set at liberty." Lachlan Mackintosh and Duncan MacDougal sailed with Kinchurdy's company at the beginning of October. If they died in the West Indies, as they most probably did, it may at least have been within the sound of Gaelic voices. There is no record of the ultimate disposal of James MacDonald, the good soldier whose blood had been stirred by the beat of Strathspey drums beyond the windows of Balmain's tavern.

In the spring of 1799, when the risk of invasion or insurrection seemed less strong than the desperate need for military economies, when the Government decided to disband those fencible regiments raised for service in Scotland only, their colonels were told that their corps would remain upon the establishment if they could persuade at least three hundred men to re-enlist for field action against the Irish rebels. The Strathspey Regiment was quartered about Irvine, once more in the south-west, and the Laird was confidently assured by his officers that the required number of volunteers would be easily found, that a hundred and fifty had already declared their willingness to re-enlist. On a blustering day in March he addressed the whole battalion on the field of exercise above the town. His words had been carefully written at his lodgings the night before, no doubt with uneasy memories of a similar appeal five years ago above the loch at Linlithgow. He called the soldiers his brave and honourable friends. He asked for their loyalty and begged them not to be disappointed by the Government's refusal to pay a new bounty upon their re-enlistment. He told them that all their officers would accompany them to Ireland, with the exception of Lieutenant-colonel Cumming Gordon whose private affairs required his resignation.* Sir James was happy to announce, however, that his young son Frank would be their new Lieutenant-colonel and would go with them most cheerfully.

> Let me now, my brave fellows, express the great esteem I have for you, and call upon all who are willing to preserve the character and existence of the Regiment to come immediately forward, that I may be impowered to inform the Commander-in-Chief accordingly.

That evening he informed the Commander-in-Chief that less than a hundred volunteers had stepped from the ranks, most of them sergeants, corporals, drummers and fifers. Like the first

---

* Alexander Cumming had now extended his name, having become the sole heir and representative, through the female line, of the Gordons of Gordonstown.

battalion of the Breadalbane Regiment, the private men of the Strathspey Fencibles would soldier no more. Within a month they had lodged their arms in Stirling Castle and gone home. Each man was allowed to keep his red coat, his little kilt and his knapsack. He was given enough subsistence money for two weeks, one hundred and forty pence, and a written discharge to protect him against predatory recruiters from other regiments.

4
STRANGERS TO DANGEROUS
PRINCIPLES

The Perthshire Militia Riots
September 1797

"How little influence the chieftains retain at this day"

THE INSOLENT LETTER was taken to John, Duke of Atholl, at noon on Sunday. His sylvan castle of Blair was at that moment in a state of siege and closer to humiliating surrender than it had been fifty years before, when a Jacobite demand for its submission was brought by a serving-girl from the village inn. Past ten o'clock on the previous evening an angry crowd of the Duke's tenantry, six hundred men and seven hundred women he was informed, had gathered in and about the kirk on Banavie Burn, joined since by many more and all determined that no man should be drafted into the new Militia. At night their menacing fires were seen on the Hill of Lude above the stone bridge, and there were no soldiers to protect the King's good subjects from the threat of arson and murder. Early on Saturday, when there was at last no doubt about the mischief intended by the common people, the Duke had assembled what force he could to impose the law, to defend his new wife, his castle and his life. He had fifty guns and one hundred and forty men, his few loyal tenants and those brought to him by his contentious neighbour James Robertson of Lude, who may have seen the irony of his own defensive position. His redoubtable mother had fired the first Jacobite gun *against* the castle when it was last invested. The plump and aging Duke was in no mood to enjoy this paradox, and he could reflect sourly upon the Lord Advocate's recent instruction to enforce the Militia Act without fear. "Go on firmly," Robert Dundas had cheerfully written, "and I am confident you will succeed without much or perhaps any difficulty." His Grace would have preferred a squadron of English dragoons to such complacent advice from the serenity of Arniston House. He and Lude had failed to explain the Act to the gathering crowd on Saturday, he did not believe his garrison would be able to resist an assault, and now this anonymous letter, boldly delivered to his door and distastefully reminding him of that unhappy mutiny in Portsmouth fifteen years before.

Blair Atholl
3d Sept. 1797

Unto the Duke of Atholl

May it please your Grace, – We your dutiful Tenants and all the country people round about, do not at all approve of Militia in Scotland, whatever encouragement you may show us; because we do not at all wish to serve against our inclination, because our most brave ancestors and forefathers would not suffer such usage, and we your above named are surprised that you would endeavour to make slaves of brave Atholl Highlanders.

May it therefore please your Grace to abolish the Act from us, and give security for it, as we will lose the last drop of our blood before we yield to such oppression.

He sent an equivocal reply to the kirk-yard, hoping it would calm the rioters, but at two o'clock he was told that they were now advancing southward upon the castle. The men, it was said, had put the women in the van, believing they would not be fired upon, and these amazons had removed their stockings and filled the feet with stones and broken glass. The garrison stood to arms, but the Duke capitulated before the mob had come half-way up the nave of trees to his slate-tiled fortress. Dressed in his favoured hunting-grey he stood at the foot of his grand stairs, watching through the open door as Robertson went to meet the tenants. When Lude had signed a declaration, giving his word as a deputy-lieutenant of the district that no steps would be taken to impose the Act, the paper was brought to Atholl and he scrawled his confirmatory signature upon it. That evening, as the victors celebrated at the inn of Blair, he wrote to Robert Dundas, telling the Advocate that in every parish across the county of Perth, from Alyth to Glen Dochart, the same riotous spirit was in the ascendancy. The lists of militiamen to be drafted had been torn from church doors, session books from which those lists were drawn had been destroyed, and ministers or schoolmasters responsible for the books had been abused, wounded, and threatened with death if they resisted. Such was the flame of misrepresentation and discontent, he said, that had he succeeded in driving off his attackers there would have been five times as many at his door the next day. He promised to bring his wayward tenants to their senses, and like other landowners throughout the county he believed that the disaffection was due to mischievous men from other parishes, for whom high rewards should be offered. "But at the same time, in the present temper of the country, we must have a military force here before such people can be safely apprehended. And where is it to come from? In Scotland we have it not."

Richer now than most of the English land-owners he envied and imitated, his mind and body dedicated to Improvement, to public roads and parklands, afforestation and grouse moors, stable banking and the Tory interest, Atholl had no real understanding of the people over whom he stood in awesome superiority. He agreed with many great men of his class, and persuaded the administration to agree also, that not only were the Highlands still an abundant source of man-power but the Gaelic race was as willing as ever to answer any military call upon it. The Government's eagerness to exploit this happy anachronism by the Militia Act is all the more remarkable in view of the chilling lack of enthusiasm the little chiefs had shown for an earlier scheme, put before them in February that year. At the instruction of the Duke of York, now Commander-in-Chief, Henry Dundas sent a circular letter to such feudal superiors as the Dukes of Gordon, Atholl and Argyll, asking their opinion upon a proposal to enlist sixteen thousand men in a Highland Corps. The soldiers would be raised as clan contingents under their own chiefs and

serve in district brigades, "to be employed in Great Britain or
Ireland, in case of actual invasion or civil commotion or the
imminent danger of both or either". It was a fanciful, dream-like
proposition for any public man to sponsor so soon after the
Fencible mutinies and at a time when further recruiting for
Highland battalions was becoming increasingly difficult, yet
Dundas confessed himself very struck by it. He told the Duke of
Gordon that although there had once been good reasons for
restraining the spirit of clanship, "It has for many years been my
opinion that those reasons have ceased, and that much good,
instead of mischief, may on various occasions arise from such a
connexion among persons of the same Family and Name". Like
Breadalbane, Forbes and Pitt before him, he too wished to
exploit the special qualities of a clan society, but the ancient way
of life that had given their schemes some substance no longer
existed, and even his shrewd eye did not see that what the victors
had destroyed might not now be resurrected to serve their future
conquests.

The proposal had come from the King's tall and ugly son, but
had not originated in his mind which, however imaginative in
many ways, knew little of the Highlands.* Upon his appointment
as Commander-in-Chief at the age of thirty-two, the Duke of
York had set aside, if not behind him, his delight in vulgar
debauchery. He applied himself to his new duties with zeal, and
although the shortest route to military advancement would soon
be through the drawing-room of his greedy mistress in Gloucester
Place, he was sincerely concerned to improve the efficiency of his
officers and the conditions of his private men. This concern came
from bitter experience. The army he had recently commanded in
the Low Countries had been officered by juvenile innocents or
senile incompetents, and so cruelly ill-equipped that its hungry
and demoralised soldiers had fought a winter campaign in linen

---

* It may have been suggested by the Laird of Grant. The fullest account of it,
with a table of the presumed fighting-strength of individual clans, the chiefs
who might command them and the districts from which they could be drawn,
is among the Laird's military correspondence in the Seafield Papers.

uniforms, without waistcoats, stockings or drawers. He respected
good soldiers, brave soldiers, and the thought of sixteen thousand
Hectors and Alexanders enlisted in a Highland Corps excited his
eager enthusiasm. Each brigade, as proposed, would be commanded by the noblest gentleman of the district in which it was
raised, and each clan battalion led by its chief and his kinsmen.
Thus the First or Isles Brigade, drawn from the MacDonalds of
Sleat and Clanranald, MacLeods, MacNeils and Mackinnons, was
to be mustered under Lord Macdonald, twenty-three years of age
and the son of the man whose mercenary military career had
ended ignominiously on that hill above Burntisland. The Argyll
Brigade, composed of twenty-one hundred Campbells, Macleans, MacDougals and Stewarts of Appin, could be led by the
Duke, Colonel John of the 'Forty-five who was now halfway
through his eighth decade. Atholl was presumed to be capable of
enlisting eighteen hundred men for a Perth Brigade from his own
people, the MacGregors, Robertsons and Macnabs. And the
Laird of Grant, upon his own assumption perhaps, could raise the
Frasers and Chisholms as well as the young men of his own name.
Every Highland clan was to be called to arms, a gathering which
even the most optimistic of Jacobite agents had never believed
possible. The author of the rhapsodic proposal referred His Royal
Highness to the enduring attachment between Highlanders and
their chiefs, their admiration of the warlike exploits of their
ancestors, and their burning desire to restore the ancient order of
Kings in Europe. York and Dundas did not believe this last
nonsensical claim, of course, but they were impressed by the
assurance that such a corps could be raised with the least injury to
agriculture and industry. And, more appealingly to men
frightened by the great ogre of Democratical Thought . . .

At this moment they may be justly considered the only considerable body of men in the whole Kingdom who are as yet
absolutely strangers to the levelling and dangerous principles
of the present age, and therefore they may be safely entrusted
indiscriminately with the knowledge and the use of arms.

Flattered though they were by the suggestion that they could still exercise an influence long eroded by the law and their own self-indulgence, the response of the chiefs was unenthusiastic. Replying significantly from London and not from his green home above Loch Moy, Aeneas Mackintosh of Mackintosh told the Duke of Gordon that without the advice of other gentlemen of Clan Chattan he could give no decided opinion. Yet he could say his country had already been drained of recruits and it would be almost impossible to raise more if they knew they would be sent to England or Ireland. "I need not remind your Grace how little influence the chieftains retain at this day in comparison to what it was half a century ago." Duncan Macpherson of Cluny had only recently recovered the estates lost by his father in the 'Forty-five and after a lifetime of ill-rewarded military service he now wished to enjoy them. "This country," he said, echoing the words and opinion of Mackintosh, "has already been much drained by different levies, so much so that if the number now proposed were taken out of it there would be a great danger of a total stop being made to the operation of husbandry." Alasdair Ranaldson would give no positive answer, cautiously saying he had as yet seen parts of the plan only. Lochiel declared himself happy to come forward, if thereby he could be quit of distasteful service with the Gordon Fencibles, but he did not think his clansmen would serve in Ireland, indeed they had already refused to go.

There was more of the same from other chiefs, and the grandiose scheme was abandoned, but the need for men remained, a military force for the defence of the United Kingdom against invasion and more urgently for the suppression of insurrection. There was reason to fear a civil revolt. By mid-summer the nation's economy was badly strained by the war, and loyalty to the constitution depended upon the price of a loaf. The Bank of England had been compelled to suspend payments, the French had made a ludicrous but alarming landing upon the coast of Wales, the Navy had mutinied at the Nore and Spithead, and Ireland was moving toward rebellion. It was innocently hoped that the old prejudices against the raising of militia in Scotland, once as strongly felt by the English as by the Scots, were now past, and in July, 1797, a new Act proposed the compulsory enlistment of six thousand men. They were to be chosen by ballot from parish registers, young men between the ages of nineteen and twenty-three, excluding those already serving in volunteer regiments or who were married with more than two children, and the names of those selected were to be posted on the kirk doors of their parishes. The newly appointed Lord Lieutenants of the shires and their district deputies were to be responsible for the proper conduct of the balloting.

The people's response was passionate and violent. There was perhaps little clear understanding of the Act, and in the Highlands it was widely suspected that it was yet another device to send young men to the Indies. It was plainly seen, however, that while the rich and the well-to-do could hire substitutes for their sons, there was no escape for the poor. Weaver and miner, ploughman and cowherd must wear the red coat, and they were not encouraged by the Duke of Hamilton's assurance that a militiaman's pay of a shilling a day was more than they could expect as labourers, or by his stern advice to consider how happily they lived under the constitution they were now called upon to protect. Accepting the frightened opinion of his nephew Robert, Henry Dundas was satisfied that the bitter resistance was due to the influence of Jacobinism, but although he correctly brought cart and horse together the harnessing of one to the other was beyond his understanding. It was the fury of the Militia Riots that changed the ineffective semi-literary associations of United Scotsmen into a revolutionary society. Throughout the Lowlands that August working-people rose upon impulse, burning the ballot lists and mobbing the schoolmasters who kept the registers. At the colliery village of Tranent in East Lothian the revolt was begun by miners' wives and children. Encouraged by their example, the young men also defied the balloting officers and presented a resolution of protest. Though they might be overpowered, they said, dragged from their parents and friends to become soldiers, the officers should learn from their present behaviour what little trust might be placed in them were they ever called upon to suppress their own countrymen. It was thus at Tranent, upon a windswept and unlovely landscape, that a bloody lesson was imposed. English horsemen of the Cinque Port Volunteers rode upon the colliers, driving them into the harvest corn beyond the pitheads. Eleven died under the long sabres, or that was the number officially acknowledged, but when the yellow fields were scythed, more bodies were found by the anguished reapers.

Incendiaries of the worst description were at the bottom of this bad business, said Lord Adam Gordon, what else could explain such wide, unanimous defiance? He asked Henry Dundas for three thousand soldiers from the south, "English Fencibles would suit us better than Scotch ones at this time". The resistance in the Lowlands was soon broken by the dragonnade, but before it was over Edinburgh was startled to hear that the Highlanders, who were expected to accept the ballot without protest, were also in revolt. Some men had foreseen this. George Haldane of Gleneagles wrote wisely to Dundas after the event, but the clarity of his opinions suggests that they had been long-held. In so far as a Democratical Spirit did prevail in the north, he said, it was in the people's wish to be treated with respect and not as if they had been born only to pay taxes. They hated the name of soldiers. They believed that the Government would not keep faith with them. They recalled the attempt to send the Fencibles out of Scotland contrary to the terms of enlistment, and they feared the same would be done with the Militia. Their sons would be taken from the land at a time they were most needed, without compensation or bounty. There were other objections but these, said Haldane as if he had suddenly remembered his superior station, were due to ignorance, stupidity and obstinacy. He thought it would be unwise to send horsemen from the south, and he reminded Dundas of the Lowlanders' fierce resistance in the killing-times of the last century. "Remember Pentland and Bothwell Bridge, and keep your dragoons to yourself. You may have need for them."

For the first time, indeed, Gaelic opposition to military service was influenced by that terrible democratical spirit, if only in the acceptance of tactics proposed by two or three politically conscious men. When the voice of revolt began to cry against other injustices its heart was already dying. The presumed leaders of the riot in Strathtay were Angus Cameron, a wright of Weem, and James Menzies, a small merchant of the same village whose early wanderings had given him the name of "The East Indian". They would be accused of seducing the loyalties of simple people, and the administration forgot, as it always does, that yeast alone does not make a loaf. Both men were Highland, but both had worked in Glasgow, had met members of the reforming societies and had read the inflammatory works of Thomas Paine. To sustain his heart and energy a revolutionary zealot must believe that all he desires is but a hand's-grasp away, and Angus Cameron, who was the more able of these two shadowy figures, may have thought that the great army of men and women who assembled on the torch-lit braes would shortly overturn the earth and create a world without master and servant. The real aspirations of the people, however, were not expressed in the language of Paine's *Rights of Man* but in the words of the letter they sent to Blair Castle, their melancholy longing for a brave past and their acceptance of the Duke's authority even when they stood in defiance of it. Cameron had escaped from the husk of a dying clan society, but the spirit of others was still the prisoner of its sweet decay. Yet it was no accident that Gaelic opposition to the Militia Act should be strong in Perthshire, the most densely populated and the richest of the mountain counties. Here the proprietor had most to gain from the future and the landless man had most to lose. From its glens had come the greater part of the men extravagantly expended in the wars of the past half century, and from Blairgowrie to Bridge of Orchy, Loch Rannoch to Strathearn, living men remembered the bitter waste of the Rebellion, the cynical betrayal of the Black Watch, the bold defiance of the Atholl and the Breadalbane Highlanders.

The first resistance came to the east of Atholl's grounds. For some days, the Duke was told by Sir William Ramsay of Bamff, the people about Blairgowrie had been murmuring against the Act, threatening to burn manse and schoolhouse if thereby they destroyed the hated lists. Ramsay thought the trouble would subside, but on the morning of Sunday, August 27, when the ballot was pasted upon the kirk door at Alyth, a great crowd gathered about the ale-house, refusing to enter the church and declaring that they would pull Bamff House to the ground before they accepted the list. He thought that his elegant home, on high ground to the north of the village, was safe enough from their ill-temper, and on Monday morning he rode north-westward over the bare hills to the narrow valley of the Blackwater where he asked the advice of Farquharson of Persie, another deputy-lieutenant of the district. Persie was in a melancholy mood, and desperate for advice himself. His tenants were hostile, and both he and the schoolmaster had received threatening letters. While both gentlemen were wondering what should be done, a sweating rider came from Ramsay's sister at Bamff. The mob had marched upon the house after all, dragging a schoolmaster with them. They had burnt the man's list and now demanded a copy which they believed to be held by Sir William. Katherine Ramsay bravely faced them and persuaded them to leave with no damage or injury done, but both gentlemen were alarmed by the news and filled with gloomy thoughts of what might happen if they proceeded with a meeting of deputy-lieutenants at Blairgowrie the next day. Advice must come from the font of power, from the Lord Lieutenant, and Ramsay sat at Persie's writing-desk. "I must trouble you," he begged the Duke, "for further instructions before I can proceed . . ."

He wrote again, to Colonel Allan Macpherson of Blairgowrie who was also a deputy, telling him that the countryside was in a state of tumult. The warning was unnecessary. The windows of the old soldier's house looked across the twin towns of Rattray and Blairgowrie upon the river Ericht, and all night he had watched the dancing torches and listened to the threat of angry voices. He sent a reply to Persie House, advising Ramsay that there should be no meeting until copies of the Act had been sent to every parish, that the people might properly understand its terms. Monday night passed without violence, although the mob did not disperse. At eleven o'clock on Tuesday morning Macpherson heard the beat of a rallying drum, and then the ringing of a church-bell in Rattray. He was a brave man, proud of his father who had died fifty years before with the clan regiment at Falkirk, and as a boy he had himself fought with Fraser's Regiment at Quebec. He now rode boldly into Blairgowrie, gathering what gentlemen he could. There was a crowd of five hundred men and women in the town, more coming across the river from Rattray, and soon the gentlemen and ministers were surrounded by waving sticks and weaving scythes. Ramsay and Farquharson arrived at one o'clock and they too were caught by the swirl of the mob, drawn into an island with the other mounted gentlemen. Macpherson shouted from the saddle, saying there would be no meeting of deputy-lieutenants, no more posting of lists until copies of the Act arrived, but he was ignored. A storm rolled out of the mouth of Strath Ericht and although the rain was heavy, falling without stop for three hours, the horsemen were not allowed to leave the street. Sodden papers were thrust at them, the blurred ink almost unreadable, and when they asked for an explanation they were told that they must sign a declaration that they would never impose the Act upon the people. For a long time they refused, but at last they submitted, and put their names to a second paper which said that they had willingly signed the first. Then were they allowed to ride home through the rain. Macpherson felt himself miserably dishonoured, and yet by honour bound to keep his word to the people. That night he wrote a painful letter to Atholl. It had ever been his earnest wish, he said, to be useful in the service of his King and Country and he would not have surrendered to the mob had it not been plain to all the gentlemen that they were prisoners without hope of relief, that with darkness coming there was a great threat of drunken violence. "So we thought it prudent to yield to this most humiliating act of my life . . ."

All across eastern Perthshire there was the same tumult. By Coupar Angus a mob came to burn the house of Mungo Murray of Lintrose who had rashly declared his enthusiastic approval of the Act. But he had also the foresight to call out a local company of the Perthshire Volunteers, merchants' sons in white and blue, and he led them in a charge upon a crowd of five hundred, taking six prisoners and carrying them in triumph to gaol. At Auchtergaven below Dunkeld the schoolmaster was awoken at night by the prick of a knife on his throat, and he looked up to blackened faces, to unrecognisable men who wore their shirts outside their clothes. They demanded the session-book and he gave it to them. Black faces and shirted men were also seen in candle-lit bedrooms at Kirkmichael and Meigle, Gourdie and Logierait. To the south by Doune, Colonel Alexander Murray of Rednock asked for dragoons to punish the insolent rioters, many of them women, who had stoned him and other deputies at a road meeting. In the city of Perth the constables refused the Lord Provost's orders to post the lists, declaring that their lives and property were forfeit if they did so. Besieged in his house above Strathearn, Sir William Murray of Ochtertyre had no faith in the seventy loyal tenants of his garrison and was mightily relieved when they were reinforced by twenty dragoons from Crieff. Even so, he was forced to receive a delegation from the mob and accept an impudent petition they had written to the King. As far south as Callander honest gentlemen were being stoned and insulted, their houses menaced by fire. With few exceptions the gentry everywhere surrendered to the mob, quickly signing the declarations demanded, and comforting their consciences with the thought that they were thus saving their women and children from the worst excesses of Jacobin terror.

There was worse to be heard from the west, from the upper strath of the Tay between Logierait and Kenmore, until now a peaceful valley of white birch and scarlet rowan. Before August ended the riders who came from Breadalbane to the slated turrets of Blair reported that there were indications of an organised and absolute resistance. David Campbell of Glenlyon, the last of his blemished name, said that although the lists had been pasted to the door of Fortingall kirk without incident he was certain that the men named in them had taken to the hills. In Appin of Dull, where Garth's uncle had schooled his young pipers for the 77th, men with blackened faces tied the schoolmaster to a horse and danced about him into Aberfeldy where he was not released until he told his captors where they might find the session-book. At Killin on the western end of Loch Tay the trap-mouthed Laird of Macnab, immortalised by the brush of Raeburn and the lids of subsequent biscuit tins, told the Duke that a violent mob had thrown the schoolmaster without his door and marched into the hills. There was also an alarming report, not yet proved, of an ugly, brutal killing. To the north by Tummel, it was said, a schoolmaster's ear had been cut from his head by a scythe, from which injury he had bled to death.

An army of men and women, loosely grouped into companies and numbering sixteen thousand it was believed, now controlled the long valley and lit the moonless nights with the joyous fire of their torches.

"*An extreme bad lesson to learn the common people*"

ON SUNDAY THE third day of September Angus Cameron left his cottage at Weem in Strathtay and walked two miles westward to hear the afternoon sermon in the church at Dull. When it was over he joined a great crowd about the Cross, where agents of the Duke of Atholl were posting a printed explanation of the Militia Act. The paper was roughly taken from them and they were driven away. Some men in the crowd told Cameron that the same had happened that morning at Kenmore and Fortingall. When he was later examined by the Sheriff-Depute in Perth he said he had gone to the kirk-yard from curiosity, that what he had done there and thereafter had not been upon his own will but at the earnest request of the people. He was not believed then, nor need he be now, but under threat of transportation or the gallows his dishonest evasion is understandable. The parish of Dull was the centre of all resistance in Strathtay and the men who came to church that day, some in the little kilt and others in black coats and vests of striped cotton, were determined upon revolt. It was a large parish, seventeen miles from Loch Tummel in the north to Strathbraan in the south, twelve westward from Grandtully to the blue opening of Loch Tay, and a great part of it was owned by the Chief of Clan Menzies and his kinsmen. At ten or fifteen shillings an acre it produced an annual rental of £4,500. It had grazing for fifteen hundred horses, five thousand black cattle and twenty-four thousand sheep, all of superior quality. It also maintained four thousand six hundred people who slept on damp heather in mean hovels which Thomas Pennant said were a disgrace to the magnificent scenery about them, and who suffered greatly from rheumatism and pleurisy as a result. They were as much attached to these smoke-blackened cottages as they were to their old ways, to their songs, their legends and their language. Those who lived in the high hills rarely went to kirk, burying their dead outside their townships, and waiting upon itinerant ministers for the solemnisation of birth, marriage and death. There were three schools, dry-stone and sod-roofed buildings supported by the proprietors of the land on which they stood. Their God-obsessed teachers were appointed by the Society for Promoting Christian Knowledge, dedicated men who taught the simple fabric of learning to four hundred pupils, using hard knuckles or the stinging tawse upon any child who spoke Gaelic in their presence.

The minister at Dull was Archibald Menzies, and the deputy-teacher at Dull was Donald Fleming. Three days before the Duke's agents came to the Cross both men had been dragged from their houses and brutally handled until they promised that they would take no further part in the imposition of the Act. It was Fleming who had been set upon the bare back of a horse and paraded through the mud streets of Aberfeldy until he surrendered the session-book, even though this was too late to prevent the balloting.

The news of the gathering at the church, and the outrages that followed, would not reach the Duke of Atholl before Monday evening, spoiling his enjoyment of the best shooting his moors had provided for some years. Though his castle had been saved from the mob he did not believe that his wretched surrender would bring an end to the trouble in his country. He had been warned how widespread this might be. Hope Steuart of Ballechin, a Volunteer captain whose wooded estate was held in the fork of the Tay and the Tummel, had sent him the names of twenty-three common men, all from townships between Logierait and Blair. Four days before the assault on the castle they had boldly gathered in Widow Duff's ale-house at Ballinluig, to plan the deforcement of ministers and teachers, to phrase the declarations the lairds must be forced to sign, and to send a rallying cry westward to the young men of Strathtay and Breadalbane. Their daring leaders were the Maclaggans, father John who impudently styled himself "The Duke of Lennox", and two sons Alexander and Donald who were travelling tailors with no fixed habitation. Atholl had first thought of calling the three men before him and lecturing them upon their villainous behaviour, but since they were now plainly responsible for the advance upon Blair he agreed with Steuart that a harsh legal example should be made of them. How this could be done he did not know, and he had no hope of an early arrival of soldiers. On Saturday evening, before those bare-legged women had come with their terrible weapons, he had received a discouraging letter from Perth. The county Volunteers, said their merchant major, Thomas Marshall, would not march from the city until they were assured that such active service entitled them to full pay under the terms of the Volunteer Act. "Upon this subject, we should wish to be honoured with your Grace's opinion . . ." The appeal was still unanswered at noon on Monday, and the Duke could not know what was happening in Strathtay.

The printed paper taken from the Atholl agents at the Cross of Dull was then brought to Angus Cameron who stood upon the kirk-yard wall and read it to the people, explaining its meaning in Gaelic. He later told the Sheriff-Depute that he had never seen a copy of the Militia Act but he had studied an abstract in the Edinburgh *Courant*. When he had given what answers he could to the people's questions he went to his home, and he said he would have taken no further part in the riots had many persons not come to his lodgings before sunrise on Monday, threatening him with violence if he did not join them. He told the Sheriff that he had thought it prudent to say that he would go willingly. The crowd was led by James Menzies, the East Indian. There were a thousand men and women armed with clubs and torches, and they filled the little street of Weem from General Wade's great inn to the Aberfeldy toll-road. Most of them were from Dull, Fortingall and Kenmore, but three hundred or more had come from the north, down the green-black fall of Keltney Burn, bringing two gentlemen who had refused to oppose the Act and were now the crowd's prisoners. One was William Stewart the heir to Garth, and the other was Joseph Stewart younger of Foss. William's brother David, a captain-lieutenant of the 42nd, was in the West Indies suppressing the last resistance of a Carib insurrection. He admired these Indians' fierce defence of their independence, but what he later thought of the riotous behaviour of his father's Gaelic tenants is not to be found in his *Sketches*.

Two hours after dawn the crowd had increased, and upon impulse or design it marched westward a mile to Castle Menzies, taking with it James MacDiarmid the minister of Weem, Robert Menzies a lawyer, and his father the factor of the Menzies estates. They walked in the middle of the mob with the young Stewarts, surrounded by waving sticks and jeering faces.

The castle was not a fortress but a fine mansion-house of yellow stone and elegant glazing, dwarfed by the wooded rock-wall of Weem Hill behind it. Its parklands stretched southward over the valley floor to the Tay, and its gardens were rich with fruit – pears, apples, red and black geans, and a wall of damask peaches. Its owner, Sir John Menzies of Menzies, was the son-in-law of Atholl whose doe-eyed daughter Charlotte he had married six months before, a union of profit rather than love for he was almost three times her age. He was a deputy-lieutenant of the county, a hard man and a rich man, round-bodied and round-faced with a nose like the coulter of a plough. His rent from his nearest tenants in Weem was £1,613 alone, but his great fortune had come from the West Indies where he had served the Government's interest and his own until he unexpectedly inherited a chief's title and the Menzies lands. When he took possession of them, and as if he were still master of a Caribbean plantation, he had hung a great bell from the branch of a tree at the eastern gate to his policies, that callers might give him early notice of their arrival. It was not rung this day, nor did he need such a caveat. On their way to Angus Cameron's house the crowd had stopped at Castle Menzies, shouting a demand for the repeal of the Militia Act. Sir John sent a message to them, telling them to be gone, to submit a petition in a proper manner, and since then he had been standing to arms with his guests and servants.

Now the mob formed a wide half-moon on his sheep-cropped lawn. Factor Menzies was sent into the house with the blunt warning that if Sir John did not wish its roof to be fired above his head he should give a written undertaking not to execute the Act. While the crowd waited for a reply it was increased to two thousand by the arrival of men and women from Grandtully under the leadership of the Maclaggans, and at this Sir John submitted. He did so with what dignity was left to him, insisting upon respect for his authority. A table was brought from his kitchens to the gravel before his door and he sat behind it with James Robertson, the session-clerk of Weem. He asked who was to be spokesman. James Menzies came forward, but what the East Indian said, or how he said it, did not please the people and they deposed him with a great shout, saying that Angus Cameron must be their man. He agreed without hesitation, and as if he had expected the responsibility he produced a sheet of stamped paper, ordering Robertson to write a petition for relief from the Act. The terms were suggested by the people, the words translated into English and dictated in proper form by Cameron. When it was done Sir John accepted it without comment, suggesting only a correction in spelling, but he found it harder to stomach the attached declaration which he and other gentlemen were to sign and which would compel them to renounce the Act. The people insisted that it should contain a clause obliging him not to admit soldiers to the valley, and he protested that he had no power to prevent their coming. Cameron was anxious that nothing should be written that would show obvious duress and he argued with the people, finally asking them to vote upon the matter. By a show of hands they agreed that the clause could be rephrased.

The nature of the declaration resembled all such papers the Highland proprietors were forced to sign, and gives support to the administration's belief that they were inspired by a co-ordinating influence beyond the hills. But the articulate and unequivocal language was Angus Cameron's and is a brief insight into an extraordinary mind, exposing an intellect and knowledge beyond his trade and station. It disproves his claim to have been fortuitously involved, it implies forethought and careful consideration, it suggests that he had read or listened to the young reforming advocates of the south. He was a craftsman, a skilful worker with wood, and like the merchant James Menzies he was a man of substance, set apart from the people he led by a little money, some schooling and a wider experience. But he was socially despised by the gentry he humiliated, and what they could not now patronise they must eventually destroy. Like all men who turn to violence in outraged compassion he nobly and naïvely believed that the word should prevail in the end, that the promises he was obtaining by force would be honourably kept. When he realised too late that these gentlemen's honour was not indivisible he would deny the word and break his own promise in order to escape their vengeance. But this Monday noon the word was surely triumphant, and one by one the Laird of Menzies, the young Stewarts, the ministers of Weem and Dull put their signatures to the declaration, affirming their abhorrence of the Act and swearing to oppose it with all their legal and constitutional power.

We hereby solemnly declare that we shall use no forcible means to apprehend, confine, or imprison any person assistant whatever who has appeared at Castle Menzies or elsewhere, or in any part of Perth on prior days; further that we shall petition government for an abolition nullifying of the foresaid Act from the records of British parliament; that the members of parliament for this county shall present this petition, or any annexed thereto, to the two Houses of Parliament, to the privy council, during the prorogation of parliament. This we shall do of our own free will and accord, as we shall answer to God.

When the last signature was written by the minister of Dull, Cameron asked the people if they would now protect Sir John against all hurt and indignity. They held up their hands, shouting that they would. He led them away and at the east gate below the great bell, he climbed upon a post and according to the charges laid against him "he did most seditiously and wickedly administer an oath to the people thus riotously assembled, to stand by one another in their illegal endeavours to resist the authority of the established law of the country".

Every proprietor at present in Strathtay was now compelled to sign the declaration, that none might feel himself morally free to call upon the Government for dragoons. More men and women were coming from other parishes in the east and the west, and a crowd of four thousand followed Cameron and Menzies through the sunlight of the valley floor to the south bank of the Tay. There on a green slope opposite the castle of his kinsman and chief lived Alexander Menzies of Bolfracks, with a walled enclosure for the graves of his ancestors, a profitable quarry that had supplied the stones for Wade's bridge at Aberfeldy, and rich grazing over the hills to Glen Quaich. When the mob came to his door, wet to the waist with Tay water, he signed the declaration without dispute, but his son William, a surgeon in the Army, angrily refused. He would sign nothing, he said, that obliged him to disobey his superior officers should they order him against the rioters. The people took him by the arms and legs and dragged him a gun-shot from the house to the river, where they might have drowned him had not Cameron stopped them. "To compel an *officer* to act so," he said, "is treason as well as sedition." The people may not have understood the nice distinction, but they allowed Doctor Menzies to live, to sign the declaration with the qualification that he was not thereby prevented from obeying his commanding officer.

The crowd was now divided into two divisions for the march eastward. Cameron mounted a horse that Menzies had given him and led one back across the river to the north bank. The East Indian took the other through Aberfeldy on the south. On both sides of the water more people were gathered in, and before Cameron had gone ten miles there were almost five thousand men and women behind him, filling the rowan-berried lane and spreading across the hillside. Everywhere the gentry were forced to stand at their doors and put their names to the declaration. It was past nine o'clock and dark when Cameron's division reached Hope Steuart's land at Ballechin, three miles from where the Tummel meets the Tay. Here he was joined by Menzies who had crossed the river to Logierait further down, bringing with him the people of that village and three prisoners – Thomas Bisset the minister, John Thomson the constable, and Major Alexander MacGlashan the Laird of Eastertyre. In a bizarre ceremony, lit by a thousand torches, MacGlashan was compelled to administer the rioter's oath to the minister and constable. The combined divisions, perhaps ten thousand people, then marched upon Ballechin House. Hope Steuart's temper was hot enough to tell them to go to the devil, but he was at once bludgeoned to the ground and dragged about his house until it cooled. When the people were gone he left at once for Perth and there wrote to the Duke saying that concern for his personal safety obliged him to be absent from his property for some days. Although his signature had been extorted by force, he said, "I am not at liberty to take any concern in carrying the Militia Act into execution."

There was no sleep in Strathtay that night. At two o'clock on Tuesday morning the triumphant army returned to Weem and Appin of Dull. The houses of the gentry were scattered islands in a terrible loneliness. Numbed by the astonishing hostility of their tenants, their honour compromised by those humiliating signatures, they watched the burning torches and prayed for delivery.

Early on Tuesday there was another alarm at Blair Castle. The Duke was told that a great crowd was coming through the deep gorge of Killiecrankie, men and women from Strathtay, from Tummel Bridge and Rannoch. With more hope than faith he called upon his nearest tenants, and to his delight the response was strong. "In the course of an hour and a half," he told the Lord Advocate, "I assembled about four hundred able bodied men who are all loyal, zealous and attached." The people came no closer to Blair than the lower slopes of Creag Eallaich, where their great-grandfathers had helped to destroy a British army more than a century before. Their retreat is unexplained, but is an example of the indecision that crippled almost everything that Cameron proposed. He said that the people should henceforth assemble in small parties only, never more than forty-nine, for if there were fifty of them together they could be dealt with as a mob under the Riot Act. He said that delegates should go to Campbell of Glenlyon and Stewart of Garth, asking these lairds for warrants entitling such groups to meet and petition. But the Highlanders neither understood his tactical caution nor had the self-discipline to observe it. Their courage was sustained by their great numbers, and if Glenlyon or Garth were asked for the warrants there is no record of them. The people were frightened by the thought of dragoons, but Cameron told them they must expect force and should prepare themselves to meet it. They need not fear, they could retire to the hills as their fathers had once done, falling upon the soldiers at night. When they asked how they were to fight with sticks and clubs he told them that there were arms to be had, muskets, swords and powder in Glenlyon House, in Lord Breadalbane's glittering armoury at Taymouth Castle. His lordship was in London as usual, of course, and if the people came to his grounds, down his noble avenue of limes and through his gentle herd of fallow deer, they got no weapons, or none that was seen in their hands.

And then there were days of quiet, no sound of drums or bridle-chains, no red coats or black horses coming northward from Dunkeld and Crieff. Although a resolute number of the people still assembled, and their torches burned at night, others were easily persuaded that they had won all they desired, that their young men would now be left in peace. According to his sworn statement, Cameron returned to his work, to joy in the wedding of a friend, but it would be charged against him that he spent those days exciting the people to further resistance. In the hearing of the schoolmaster Fleming he said that he knew that soldiers must come, but the people would be ready to meet them. He boldly proposed that a number of gentlemen should be taken prisoners to Blair, where Atholl himself should be asked to

give his written approval of their declarations. At Blair the Duke
fretted over the continued insolence of the man and the insufferable absence of force to apprehend him. The commander of some
English dragoons newly arrived in Perth promised to send arms
and cartridges, but Atholl wanted troopers. He told the Lord
Advocate that although he and others had been compelled to
sign the declarations such a submission of authority would have
a calamitous effect throughout the nation if it were not soon
corrected. "It is an extreme bad lesson to learn the common
people, that by tumultuous assembling they can with effect
oppose the law of the land."

"How happy I am that we have got so well rid of Mr. Cameron"

THE DUKE WAS told that the rumour of a schoolmaster's bloody death was unhappily true. He was Mr. Forbes, a Society man who taught a few children at Fincastle, in a pleat of hills between Blair and Tummel. When awoken by a mob he had resisted bravely, whereupon one MacGregor struck him with the blade of a scythe, cutting off an ear, from which wound he languished and died. The murderer was known to be deranged, but his madness strengthened the demand for his early departure through the gallows' trap.

The devil at the head of the Strathtay men was also marked down for merciless punishment, and Atholl told Robert Dundas that it was highly incumbent upon the Sheriff to be at hand in Perth to take any precongitions that might be necessary. With more fear than contempt or mockery, the gentry were now calling the wood-worker King Cameron and The Rebel Chief. He was said to have "unknown faces" about him at all times, and that prior to the beginning of the riots he had held midnight meetings and administered seditious oaths. At the end of August, it was said, he and James Menzies had gone to MacNaughton's tavern in Aberfeldy, there to meet Winlack, a hatter from Perth with whom they discussed religion and Thomas Paine's *Age of Reason*. The taking of oaths, their chilling reminder of the Parisian Terror, obsessed the Duke's High Tory mind, and he told the Lord Advocate that representatives of the United Scotsmen were undoubtedly responsible for the mobbing and rioting, that the root of tumult lay much deeper than opposition to the Act. "I would certainly wish that some infantry were at Perth, as well as cavalry, for threats of burning houses and making people take oaths must be nipped in the bud."

By infantry he plainly meant marching-regiments, not the laggard Volunteers of his county. The Maclaggans had gone into the hills and the people about Blair were now calm. There was no attempt to stop the post-riders between the Castle and the south but the letters that came were disheartening. There was a great marching and counter-marching of battalions across the Stirling plain, brave musters at Callander and Crieff, but none advancing up the Dunkeld road. Now fearing a sudden descent by wild Breadalbane men, the magistrates of Perth were unwilling to part with the Volunteers, who were themselves reluctant to march before they were assured of their pay. Colonel Charles Rooke, commanding a regiment of bucolic English horsemen called The Windsor Foresters, was still delayed in the city for no clear reason. The arms he had promised to send for the defence of Blair Castle – forty stands of muskets and a chest of cartridge and ball – at last left on Thursday, September 7, in the charge of James Stobie, one of the Duke's factors and an amateur cartographer. Captain Stobie was proud to be played out of the city by the Volunteers' band, cheered by thousands of its inhabitants, but he travelled no more than fifteen miles to Dunkeld where he was advised by young Lord Rollo that since the country was quiet there was need for him to proceed further. While he waited for a cart to come from Blair for the arms he wrote to the Duke upon the urgent matter of the Volunteers' uniforms, their blue coats, white breeches and varnished black hats. He thought that some men might need money for the clothing, and he respectfully awaited his Grace's directions. He was exceedingly glad to hear that the north country was now quiet. It was unpleasant, he said, for it to be otherwise.

On the morning of Sunday, September 10, Angus Cameron and James Menzies went to hear the Gaelic sermon at the kirk of Kenmore, upon a green headland above Loch Tay. When it was over, said Cameron, he talked to the congregation, explaining the Act and saying that it was the people's right to meet and petition, providing such a petition had no more than forty-nine signatures. But the charge against him, upon the evidence of

informers, was that he and Menzies excited the people to further
resistance, warning them that sixteen thousand men were ready
to oppose the enlistment of a militia and those who would not
willingly join this army would be forced into it. Later that
afternoon both men went up Strath Appin by the old military
road, northward past the white cataract of Keltney Burn to a
bare heathland, and thence down to Tummel water. Their
departure was watched by a number of Strathtay gentlemen who
had come to the little kirk of Weem to honour God and to pray
for delivery from His meaner servants. They questioned some of
the people of the village and were alarmed by what they were
told. One of them wrote at once to his friend Henry Butter, the
Laird of Faskally below Killiecrankie, hoping that Mr. Butter
would pass the information to the Duke.

> It is said that Cameron is off to collect the Rannoch people,
> and that the different agents are to set on foot the whole
> country from Logierait to the top of Breadalbane, Glenlyon,
> etc. – all to meet at or about Weem, for the express purpose
> of getting possession of all the arms in the different houses,
> and Taymouth, from thence to Blair etc. In consequence of
> this report I can assure you of the gentlemen who intend this
> very night to hide whatever firearms they are in possession
> of. . . . Be assured that the incendiary Cameron and his
> agents are at work.

Butter forwarded the letter at once to Atholl who had already
received a similar report from Sir John Menzies. Cameron later
denied this account of his visit. He said that he went to the
Government saw-mill on Loch Rannoch, to the forest of red fir
and white birch where two men were cutting wood for his use.
He admitted that he had told some of the people that there was to
be a meeting in the kirk-yard of Fortingall on Monday, but no
more. He drank with the sawyers until past three o'clock in the
morning and then walked homeward over the dawn hills.

Some young gentlemen were angered by their fathers' decision
to hide the arms that should more properly be used against King

Cameron and his mob. They believed that the rogue had done all
the mischief he could and if he were not soon taken up he would
flit from the county. Faskally's son Archibald, a brevet-major of
light dragoons on furlough, wrote an acerbic letter to the Duke.
"I trust your Grace will pardon me in saying that I think the
honour of the country materially concerned in preventing the
escape of a notorious offender." There were at least thirty
gentlemen ready to arm and ride, and it would give Brevet-major
Butter particular satisfaction to be their leader. Despairing of help
from the south, the Duke was ready to accept this zealous offer,
and then, before dusk on Tuesday, a party of fencible horsemen
rode down the dappled drive to Blair Castle, blue coats, black-
roached helmets and burnished scabbards. Ten days after the
beginning of the riots in Strathtay, Captain Samuel Colberg of
the Windsor Foresters had come to the defence of the Crown and
the relief of men of property.

He was a young and high-spirited officer, eager for action and
ready to pluck King Cameron from the midst of his followers. He
did not believe that it would require an invasion in force. He had
already left a third of his troop at Dunkeld, and now he proposed
to leave all but eighteen of the remainder at Blair, for the protection of his Grace. He dined with the Duke that night and in the
morning he waited impatiently for the arrival of the sheriff-
substitute, James Chalmers, and the completion of the necessary
warrants. He put his small detachment on the road before sunset,
taking it over the heather-blue shoulder of Tulach to Loch
Tummel and then southward by Strath Appin to Castle Menzies.
Mr. Chalmers rode at one stirrup and at the other was the Duke's
brother, Lord Henry Murray, a major of Volunteers and not
much older than his niece Lady Charlotte who welcomed him
with emotional affection. Sir John was also glad to see these big
English dragoons, and while he approved of Colberg's plan to lift
the Rebel Chiefs from their beds before dawn on Thursday he
did not believe there were enough horsemen to take them from
the valley without a fight.

The coming of the soldiers was known to Cameron before they

rode past the Falls of Keltney. He and Menzies also knew, from the presence of Chalmers, that there would be an attempt to arrest them. Their curious inaction may be explained by the fact that they were indeed not guilty of the charges against them, and thought that their innocence alone would protect them. They may have believed that the promise exacted from the Laird of Menzies, his oath before God that he would use no forcible means to apprehend or imprison them, was security for their safety. In view of what happened later at Grandtully they may have been confident that so small a detachment of Horse could never remove them from Strathtay, and that their arrest would bring a necessary clash with the soldiers. They believed, as others less sophisticated believed, that the common men of Inverness, Ross and Argyll were ready to support them, and a bloody encounter with the Foresters would thus inspire a greater revolt in the Highlands. Simpler men, wiser men perhaps, would have used this hour or two of grace and slipped westward by Glen Lyon to the moor of Rannoch, to the roadless wilderness of Mamore. But they did nothing, and there was no resistance when a dragoon broke down their doors with the butt of a carbine.

A file of troopers brought a post-chaise from the inn, and both men were quickly thrust inside. Colberg placed himself by the side of the coach and ordered a march at the trot. With twelve riders before and six behind, the party moved eastward along the north bank of the Tay, the dark leaf and red fruit of the roadside already touched by the coming light. His warrants served, the Sheriff-substitute remained in the cottage, examining the books and papers he found there, the detritus of Cameron's humble scholarship. Much of it was of no consequence, or at least irrelevant to the charge, but there were some yellow sheets that excited Mr. Chalmers' professional interest and he placed them in a sealed bag with an inventory. "*Nine letters, two songs, a draught or copy of a letter, and some jottings . . .*"

The alarm was now up, shouting voices in the half-light, the blowing of whistles and the strident bray of a horn. Colberg was reluctant to increase the pace lest the horses be winded before they were out of the valley, and because of this the party was quickly overtaken by small groups of pursuers, shadowy figures moving swiftly on foot, and sometimes mounted men, white faces turned to the officer as they passed. They shouted, not to his prisoners Colberg thought, but to the braeside, to the bright gleam of the river on his right. They called *"En mass Cameron!"*, or thus the words seemed to him, and he did not know what the Gaelic meant. The cry was taken up by other voices, and as the light grew stronger he saw that the valley was alive and black with movement. "We observed hundreds of people, with forks, fowling-pieces, pikes and scythes fixed on poles, pouring from the mountains and from the water side, and the road covered with men, women, and children." He kept the coach-horses moving at a trot. The crowd parted before, and closed behind. He looked back. His six troopers at the rear were now riding in a mob of perhaps two hundred men, all but the tossing heads of their horses hidden, their blue figures apparently carried on the shoulders of the Highlanders. He was afraid that one of the dragoons might snap a pistol at these angry faces, or draw a sabre against a threatening scythe. He fell back, warning the mob to stand off, but it ran past him as if he were not there. He spurred on to the coach and spoke to Cameron, and what he shouted was probably less literate than the words he put in his report. "You see the wretched situation you have plunged yourself in, by interfering in political affairs?" Cameron did not answer, but he called to the Highlanders in Gaelic, and Colberg had no doubt that he was exhorting them to violence. "Persuade them to go peaceably to their homes," he said, "my men will not fire first. If yours do I know I shall fall, but I shall send a ball through them first!"

Six miles from Weem at Grandtully, where the river curved to the south, the road also turned sharply to the right and crossed a stone bridge to the other side of the water. The sun was now above the hill at Logierait, filling the valley with golden light, clearly showing Colberg that he must be surrounded by no less than five thousand men and women, all armed with savage weapons. He wondered why they had not yet attacked him and the question was soon answered. Less than a mile from Grandtully a mounted gentleman was waiting at the roadside, thighs and saddle wet from his crossing of the river. He was Captain Grant of Pitnacree and he turned to ride beside Colberg, telling the officer that a great crowd of men were holding the bridge, determined to dispute its passage. They had assured him that they would have Cameron and Menzies delivered to them peaceably or they would kill the dragoons. Pitnacree appealed to the prisoners, asking them to tell the mob that they went willingly with the soldiers, but Cameron refused. Grant would stay no longer, afraid that his house would be burned and himself killed if he remained with the coach. "You must cut your way through" he said, "or draw them off." And he rode away.

Colberg accepted the challenge of the people with enthusiasm. "The lucky moment of thought came into my memory," said his report, "which was to speak to them but show no fear, and as lenient measures with the untaught and illiterate are always best." He ordered his riders to load their pistols, all but three whom he suspected of being drunk, but warned them not to fire until he gave the order. He then told his sergeant and the coachman what he intended and rode on alone to Grandtully. He halted at the top of the slope, where the road dropped steeply for ten yards to the bridge. There he was surrounded by its hostile defenders but he smiled at them amiably, leaning forward on the pommel of his saddle as if they were neighbours met casually on a journey. "I don't wish to hurt Mr. Cameron or his friend," he said, "nor do I wish my party to be hurt by you. Give me leave to explain this business." The Highlanders were disarmed by his manner, surprised that he had come alone, and one impulsively put up a hand in greeting. Colberg shook it warmly and at that moment he heard the sound of wheels and hooves behind him. He looked back casually and then, when the first file of his escort was on the tip of the slope, he winked, shouted gaily, and spurred into the crowd. Carriage and dragoons came down the rise behind him in a yelling charge, the coachman standing on the box with whip lashing. They scattered the defenders of the bridge, bounced over its arch and were away down the open road beyond. Colberg kept the pace at a gallop for eleven miles, out of Strathtay by Balnamuir and southward through the trees to Inver opposite Dunkeld. There he halted at MacGlashan's Tavern.

The coach-horses were winded, and the trooper's mounts were also spent, necks stretched and nostrils wide. The tavern was an ale-house with no post-change, and since there was no sound of pursuit on the wooded road behind Colberg decided that his party was now safe. He told Cameron and Menzies that they might dismount and take a pot, and when he had ordered his escort to feed and water he crossed the Tay by the ferry. He hoped for fresh coach-horses at Dunkeld House, a red-brick English building and one of the Duke's homes, but there was none to be had. He came back, and as he leapt ashore he heard a great shout to the north. The Strathtay men, several hundreds of them he believed, came out of the trees and ran swiftly toward the inn. Colberg shouted for the prisoners to be put in the coach. He ordered four troopers to leave at once with the carriage, to ride at the gallop and to kill the horses if that would get them quickly to Perth. He then placed the remaining dragoons in line across the road and walked his horse forward a few paces to meet the Highlanders. They came on slowly now, alarmed by the resolute troopers, and they stopped when Colberg drew his sabre, sloping it on his shoulder. He warned them that he would cheerfully cut down the first man who attempted to pass him. They could have shot him out of the saddle with a fowling-piece, or unseated him with a scythe before he could touch them, but instead they argued with him, pleading and threatening. "They said if Cameron was confined they, the Atholl, Ross and Argyll Highlanders would rise in a mass and burn all before them." Colberg laughed at them, asking what they feared. Cameron was only going to give bail for his appearance at the assizes, and would probably return to them when that was done. He shouted to the troopers behind him, "*By twos . . . to the right about. March!*" His smiling eyes on the mob, he heard the response to his order, the clatter of departing hooves, and he was alone. He argued for a few moments more and then he turned suddenly, galloping after the detachment. "They followed us some miles beyond Dunkeld, when we heard some guns fire, but I proceeded and arrived fatigued, but safe."

He brought his command into Perth shortly after four o'clock in the afternoon and was escorted through its streets by the noisy drums of the Volunteers. Cameron and Menzies were placed in the town gaol, guarded by forty soldiers, and were examined that night by the Sheriff-depute, Archibald Campbell younger of Clathick. He was shocked by what their statements revealed, and when they were at last returned to their cells he wrote at once to the Duke. Although Cameron had accepted his imprisonment with dignity, he said, the man was a hardened fellow and should be sent to Edinburgh as soon as possible, that his trial might strike terror into his misguided followers. Part of Cameron's statement confirmed Atholl's opinion that the root of the tumult lay deeper than opposition to the Militia Act, that the people had begun to express more bitter and more fundamental grievances, too late to be effective, perhaps, but questioning the principles of government and society. The extent of this is indicated rather than defined in Cameron's statement. He stubbornly insisted that he had refused to act as the people's leader unless they proceeded constitutionally, and he denied that he had impudently and impertinently drawn up an Act of Parliament that would redress their many wrongs. "He had heard rumours," it was written by Campbell's clerk, "but no resolutions actually formed about reducing the ministers' stipends, the schoolmasters' salaries, and the lairds' rents, and he never heard any proposal about the King being obliged to reside at Edinburgh, or about the excisemen not being allowed to go above a mile from their own houses."

The power of Cameron's influence became clear at the moment it was removed by his arrest, for the co-ordinated resistance of the people now collapsed. When Samuel Colberg galloped out of history along the Perth road the Strathtay men remained at Inver for the rest of the day, some about MacGlashan's tavern and others patrolling the river-bank, shouting threats across the water. Their presence was reported to Captain Stobie, who having at last delivered the muskets and powder to Blair was now returning to Dunkeld. He and his detachment hid in the roadside trees until dark, coming into the town past ten o'clock. What leadership now remained in the mob was exercised by three men whom the warrants would later describe as King Cameron's Lieutenants. Two of them were roadmenders and the third was The Duke of Lennox. John MacLaggan had come from hiding in the hills of Rannoch to command the defenders of the bridge at Grandtully, and may have been that "very stout man" who grasped Colberg's hand in impulsive friendship. None of the three had the intelligence or skill to impose a discipline that would compensate for the shock of Cameron's arrest. James Stewart, the Duke's factor at Dowally on the left bank of the Tay, had watched the coach rocking through the trees on the opposite bank, the galloping dragoons and the mob in shouting pursuit, and toward dusk he stiffened his courage and went to Dunkeld to learn if further mischief was planned. What he discovered he reported to Atholl the next day. A man he knew, one of the rioters, came over the ferry from Inver

> ... and frankly told me that their plans were to raise up all the people in Grandtully and Strathtay, and to proceed to Castle Menzies, and if Sir John did not give them his obligation that he would relieve Cameron that they were fully determined to burn Castle Menzies. That they were also to go to Taymouth and brake open Lord Breadalbane's Armory, and take all his arms, and that this day they were determined to come down in a body to raise all the men on the north side of the Tay and Tummel, and proceed to Atholl House.

But the brave talk came to nothing, and the mob broke into small groups, moving aimlessly back to Strathtay. Those who came to Castle Menzies on Friday found that it was now protected by Major John Atherton and two troops of the Lancashire Light Dragoons, big fencible men with leather helmets and long straight swords. They had come from Crieff, by the Sma' Glen and the bleak pass of Cachill Burn, cantering to Sir John's door an hour or so after the post-chaise left the kirk-yard of Weem. Protected by these red-faced Englishmen and reassured by the sight of their horse-lines on the grass below her window, Lady Charlotte wrote gaily to her dearest papa, "I cannot tell you how happy I am that we have got so well rid of *Mr. Cameron* and his friend. How anxious you must have been to hear of the success of the party dispatched from Blair . . ." Her husband was equally pleased to have his humiliation revenged. The Lancashire troopers, he told his father-in-law, were fine-looking and well-mounted fellows, and he was full of admiration for Major Atherton who rode about the valley with no more escort than a sergeant's guard. "After Sunday is over, without any apparent disposition of the people to rise, I should think one troop a sufficient force for protection."

There was no further disposition to rise. That week-end there was indeed a midnight alarm, a report that the Duke of Lennox and the Grandtully people were again advancing on Castle Menzies, but the troopers who rode to meet the threat found nothing on the road but the marauding fox, and heard nothing in the hillside pines but cry of the long-eared owl. Now and then on following nights there were torches on the braes, voices calling in dark defiance, but resistance and revolt were over. More dragoons came from the south, English and Lowland fencibles who filled the inns and cottages of Aberfeldy and patrolled the gentlemen's estates. The greatest blow to the people's spirits, to their belief that all Highlanders would stand by the men of Strathtay, was the arrival of the Sutherland Fencibles, four companies to beat the heather of Schiehallion, Rannoch and Lawers as the Jacobite-hunters had done fifty years before. Behind the soldiers came Sheriff Campbell with warrants for the arrest of all rioters and all ringleaders known by name. At noon on Saturday, September 23, he took lodgings at MacGlashan's tavern and before nightfall he sent a bundle of these warrants to Lieutenant Peter MacRaw of the Volunteers at Logierait. "If you can find out the name of the man who is mad, and who killed the schoolmaster, you will fill up the blank, and if you miss the other persons in the riot who are of more consequence to be laid hold of than the madman, you may apprehend him . . ." Like MacGregor the murderer, most of the men marked down in the warrants were given no Christian names. They were weavers and farmers' sons, roadmenders, labourers and wandering tailors, all betrayed to the Sheriff's officers by anonymous informers. The most notorious had already been taken up. At dawn on Saturday a party of Sutherland men under Captain Hugh Mackay had found the Duke of Lennox, alone on the hills above Grandtully.

The Highlanders' resistance to the Militia Act was receding quickly, an ebb-tide across the low flats of bewildered despair. Before the month was out Major-general Alexander Campbell of Monzie came from Edinburgh to command all the dragoons, fencibles and volunteers in Perthshire. He was a sick man, his health ruined by service in the Caribbean, but he was firm and resolute, and he ordered his command as if he were on campaign, cowing the people by a mighty exercise of force. Now that they were safe, the gentry wondered at the fury that had so briefly threatened their security and their lives. It was agreed that outside influences had been responsible, those "unknown faces" which Mr. Butter said were always to be seen behind the shoulder of Angus Cameron. It was further agreed that had greater efforts been made to explain the Militia Act to the people they would have accepted it peacefully and willingly. No one, except Atholl and Gleneagles perhaps, looked for deeper reasons: the Highlanders' intense hatred of compulsory military service, their resentment of increasing rents and excise taxes, their hatred of schoolmasters who forbade the speaking of Gaelic, and their outraged contempt for ministers appointed by the Laird and not by the congregation. Lord Fife, the Lord Lieutenant of Banffshire, understood something of this complex discontent, or at least recognised the danger in it. He thought it lunatic that such disaffected ingrates should be entrusted with the defence of the kingdom. He had been at his shooting-lodge on the Braes of Mar when the men of Deeside rose against the Act. None of them threatened him, he told the Lord Advocate, but even so he had been inadequately protected by a few servants and friends while all the country was in a state of ferment.

> I have for forty years past uniformly advised that these people should never be trusted with arms. I hope this is but one example of many that will convince those who either advise to arm them, or to raise them, to alter their opinion. I will venture to decide that, if ever the measure is gone into, it will be a fatal one. They are good soldiers under proper military discipline abroad; at home, they are in mountains with very little society in the neighbouring country, and speak a different language. If ever they are armed, they will only do mischief.

Six months later, when he came again to shoot at Mar Lodge, he instructed his agents to evict and remove all those tenants who were known to have taken a forward part in the riots. He advised his neighbours to do the same, telling them that he knew from long experience that it was necessary to make examples of such men.

General Campbell kept his dragoons and fencibles on patrol and search until the first October snows closed the high valleys and gave a brief security to the men named in the warrants. No such display of punitive force had been seen in the Highlands since the harrying of the glens after Culloden, and although it was not brutal like that fearful experience it recalled a bitter memory and finally broke the will to resist. The Duke of Atholl asked Henry Dundas to suspend the ballot in Perthshire, to allow men to come willingly into the new Volunteer regiments, but the advice was rejected. When the Act was again imposed it was accepted without violence, or none significant enough to be recorded. Some of the gentry who had been forced to sign those degrading declarations, swearing to oppose the raising of a militia, now became captains and majors in that corps, and would in time order it to disperse the mobs of hungry men and women who rioted against the starving price of meal.

On the morning following their examination by the Sheriff in

Perth, Angus Cameron and James Menzies were sent to Edinburgh, escorted by a troop of Foresters with carbines loaded and primed. They were not gone an hour when Colonel Rooke was told that there would be an attempt to rescue them at Bridge of Earn, four miles to the south. He sent another troop in support and either because of this, or because the alarm was false, the attempt was not made. The prisoners were placed in the Tolbooth at Edinburgh and four months later on Monday, January 15, they were at last brought before the High Court of Justiciary, charged with sedition, mobbing and rioting. That same week a company of the Sutherland Fencibles was marched back to Weem, to maintain the peace should the Strathtay people rise in anger against the inevitable sentences of the court. Both men pleaded not guilty to the charge and were returned to the Tolbooth to await their trial. On Tuesday Cameron applied for bail, which was surprisingly granted, but there was no answer in the court the next day when his name was three times called by the macer. He was gone and was never heard of again. Sheriff Campbell thought he had fled to the Highlands, and James Chalmers was ordered to search for him, but no man believed that the runagate would remain long in Scotland. "I suppose," the Sheriff wrote to Atholl, "he will make off for Ireland or America. Such is the termination of all that trouble and expense which has taken place." The court was unwilling to proceed against Menzies, since the charges against both men were interdependent. Although the East Indian was re-committed on a new warrant and later admitted to bail, nothing is known of his ultimate disposal. With thunderous solemnity the court declared that "Angus Cameron is an outlaw and fugitive from His Majesty's laws, to be put to the horn, and all his moveable goods and gear to be escheat." The empty words echo in the darkness that now hides King Cameron, the Rebel Chief of Strathtay.

Four months later eight other men appeared before the circuit court at Perth. The Duke of Lennox was not among them, nor MacGregor of the murderous scythe. There was a farmer and a weaver, a shoemaker, a miller, and men of no declared trade or occupation. In the context of the charges and the temper of the times the sentences were lenient, perhaps from compassion but more probably from the cautious realisation that harsher treatment would worsen the sullen acceptance of the Militia Act. They received a year's imprisonment, three of them to be banished from Scotland at their release. In August they were offered and accepted a remission of their punishment upon their willingness to join one of the King's marching-regiments or serve in one of his ships of war.

Above the Tay at Aberfeldy, near the grey span of Wade's noble bridge, is the heroic figure of a Highland soldier, his musket slanted on his back and his hand in the hilt of his sword. The cairn upon which he stands marks the spot where the men of the Watch were remustered as the 43rd Regiment of Foot. There is no tangible remembrance of the fact that sixty years later some of their sons and grandsons were among the thousands who passed this way under the leadership of Angus Cameron and James Menzies. But history has its quiet ironies. The model from which the Victorian sculptor innocently worked was an 18th century engraving of the mutineer Farquhar Shaw.

5
A FEW GOOD HIGHLANDERS

The Canadian Fencible Regiment
Glasgow, August 1804

"So much for Highland attachment between Chief and Clan"

A SENSE OF betrayal was common to both, bitter anger their motivation, but the differences between the mutiny of the 43rd Highlanders in 1743 and the revolt of the Canadian Fencibles in 1804 are more significant and demonstrate the harsh changes that had taken place in less than a man's lifetime. The soldiers who stood to arms that May night in Ladywood were proud of the ties of clanship, united in a love of their land and arrogantly sure of their superior way of life. The Fencibles on the Low Green at Glasgow were disorganised and bewildered, abandoned by and abandoning their hills. The Highlanders of the 43rd were young, dressed in bonnet and plaid and armed with the three-grooved swords beloved by the bards. The Fencibles spanned two generations in age, fathers were flanked by their sons when they came to the morning and evening parades. They were without weapons and uniforms, and their officers were alien to them. They supplemented their soldier's pay by casual labour for the small tradesmen of Glasgow, and they denied themselves food that their families might not starve in the Highland ghetto of the city. The mutineers of the Black Watch wished to return to the mountains from which they believed they had been dishonourably seduced, but the Fencibles were ready to be gone for ever from their hills and islands. Old loyalties were now meaningless, and the chiefs were despised by the poets who had once honoured the valour of the *ceann-cinnidh* and his kinsmen.

> Their land and they themselves
> will die together,
> since they have become hard monsters,

435

> stiff-necked, cruel,
> with no mercy or remorse;
> poisonous, cold
> to inferiors and tenantry,
> slaughtering them with heavy burdens.

There was a change too in the attitude of Government. The scheme for a Highland Corps, Henry Dundas' bizarre proposal to revive the clan system in order to harness its strength to a war-chariot, had been the last indication that authority might be willing to respect the peculiar qualities of the Highlander. In the King's diminishing periods of rational thought, which his physicians' terrifying treatment would eventually remove altogether, he had declared his resolute belief that civilians should not be given the command of the regiments they raised. Although they were still required to find men, the chiefs could no longer preen their military vanity or profit from docked bounties and clipped clothing contracts. The War Office was now of the opinion that the Highlander's attachment to his native dress, to the company of his fellows and the leadership of men of his own race, was more hazardous than useful, encouraging a perverse spirit of insubordination and mutiny. This fear contained a half-truth, and led inevitably to the conclusion that Highland regiments should be made indistinguishable from an English battalion of the line. One of the last marching-regiments to be raised as a clan contingent was the 79th Cameron Volunteers in 1793. Its Colonel was Alan Cameron of Erracht, once a fugitive duellist, a Customs clerk in Greenock, and a soldier of the American wars. In less than two months he enlisted seven hundred and fifty men from Lochaber, Appin, Morvern and Mull, including two hundred sent to him by the MacDonell chief of Keppoch, and the bounties he paid came from his own pocket or those of his officers. The battalion served in Flanders and was then sent to the West Indies where inevitable fevers destroyed its spirit and efficiency. The survivors either took their discharge in the islands or were drafted into the 42nd and Erracht came home to recruit

another battalion. When this was done he was told that since it
now contained so few men of Scottish birth it must abandon the
kilt and "be cloathed strictly according to His Majesty's regulations for cloathing the Regular Infantry of the Line". He appealed
against the decision and went quickly to the Highlands where he
raised seven hundred replacements from the distressed people of
Lochaber. The regiment was then wasted in a cruel autumn
descent upon the Low Countries. Five years later, when the War
Office proposed to replace the belted plaid of all Highland
regiments with what Erracht called "harlequin tartan pantaloons",
he wrote an impassioned letter of protest. It is still quoted in
defence of the kilt, and by some who forget that it also condemns
the gentlemen of Erracht's class and admits that they had shame-
lessly exploited the Highlander's love of his native dress.

> From my own experience I feel well-founded in saying that
> if anything was wanted to aid the rack-renting landlords in
> destroying that source which has hitherto proved so fruitful
> for keeping up Highland corps, it will be that of abolishing
> their native garb, which his Royal Highness, the Commander-
> in-Chief, and the Adjutant-General, may rest assured will
> prove a complete death warrant to the recruiting service in
> that respect.

The last regiment to be raised as a clan levy was the 93rd,
drawn from the valleys of the far north in 1800 and by methods
uniquely despotic. The young men of every parish were summoned and inspected by William Wemyss, Colonel of the new
corps, and those who were offered a pinch from his snuff-mull
and a dram from his flask were taken as soldiers. They were told
that military service was a binding obligation required by their
chief, the Countess Elizabeth. She was *Ban mhorair Chataibh*, the
Great Lady of Sutherland, whose rich English husband could
spend more in one morning at Christie's than the yearly rental
of her Highland estates. If she had any uneasy doubts about the
manner of recruitment they were soothed by one of her law-
agents, and in words particularly pleasing to her taste for romantic

history. According to the ancient customs of her people, he said, service in war was the qualification for the possession of land under a lord, and this musty precept was zealously applied by the recruiters of the 93rd Sutherland Highlanders. Enlistment under threat of eviction, summonses of ejection against the obstinate, were now commonplace, but no more relentlessly exercised than on her ladyship's lands where the pace and pattern had already been set by the raising of fencible regiments in 1779 and 1793. John Matheson was a farmer's son in the parish of Dornoch and in the employ of old Rearquhar when he was enlisted in the Fencibles. "I entered not as a matter of choice," he wrote in his *Memorandum Book*, "but owing to the old feudal system of the country I was obliged to go to please the Lord. Plainly, every farmer was under the necessity of giving at least one of his sons if he had any fit for service." The people of the county were remote from the dangerous levelling principles of the south, and it was perhaps not military necessity alone that selected the Sutherland Fencibles for the suppression of the Militia Riots in Perthshire. Even so, three months before the regiment marched into Strathtay it had come close to revolt against the brutal behaviour of its Adjutant. "The judicious interference of the commanding officer," said Garth, "checked the proceedings of the Adjutant, and this threatening storm instantly subsided."

The sergeants and corporals of the battalion then raised the sum of two hundred guineas, from among themselves and the more tractable private soldiers, offering it as a reward "for the apprehending or detecting any person or persons who has, or shall, attempt to seduce soldiers of our own, or any other corps, from their duty". This generous spirit would later turn sour. When the Fencibles were disbanded, two hundred and sixty of them were offered the snuff-mull and the whisky-flask and taken into the 93rd. Those who came home from a long exile on the Cape of Good Hope, the few who survived a killing advance against American riflemen at New Orleans, discovered that their service had given their parents no security of tenure. Sheep had already replaced men in Rogart, Loth, Clyne and Assynt.

Southern graziers were leasing the braes of Kildonan, and within a year the first cottages would be burning in the great clearances of Strathnaver.

By the end of the 18th century the morale of all Highland regiments at home had reached its nadir. Even the Caithness Fencibles, recruited by the progressive Laird of Ulbster, had mutinied at Berwick, mauling the Town Adjutant and rioting in the streets. The Duke of York was shocked to hear that "The Caithness officers took no steps to rescue Adjutant Smith from these ruffians, whose attack he was the less able to resist from having lost a limb in the service of his country." The Earl of Breadalbane's 116th Regiment joined the mutiny of other regiments in Dublin in August, 1795, a violent protest against a proposal to disband them and disperse them among other corps. The scheme was no more than good sense, for the Army now had more battalions than men to bring them to strength. The veteran Old Regiments, those numbered below 100, were often a third or two-thirds under their establishment, while the inexperienced New Regiments were almost all complete. The increasing demand for seamen in what was largely a naval war at this time had gravely reduced recruiting for the Army, and the Duke of York decided to draft the men of the New Regiments into the Old. He did not think the disbanded battalions would be a great loss. "They are generally composed of very bad materials," he told Henry Dundas, "and from the ignorance and inexperience of the officers are very slow in obtaining a degree of discipline and in being in other respects fitted for service." Fifty-three battalions were thus to be removed from the establishment, and when this became known in Ireland four of them mutinied in protest. For two days they rioted in the streets of Dublin, boasting that they would storm the Castle and take the Customs House, and were only subdued by the arrival of two thousand Irish Militia and the third battalion of the Breadalbane Fencibles. For a week the lash was heavy upon the backs of the ringleaders.

The part played in the mutiny by the men of the 116th is obscure, although their motives can be understood. They had been enlisted on Campbell lands in Breadalbane and Argyll. They wore the black tartan and white-faced scarlet, and they believed as others before them had believed that they could not be required to serve in any but a kilted Highland battalion. Some at least were granted this privilege upon the disbandment of the regiment, but when Captain Stewart of Garth came to collect them for the 42nd he thought they were very poor cattle. "They had lost much of their original manners, and that strict attention to religious and moral duties which distinguished the Highland youths on quitting their native glens." He attributed their sad decline to the corrupting influence of their Lowland, Irish and English comrades, but it was also true that the Highland recruit was no longer a brave innocent looking backward to the warrior past of his fathers. He had seen the future and wished to escape from it.

The passionate desire to be gone from the Highlands was an emotion new to the people, although emigration had a long history and was inevitable in a land where the population had always over-reached its resources. Before the American Revolution the small tacksmen who crossed the Atlantic to escape the rack-renting of their chiefs had taken their reluctant sub-tenants with them, and if there is a common well-spring for that enduring nostalgia among the Scots of America and Canada it flows from the sorrow of those early emigrants. In the last two decades of the century, however, under the increasing pressure of over-population and under-production, of harsh social changes, high rents and eviction, it was the people not the gentry who had the strongest desire to leave the mountains. The great famines that followed the American wars had wasted the northern Highlands, and the Sheriff of Caithness reported that not only were the common people of Ross dying of starvation but farmers of substance were also begging for bread. Rents rose in staggering lunacy, as much as two hundred or three hundred per cent in some parishes. "It need be no matter for surprise," wrote the philanthropist John Knox in 1786, "if gentlemen should embrace the tempting offers from sheep-farmers. One man will occupy land that *starved* fifty or more families; he gives double or treble rent, and is punctual to the day of payment."

Donald Cameron of Lochiel was a gentleman who embraced these offers with enthusiasm. Having abandoned his unsuccessful and unpleasant career in the Gordon Fencibles he was now rebuilding his woodland home at Achnacarry, and at a cost of £10,000 which would not be recovered from the meagre rents of his clansmen. With the beginning of the new century his factors and agents began the clearance and sale of grazing land in Glen Dessary, Glen Kingie and Locharkaigside. Common men and tacksmen were uprooted by the change, among them John Cameron of Kinlocheil who would later save some of his self-respect by taking a captain's commission in the Canadian Fencibles, buying it with coin and with the sons of the landless men who had once been his dependents. The small gentry of Lochaber were bewildered and they left the land without regret. A MacMillan of Murlaggan who went to exile in North America said that because the old ties between clan and chief had been totally extinguished he was now fortunate to be so far removed from unnatural tyranny. Alexander Cameron younger of Invermallie told a friend in Surinam that the world had been turned upside down.

> Families who have not been disturbed for four or five hundred years are turned out of house and home and their possessions given to the highest bidders. So much for Highland attachment between Chief and Clan, but my own opinion is that the great gentlemen are doing a general good without any intention of doing so, by driving these people to desperation and forcing them to quit the country.*

Three-fifths of the Highland proprietors were now absentee landlords, and their dispossessed or unwanted tenants were dregs in the cup of their good fortune. The spirited reel which Boswell had watched on the sands of Skye, the turning whirlpool called *America*, had spread westward to the blue Hebrides and eastward

* Quoted in Somerled Macmillan's *Bygone Lochaber*.

into the brooding mountains of the mainland. An abandoned people were either in movement already or were eager to join the phrenetic dance.

Mass emigration is not an act of adventurous courage, the joyous rejection of security for the challenge of the unknown. It is the choice of what is hoped will be a lesser evil, and as such it is a cry of protest which later generations stifle into a statistic. Knox said that twenty thousand people left before the Revolution, and there was a fear that large areas of the Highlands would be depopulated. In the last decade of the century an average of one thousand emigrants a year sailed from the western sea-lochs, and although the French wars stopped some of the flow the drain continued. In 1801, according to Thomas Telford's *Survey*, three thousand men, women and children emigrated, and in the following year three times as many declared their willingness to leave. His estimate was perhaps exaggerated, but the figures given in a Parliamentary report of 1803 suggest that at least ten thousand people had gone from the Highlands and Isles in the previous three years. Upon each turn of the dance a hand was outstretched for a new partner, and the letters of the departed exiles called upon their friends and kinsmen to take ship and join them.

The proprietors were at last moved to check or stop the great exodus. The complexities of the economic situation, partly created by their unthinking greed and partly by the inexorable nature of the economy, paradoxically compelled them to oppose what their successors would recognise as a providential solution to the problems of over-population and the need for sheep-walks. "Ascribing the spirit of emigration to mere capriciousness," said Lord Selkirk, "they deprecate in it the loss of a nursery of soldiers that has hitherto been found in the Highlands, not adverting to the decay of those causes from which the advantage was derived." It was not only the loss of soldiers that was feared but also the loss of a residual tenantry still required on those estates yet to be delivered to the Great Cheviot. Some of the more prominent Highland proprietors sat upon a commission at the Government's request, to consider the grievous evil of emigration and to propose methods of restricting it. This could not be done by simple prohibition, unacceptable to common sense and the conscience of the nation, but an alternative had been suggested by the improving members of the Highland and Agricultural Society. With commendable insight into human nature, they declared that the most effective course would be to reduce the profits that were being made from emigration. Ship-owners and ship-masters had grown rich in the trade, filling their leaking and fever-rotten vessels in a manner that would have shocked a slave-runner, and leaving a wake of corpses across the Atlantic waters. Profit demanded that minimum thought should be given to the comfort, health and survival of the passenger. Profit created crimps and swindlers who preyed upon the waiting people in the seaports. Profit came from so delaying a ship that the emigrants exhausted the little food they had bought for the voyage and were now forced to buy more from the captain. There was profit also in those who died before departure, for their fares were unredeemable and the miserably small deck-space they vacated was quickly filled. The Passenger Act of 1803 suppressed some of these abuses and reduced the traffic by imposing conditions that put the cost of the voyage beyond the means of many, but its humanitarian mask concealed the fact that its real design was not to protect the emigrant but to prevent him from leaving altogether. Removing the treatment could not lower the temperature of that emigration fever, and public works like the Caledonian Canal, which gave employment to some dispossessed Highlanders, were no general cure. The people were many and wished to be gone. In that wish, and in a new and pressing need for a defence force in British North America, Lieutenant-colonel Thomas Peter saw and took his opportunity.

He was a middle-aged half-pay officer and fretting against idleness. He came from a Lowland family with a merchant house in Glasgow and land in Renfrewshire. For twenty-five years he had soldiered in the Royal Welch Fusiliers, and at the wretched surrender at Yorktown he had wrapped the regimental colour beneath his shirt to save it from the Colonials. He had risen by purchase rather than preferment, his body was scarred by wounds and weakened by camp fevers. His long years in America had given him an attachment to that continent and influential friends among its Canadian inhabitants, but now he was without a command and without prospects, passing the useless days in the Lowlands or at his lodgings in London. His hope of profitable employment in the only trade he knew was first aroused in the early summer of 1803, when the Duke of York approved a plan for raising four fencible regiments from the people of Newfoundland, Nova Scotia, New Brunswick and Lower Canada. They were to hold the border and garrison the forest forts, thus releasing British infantry of the line for more urgent service in Europe.

Peter was not the only officer who saw an opportunity for personal advancement in this need. Within two months Lieutenant-colonel Charles Williamson had asked for and received permission to raise a British Emigrant Regiment in North America. After his resignation from the Army at the end of the Revolution he had spent twelve years as a farmer on the western borders of New York State, although he does not seem to have accepted the authority of the new nation to which he was subject, nor to have believed it could long endure. His intention, which received the astonishing approval of the Duke, was to recruit most of his men in the United States and thus, he said, open a door for British subjects to return to their allegiance. "No men," he wrote with feeling, "know better how to value the British Government and constitution than gentlemen who have passed some years under a Republican Government." His fellow-citizens, however, were presumably not gentlemen since they were indifferent to his felicitous invitation, although they tolerantly allowed him to conduct his recruiting from the city of New York. In a truly British if not American manner, he put his failure down to the weather which prevented him from carrying his volunteers across the border and sea to Canada. "The bounty affords sufficient money both for the soldier and the procurer, but there is still a difficulty as to the transport to the rendezvous." The soldiers he had hoped to recruit were men of Highland descent who were thought to be groaning under severe conditions of labour and climate as well as the perfidy of republican rule. He had sent a captain to the Highlands to find discharged soldiers who might serve as sergeants and corporals, but he had not believed it possible to raise a whole regiment there. "Probably no time ever," he told the War Office, "was more difficult to engage men than at the present in Scotland."

Closer to that land and the distress of its mountain people, Thomas Peter knew that while there were indeed few Highlanders who would volunteer for a marching-regiment there were many thousands whose hope of emigration was now choked by the Passenger Act, and who would accept military service if it offered them some escape to British North America. The letter of service sent to him on August 8, 1803, approved his plan and authorised him to raise ten companies, nine hundred and fifty private men with equivalent officers, non-commissioned officers, drummers, fifers and surgeon's mates. It contained no reference to special conditions of service, no indication where the regiment was to be recruited and none where it was to be sent. These matters, however, were fully understood and accepted by Lord Hobart, the amiable and well-mannered minister who straddled two uneasy horses as Secretary at War and Secretary for the Colonies. Eleven days after the signing of Peter's letter of service, his lordship's senior clerk informed the Duke of York's *aide* of the peculiar nature of Colonel Peter's regiment. In effect the memorandum said that the Secretary at War and for the Colonies was pleased to take advantage of the restrictions which the Secretary for the Home Department was now placing upon emigration.

His Lordship is of opinion it would be advisable under present circumstances, that those of the Highlanders who had withdrawn from their former establishments for the purpose of going to America, and who having been disappointed in that object, are now without occupation, and in distress, should be enlisted into the Fencible Corps that is now raising for

American Service, and that they may be encouraged by an assurance that their Families shall be allowed to accompany them to Canada, and that if, after the War, the Regiment should be disbanded in America, Allotments of Land in one of His Majesty's Provinces there, shall be made to such of the Officers and Men as may be desirous of establishing there, in the proportions and under the conditions upon which Allotments may at the time be made to other Settlers.

The letter of service was sent to Peter at Crossbasket House by Hamilton. Elated by an assurance that he would shortly be confirmed in the rank of Brigadier-general as well as Colonel of the Canadian Regiment of Fencibles, he had already selected most of his officers and secured commissions for them. Some were men of Canadian birth or residence, with past frontier service in the 60th, the Queen's Rangers and Champagne's Regiment. The subalterns were ambitious young men from English or Welsh battalions of the line, and a minority only were Scots or of Scots descent. None who were yet commissioned could speak Gaelic and none had been north of the Highland Line. The Lieutenant-colonel was David Shank from the Rangers, the son of a naval officer in Nova Scotia, a hard man and a stern man, skilled in forest fighting and soured by years of half-pay. The only contact between such officers and the men they were to recruit and train was an experienced core of Gaelic-speaking sergeants with long service in Highland regiments.

Before the northern hills were turning brown, before snow had fallen on the high peaks, Peter's recruiters went north to drum up their companies. He had received Lord Hobart's approval of a hand-bill he proposed to circulate in the townships of Inverness, Ross, Argyll and the Isles. It promised all recruits that they would be granted land upon their discharge in Canada, and it assured them that their wives and children would be allowed to accompany them. When the bill was reprinted by his officers, or by their crimps and agents, there was a small change in its wording.

G. R.

WANTED

for his Majesty's Canadian Regiment, a few
good Highlanders

The Regiment is to serve in America only. Therefore
natives of this country as are desirous of going to America
with their Families have now an excellent opportunity of
accomplishing their wishes by inlisting in the said Regiment, as Government will carry the Wives and Families
of the Soldiers free of expense to that Country, and when
the Regiment is disbanded, the Soldiers will be entitled to
such allotments of Land as are granted by Government to
Soldiers who settle in America. Every man who inlists will
receive a bounty of six guineas to be appropriated according to the recruiting instructions. Men who are desirous
of embracing this opportunity will apply to——————.

The disastrous change was in the appeal to men who wished to
go to America with their *Families*, and in the following use of
Wives and Families where Peter's original bill said *Wives and
Children*. The alteration was perhaps of no consequence in
English, indeed Hobart's clerk had referred to families in his
memorandum, but the Gaelic word for family is warm and
generous, and when used by the interpreters it was taken to mean
all dependants of the recruit, his aged parents, his brothers and
sisters, his deserving kinsmen. Peter and his officers were at first
unaware of and later indifferent to this meaning, but the Highland
agents they employed cynically exploited it, knowing that it
spread the net of profit still wider. It was one of the many deceptions they practised upon an ingenuous people, yet perhaps more
cruelly dishonest than other lies they told: that provisions and a
cow would be given to the soldier's family in Canada, that he
would receive a grant of money upon his discharge, that he would
be required to drill for two days only in seven, and that for the
rest of the week he might work upon the land he had been
promised.

"All the people in this island are upon the wing"

LIEUTENANT JAMES PENTZ, an aging officer of the Royal Americans, was happy to be removed from the half-pay list and gazetted to the Canadian Fencibles. In March, 1804, he was the zealous commander of a recruiting-party at Greenock where he was told by Mr. MacEachen, a gentleman of Clan Donald and Clanranald's house, that the island men of the Uists were so attached to his own person and so hot for emigration that he could enlist as many as the Lieutenant would desire. Pentz gave him papers of authorisation and a pass to the isles from which MacEachen returned a month later with the news that two hundred men, with their families and baggage, would be ready to embark for the mainland on the first day of May. They were willing to pay their own passage to the Clyde, and upon this encouraging assurance Pentz hired two small sloops against a guarantee of seventy-seven guineas, which he was confident the Crown would honour. The ships sailed with MacEachen in the last stormy week of April, tacking about the Sound of Bute to Loch Fyne, through the green throat of the Crinan Canal and thence across the black sea to South Uist. Pentz did not go, he sent Sergeant Nathaniel Cameron of his command, with a corporal and two private men, charging them all to abide strictly to the recruiting instructions.

Ranald MacEachen was a younger son of the little tacksman of Howbeg on South Uist, a wind-drift holding above the Atlantic, low hill-grazing and a yellow-green machair of marram grass and sand. His family had held the lease for two hundred years, and like all gentlemen of his name he claimed descent from a 15th-century chief of Clanranald. Under the extortionate rule of the

448

present chief and his factors this distinction would not entitle him to much of the islanders' respect, but there was a warmer claim upon their affection. His uncle or great-uncle Neil had been one of those who took that bonny boat over the seas to Skye, and had then gone into unrewarded exile with its passenger prince. Time can balance all misfortune. The exile's son was now a general in the armies of Bonaparte, and the exile's nephew was beating up recruits for George III in the hope of a few guineas. MacEachen's motives in becoming an agent for Pentz are obscured by the fact that the only surviving records of his activities were written by men who thought his conduct outrageous, a grievous threat to the economy of the nation. It is possible that he sincerely intended to help the islanders, but more probably he wished to turn a profit from their desperation and Thomas Peter's needs. A recruiting-officer could hope to purse a guinea or two from the public funds for every man he enlisted. That much was his accepted right, but there was more to be got if company and regimental officers increased the bounty in desperate competition to complete their commands. The difference between the full sum and what the recruit finally received was shared between the officer, his agents and his crimps. Highlanders like MacEachen, with threadbare gentility and a vestigial influence over the people, were invaluable to a Canadian recruiter, and it was they who first made the significant change in Peter's hand-bill, and then improved on it with beguiling lies. MacEachen's activities toward the end of March aroused immediate alarm among the servants of the mighty. On Benbecula, the island knee-joint between the thigh and calf of the Uists, a clergyman wrote to Clanranald's agent, saying that Howbeg's son had completely deranged the minds of simple people.

They follow him in great numbers wherever he goes, and are as much determined to engage with him as ever they were with any emigrant agent who has yet appeared in the country. He seems to promise them very ample conditions, and they imagine his promise a sufficient security for all. How far this

may go on, it is impossible for me to say . . . All the people in
this island are upon the wing, and as they themselves say
determined to follow him in a body, but few have as yet (not
above six or seven) actively enlisted with him.

When MacEachen returned with the sloops, those six or seven
recruits became one hundred and fifty, three-quarters of the
number he had promised Lieutenant Pentz. With their wives,
children, dependants and baggage, they gathered on the low hills
above Lochboisdale where the ships were anchored. But Clanranald's factors had called upon the power of the Law to prevent
their departure. Between the brae and the ships' boats were two
lines of constables and Sheriff's officers, and after the magistrate's
orders to disperse were ignored they advanced upon the emigrants, driving them away with blows and curses. MacEachen
protested and was immediately arrested, accused of making
promises that were not supported by Peter's hand-bill, and when
Sergeant Cameron boldly demanded to see the written charge he
was told that the matter was not his concern. MacEachen was
taken to the mainland, across the mountains to Inverness Gaol,
and the passing years have not only destroyed any papers that
might show what happened to him, they have also removed his
name from any history of Clan Donald. Sergeant Cameron
returned with the empty sloops to Greenock where the owners,
anxious for their seventy-seven guineas, threatened Lieutenant
Pentz with a debtor's cell if they were not paid. Four months
later he was still writing urgent appeals to his superiors, asking
them to save him from imprisonment. "Should it unfortunately
fall on me, it will inevitably reduce me and my family to the
greatest state of misery . . ."

The magistrates at Lochboisdale had not prevented the people's
departure in order to protect them from the misery that might
have befallen them. The Great Cheviot would not come to the
Outer Isles for another quarter of a century, and nowhere was
there a greater shortage of labour than in the Hebrides, nowhere
was it more acute than on the estates of Ranald George Mac-

Donald, sixteen years of age and the twentieth captain of Clan-ranald. The fortune he would later squander in London as a Regency buck was being built upon a harvest of kelp, the glistening vegetation which a restless ocean spewed upon the islands and which, when calcined in primitive kilns, provided a rich source of materials for fertilisers, for the manufacture of soap and glass. The great warrior chiefs had become sea-weed farmers, forcing tenants from the hill-grazings and compelling them to work from dawn to dusk on the shore for impoverishing wages. The native islanders were not enough for the labour, and all the landlords imported more harvesters from the dispossessed of the mainland. Kelp had sold for seven pounds a ton in 1790 but was now bringing twenty. Clanranald's rents from South Uist had been little more than £2,000 in that same year and had now risen to £15,000. Less than a quarter of the return from the sale of the weed went in the cost of labour and transport, and as the price rose it was not shared among the men, women and children who worked with hook and sickle upon the rocks. It is not surprising that some of them wished to be gone with Ranald MacEachen, and it is not surprising that they were prevented by Clanranald's factors and Clanranald's Law.

Other recruiters were more successful than Lieutenant Pentz, and as the soldiers and their families began to arrive at Thomas Peter's headquarters in Hamilton his early dreams became a nightmare. He had no subsistence money to give the dependants, and not enough to keep the soldier's pay from falling into arrears. He had no uniforms to clothe them, no arms to equip them, and no power to demand quarters for their families. He wrote earnest letters to Edinburgh and London asking for guidance, and every morning there were dark, softly spoken men at his lodgings, telling him of their poverty and hunger, asking where they might store their meagre furniture, and who was to pay for such storage now that their bounties were spent upon food for their children. There were no proper medical supplies. Used to the wide sea-skies of the islands, the rain-cooled air of the mountains, the soldiers and their families sickened in their foetid lodgings, and suffered still more when the companies were marched from Hamilton to Glasgow. Since the magistrates of the city also had no power to enforce the quartering of the dependants, the despairing soldiers found what shelter they could, and paid for it by casual work as building-labourers, as ale-house-messengers, pot-cleaners and stable-men. They listened with unbelieving eyes when Peter told them that the promises made to them had no authority. He was frustrated by the responsibility of so many unwanted dependants. "May I beg to know," he had written to the Secretary at War as early as January, "if it is meant that Government will be at the expence of carrying them all? Another question which is always asked me is *Are our wives and children, after their arrival, to have any provisions allowed them by Government, and in what proportion?*" He was bluntly informed that his soldiers should be told that wives and children only would be given a free passage, that no others would be taken aboard the transports at Greenock, that there would be no provisions allowed. But he was not told how he was to explain this apparent breach of faith. At the end of May his adjutant, Lieutenant John Wilson, reported the first miserable deaths from sickness and starvation.

The King's ministers were now regretting the establishment of the Canadian Fencibles, and the failure to speed the dispatch of clothing and equipment may be explained by their cooling enthusiasm. They were not yet disturbed by the condition of the soldiers and their families, but they were alarmed by the unexpected and angry reaction of Highland proprietors. Charles Hope, who had succeeded Dundas as Lord Advocate, was the first to hear of the Lairds' furious opposition to the regiment. He was a tall, handsome lawyer, a stubborn Tory with a stentorian voice that was less effective in court or Commons than it was on St. Ann's Yards, where he wore a cocked hat and crimson sash as Colonel of the Edinburgh Regiment of Gentlemen Volunteers. Holiday soldiering delighted him as much as the subtleties of Law, but the Canadian Fencibles gave him no comfort of mind. In March he informed the Home Secretary, Charles Yorke, that he had received unsettling complaints from many Highland gentlemen who not only objected to the behaviour of Peter's recruiters but also to the regiment itself. His own opinions were less than impartial. He had been what he was proud to describe as "the chief hand" in the preparation and moving of the Passenger Act, and his strong disapproval of Peter's recruiting was undisguised in his letter to Yorke.

> Considering the numbers that have lately emigrated to America, the natural disposition of the people to do so, the evident loss to this country arising from the depopulation of its most warlike districts, it is not easy to conceive a measure more calculated to increase the spirit of emigration. It is giving great disgust to the Highland gentlemen and to the lieutenants of the Northern Counties, who find it impossible to complete their quotas for the Militia and the Reserve, under the disadvantage of such a competition; and as to the Regulars, it is impossible to expect that a single man will enlist, while entering into the Canadian Regiment they can, at once, obtain an easier service and indulge their propensity for a wandering and idle life.

One of these disgusted Highland gentlemen was the Good Sir James Grant who had done more than most proprietors to supply the Crown with soldiers, albeit with some heartbreak. "The consequences of recruiting for an American regiment," he told Charles Hope, "at a time when Britain requires all its inhabitants for its own defence, and for the considerable works which Government are carrying on for internal improvement, might be very prejudicial and fatal in the West Highlands where the people are but too prone to emigrate." He sent the Lord Advocate a copy of a letter he had received from James MacDonald of Greshornish on Skye. Mr. MacDonald had been watching the recruiting of Dugald Campbell, a middle-aged company commander in Peter's regiment. The Captain was a native of the island who had emigrated to America with his family in 1772 and who had recently returned to persuade others to follow his example. MacDonald was alarmed by the fact that few young men were enlisted by Campbell, that almost all his recruits were the heads of large families. "If my information is correct, the number inspected and approved already exceeds a hundred, and is daily increasing as numbers flock in from all corners of this Isle, and some from the Long Island and adjacent parts of the mainland. Thus have such of our valuable inhabitants as incline to emigrate disposed of themselves." Forwarding this letter to London the Lord Advocate said that the minds of such people had been unhinged by "the lies and nonsense told them by the agents of Lord Selkirk and other emigrant-mongers". He accused Thomas Peter, whom he sometimes referred to as Porter until corrected by his clerk, of taking none but the nation's finest men, leaving the "refuse" for other corps.

From his London house by the Haymarket Lord Seaforth sent the Home Secretary a sheaf of recruiting-bills, so pregnant with the inevitable ruin of the country, he said, that his public duty obliged him to protest. Francis Humberston Mackenzie was a newly created baron, a cousin of the last Earl long buried in the south Atlantic, and a brother of the first-major of the old 78th, long dead from a Mahratta sword. Survival had brought him the Seaforth estates and the thinnest shadow of their great titles, but since he had failed to provide himself with an heir, and had small inclination to do so now in his sixth decade, they would die with him. The thought of other men's children, however, obsessed his thoughts, and he was shocked by the infamy of anyone who permitted them to be taken from the country.

The Canadian recruiters carry off, not only the able and valid part of the population and their wives, but also their children; that is, the future Stock on which the existence of the Country depends!! The consequence is this:—the parents, uncles etc., and the invalid part of the population, will be left behind, a dead burthen on the Land; for the Children going, there is not even the future prospect of relief. The landholders must either starve themselves, or turn these poor wretches out to starve and make room for sheep.

His lordship's argument that the fear of starvation would force the lairds to introduce the Great Cheviot is unique, and one overlooked by later defenders of the clearances, but the loss of a future labour-force alarmed all proprietors. Some of them met at Inverness and addressed a resolution of protest to the Member for their county, Charles Grant. He was a descendant of the warrior Grants of Sheuglie in Glen Urquhart where he had been born on the day his father, Alexander the Swordsman, was fighting at Culloden. He had restored his family's name and more than recovered its fortunes by service with the East India Company, and could now spend £600 to win himself a seat at Westminster and £16,000 for the handsome estate of Waternish on Skye. He was a gentle man, and his protest to the Home Secretary was more civil than the enraged language of the last Mackenzie of the Cows. He deplored the deceptions practised by MacEachen and Dugald Campbell, and was moved by the probable hardships of the women and children, but in the context of his age, and the bi-focal vision of his humanitarian principles, he too placed the risk to the economy above all else. Yet his conscience compelled him to fight for the disbandment of Peter's soldiers by emphasising the sorrow and the misfortune their departure must cause to their abandoned dependants. "Many have enlisted under the idea of being allowed to take their *families*, that is to say not only their wives and children, but their parents etc., with them, so that at the time of embarkation much confusion and distress may arise, and the aged persons left behind to become a burden to the country."

Some proprietors wasted no time with letters to Edinburgh or resolutions to their Members, but dealt summarily with any of their tenants who were inclined to enlist in the Canadian Regiment. Sir Hector Mackenzie of Gairloch on the western seaboard of Ross was known to his people as The Buck-toothed Laird, and he was accustomed to dispensing justice as if he and they were still living in the 17th century without civilised access to magistrates and courts. Sixteen of his tenants told a recruiting agent that they would enlist if a ship were sent for them, and one of them, Donald MacDonald, went by foot to Glasgow to repeat this promise to Captain William Ellice.* The officer sent him back to Gairloch in a sloop but there he found that the other fifteen had now changed their minds and would not enlist. The Buck-toothed Laird had ordered them, under threat of his displeasure, to remain in his employ, and after a day or two of reflective thought he had marched them all to Inverness where the magistrates he despised obligingly accepted his claim that if enlisted they would be illegally taken from his benevolent care. Donald MacDonald sailed for Glasgow with his family and before long he would regret that he had not remained with the others. The sub-tenants of Gairloch, who had endured crippling increases in their rents and who had feared that Sir Hector would evict them altogether, soon discovered why he had prevented them from leaving. His improving ambitions had been excited by the thought of a cod-fishery on his seaboard, the successful operation of which would require all the labour and loyalty of his people.

The protests of the proprietors finally persuaded the Government to ask for a full report from the Lord Advocate and the Earl of Moira, Commander-in-Chief in Scotland. They were required to investigate the manner of enlistment and to inform the Home Secretary of any hardship that might be caused to the families and dependants should His Majesty's ministers decide to disband the regiment. Events would outpace the Lord Advocate's slow response, and his report was not sent until some days after the mutiny. In his opinion no suffering would be caused by discharging the Canadian Fencibles and there need be no uneasiness about their families. All Highlanders removed from their ancient lands could be usefully employed as common day-

---

* The Ellice family was rich and influential in Canada. The Captain's brother would shortly make a greater fortune in the fur trade and eventually become Secretary of War at Westminster. His nephew Edward, a progressive humanitarian and a founder of the Reform Club, had a distinguished career in British politics. In the middle of the 19th century he bought a large part of the Glengarry estates when the last of the MacDonells were cleared.

labourers on the Caledonian Canal, the docks at Leith, the continued building of Edinburgh New Town, where they could earn at least two shillings a day and as much as three shillings and sixpence by piece-work. It had always been the Lord Advocate's opinion that the discontent and delusion of the Highland people were only temporary, that "if time were given to them for reflection, and employment found for them at home, their natural good sense would prevail and retain them to be the most useful subjects". Instead, the Spirit of Emigration had been revived.

> The whole Highlands were thrown open, and were immediately over-run with agents and crimps, who had recourse to the very misrepresentations and falsehoods as to this country, and held out the same delusive prospects as to America, which had been done by the agents of Lord Selkirk and others . . . The consequence was that thousands instead of hundreds were eager to enlist in this regiment. All other recruiting was totally at a stand, for it was vain for any officer to offer his paltry bounty in competition with the paradise of America which the agents of the Canadian regiment promised to their followers.

Throughout the early summer Thomas Peter struggled to create a disciplined force from his recruits, his efforts harassed by their increasing discontent and despair. The battalion was not yet complete, more drafts were to come from the Highlands and Isles, but by the middle of June its strength was 683 private men. There were also 432 wives and 1,069 children, and with others not accepted by the Government the total number of dependants may have been above two thousand. To relieve some of the pressures upon them, Peter asked permission to recruit a number of the elder boys as drummers, but he received no positive reply. He and his officers were now clothed in splendid regimentals, his sergeants and corporals in red coats, white breeches and varnished hats, but his soldiers wore the ragged clothing in which they had come from their glens, and they still paraded with sticks for musket drill. The dirks which some of them carried were their own, and they wore them in brave defiance of regulations which Peter had no heart to enforce. A city mob gathered about every parade to jeer at his command, but this worried him less than reports that some of the Highland people in Glasgow were urging the soldiers to rebel against their humiliation, telling them that they would be betrayed.

Late one evening at the beginning of July, past supper-time when the officers sat at their wine in the Star Inn, they heard a great shouting in Glassford Street. They went to the windows and looked down at a crowd of civilians who shouted again when the gentlemen were seen. The cries were in Gaelic and meant nothing to the officers, but they were understood by Sergeant-major John Maclean in the tap-room below. He came to the door and saw one man who shook his fist at the officers above and cried "Bad luck to them if they come out of doors!" Maclean took the fellow to be a townsman, but the next day he saw the same face in the ranks of the grenadier company. He asked for a name, and was told that the soldier was Donald MacDonald from Gairloch.

On July 17 the regiment was inspected and approved by Major-general William Wemyss of that Ilk, the heavy-jowled Deputy Commander-in-Chief whose abundant snuff-mull had raised the 93rd for his cousin the Countess Elizabeth. It was a warm, sunlit day and he sat on his horse in the shade of a great elm where the Young Pretender had reviewed his Highlanders sixty years before. He said that he was much impressed by the battalion, and he asked Peter to make his approval known to the men. It was perhaps later that day, when the General dined with the officers at the Star, that Peter was told he would shortly receive his marching-orders, that the battalion would now go by road to Portsmouth and thence to the Isle of Wight where it would embark for Canada. The soldiers still believed, as they had been promised at their enlistment, that they and their families would leave together from the Clyde, and they were already angry that they had not left on the date promised, the last day of June. Thomas Peter may have known, and in view of past experience the Government should have known, that such marching-orders would mean one thing only to the Highlanders – they were indeed betrayed. They knew nothing of Wight, and some believed it to be far across the sea from England, as far as the Channel Islands or beyond the coast of France. But all Highlanders knew that the East India Company used the island to train the soldiers it recruited for its own regiments. It was more than this. "It is a place," Private William Stalker would soon write in his halting petition, "that some regiments went to, and in place of the place or places they were engaged for, was sold and sent off to the East Indies." Peter protested against the marching-orders, but not because they would alarm his command. He argued that a long journey through England with so many women and children, and so much baggage, would be a great inconvenience. He suggested that the families should travel by sea from the Clyde. This too, when it was known by the men, would prove to be an error, for the separation would be taken as further evidence that they were to be sent alone to India.

No orders, proposed or unconfirmed, are for long secret in a regiment, and within two days of the inspection a rumour of the new destination was current in the battalion. The next morning at six, when the soldiers came to parade on the Low Green and were called upon their markers, some of them sat in a silent circle on the grass. Sergeant-major Maclean spoke to them, asking why they would not obey their officers. "Nothing is the matter with us but hunger," said a grenadier, James Bruce, "and we shall not fall in until we get what is due to us." Maclean told them that if they did their duty as good soldiers they would get all that was due, to the uttermost farthing, but not until the promise was repeated by Adjutant Wilson did they rise and join their companies.

Fifty of the dependants were now dead and buried in paupers' graves, wives, children and the aged. Peter's spirits had reached their lowest ebb. He rarely came to Glasgow, leaving his command to David Shank and preferring the protective comfort of his family home. He asked for a brief leave of absence to attend to personal affairs in Ireland, but before the request was granted his regiment was in a state of mutiny.

"Out Grenadiers . . .! Out Grenadiers . . .!"

BETWEEN THREE AND four o'clock on the morning of Tuesday, August 7, the insensible body of a middle-aged man was found on Glasgow High Green, in the darkness of the trees and by the wooden bridge across Camlachie Burn. His head and face were severely bruised, and he did not recover consciousness before he died at seven that evening in the Infirmary. By then he had been identified as John Campbell, a private soldier of the Canadian Fencibles. His wife Catherine was at his bedside with their son David, who was also a soldier of the regiment. There was no evident reason for his death. His comrades said that he was a sober and inoffensive man. He had not been robbed, for although he had no money to be taken his watch was still in his pocket when he was found. His family believed that he had been maliciously attacked, but others said that he had collapsed from sickness or hunger, fatally injuring himself when he fell upon the large stones about the burn. His death was briefly reported in the *Courier*, and its effect upon his miserable family would have concerned no one else had it not been for a petition written by the hand of David Campbell and signed with his mother's mark. She clearly understood that she and her dependant family could not now be taken to Canada, although two of her sons were serving in the regiment. The two young men were her only support, she said, without them she would be thrown upon the wide world and reduced to the miserable necessity of begging for her livelihood. She asked Lieutenant-colonel Shank to discharge them, that they might provide for the family upon its return to their native country. Enclosed with the petition was a bleak addendum also written by her eldest son.

A list of David Campbell's family son of the deceased John Campbell is as follows viz.

David Campbell	private
Archd. Campbell	Drummer
Dond. Campbell	my brother a boy of 8 years
Anny Campbell	my sister 12 years old in bad health
Mary Campl.	6 years old
Cathrin Campbell	My Mother
Flory McKinnen	my Grand-mother who was promised faithfully to be brought along with the family

The petition was forwarded to General Wemyss who passed it to Lord Moira who sent it to the Home Secretary who returned it to Scotland for the Lord Advocate's information. Charles Hope was by then writing the report required of him, and in the confusion of papers upon his desk David Campbell's addendum became detached from his mother's petition. The Lord Advocate did not read it carefully, nor understand it fully, but he recalled it to the Home Secretary's attention as an example of the flagrant manner in which the word *family* had been interpreted, and to the detriment of the Kingdom. "In short all whom the recruit chose to take, or who chose to go with him . . . You will see that his Grandmother (probably no great loss), his mother, his father, his children, his brothers and sisters are included."

Catherine Campbell's petition and its addendum were thus abandoned in the labyrinth of ministerial correspondence, and the death of her husband was forgotten in the violent events that began while his body still lay in its shroud at the Infirmary. The men of the regiment were now despairing. Few of them were as literate or as articulate as Private William Stalker, but the petition he was writing to General Wemyss spoke on behalf of them all, for their experience was common. He said that he and others had been enlisted by James Pentz who had promised that their families would receive a year's provisions upon arrival in Canada. Each man would be given two and a half acres to work while he was soldiering, and upon his discharge he would receive forty more, to belong to him and his heirs in perpetuity.

> At Lieut Pink or Spences Desire we sold of all our Furniture Cattle & Effects except our work materials bed cloths & bed & Table linens, which are all store-housed at Greenock and none to look after as they are Parishable Articles we have reason to believe by this they are mostly consumed. The greatest part of us are married men our Money is now gone to support our wives and Families as it is well known a Shilling perchis little enough to support a Soldier, our wives and Families are Crying aloud for Food and little or nothing to give them. Our situation at first outgoing is truely lamentable we have been here near Three Months at hard Dreel, nothing given to our Wives and Families . . .

The hard drill, which now prevented most of them from finding work to feed their dependants, was imposed by Shank as a corrective to the mounting discontent. It began at the misted morning hour of six on the Low Green, eastward of the Shambles, the stench of which convulsed the soldiers' empty stomachs and filled their mouths with bile. Carrying their mock firing-pieces, some with ancient dirks thrust into their belts, they marched and counter-marched until noon, and an hour later they marched again until three. Then they were at last drummed away to their quarters, leaving the Green to the city's herd of milk-cows and its bell-loined bull, to bare-thighed women in the Wash-house tubs and boys fishing for eels in the burn, to old men drinking herb-beer at the tavern and golfers coming to play in the last light of the day.

Word of the soldiers' rebellious ill humour was sent to the Earl of Moira at his house on Queen Street, Edinburgh, where it was received with little sympathy. He disliked the methods used by

Peter's recruiters, but said he did not think it his duty to judge a civil policy that offered emigration in return for enlistment. However, he believed the Fencibles would be of little value in Canada. "Were I governor of that province," he told the Lord Advocate, "I should feel my safety just the reverse of confirmed by the arrival of such a regiment." He was a handsome and profligate Anglo-Irishman of the ascendancy, a thin-fleshed, hot-tempered and tight-breeched cavalryman with a taste for duelling, and he had once acted as the Duke of York's second in a dawn encounter on Wimbledon Common. Although he believed that Ireland suffered under a disgusting tyranny he despised all rebels, and he once put a price upon the heads of those in America. He was amused when colonial girls were ravished by his soldiers, saying that an issue of fresh meat had turned the men into riotous satyrs. He was exact in chivalrous conduct, but exclusive in its exercise. Surrounded once by Washington's dragoons he bowed in surrender, but pretended difficulty in drawing and delivering his sabre, thus delaying his captors until the arrival of his command. The behaviour of the Canadian Fencibles this August was an intrusion upon his uxorious bliss. At the age of forty-nine he had just married a young Campbell of Loudoun and would remain so besotted with her that papers found at his death asked for his right hand to be severed and preserved until it could be buried with her. He was alarmed enough by reports from Thomas Peter, by the evidence of unwarranted promises made to the recruits, to order a Court of Inquiry. It sat in the Trades Hall on Glassford Street and its report was awaiting Moira's attention when the mutiny began.

Early in the morning of Wednesday, August 8, while Catherine Campbell still keened over the body of her husband, the companies were paraded on the Green and given their marching-orders for the Isle of Wight. David Shank, who commanded that day, sent each captain to his company to tell the men that all baggage was to be loaded on the waiting wagons and carried to the Broomielaw, the quayside on the Clyde, where it would travel by lighter to Greenock and thence by ship to Wight with

the women and children. The first division of the regiment,
grenadiers and light company men, would march south on
Thursday. Before their captains had finished the men called out in
anger, shouting that they would go to Canada, they would not
march into England. Some sat in stubborn circles upon the
ground, ignoring their officers or declaring that they would not
move until they were given food for their children. James Bruce
told a sergeant that in order to keep his wife and bairns alive he
had gone without food himself, eating no more than four sparse
meals a week and spacing them over the days to give himself
what strength he could. Others protested that no man with a
throng family could support it on seven shillings a week. Now
regretting his bold decision at Gairloch, Donald MacDonald said
that it had been wrong to take him from his country when his
laird had declared that none should go, but no officer understood
what he meant. The battalion line was soon broken into a dun-
coloured mob, swirling about the scarlet figures of the officers and
sergeants. The Gaelic people of the city, running down from the
High Green, became so mixed with the soldiers that it was
impossible for many captains to know who were their men and
who were not. John Wilson walked quickly across the front of
the parade to the grenadiers, calling upon them to stand to their
duty like men. The Adjutant spoke no Gaelic and he believed
that while most of the Fencibles knew what he was saying they
pretended not to understand his English. Because Bruce and
MacDonald were more angry than the rest, more noisy Wilson
said, he asked them if they would set an example and obey their
orders, but Bruce shouted "*No!*", and MacDonald shook his head,
holding up a hand in angry refusal. Lieutenant-colonel Shank had
endured enough from his undisciplined command and from the
jeering mob. He ordered the companies to be dismissed, to break
ranks here and not in the streets where they lodged, but his
drummer beat for some minutes before the order was obeyed. As
the men moved westward in small groups, Wilson caught at
Bruce's sleeve, warning the grenadier of the dreadful consequences of any act of mutiny. "His reply to me," reported the

Adjutant, "was that he was perfectly aware, but was determined not to march, or words to that effect."

When Shank came in anger to Thomas Peter at the Star the Brigadier at once appealed to General Wemyss for guidance. He was told to parade the men again the next day, and if the first division remained obstinate it was to be marched to the guard-house at the Circus, an old riding-school near the inn, where Wemyss would address it and recall it to its duty.

The battalion came to the Low Green late in the afternoon of Thursday. The day was unseasonably cold and the morning's rain-squalls had now settled into a steady fall. Despite the weather a crowd was again gathered on the upper slopes of the Green and in the shelter of the trees, cat-calling the soldiers or urging them to resist the cruelty of their officers. David Shank wasted no time after the company officers had reported to him. He ordered the first division to march to the Old Bridge and the road to the south, and when it hesitated he called upon Captain William D'Haran of the grenadiers to lead it to the Circus. The abrupt change in orders confused the soldiers, but once they understood that the march had again been abandoned they went willingly. The sky was now so heavy with clouds, the air so darkened with rain, the dank smoke of peat and coal, that little could be clearly seen in the narrow streets north of the Shambles. As they arrived at the arched and open doorway of the Circus the leading grenadiers halted, calling to their officers and asking if they were to be imprisoned. D'Haran seized two stubborn men by the arms and pushed them into the building, shouting to his sergeants to do the same, and by this rough compulsion the whole company was got inside. The Light Company men would not enter, and reinforced by a growing mob they called upon the grenadiers to come out. Donald MacDonald heard them, slipped past his captain and ran to the street. "Where has that man gone?" said D'Haran. "To make water, sir!" said a sergeant.

When he realised that the officers of the Light Company had lost control of their men D'Haran also went outside, and his grenadiers immediately followed him. Once more, by oaths, threats and blows, he and his officers got them back into the building, including Donald MacDonald, and this time the doors were closed behind them. For fifteen minutes, or so it seemed to D'Haran as he faced his wet and sullen company in the stone-flagged arena, the soldiers outside did nothing. Then their shouting and their calling, the hammering of their sticks upon the walls, changed to a sustained chant of "*Out Grenadiers . . . ! Out Grenadiers . . . !*" They threw themselves again and again upon the doors until the lock broke. This time the grenadiers could not be restrained. Determined to hold one man if possible, and he the most villainous, D'Haran grappled with MacDonald. They struggled in angry silence until the Highlander raised a hand, broke the Captain's hold with a blow, and ran into the rain and the cheering crowd.

At the Star Inn that evening the officers gloomily debated the puzzle of a regiment that would willingly parade when called, but would not march where it was ordered. They had yet to read the petition of Private William Stalker which would contain something of an answer to that paradox. "*We are all true lovers of His Majesty,*" he said, "*and our hearts beat big for the support of our noble Constitution, no disunion or animosity will be amongst us which, if done, will not be friends to our Brotheren of Mankind.*" Peter knew that the battalion must be considered in a state of mutiny, that enough trouble had been caused by men like MacDonald to bring them before a firing-party. D'Haran was particularly bitter. He had sat upon the Court of Inquiry and had apparently learnt nothing from it, believing that the complaints made to it were either unfounded or trifling. He said Bruce had repeatedly told him that he would rather die than go to the Isle of Wight. Furthermore, the soldier had said, some men in the regiment had received letters from kinsmen on that island, warning them not to come there or they would be lost. There was nothing any of the officers could do with such men and such ignorance, but when David Shank reported that night to William Wemyss the General seemed unconcerned, or at least still certain that his influence – with or without the assistance of a snuff-mull and a whisky-flask –

was strong enough to compel the obedience of Highlanders. He said that he would now address the battalion at its morning parade.

He came to the Green at nine on Friday, wearing a cocked hat, crimson sash and a tail-coat of braided scarlet. The soldiers were drawn up by companies facing the river, each man with his musket-stick or dirk. They were quiet and obedient, but before they fell in upon their markers Bruce and MacDonald had gone from group to group, talking earnestly with each. The rain of the previous day was past, the sun bright on the grass and upon the white sheets laid out to bleach by the Wash-house. A greater crowd had come to watch, and the mob was outnumbered by the sympathetic Highland people of the city and by respectable folk from the Gorbals and the eastern suburbs. The tall timber gate to the High Green had been opened for them, as if this were a holiday or a grand review, and the milkherd had already been brought to the turnstile, watched by a waiting line of old men and children, each with a japanned tin. When he had ridden to the front of the battalion William Wemyss dismounted and walked to within five yards of the centre company. There he lectured the regiment, and Sergeant-major Maclean translated his sorrowful words. He said that the soldiers had behaved outrageously and shamefully, bringing upon themselves the most severe penalties prescribed by the Articles of War. He was confident, however, that he could reassure their doubts and promise them a settlement of all just grievances. He then walked along the line, his hat beneath his arm, inviting any man who so desired to step from the ranks and speak candidly with him. Both Bruce and MacDonald came from the grenadiers, politely removing their knitted grey bonnets, but only a bitter fragment of their conversation was recorded, and that in MacDonald's defence at his court-martial.

"You are guilty of disobedience," said the General, "by being laggard in falling into the ranks."

"If I was laggard," said MacDonald, "it was not from lack of obedience, but from weakness and hunger."

When the parade was over, and the General was gone at a canter through the trees to Barrowfield, the soldiers did not know whether or not they would again be ordered into England. Wemyss had told them that there was nothing to fear, that their wives and families would join them aboard the transports at Wight, but he was not believed. As the companies were marched away many people walked beside them, calling to them with great emotion. "Poor men! You are sold to the East Indies! What will become of your wives and children?"

"Damn you for dogs and cowards! Rescue Maclean!"

SEVENTY MEN WERE now absent when their names were called at the morning parades. They were marked down as deserters but it was known that most of them were in the city and could be found any night at their lodgings. They told their sergeants that they knew they risked the lash by their continued absence, but desperate need again drove them to find work to feed their families. The rest still assembled to the beat of the company drums and drilled when required, but their spirits were sluggish and their stubborn hostility increased as the marching-orders for the south remained in suspension. The Earl of Moira was forced to agree that they must be considered in a state of mutiny and the peace of the city at risk, yet he hesitated to send in the Horse and Foot which Wemyss held in readiness to the south of Hamilton. These were days of sleep-walking, and the mind of authority was the prisoner of inaction. Thomas Peter had been told that his appointment as brigadier-general had been confirmed on the Irish establishment, and he seemed anxious to be gone from Scotland and his demoralised regiment. The junior officers, upon whom Moira hopefully relied to restore order, kept to the Star Inn or their own quarters, for when they appeared alone in the streets they were pelted with mud, with vegetables and stones, and were accused of murdering the dead wives and children of their soldiers. Provost Laurence Craigie issued a useless proclamation against such insulting behaviour and he told Wemyss that the Trades Battalion of the Glasgow Volunteers, due to stand down that week, had gallantly offered to remain under arms, to maintain order in the city and to march against the Fencibles if required.

The General accepted the offer, but with more diplomatic politeness than faith in these amateur soldiers.

Moira's indecision was contrary to his impetuous nature. Like others who held his office before him, Oughton and Lord Adam Gordon, he believed that mutiny should be immediately and inexorably crushed before it poisoned the body of the Army, but the deepening dichotomy of Government opinion disarmed this instinctive reaction. He had told Hobart that the regiment would be of no value in Canada, that it should be disbanded, and he knew that such good advice and the protests of the land-owners were bending the King's ministers to the same view. Yet his orders for the march into England remained unchanged. Against his judgement and experience, he had thus decided to postpone the use of force. "I have wished to avoid the crisis," he told the War Office, "till private remonstrance with the individuals may have had effect." These individuals were those whom the Canadian officers named as leaders of disaffection and insubordination, principally Donald MacDonald and James Bruce. Whatever the present need to temporise, Moira believed that they must eventually be tried and punished, and it was perhaps no accident that the steps taken to bring them to that private remonstrance also served to entrap their words and provide the evidence against them at their inevitable court-martial.

Angus Gordon kept an inn at Airdrie, a mean staging-house on the Edinburgh road twelve miles from Glasgow. He was also a King's Messenger, a letter-carrier and a thief-taker, and by common custom he acted as a spy and informer. He was a Gaelic-speaker from Sutherland and he believed himself to be held in esteem by his noble countryman William Wemyss for whom he sometimes delivered dispatches. On Monday, August 13, the General asked him to remain in Glasgow for three or four days more – "as a particular favour" Gordon said – to talk to Bruce and MacDonald and to report upon the behaviour of the regiment. That evening he went to the Low Green and when the parade was over he had no difficulty in finding MacDonald for the soldier was haranguing the grenadier company, urging it to be bold in resistance to the marching-orders. Gordon introduced himself as a Highlander who wished the Fencibles well and he invited MacDonald to a tavern on the Gallowgate. There they were joined by Hugh Mackay, another Sutherlander and the Paymaster-sergeant of the regiment, whom Gordon had cautiously insisted should be a witness of the meeting. Both advised the Gairloch man to do his duty as a soldier, warning him of the dangers of mutiny. Angus Gordon carefully remembered the soldier's reply. "I'd rather suffer death on the Green of Glasgow," said MacDonald, "I'd rather be tied to the muzzle of a cannon and be blown up than go to the Isle of Wight." The next morning, when Gordon came again to watch the parade, he saw MacDonald run from the ranks of the grenadiers and stand before them with his arms wide, calling upon all good men to fall in behind him. Some did so, shouting at their silent officers, but the unexplained fire of anger soon died and they returned to the ranks, performing their drill without complaint.

James Bruce was also taken to the tavern on the Gallowgate and he was frightened by Gordon's dark warnings. His family was ill, he said, and he had no money to buy food, but he was entirely innocent of any charge and wished his General to know this. So Gordon took him to the great house where Wemyss was grandly lodged and he again declared that no man could justly accuse him of mutiny. The General listened to his halting English and then dismissed him. "I am satisfied that you mean to be honest," he said with too subtle ambiguity, "but take care of yourself in all the time coming."

Gordon was not satisfied, and he came each morning and evening to the Green, talking familiarly with both Bruce and MacDonald and with all the men who were loud in resistance to the marching-orders. On Wednesday the soldiers were told by seamen that the transports had sailed from Greenock with some of the baggage, but no officer or sergeant would tell them where the ships had gone, or if they had gone. That night William Stalker wrote his petition to the Duke of York and it was delivered to Wemyss the next day with another that had no names attached, only a subscription: "*Signed by Mutual Consent of His Majesty's Canadian Regiment*". This second petition accused Captain Dugald Campbell of enlisting men upon a promise that they would sail from the coast of Argyll on June 24, that once in Canada they would be freed from military service during the time needed for sowing and reaping the land granted them. Now they were to be sold to the East India Company.

> Our officers do not hesitate to tell us that your royal highness or Government has nothing to do with us any further nor will look any more after us, which we do not believe, neither do we insist upon any thing more than our bargain which we humbly hope your royal Highness will fulfill unto us as we do not consider ourselves accountable for the misconduct and imposition of Officers in representing your royal Highness's commands unto us with a falsehood ... We most humbly beg if it is too late for transporting us that your royal Highness will grant our continuing here till spring next, as our removal to any other part of Britain will terminate in our immediate ruin, our families being severally feverish and numberous in a dying situation ...

Moira sent the petition to London, and lest the Duke of York should suffer an aberration and grant its farcical request he decided to be quit of the regiment, to send it where other men might now be troubled by its mutinous conduct. Thomas Peter was told to bring the ringleaders to immediate submission by persuasion, or deal with them summarily. At three o'clock on Sunday the Brigadier ordered Sergeant-major Maclean to go to Donald MacDonald's lodgings with Doctor James Muir, who had been treating the soldier's wife, and James Macintosh adjutant to the Highland Battalion of the Glasgow Volunteers, both men having some influence over the men of the regiment. The gentlemen remained in the street while Maclean went up to the small, dark garret where MacDonald's sick wife lay beneath a thin plaid and his three children were crying for food. He persuaded the distraught soldier to speak with Macintosh below, and both Muir and the Adjutant urged MacDonald to come with them to Peter. He was taken to a large room on the first floor of the Star where the well-fleshed Brigadier sat in the fine regimentals of his new rank. MacDonald spoke no English and what was said to him was translated by Macintosh. His lonely spirit, already weak from hunger and despair, was perhaps unnerved by the contrast between his own lodgings and this clean white room, by the smell of rich food from the dining-chamber below. He was asked if he would march, and he said that he would. He begged Peter to forgive his behaviour and was told that this would not be enough, he must also beg forgiveness from General Wemyss. He said that he would do that also, and was willing to be taken before the General now. He was asked if he would advise others to march. "I cannot do that," he said, "but I will march myself." He could not be moved from this answer, and Peter sent him away.

That evening sergeants and corporals went from lodging to lodging, telling the grenadiers and light company, the men of four battalion companies, that they would form the first division of the regiment for a march to Ayr the next day. The new orders were an addled compromise, and when some of the sergeants admitted that the ships from Greenock may have gone to Ayr no one believed that this meant they were to sail for Canada. The soldiers said that they would be tricked, that they would now be taken by sea to Wight and there delivered to the East India Company. When they came to the Green the next morning only a few brought their families and baggage to the waiting wagons. Upon his now customary watch, Angus Gordon did not see MacDonald among the grenadiers but found him at last with some civilians at the turnstile gate. He advised the soldier to join his company and march peaceably, but MacDonald said that his wife and children were too ill to be moved and no man would make him leave them.

The battalion paraded upon its markers and at first listened silently to the reading of the marching-orders. The first division of six companies was to march that morning for Ayr with the baggage-wagons, a further two for Kilmarnock the next day, and the remaining two for Irvine on Wednesday. The men now cried out in protest, some breaking ranks to step forward and shout in their captain's face. Shank ordered the drums to beat, call by call until the angry men were exhausted by the noise. They were at last silent, but when D'Haran ordered the first division to move, only one hundred and fifty men obeyed. They followed the wagons westward past the Shambles to the Old Bridge, their musket-sticks at the carry and many looking backward to the Green as if asking for help. Before the first files wheeled left to cross the Clyde a great crowd came down Stockwell Street, hurling stones at the officers and calling upon the soldiers to stay. Angus Gordon said that MacDonald was with this mob, a stick in his hand, but he could not swear that the soldier's intention was not to fall in with his company. As the crowd ran on to the narrow bridge it was joined by soldiers from the Green and in the struggling, shouting mêlée most of the division was dragged back or turned back to the north bank. D'Haran marched on with his head up, refusing to halt until he had passed through the Gorbals to the suburbs. He then saw that there were less than fifty men behind him. He took them on to Ayr, and that night some of the men who had put their grieving families on the wagons slipped away from Glasgow to join them.

Wemyss wrote to Moira in rage and frustration. The conduct of the regiment was more shameful than ever and its usefulness to His Majesty was surely now at an end. "They will remain in a constant state of mutiny and will oblige your Lordship at last to come to some final measure with them." He had not used the force he had drawn up in readiness and he was now ashamed of his tolerance which was almost, but only almost, excused by his own and his Lordship's humane concern for the miserable condition of the soldiers' women and children. He was determined to proceed with the march to Ayr and the voyage to Wight, and he had given orders for the arrest of the known ringleaders and the listing as deserters of all those who refused to go. But in the morning the enormity of the problem, the weight of such hostile misery, seemed to rob him of strength and decision, and again the marching-orders were left in suspension.

At noon on Tuesday Donald MacDonald was once more called before Peter at the Star Inn. This time he was brought by Quartermaster-sergeant Alexander Macmillan, a gentle Lochaber man who acted as the Brigadier's interpreter. Peter was no longer direct in appeal, but cunningly questioned the soldier in an attempt to trip a simple mind into its own betrayal. If the whole regiment marched, would not MacDonald march with it? He would march if it marched, he said, and if it stayed he would stay. If Peter came to the front of the battalion and asked all those willing to march to step forward, would MacDonald be among them? That he could not say, until he saw how many came forward. If six grenadiers of his company stepped forward, would he join them? No, he did not think six grenadiers would be enough. If twelve grenadiers came forward, would he join them? "I don't know," said MacDonald in sudden anger. "Plague me no more upon the subject!" Peter amiably excused the insolence, saying that he understood its cause. He had given MacDonald the best of advice, and if the grenadier now marched there would be no memory of what had passed between them. MacDonald misunderstood, or was as cunning as the officer. He would be quiet, he said, he would not say a word for or against marching. No, said Peter, that was not what he meant. MacDonald must now be as ready to persuade his comrades to march as he had been in dissuading them. When this was translated, the Highlander's pride was hurt. He would be a very bad man indeed, he said, if he turned his coat so easily. Now Peter was angry. MacDonald must obey orders or he would most certainly suffer. "I can only die once," said the soldier. He thanked the Brigadier for his advice and asked to be dismissed.

As if each were thus a key that might turn of its own will and could be left alone to unlock a solution to the mutiny, Bruce and MacDonald were not included in the arrests ordered by the General. But other men were taken, by constables from their squalid lodgings at night or in the street as they left the Green.

Some were not held in the regimental guard-house at the Circus,
but in the Town Gaol or the new barracks at the eastern end of the
Gallowgate, and no word was heard from them. This measure
was perhaps designed to unman the soldiers but inevitably it
deepened their hostility. At the evening parade on Thursday,
August 23, as the officers were entering the Green by the turnstile
gate, Drill-sergeant David Cumming was angered by what he
thought to be the insolent manner of the Light Company, and he
called upon John Maclean to fall out and follow him in arrest to
the guard-house. The soldier did so and his companions moved
forward in protest until Sergeant Duncan MacInnes cried "*Stand
fast . . . Officers on parade!*" The ranks were re-dressed, but Angus
MacFarlane ran to their front and turned upon them. "Damn you
for dogs and cowards!" he shouted. "Rescue Maclean!" He was
very young and had not been in the regiment six weeks, and
when no one responded he laughed nervously. "Fall in, boy,"
said MacInnes. MacFarlane laughed again, as if his appeal had
been a jest, and still laughing he returned to his place.

But John Maclean was a popular man, and his arrest was
bitterly resented. Later that evening, when the big whale-oil lamp
was being lit outside the Circus, all the men of the Light Company came to the building with a mob behind them. The eight
soldiers of the Guard, under Sergeant Lachlan Maclean and
Corporal John MacDonald, had no arms and no wish to resist
their friends. The Sergeant decided that there must be two or
perhaps three hundred men and boys in the following mob, all
carrying sticks and stones. He called uneasily to the Highlanders,
asking what they wanted, and was answered by another young
recruit, Roderick Fraser. "*We want the prisoner!*" Having shouted
this Fraser led a charge upon the open door, pushing the Sergeant
and the Guard aside. Corporal MacDonald attempted to stop
them, but he was taken gently by the arms and held against the
wall where earnest voices told him that John Maclean must be
released, that they would not suffer him to be removed to hidden
places like other poor men. Maclean was brought out in triumph,
and in the weak light the Sergeant could not be sure of all the men

who took him into the street, but he was certain that Fraser and MacFarlane were holding the prisoner's arms.

Two days later both young men were taken up by constables and delivered to the Town Gaol. The Earl of Moira realised that if there were not to be another outrageous incident, and the next a bloody one, he must put a decisive end to the mutiny. He sent Thomas Peter a letter which he said was to be read at the head of the regiment. It promised the soldiers that all their previous indiscipline would be overlooked if they now marched upon their orders. If they refused, force would be brought against them and they would be tried for mutiny under the Articles of War.

"Without fraud or guile, sincerely and firmly . . ."

LORD MOIRA'S LETTER was read to the regiment on Sunday, August 26. It was heard in silence and its threat of force was known to be real. A battalion of the Stirlingshire Militia had been drawn in to the eastern suburbs and patrols of English dragoons were riding the northern bank of the canal between Port Dundas and Craig Park. Their officers came to dine at the Star, and the menace of their drums and trumpets was distantly heard at sunset. The reading of the letter was followed by new marching-orders. The regiment would leave for Ayr in two equal divisions headed by the Grenadiers and Light Company, Lieutenant-colonel Shank to lead the first on Tuesday and Brigadier Peter to march with the second on Wednesday. Baggage and families would go with the first division, the bat-wagons to be loaded at dawn outside the Circus. Those men whose wives and children were grievously sick would be allowed to march with the wagon party if their names were approved by their company sergeants. For the first time, as they moved along the ranks with an interpreter, the officers made an earnest attempt to assure the men that all would be well, that their fears were groundless and that they were indeed to be carried to Canada. But these captains and lieutenants, Dugald Campbell, James Pentz, William Ellice and others, had given earlier assurances, false promises since betrayed. They had threatened the soldiers with force and damned them for ingrates justly abandoned by the Duke and the Government. Few could now believe such men, but there was no protest and the Highlanders' silence was a sullen acceptance of the inevitable, whatever it might be.

Donald MacDonald's mind was sadly confused. In her sickness

that morning his wife had reminded him that she had only agreed to his enlistment because her brothers were among those recruited at Gairloch, and once they were restrained by the Laird she had no further wish to go to Canada. Upon an impulse, however, in despair or the realisation that there was no alternative, he went to Sergeant Cumming and asked leave to march in the wagon party with his family. His name was so entered in the Sergeant's book. The omnipresent Angus Gordon advised James Bruce to do the same, but the soldier protested that his wife and two of his five children were too sick to travel and he would not leave them. There was more to keep him. He had borrowed thirty shillings from a sympathetic tradesman and he could not march with an debt unpaid. Honour obliged him to stay, and also the fear that his few possessions might be taken to defray the money. And still more. He said that other soldiers had threatened him with violence if he marched. When the parade was dismissed he went to the house on Shuttle Street where he lodged with the Widow Duffie, and there his wife was weeping, believing that he had left her. He explained that if he marched she would indeed be deserted, but if he stayed he would be arrested and she would still be abandoned. The Widow Duffie, anxious to be quit of tenants who paid no rent, called Bruce a fool for not going with his comrades, and his wife cried "If they take us out of Glasgow they will do what they please with us!" Bruce turned to a friend in frustration. "This is the way with me!" he said. "There are two women in the house and they get one on each side of me, and bother me that I don't know what I'm doing, and when I go among the men they do the same."

The first companies of Shank's division assembled at five o'clock on Tuesday morning. Dawn was delayed by an overcast sky, the air heavy with misted rain. In the shelter of the great elm and wrapped in a blue cloak, Thomas Peter grew impatient with the laggard arrival and surly indiscipline of the soldiers. The companies were still not complete when the second division came to drill on the High Green four hundred yards to the east, and it too lacked order, breaking into noisy groups as soon as it halted.

There were many civilians abroad, most of them on the High
Green where they walked before and behind the division, and
some between its open ranks. Peter sent the Adjutant to discover
what was happening, to ask the officer of the day, Captain Ellice,
why he had not begun the exercises. When Wilson reached the
Green, before he approached the idle officers beneath the trees, he
saw MacDonald and other grenadiers talking to men of the Light
Company. He spoke to them angrily, ordering them to join the
first division, and when they ignored him he seized MacDonald's
sleeve. He was immediately surrounded by angry men, deafened
by their Gaelic voices. He became alarmed for his safety, then
Sergeant-major Maclean was at his side, tall and calm, telling him
that the Brigadier wished him to return, that he would himself
bring the second division to order.

With his fist and cane the Sergeant-major drove away the
civilians, and he called upon the sergeants to straighten the
dressing of their companies. As if removing a thorn from inflamed
flesh he then took MacDonald by the shoulder and drew him
away to the trees, asking him why he was not with the grenadiers
in the first division. The soldier said that he had permission to
march with the wagon party, but this morning his wife had been
too sick to rise and he would not leave without her. "Go to your
officer," said Maclean, "and tell him that I shall be answerable for
you. You'll get furlough to remain until she is recovered."
MacDonald did not believe him. He would not be allowed to
stay, he said, and he would not ask. "Then your blood be on your
head!" said Maclean, and turned away in disgust.

At seven o'clock, more than an hour after it was due to march,
the first division was still in disorder, and although the men had
fallen in upon their markers they argued and shouted in the ranks,
turning their backs upon their officers. Thomas Peter was afraid
that if there were further delay they would break away and leave
the Green. He told Shank to order the march, and upon the
Lieutenant-colonel's command the Highlanders turned obediently
from line to column of companies, still shouting above the beating
of the signal drum. Shank moved to the column-head and lifted

his voice again. "Canadian Regiment . . . *Forward!*" As the division moved Donald MacDonald ran along the left flank of the grenadiers, his bonnet clenched in his fist, calling with great emotion for all good men to stand with him. Less than a score did so, and most of them soon slipped away to the city or to the rear of the departing column. Lieutenant Wilson roughly ordered the rest to do their duty, but MacDonald shook his bonnet in defiance and they ran to the High Green. The second division was now drilling in column of fours, and when the grenadiers joined the rear files of the Light Company they were seen by Maclean. He told them to be gone. They turned about and were lost among the civilians now moving toward the Low Green. "It would be a bad thing," said Maclean to Captain Ellice, "if the revolters got among us."

The first division was away, all of its drums beating and carrying it over the white bridge to the Gorbals. No roll had been taken and Peter believed that many soldiers had dropped away into the anonymity of the crowd. But the division was gone without violence and he knew that the back of resistance was now broken, that his own column must march without protest the next day. Before then he was obliged to obey the orders sent by Wemyss on Monday, to arrest all those who had failed to march this morning. MacDonald and Bruce had been included in Moira's conditional amnesty, but when Peter was informed that they had not gone with the grenadiers he told Wilson that they had now put themselves beyond this clemency and must be taken up.

MacDonald was easily found. When he left the Light Company he wandered alone through the city until past eleven. Returning to his lodgings he comforted his wife for another hour and then went to the Gallowgate with a bundle of clothes which he sold, buying a little food and also a chest in which he intended to pack the rest of his belongings. He still needed two shillings for the full price of this chest, and to earn it he went to a merchant for whom he had previously laboured, and who was now building a new house. He was given work there and at three o'clock in the afternoon, when he was wheeling a barrow of rubble, he was found by Sergeant-major Maclean, a party of men from the Stirlingshire Militia and two constables, one of whom was a Highlander of his own name. He was surprised when he was told that he was under arrest. He said that he had leave to stay from Sergeant Cumming, that only his wife's illness prevented him from marching with the first division. He asked for word of his arrest to be sent to his wife, and he did not resist when he was taken to the Tolbooth. That evening the merchant sent one of his workmen to tell Mrs. MacDonald what had happened, but she had already heard from Maclean. She was in convulsions and three women were holding her upon the floor.

No officer or sergeant had seen James Bruce at the morning parade, but Angus Gordon found him among the civilians on the High Green and told him that he was a fool not to join his company. If he now ran as fast as he could he would soon come up with the first division. Bruce was unhinged by hysterical fear. He could not leave his family without money and food. "I might as well drown them as leave them to starve!" He complained bitterly that he and his family had been betrayed, that upon his enlistment Quartermaster-sergeant Macmillan had promised him that those of his sons over the age of ten would receive the same allowance as a man of the regiment, and those under ten would receive half. He had also been told that he would embark for Canada in June, "to strengthen the country and cultivate the waste lands". He pushed Gordon aside and went from the Green to the city. At his lodgings he sat beside his wife and told her that he should have gone with the grenadiers. "Look at your children," she said, "will you leave them to starve?" He could not endure her bitter tears and he ran out, looking for a friend who might lend him money. He saw Donald Gunn, a Highland street-porter who had once before given him a guinea and who had been with him on the hopeful day of his enlistment. But now Gunn would lend no money, and had what he thought was the best of reasons for refusing. He and his wife, he said, were agreed that they would help Mrs. Bruce, but not until the grenadier had gone with the regiment, for they could not encourage him to disobey his officers and thus bring greater misery upon his family.

An hour later Bruce went to the house of a Highland woman, Catherine Mackay, where some of the Canadian Regiment were lodged and others came to drink. Angus Gordon knew of this meeting-place and when he was told that the word was out for the arrest of Bruce he went to it at once. Mrs. Mackay was standing in the doorway and she admitted that Bruce was above, with three or four soldiers and a gentleman or two of the town. She took Gordon to the door of the room but he would not enter. He asked if there were an adjoining chamber where he might hear what the soldiers were saying. She said there was a back room and he could do what he wished. The partition wall between the two rooms was made of thin slats of wood, and as Gordon crouched beside it he clearly heard all that was being said. It was bold talk, brave words to sustain the courage of unhappy men. He did not think that anything was said by the citizens, but the soldiers declared that they would not march the next day, that they would not go to the Isle of Wight until the Duke himself answered their petition, promising them a passage to Canada. Then one of them began to sing. Angus Gordon from the parish of Farr in Sutherland could not understand all the words of the verse because the singer was a West Highland man whose Gaelic was unfamiliar. But he understood enough to know, and later to swear on oath, that they were very seditious, that they spoke of the soldiers' determination not to go to Wight, not to be sold to the Indies, not to leave Glasgow until they were given a paper signed by the Duke of York. After a cramped quarter of an hour Gordon went down to the kitchen where he asked Mrs. Mackay to go above and tell Bruce that there was a friend below who wished to speak with him. She went grudgingly, and when Bruce came down Gordon invited him to share a bottle of porter at the tavern across the street. The soldier said he could not leave, he was engaged in business with two townspeople, but if Gordon wished they could meet later at the Cross. The spy agreed, touched the grenadier's shoulder in friendship and left.

Catherine Mackay would later swear that Bruce had been in her house with other men of the regiment, and that the reckoning for what they drank was paid by a man of the town. She had heard no song. If there had been singing, she said, she would surely have heard it in her kitchen. But the report which Gordon carried to Wemyss within the hour convinced the General that a dangerous committee of action had been formed and that Bruce was a ringleader. His fear of sedition and civil revolt, of collusion between the levelling societies and disaffected soldiers, was strengthened by reports that a mysterious "man in a cloak" had frequently been seen on the Green, talking to the Fencibles. Later that afternoon, when Bruce returned to Shuttle Street with a little food and a few shillings he had at last borrowed, he was stopped at the door by soldiers of the Stirlingshire Militia and was taken to the Tolbooth.

The second division left the next day. There was no protest, no defiance of the order to march, the brave song above Catherine Mackay's kitchen had been a cry of protest only. Many men were absent from the parade. Some were taken up as deserters and sent to Edinburgh, some disappeared for ever into the darkness of the city or went homeward to their mountains, but by the week's end almost all of those with families had followed them or taken them to Ayr. On Wednesday evening Wemyss went by coach to Edinburgh where he and Moira agreed that the Duke of York must be urged to disband the regiment. The Commander-in-Chief sent the relevant papers to the War Office, the reports of Peter's officers, the recommendations of Wemyss and the Lord Advocate. "The enclosed," he said, "will justify the opinion I had formed of the hopelessness of getting a corps so constituted into any kind of order. It will be necessary to prevent the mischief of the example to other troops, to try and punish some of those who have been most marked for turbulence." He was confident that if and when proper explanations were made to the soldiers they would be satisfied that the Government was innocent of any breach of faith. When this dispatch reached the Duke of York he had already decided to discharge the regiment and he cancelled the orders for its embarkation. With genuine compassion he suggested that a full inquiry should be made into the probable state of the women and children once the men were disbanded, but little attention was paid to this recommendation, and other problems soon drove the matter from his royal mind.

The soldiers most marked for turbulence were carried to the casemates below Edinburgh Castle. Those taken up as deserters were soon returned to the regiment without trial, but not before Angus Gordon had spoken to many of them and reported to General Wemyss that the common and only cause of their desertion was their foolish fear of the Isle of Wight. Four men were brought to trial in the second week of September: Roderick Fraser, Angus MacFarlane, James Bruce and Donald MacDonald. The court sat above Palace Yard under the presidency of a dragoon colonel and none of its fourteen members was an officer of a Highland regiment. Fraser and MacFarlane were quickly disposed of, the first being sentenced to a thousand lashes and the second to five hundred, but the court-martial of Bruce and MacDonald was one of the longest and most exhaustive ever held. Evidence was not only heard from officers and men of the regiment but also from many civilians, from Gunn the street-porter and from Mrs. Mackay, from Doctor Muir and the Highland constables, from Lieutenant Macintosh and of course Angus Gordon. At the end of two weeks the court listened to the impassioned and reasoned address by which the prisoners' advocate introduced their defence. He dealt with, and to his satisfaction demolished, the evidence given by each witness for the Crown. He said the prisoners were now aware that they were not entitled to question the good faith of the Government or disobey their officers. But neither of them, he said, was familiar with military custom and it should be remembered that they were without the arms and uniforms that might have given them a lively sense of their duties and responsibilities.

The mutiny with which they are charged did not consist in their originating the spirit of discontent or resistance which arose in the Regiment; for it has been shown that this spirit was produced by circumstances totally independent of them, and above their control. The mutiny with which they are charged did not consist in their having struck a superior officer, or having drawn or lift up any weapon, or offered any violence against him. For any offence of this kind there is not a trace to be discovered upon the face of the whole evidence. What then is the real nature of the offence charged? It is entirely the effect of ignorance, practised upon by gross imposition and delusion. By these means, aided by circumstances, which gave an appearance of probability to the delusion, the prisoners were induced to form a fixed and decided opinion that the regiment was to be sent to the Isle of Wight, and from thence to the East Indies; whereby they would be separated from their wives and children who would be left in a state of absolute misery. Under this condition they opposed not anything which they were conscious was right. They only for a time refused obedience to orders which they, bonafide, without fraud or guile, sincerely and firmly believed to be contrary to the faith of the Government. If an offence of this nature must be made the object of punishment by the strict rules of military law, no case ever occurred which called more loudly than the present for the exercise of mercy in the judgement to be formed.

On the last day, and in concluding the exculpatory evidence, the young advocate asked the court's leave to lay before it certain papers which would prove the gravity of Mrs. MacDonald's illness, which would prove that many soldiers had been forced to sell their clothes and furniture to support their families, which would prove that fifty women and children had died from privation and hunger in five weeks. There were also papers, particularly a letter written by Captain William Ellice now in the possession of General Wemyss, which contained promises not included in the handbills and which assured the recruits that they would embark from Greenock for Canada within twenty days of leaving the Highlands. At this point the President adjourned the court. When it reassembled at ten o'clock the next morning he declared that after mature deliberation on the whole evidence it was satisfied that the charge of repeated disobedience in refusing to march was proven against both prisoners. A second charge of incitement to mutiny had not been proven against James Bruce, but the court was satisfied that Donald MacDonald had been several times guilty of this offence. Both prisoners were therefore guilty of a breach of the Articles of War, for which James Bruce was sentenced to five hundred lashes and Donald MacDonald to eight hundred lashes, to be administered at such time and place as General the Earl of Moira should be pleased to direct.

The sentences were lenient, no worse than a soldier of the line might expect for a less serious crime. The President of the court added a qualifying rider to its decision. He said that both men may have believed that since they were neither uniformed nor armed they were not subject to that military discipline they might otherwise have accepted. He also believed that the distress of their families was responsible for the bewildered state of their minds, and was indeed the cause of their remaining behind when the divisions at last marched for Ayr. Because of these circumstances, he said, the court asked for mercy, a recommendation which Moira was happy to extend to Fraser and MacFarlane. The circumstances of the mutiny and the evidence to the court-martial had put the reputation of the Government and the Army at risk, and that risk might have been greater had the prisoners' advocate produced the papers he proposed. Such unhappy, unsavoury matters were best concluded and forgotten. Three of the men were unconditionally pardoned and returned to their regiment at Ayr. The fourth, the boy Roderick Fraser, was told that he would escape the lash if he enlisted for unlimited service in a regiment of the line, a clemency he willingly accepted.

Winter came early that year and was particularly harsh in the south-west where the companies were quartered. There was no relief from the hunger and hardship of the families, although the soldiers' subsistence money was now more regularly paid. Before the beginning of another year the battalion was at last disbanded. It was not removed from the establishment, Thomas Peter was free to recruit another nine hundred and fifty men if he wished, but the Highlanders were told that they were discharged from the Canadian Regiment of Fencibles. Their release was without joy, the final breach of faith. They were far from their land and now denied the emigration they had been promised, the powerful and principal reason for their enlistment. The immovable fabric of their homes, their furniture and their stock, had been sold before they left, and the few possessions they had brought with them were long since exchanged for food. Although their lairds had violently protested against their recruitment there was no eagerness to welcome them back. A few found the money to buy a coffin passage to America, but the rest were soon begging in the towns and villages of the south-west. They were no man's responsibility and no man's pen recorded their suffering.

Two Highland regiments were at this moment raising second battalions, the 78th Ross-shire Buffs and Erracht's 79th, and since it was no longer easy to find willing young men or pliable parents in Kintail and Lochaber, their recruiters came to Ayr like hungry crows. They took the young, the fit and the despairing, all who chose to soldier again rather than beg. Men who had followed one drum in the hope of land in Canada would now march to another by the waters of the Nile or the bloody snow to Corunna. David Stewart of Garth, home from Egypt and recovered from wounds taken at Alexandria, required ninety men for his major's commission in the 78th and he completed the number with twenty-two discharged Canadians. Fifteen years later, at work on his *Sketches* in the quiet of Strathtay, he wrote briefly of this last Highland mutiny that had indirectly helped him to secure his coveted majority. He remembered the soldiers with sympathy but he deplored their lack of manly spirit, and he primly disapproved of the manner in which they had accepted their misfortune.

"They spread themselves all over the country proclaiming their wrongs, and thus helping to destroy the confidence of their countrymen, not only in Government but in all public men, whom they now began to think totally unworthy of credit."

APPENDIXES

APPENDIX

A Letter of Service

War Office
8th January 1778

The Earl of Seaforth

My Lord, – I am commanded by the King to acquaint you that His Majesty approves of your proposal for raising a Regiment of Foot in the Highlands of Scotland, to consist of Eight Battalion Companies, one Company of Grenadiers, and one of Light Infantry: The Battalion Companies to consist, each of 1 Captain, 2 Lieutenants, 1 Ensign, 5 Serjeants, 5 Corporals, 2 Drummers, and 100 Private Men; the Grenadier Company of 1 Captain, 3 Lieutenants, 5 Serjeants, 5 Corporals, 2 Drummers, 2 Pipers, and 100 Private Men; the Light Infantry Company of 1 Captain, 3 Lieutenants, 5 Serjeants, 5 Corporals, 2 Drummers, and 100 Private Men, with the usual Staff Officers. The Regiment to have one Lieutenant-colonel Commandant and two Majors each having also the command of a company.

I am to inform you that Levy Money will be issued to you at the rate of £3 per man for 1082 Men, and that His Majesty has been pleased to direct that the Pay of the Regiment shall take place from the date of your Beating Order, and shall be allowed you in aid of recruiting; on condition that you do render an exact Account of the said Levy Money and Pay that shall be issued to you, charging against it five guineas for each Man reviewed and approved, together with the subsistence of the Non-Commissioned Officers and Private Men from the day of their respective attestations; and if there should be any balance remaining, it is to be considered as a Saving to the Public, to be hereafter disposed of as shall be thought proper.

No more than Three Guineas will be allowed to be given to each Recruit.

None are to be enlisted under five feet four inches, none under Eighteen Years, or above thirty.

It is required that the Regiment shall be actually raised and approved (after being reviewed by a General Officer) within four months of the date hereof.

Having laid before the King Your Lordship's representation that your having the Command of this Corps will considerably accelerate the raising & completing it; and that desirous of showing your attachment to the Cause by personal Service, your Lordship hoped H.M. will not object to your being appointed Lieut. Col. Commandant, on condition that you do renounce all Claim to future Rank or Promotion in the Army; and in case of a reduction, that you do not desire Half Pay, or any other Emolument whatsoever; I am to acquaint you H.M. is pleased on those conditions to approve of your Lordship as Lieut. Col. Commandant, with the Command of a Company.

H.M. reserves to himself the nomination of the two Majors, but I leave to your Lordship the recommendation of the other officers, being such as are well affected to H.M. & most likely by their Interest and Connections to assist in raising the Corps without delay, who if they meet with His Royal approbation may be assured that they shall have Commissions as soon as ever the Regiment is completed.

I am likewise authorised by H.M. to acquaint your Lordship, the Officers will be entitled to Half Pay in case the Regiment shall be reduced after it has been once established.

H.M. consents that on a reduction the Corps shall be disbanded in Ross-shire.

I am to add that it is H.M. pleasure that, from the date hereof, and during the continuance of the Rebellion now subsisting in North America, every Person who shall enlist as a Soldier in any of his marching Regiments of Foot, shall be entitled to his discharge at the end of three years, or at the end of the Rebellion, at the Option of H.M.

> I have the Honour to be,
> My Lord etc.
> BARRINGTON.

CHRONOLOGY

Date	National Situation	Highland Regiments Raised (* Mutinied)
1689	Revolution, accession of William and Mary, war with France	1 The Earl of Argyll's 2 Hugh Mackay's 3 Lord Strathnaver's 4 Independent Companies
1725	Policing of the Highlands	5 Independent Companies (Black Watch)
1739	War with Spain	6 The Black Watch re-formed into a regiment of the line, the 43rd Highland Regiment*
1745	War of the Austrian Succession Last Jacobite Rebellion	7 64th Loudoun's Highlanders 8 Argyll Independent Companies

1757	The Seven Years' War
	9 77th Montgomery's Highlanders
	10 78th Fraser's Highlanders
1759	"
	11 87th Keith's Highlanders
	12 88th Campbell's Highlanders*1
	13 89th Duke of Gordon's Highlanders
	14 The Argyll Fencible Regiment
	15 The Sutherland Fencible Regiment
1760	"
	16 101st Johnstone's Highlanders
1761	"
	17 100th Campbell of Kilberrie's
	18 105th Queen's Highlanders
	19 Maclean of Torloisk's Highlanders
	20 113th Royal Highland Volunteers

Date	National Situation	Highland Regiments Raised (*Mutinied)
1775	The American Revolution	21 71st Fraser's Highlanders*
1777	,,	22 73rd Lord MacLeod's Highlanders
1778	,,	23 74th Barbreck's (Argyll) Highlanders
		24 76th Lord Macdonald's Highlanders*
		25 77th Duke of Atholl's Highlanders*
		26 78th Lord Seaforth's Highlanders*
		27 81st Aberdeenshire Highlanders*
		28 84th Royal Highland Emigrants
		29 The Western (Argyll) Fencibles*
		30 The Northern (Gordon) Fencibles
1780	,,	31 73rd Perthshire Highlanders

| 1787 | War in India | 32 | 74th Highland Regiment |
| | | 33 | 75th Stirlingshire Regiment |

1793	War with France	34	78th Ross-shire Buffs
		35	79th Cameron Highlanders
		36	1st Strathspey (Grant) Fencibles*
		37	2nd Sutherland Fencibles*
		38	4th Breadalbane Fencibles (3 Batts.)*
		39	5th Western (Argyll) Fencibles (2 Batts.)*
		40	6th Northern (Gordon) Fencibles*

1794	,,	41	97th Strathspey Highlanders
		42	98th (91st) Argyll Highlanders
		43	100th (92nd) Gordon Highlanders
		44	116th Perthshire Highlanders*
		45	132nd Cameron's Highlanders
		46	133rd Fraser's Highlanders
		47	The Aberdeen Highland Regiment
		48	8th Rothesay & Caithness Fencibles*

Date	National Situation	Highland Regiments Raised (*Mutinied)
	War with France	49 The Glengarry (British Highland) Fencibles
		50 The Dunbartonshire Fencibles
		51 Lord Reay's Fencibles
		52 The Loyal Inverness Fencibles
		53 The Earl of Elgin's Fencibles
		54 The Perthshire Fencibles
		55 The Caithness Legion of Fencibles
		56 The Fraser Fencibles
1799	,,	57 The Argyllshire Fencibles
		58 The Royal Clan Alpine Fencibles
		59 The Ross and Cromarty Rangers
		60 The Fencible Regiment of the Isles
		61 The MacLeod Fencibles
		62 The Lochaber Fencibles
1800	,,	63 93rd Sutherland Highlanders[2]
1803	,,	64 The Canadian Regiment of Fencibles*

The strength of each of these marching or fencible regiments was between 700 and 1,000 men, the latter figure being most common. Some of the regiments also formed second and third battalions. Not included in this list are the many units of Highland militia and volunteers raised during the Napoleonic wars. In addition to the Argyllshire Independent Companies mustered to oppose the Jacobite Rebellion of 1745 more than thirty other companies came from clans or districts sympathetic to the Hanoverian cause. The Earl of Sutherland, for example, assembled 2,400 men at his own expense, the Laird of Grant raised 1,100, and the Laird of MacLeod 1,000.

[1] This mutiny is not referred to in the text. The 88th was raised by John Campbell of Dunoon and served in Europe. It was disbanded at Linlithgow in 1763 when, says Garth, "an unfortunate collision of opinion occurred". The men demanded pay and clothing due to them, and before their complaints were met "some indications of violence very opposite to their previous exemplary conduct were manifested".

[2] Frequently described as "the most Highland of Highland regiments" it was also the last to be raised in the old way as a clan levy and thus, perhaps, the last real Highland regiment.

Acknowledgements

WITH THE EXCEPTION of the Black Watch Mutiny of 1743 the events described in this book have been largely ignored by historians, social, political and military. The revolt of the Canadian Fencibles, for example, occupies a quarter of a page in Garth's *Sketches*, and I know of no other printed reference to it. Even the most recent works on Highland history after the Rebellion of 1745, while making the customary reference to the raising of Highland regiments, say nothing of any resistance to such service or its relevance to the changing social and economic condition of the Highlands. If I say that I find this astonishing I do so with humility and respect, and with the realisation that military matters rarely interest the social or political historian, that mutiny is always a jarring note in regimental histories. Manuscript sources in Scotland and England have thus supplied the greater part of the information given here. MacWilliam's *Records of the Black Watch Mutiny*, published over sixty years ago, are of course invaluable, but in this case too I returned to the original material in the Public Record Office. A satisfactory understanding of the last stages of this mutiny would also have been impossible without a visit to Tresham's lonely, overgrown water-orchard. I began my reaserch with hope but little conviction that I would find the information I required, believing that the lack or loss of it must explain in part the absence of any other work on the subject. I was therefore delighted by what I found during two years of study, as well as unreasonably disappointed by what I did not. In many cases I opened letters that had not been disturbed since they were first read and refolded, and the black sand that had been used to dry the ink still clung to the pages. Because of this the voices of some of the mutineers, of their sorrowing friends or parents, were immediate and deeply moving. Such an experience is one of the rewards of original research, although it increases a writer's unhappy awareness that he has done less than justice to his subject.

This book is the fourth of the series I have written on the destruction of the clans and the Highland way of life, and although complete in itself it may take a proper chronological place between *Culloden* and *The Highland Clearances*. It would have been impossible without the help and advice of too many people to acknowledge in full, but I must make known my gratitude to the following: A. M. Broom, of the Scottish Record Office; the Earl of Cromartie; Sir Hew Hamilton Dalrymple; Ian D. Grant, of the National Register of Archives (Scotland); R. E. Hutchison, of the Scottish National Portrait Gallery; Dr. Mary Johstone for permission to quote from Sergeant Matheson's *Memorandum Book*; J. R. Ker, for particular guidance on the events of 1743 and further back; Miss Elizabeth Mackay, for her help with the Rearquhar Papers; Rory Mackay, for his constant and friendly encouragement, and his translation of some of the Gaelic verse used; Alex A. MacKenzie, Sheriff Clerk Depute at Lochmaddy; the Reverend Somerled Macmillan; Eòin Macpherson, of Clan Macpherson House; Sir Ewen Macpherson-Grant, for access to the Ballindalloch Papers; W. H. Makey, Edinburgh City Archivist; G. Milton, Estate Bursar of Oundle School; George Proctor, Sheriff Clerk, Inverness; Dr. Thomas I. Rae, of the National Library of Scotland, once again for his friendly help; John Steare, headmaster of Kettering Grammar School, and W. A. Thorburn of the Scottish United Services Museum whose assistance is warmly appreciated.

I am also in debt to the staffs of the Public Record Office, the Scottish Record Office, the National Library of Scotland, the National Army Museum, the London Library, and the Kent County Archives. Finally my thanks to the Scottish Gaelic Texts Society and the Scottish Academic Press Ltd., for permission to use some English translations from *The Songs of Duncan Ban Macintyre*.

LIST OF SOURCES

MANUSCRIPT SOURCES

The Public Record Office, London

Home Office Papers	HO 50	War Office
	HO 51	War Office
	HO 102	HO (Scotland)
	HO 103	HO (Scotland)
State Papers Geo. III	SP 60	
	SP 61	
War Office Papers	WO 1	Correspondence
	WO 3	Out-letters, Commander-in-Chief
	WO 4	Out-letters, Secretary at War
	WO 26	Miscellanea, Miscellany Books
	WO 30	Miscellanea, Various
	WO 34	The Amherst Papers
	WO 71	Judge Advocate General's Office, Courts-martial etc.
	WO 72	Judge Advocate General, Letters and Documents
	WO 81	Judge Advocate General, Letter-books

The Scottish Record Office, Edinburgh

Breadalbane Papers (Military)	GD 112/52
Dalguise Papers (typescript)	GD 38
Elibank Papers	GD 52
Hamilton-Dalrymple Papers	GD 24
Lord Macdonald's Papers	GD 221
Melville Castle Papers	GD 51
Rearquhar Papers	GD 1/336
Seafield Papers	GD 248
Seaforth Papers	GD 46

The National Library of Scotland, Edinburgh

Melville Papers	6 ff 207-17
	351 ff 13

Kent County Archives, Maidstone

Amherst Family Papers	U 1350

Ballindalloch Muniments, Ballindalloch Castle

	Bundle 204

PUBLISHED PAPERS

Chronicles of the Atholl and Tullibardine Families, Volumes 1–5, Edinburgh 1908

Dartmouth Manuscripts, I–III. Historical Manuscripts Commission, 11th Report, Appendix V, 1887; 14th Report, Appendix X, 1895; 15th Report, Appendix I, 1896

CONTEMPORARY NEWSPAPERS, ETC.

Aberdeen Journal
Caledonian Mercury
Dumfries Weekly Journal
Edinburgh Advertiser
Edinburgh Chronicle
Edinburgh Evening Courant
Edinburgh Gazette
Glasgow Courier
Glasgow Mercury
Hampshire Chronicle
Morning Chronicle
Ruddiman's Weekly Mercury
The Times
Gentleman's Magazine
London Magazine
Scots Magazine

CONTEMPORARY MILITARY PUBLICATIONS

A Treatise on Courts Martial, to which is added an essay on Military Punishments and Rewards, by Major Stephen Payne Adye. London, 1786

A Treatise on Military Discipline, by Lieutenant-general Humphrey Bland. London, 1759

The Military Medley, to which is added an Explication of Military Terms, by Thomas Simes. Dublin, 1767

Military Instructions for Officers, by Roger Stevenson. London, 1770

Military Antiquities, respecting a History of the English Army, by Francis Grose. London, 1801

Army Lists, Various

CONTEMPORARY MAPS

The Royal English Atlas. Bown and Kitchen, 1762

Edinburgh, 1765. William Edgar

Edinburgh, 1770. John Rocque

Linlithgow, 1773. Armstrong
Leith, 1777. Scott
Glasgow, 1807. Fleming
Edinburgh, 1817. Kirkwood
Dumfries, 1819. Wood
Portsmouth, 1762

JOURNALS

Scottish Historical Review	Vol. XVII, 1920. "The Causes of the Highland Emigrations, 1783–1803", by Margaret I. Adam. Vol. XIX, 1922. "The Eighteenth Century Highland Landlords and the Poverty Problem", by Margaret I. Adam.
Transactions of the Gaelic Society of Inverness	Vols. III & IV, 1873–5. "The Black Watch Deserters executed at the Tower", by A. Mackintosh Shaw. Vol. X, 1881–3. "The Highland Regiments", by William Mackenzie. Vol. XIX, 1893–4. "Gleanings from the Charter Chest at Cluny", by Alexander Macpherson. Vol. XXIII, 1898–9. "The Gael in Canada", by A. Fraser.

BIBLIOGRAPHY

Adam, R. J.	*Papers on Sutherland Estate Management, 1802–16.* Scottish History Society, Edinburgh, 1972
Anonymous	*A Short History of the Highland Regiment.* London, 1743.
Arnot, Hugo	*The History of Edinburgh, from the earliest accounts to the present time.* Edinburgh, 1788.
Bain, Robert	*A History of the Ancient Province of Ross.* Dingwall, 1899.
Black, George P.	*Arthur's Seat, a history of Edinburgh's Volcano.*
Boswell, Samuel	*The Journal of a Tour to the Hebrides with Samuel Johnson.* London, 1786
Bulloch, J. M.	*Territorial Soldiering in the north-east of Scotland, 1759–1914.* Aberdeen, 1914. *The Raising of the Aberdeen Militia, 1797.* Privately printed, Keith, 1915. *The Scots Fencibles and English Service, 1794.* Privately printed, Aberdeen, 1915. *The Mutiny of the Atholl Highlanders and an*

	account of the Sheelagreen Gordons. Privately printed, Buckie, 1911.
Campbell, the Rev. Mr.	*The Behaviour and Character of Samuel Macpherson, Malcolm Macpherson, and Farquhar Shaw, the Three Highland Deserters who were shot in the Tower, July 18th, 1743.* London, 1743.
Cleland, James	*Annals of Glasgow.* Glasgow, 1816.
Cockburn, Henry	*Memorials of his Time.* Edinburgh, 1856.
Fortescue, John	*A History of the British Army,* volumes 4i & ii. London, 1906.
	British Statesmen of the Great War, 1793–1814. Oxford, 1911.
Grant, James	*Memorials of the Castle of Edinburgh.* Edinburgh, 1850.
Gordon, Pryse Lockhart	*Personal Memoirs; or Reminiscences of Men and Manners at Home and Abroad.* London, 1830.
Gowans, James	*Edinburgh and its Neighbourhood in the days of our Grandfathers.* London, 1886.
Harper, Colonel J. R.	*A Short History of the old 78th Regiment, or Fraser's Highlanders, 1757–63.* Laval, Quebec, 1966.
Hibbert, Christopher	*King Mob, the Story of Lord George Gordon and the Riots of 1780.* London, 1968.
Howell, T. B.	*State Trials,* Volume XXVI, 1796–98.
Macdonald, the Rev. A. and the Rev. A.	*The Clan Donald,* Volume 3. Inverness, 1904.
Mackenzie, Alexander	*A History of the Mackenzies.* Inverness, 1894.
Mackintosh, H. B.	*The Grant, Strathspey or First Highland Fencible Regiment, 1793–99.* Elgin, 1934.
	The Northern, or Gordon Fencibles, 1778–83. Privately printed, Edinburgh, 1929.
Macintyre, Duncan Ban	*The Songs of Duncan Ban Macintyre,* edited with translation by Angus MacLeod. Scottish Gaelic Texts Society, Edinburgh, 1952.
Macleod, Sergeant Donald	*Memoirs.* London, 1791.
Macmillan, Somerled	*Bygone Lochaber, historical and traditional.* Glasgow, 1971.
Macpherson, Alexander	*Church and Social Life in the Highlands.* 1893.
Macrae, the Rev. Alexander	*History of the Clan MacRae.* 1889.
MacWilliam, H. D.	*A Black Watch Episode, 1731.* Edinburgh, 1908.
	The Official Records of the Mutiny in the Black Watch, 1743. London, 1910.

Maidment, James	*Scottish Ballads and Songs.* Edinburgh, 1859.
McArthur, Margaret	*Survey of Lochtayside, 1769.* Scottish History Society, Edinburgh, 1936.
Marshall, Henry	*Military Miscellany, a history of the Recruiting of the Army, Military Punishments etc.* London, 1846.
Meikle, Henry W.	*Scotland and the French Revolution.* 1912.
Mitchison, Rosalind	*Agricultural Sir John, The Life of Sir John Sinclair of Ulbster.* London, 1962.
Paterson, James	*Kay's Edinburgh Portraits,* edited by James Maidment, 1885.
Prebble, John	*The Highland Clearances.* London, 1963.
Reid, Robert	*Old Glasgow and its Environs.* London, 1864.
Ruvigny, Marquis of	*The Jacobite Peerage, Baronetage, Knightage, and Grants of Honour.* Edinburgh, 1904.
Selkirk, 5th Earl of	*Observations on the Present State of the Highlands of Scotland, with a view of the Causes and Probable consequences of Emigration.* London, 1805.
Stewart of Garth, David	*Sketches of the Character, Manners, and Present State of the Highlanders of Scotland, with details of the Military Service of the Highland Regiments.* Edinburgh, 1822.
Tullibardine, Marchioness of	*A Military History of Perthshire, 1660–1902,* Vol. i. Glasgow and Edinburgh, 1908.
Youngson, A. J.	*After the Forty-five: the Economic Impact of the Scottish Highlands.* Edinburgh, 1973.

PARTICULAR REFERENCES, MSS AND PUBLISHED PAPERS

I   *43rd Highland Regiment*
        Letters, orders, dispatches: SP 60, 61; WO 26/20; WO 30/43; WO 71/125; Atholl Chron. vol ii.
        Court-martial: WO 71/18.

II   *78th Lord Seaforth's Regiment*
        Correspondence, Oughton, Amherst, Seaforth etc: WO 34/111; WO 1/997.
        76th Lord Macdonald's Regiment
        Lord Macdonald corr: GD 221; WO 1/997, 998.
        Oughton corr: WO 1/1005; WO 34/147.
        42nd and 71st Highland Regiments
        Oughton corr: WO 34/114, 115, 148, 149, 229; WO 1/616, 1005.
        Orders to Innes: WO 1/1004.
        Court-martial: WO 71/54; WO 72/8; WO 81/14.

Argyll Fencibles

Corr. Oughton etc: WO 1/1003; WO 34/119; WO 71/55; WO 72/8;
WO 81/14.
Court-martial: WO 71/55.

77th Atholl Highlanders

Recruiting orders: WO 3/26; WO 4/101, 121, 122, 823; WO 3/26.
Officers' letters from the Atholl Chron. vol iv.

III   *Fencible Regiments, general*

Recruiting etc: GD 51/1/831, 858, 860; GD 112/52/1; HO 51/147;
HO 102/10; WO 4/157.

Gordon Fencibles and others

Corr. Lord Adam Gordon etc: GD 51/1/824; HO 102/10.

The Strathspey Fencibles

Formation: GD 248/213, 685.
Mutiny at Linlithgow: GD 248/213/1; GD 248/685/5; GD 248/686/1;
Melville Papers 351.
Mutiny at Dumfries: GD 248/689/4; Court-martial GD 248/689/2
Disbanding: GD 248/697/4.
Glengarry, and his company: GD 51/1/844, 849; GD 248/689/4.

The Breadalbane Fencibles

Mutiny: GD 51/1/854, 855, 857; GD 1/336/45; GD 112/52/1, 2, 2A,
3, 4, 24, 53; HO 102/11; HO 103/1; Melville Papers 6.

IV   *Perthshire Militia Riots*

Highland Corps: GD 248/693.
Riots: letters etc., from the Atholl Chron. vol. iv; State Trials XXVI.

V   *The Canadian Regiment of Fencibles*

General: WO 1/617; WO 3/119; WO 4/160.
Formation: WO 1/627, 628, 773; WO 4/280; HO 50/398.
Lairds' protest: WO 1/627, 773; GD 46/117; HO 50/398; HO 102/19.
Soldiers' protest: WO 1/773; HO 50/398.
Courts-martial: WO 71/198

Glossary of Highland Surnames

HIGHLAND SURNAMES CAN be a confusing thicket, made more
daunting by the preference for one or two particular Christian
names – Kenneth among the Mackenzies, for example, John and
James among the Grants. Some effort has been made in this book
to keep identities clear by using the territorial designations of
chiefs and tacksmen as an occasional alternative to their surnames.
This was, in any case, the custom of their time, an acknowledgement of rank and an obligatory mark of respect. The following
glossary lists some of these designations and identifies the holders
referred to in the text. It may be used together with the index. As
a secondary guide, a list of clans at the end of the glossary gives
some of the designations of their members.

Argyll	Earl and Dukes of, chiefs of Clan Campbell
Atholl	Dukes of, chiefs of Clan Murray
Auchindown	Major John Grant of Auchindown, Strathspey Fencibles
Ballechin	Captain Hope Steuart of Ballechin
Barbreck	Lieutenant-colonel John Campbell of Barbreck, 74th Regiment
Belladrum	Colonel James Fraser of Belladrum, Fraser's Fencibles
Breadalbane	Earls of, chiefs of Clan Campbell. John Campbell, 4th Earl, Breadalbane Fencibles
Chattan, Clan	A confederation including, *inter alia*, Macphersons, Mackintoshes, Macbeans and Shaws
Chisholm, The	William Chisholm of Chisholm, chief
Clanranald	Ranald George MacDonald of Clanranald, chief
Cluny	Lachlan, Ewen and Major Duncan Macpherson of Cluny, chiefs
Coll	Major Alexander Maclean of Coll, Breadalbane Fencibles
Culbin	Major George Grant of Culbin, 43rd
Delcroy	Lieutenant John Grant of Delcroy, Strathspey Fencibles
Duart	Sir Allan Maclean of Duart, chief
Erracht	Colonel Alan Cameron of Erracht, 79th
Foyers	Captain Simon Fraser of Foyers, Strathspey Fencibles
Garth	Major-general David Stewart of Garth
Glencoe	Lieutenant Alexander MacDonald of Glencoe, 76th

Glenfalloch	Captain Colin Campbell of Glenfalloch, Breadalbane Fencibles
Glengarry	Captain Alasdair Ranaldson MacDonell of Glengarry, Strathspey Fencibles. Also referred to as Alasdair Ranaldson
Glenlyon	David Campbell of Glenlyon
Glenmoriston	Major John Grant of Glenmoriston, Strathspey Fencibles
Glenorchy	Campbells of Glenorchy, later Earls of Breadalbane
Grant, Laird of	Sir James Grant of Grant, Strathspey Fencibles. Also referred to as The Laird and The Good Sir James
Keppoch	Ranald MacDonell of Keppoch, chief
Lochgarry	Lieutenant-colonel John MacDonell of Lochgarry, 76th
Lochiel	Captain Donald Cameron of Lochiel, Gordon Fencibles
Lochnell	Lieutenant-colonel Sir Alexander Campbell of Lochnell, Western Fencibles
Lude	James Robertson of Lude; Captain William Robertson of Lude, 77th
Lovat	Simon Fraser, 11th Lord Lovat; Lieutenant-general Simon Fraser of Lovat, 78th and 71st; Archibald Fraser of Lovat, M.P.
Melfort	Major John Campbell of Melfort, Argyll Fencibles
Menzies, Laird of	Sir John Menzies of Menzies
Redcastle	Lieutenant Kenneth Mackenzie of Redcastle, 78th
Scatwell	Captain George Mackenzie of Scatwell, 78th
Scotus	Lieutenant Aeneas MacDonell of Scotus, 76th
Seaforth	Earls of, chiefs of the Mackenzies. Kenneth Mackenzie, Earl of Seaforth in the peerage of Ireland, 78th
Sheelagreen	Lieutenant-colonel Charles Gordon of Sheelagreen, 77th
Sleat	Macdonalds of Sleat, chiefs of Clan Donald. Sir Alexander Macdonald of Sleat, 1st Baron Macdonald of Macdonald and Sleat, 76th
Strowan	Lieutenant-general James Murray of Strowan, 77th

CLANS

Cameron	of Callart, Erracht, Invermallie, Kinlochiel, Lochiel
Campbell	of Argyll, Ardkinglass, Barbreck, Breadalbane (Glenorchy), Craignish, Glenfalloch, Glenlyon, Lochnell, Melfort, Monzie, Stonefield
Fraser	of Belladrum, Foyers, Lovat
Grant	of Auchindown, Culbin, Delcroy, Glenmoriston, Glenurquhart, Grant, Kinchurdy, Pitnacree, Rippachie, Sheuglie

Menzies	of Bolfracks, Comrie, Invergowrie, Menzies
Murray	of Atholl, Lintrose, Ochtertyre, Rednock, Strowan
MacDonald	of Ashkernish, Clanranald, Glencoe, Greshornish, Kilmalew, Knock, Rammerscales, Sleat
MacDonell	of Glengarry, Keppoch, Lochgarry, Scotus
Mackenzie	of Coul, Gairloch, Gruinard, Kintail (Seaforth), Redcastle, Scatwell
Mackintosh	of Dunachton, Mackintosh
Maclean	of Coll, Duart
Macpherson	of Ballachroan, Blairgowrie, Cluny
Robertson	of Kindeace, Lude, Straloch

Index

The names of chiefs and lairds are listed in the alphabetical order of their territorial designations, and by chronological order within their families. An asterisk signifies a mutineer or mutiny.

MORE ABOUT PENGUINS
AND PELICANS

Penguinews, which appears every month, contains details of all the new books issued by Penguins as they are published. From time to time it is supplemented by *Penguins in Print*, which is our complete list of almost 5,000 titles.

A specimen copy of *Penguinews* will be sent to you free on request. Please write to Dept EP, Penguin Books Ltd, Harmondsworth, Middlesex, for your copy.

In the U.S.A.: For a complete list of books available from Penguins in the United States write to Dept CS, Penguin Books, 625 Madison Avenue, New York, New York 10022.

In Canada: For a complete list of books available from Penguins in Canada write to Penguin Books Canada Ltd, 2801 John Street, Markham, Ontario L3R 1B4.